Political Participation in Beijing

Political Participation in Beijing

TIANJIAN SHI

Harvard University Press
Cambridge, Massachusetts, and London, England   1997

Library of Congress Cataloging-in-Publication Data

Shi, Tianjian.
    Political participation in Beijing / Tianjian Shi.
        p.   cm.
    Includes bibliographical references and index.
    ISBN 0-674-68640-3 (cloth : alk. paper).
    ISBN 0-674-68641-1 (pbk. : alk. paper).
    1. Political participation—Peking (China)
2. Peking (China)—Politics and government.
3. China—Politics and government—1976–
I. Title.
JQ1516.S53   1997
323′.04′0951—dc21   96-53018

To the memory of my father, Daoyuan Shi,
and to my mother, Bingxian Wu

Contents

Preface

My interest in political participation was generated by a stimulating course, "Political Participation in Comparative Perspective," taught in the 1980s by Professor Andrew Nathan at Columbia University. At that time, Western scholars were beginning to see the revival of social sciences in Communist China. Liberalization for a brief period between 1987 and 1989 made many of us believe that the time had finally come for social scientists to get access to the general populace in that country. Excited by the general political atmosphere and the economic and political reforms in China, I thought the time for the first scientific sample survey of political participation had arrived. I must confess now that had I known the tremendous difficulties ahead, I would never have had the courage to launch this project.

At that time, a deputy director of the Political Science Institute (PSI) of China's Social Science Academy (CASS) was spending a year as a Henry Luce Fellow at Columbia University. I mentioned to him my wish to conduct a survey of political participation in China. He encouraged me to write a proposal and offered to send it back to his home organization (the PSI) for approval; he also assured me that I would have no difficulty getting approval from his organization. I followed his suggestions but had still heard nothing from the institute by the time he returned to China several months later. It took me another six months to realize that the silence on the other side of the Pacific Ocean should be interpreted as a negative response to the proposal.

My personal experience as a "sent-down" youth during the Cultural Revolution taught me how to articulate my interests, as ordinary citizens in China do, in this kind of situation. Rather than trying to influence or change bureaucratic decisions, people usually manage to circumvent them. I decided to adopt the same strategy to push the project through by bypassing CASS and turning to other institutions for help.

I contacted two other organizations to explore the possibility of their sponsoring my research. One was the Department of International Politics at Peking University, my alma mater, and the other was the newly established Institute on Social Surveys of China (SSC) under the authority of the Economic System Reform Institute. In the second half of 1987, I received favorable responses for both of them. Officials in both organizations sent me their formal approval, stating that they would fully cooperate with me. The letter from SSC even suggested that the survey results be sent to the State Council with policy suggestions on political reform. Hoping that at least one of these two prestigious institutions would keep its promise, I went back to China in January 1988 for fieldwork.

After returning to Beijing, however, I found that neither of them was able to work with me. SSC was in legal battle with its parent institution, the Economic System Reform Institute. Du Yan, the director of SSC, who had agreed to cooperate, was ousted from his position by the Economic System Reform Institute. He was charged with "leaking state secrets" because he provided the home phone number of Bao Tong, Premier Zhao Ziyang's secretary, to a foreign reporter. When I arrived in Beijing, Du had already been put under twenty-four hour surveillance by the police. The real problem, according to one source, was that the sponsoring institution wanted to regain control of SSC. The charge was only an excuse of course. Such a deadly political struggle would definitely handicap the working capacity of SSC. I realized that cooperation with people there could be extremely dangerous.

Peking University was unable to work with me for another reason. Before I returned to China, I obtained an official agreement letter from the Department of International Politics. The chairman of that department and the chairman of the Department of Political Science at Columbia University even exchanged letters to make the collaboration an official one between the two universities. Unfortunately, when I went to the Department of International Politics to discuss the project, I realized that its approval was not enough. I had to obtain the consent of the university, which the department assumed would be easy to get because there had been an understanding between department and university authorities on the project. After the university gave its formal approval, the department and I had to file a joint application to the State Education Commission. When I asked department officials to estimate how long I would have to wait for approval from the commission, they told me the process usually takes three to six months.

The only reasonable choice for me under such circumstances was to locate a new partner and, fortunately, I found one—the Beijing Social Economic Research Institute (SERI). SERI was a private research institution run by two eminent liberals, Chen Ziming and Wang Juntao. The organization was staffed by a group of idealistic university graduates. Chen and Wang had been involved in the April Fifth Movement in 1976 to protest against the Gang of Four and were put in jail after the first Tiananmen Incident. They were both rehabilitated after the gang's fall. Wang Juntao was even elected to the Central Committee of the Communist Youth League. Although Chen and Wang were later charged as the "black hands" behind the democracy movement of 1989 and sentenced to thirteen years in prison, they did not have much trouble with the authorities even though they were not blind loyalists.

In 1985, Chen and Wang set up a correspondence school. Within two years, the school is said to have earned 10 million renminbi (RMB), the equivalent of 2.7 million U.S. dollars. Instead of putting the money into their own pockets, Chen and Wang decided to set up a research institute—SERI—and provided no less than 500,000 RMB (135,135 U.S. dollars) per year to support social science research. Following the practice in the United States, SERI established an executive committee to evaluate research projects proposed to the institute. It also bought a national newspaper, the *Economic Weekly Review,* to facilitate publication of research results to avoid government censorship.

Because of its economic independence, the institute did not have to deal with governmental red tape and could make its own decisions on what research projects to support and whom to work with. When I arrived in Beijing, the then three-year-old institute had completed a number of survey research projects. Among them are "The National Character of the Chinese People" and "The Political Psychology of the Chinese." In an attempt to strengthen the quality of survey research, Chen and Wang invited me to join the institute to establish an independent survey research institution—the Opinion Research Center of China (ORCC)—under SERI. I managed to gather a group of Western-trained survey specialists in the institution. Among them, three people held diplomas from the Survey Research Center (SRC) of the University of Michigan, one of the leading survey research centers in this country.

The institute also provided me with staff assistance and a substantial amount of financial support for the project. I was responsible for training the staff in survey methods and helping them to design two scientific sampling frames, one nationwide, the other for Beijing. With financial support from SERI, I began to collect sampling data. The data collection for the

Beijing sampling frame was accomplished by the end of 1988. "General Interview Techniques," published by the SRC, was translated into Chinese and used to train ORCC's interviewers. With the help of ORCC, I conducted a pilot survey to pretest the questionnaire to be used in the proposed nationwide survey. For reasons to be explained below, this pilot survey became the basis of this book.

Before we had a chance to finish our job of collecting data for the national sample, students in Beijing gathered in Tiananmen Square to memorialize the late former Communist Party general secretary Hu Yaobang. The events on June 4, 1989, and the subsequent political atmosphere made the nationwide survey impossible. On June 10, I flew back to New York via Tokyo, with only the completed questionnaires of the pilot study. Given the post-Tiananmen political atmosphere in China, a nationwide survey could not be done in the foreseeable future. After returning to New York, I began the analysis of mass political participation based on the Beijing pilot study. The results of that analysis are presented in this book.

This brief history of my project reminds me how many people helped at various stages. This book developed from the research of my doctoral dissertation, completed in 1992 at Columbia University. I am most grateful to the members of my dissertation committee: Andrew Nathan, Thomas Bernstein, and Robert Shapiro. Andrew Nathan has stimulated my interests in political participation and provided invaluable support and guidance in my work. Without his encouragement, help, and various kinds of support, this book could not have been written. Thomas Bernstein read earlier versions of this book and gave me important suggestions. Robert Shapiro guided me through the process of data manipulation. Andrew Walder and Martin Whyte read the research proposal in its early stages and gave me many useful suggestions.

Some of my fellow students at Columbia deserve special mention. Wang Xi and Wu Guoguang supplied me with much inside information on the political process in China. Ren Yue gave me many fruitful ideas in our discussion of this topic. Joan Judge and Martin Rivlin helped me edit a draft of the book.

This work has been aided by a number of institutions. I would like to acknowledge the support of National Science Foundation dissertation grant INT-88-14199 and the assistance of the Opinion Research Center of China and the Social Economic Research Institute. ORCC and SERI provided not only excellent staff assistance but also substantial financial support for this project. Wen Tiejun, Bai Hua, Hao Hongsheng, Jiang Hong, Xu Ping, Ke Dongyun, Li Wei, and Meng Qingling participated in the survey. Without their courage, skill, and enthusiasm, the fieldwork could not have been successfully accomplished.

During the final stages of the making of this book, I found supportive environments at the University of Iowa and Duke University. I want to thank the University of Iowa for its support for one summer and Duke University for giving me one semester's leave to revise the manuscript. My thanks also go to Zou Weidong, Xu Ping, and Ke Dongyun for their research assistance; the anonymous readers for Harvard University Press for their criticisms; and Stanley Rosen and Melanie Manion for their helpful comments on an earlier version of this book. I thank Elizabeth Suttell at Harvard University Press for her help and Elizabeth Hurwit for her excellent editing of a manuscript written by someone whose native language is not English; I register my admiration for her although I do not envy her job.

Throughout the project, I traveled between the United States and China. My wife, Christine Chiu, and daughter, Eleanor, bore my absences and provided constant encouragement and support. They deserve more than the usual thanks that authors extend to their family. To them goes my love and deep appreciation for sharing my scholarship and my life.

Finally, I would like to thank my parents. They provided me with valuable guidance and support in the early stages of my life. And when I was a sent-down youth working as a peasant in Henan Province and as a truck driver in Beijing during the Cultural Revolution, they encouraged me never to lose hope about life. "If there is no opportunity in your life, you have nothing to regret," my father said to me at the time I was working in rice paddies sixteen hours a day; "but if opportunity comes in your life and you could not grasp it because you are not well-prepared, you would regret it all your life." Taking his advice, I spent all my spare time on study in those years, although I never knew whether an opportunity would come. An opportunity finally arrived, and I did not let it pass by me. When college entrance examinations resumed in China in 1977, after ten years of suspension, I passed and became a student at Peking University. University education opened a new horizon in my life. I am especially thankful to my parents, to whom I gratefully dedicate this book.

Political Participation in Beijing

1

Introduction

Participation is a concept derived in large measure from the notion of democracy. The two ideas have been intertwined since Aristotle's time. Democracy at its most basic level means rule by the people. Participation is a process by which "goals are set and means chosen in relation to all sorts of social issues."[1] Traditionally participation is treated as a unidimensional phenomenon. Elections are the only way for people to participate in politics.[2] By selecting among competing political leaders, people communicate their needs and desires to governments. Their elected officials obtain the consent of the governed and thus are accountable to the people.[3] In addition to its instrumental usage, participation has important psychological and attitudinal values. The act of political participation can be a source of both objective and subjective satisfaction for participants—satisfaction with the government and satisfaction with one's role in society. Political participation is thus considered a means for people to articulate their interests and an end that produces a sense of "full membership" within the political system.[4]

Studies of political participation in communist societies follow a different tradition. The totalitarian model that dominated the field in the 1950s and 1960s stressed the absolute power of the Communist Party and laid great emphasis on control and mobilization.[5] It pictured politics in the former communist countries as passive and dominated by elites determined to maximize their own power and transform society on the basis of their ideological propensities. According to this model, states in communist countries monopolize three major forms of interpersonal confrontation: "(a) mass communications; (b) operational weapons; and (c) all organizations, including economic ones."[6] The states' monopolistic control of mass communications in these societies successfully limits information flow. By limiting the right of association, governments therein effectively prevent interest aggregation, depriving people of the possibility of defeating the political authorities. The monopolistic control of operational weapons makes it easier for states to suppress *organized* opposition. It gives a state such extensive control that some totalitarian theorists believe these regimes could annihilate all boundaries between the state and other social groups, even that between the state and the individual personality.[7] What citizens then confront is manipulation by a polity coercing them into hyperactively supporting policies of self-appointed leaders who are totally impervious to public opinion.[8]

Although there are variations in totalitarian theory, the basic configuration of the relationship between the state and the society remains the same. As institutional settings not only block the way for popular demands to reach elites but also deprive citizens of any possible weapons to make elites listen to their opinions, participation in such societies can be similar to that found in liberal democracies only on the surface. There are parades, demonstrations, and uncontested ceremonial elections, but they are all organized by the regime to mobilize the support of the general populace, rather than utilized by citizens to express their opinions to authority. Mass participation in those societies is at best suspect and at worst a hoax. Widespread protests and political violence found in communist societies reflect the failure of participatory institutions and the governing process. Protest there is usually considered the antithesis of participation.

With the waning of the cold war and changes in communist societies in the 1960s, scholars have gradually become disenchanted with the rigid totalitarian model. Many studies revealed that, as political terror and mass mobilization subsided, there was an accompanying revival of genuine political competition within the framework of political controls. Research on intermediate and high-level politics clearly demonstrated the limits of party primacy and institutional control. Scholars found that not only the party apparatus but also the security police, military, industrial managers, economists, writers, and jurists in communist societies have significant input in the process of policy formulation. More important, they found that groups emerging from the temporary atomization of earlier periods of communist control had begun to actively pursue their own shared interests.[9] Contrary to the totalitarian model, communist parties in such states are pictured as possessing no absolute powers and struggling with internal divisions. Interest group theorists believe it is beyond the capability of these regimes to either assimilate all the boundaries between state and society or totally prevent interest articulation.

The interest group model dramatically improves our understanding of the state-society relationship in communist countries by showing that private life and private interest articulation also exist within those societies. Unfortunately, the model still denies the possibility of ordinary people influencing government decisions. According to both the totalitarian and the interest group models, meaningful political participation requires certain institutional arrangements in society to link people's political activities to the policy-making process. Since political outlets and organizations in communist societies—such as elections, mass campaigns, trade unions, and peasant associations—are all designed by the regime to "preempt and expropriate the formation of voluntary groups and their functions of interest articulation,"[10] the political activities of ordinary people cannot be effectively linked to the policy-making process.

But all other important theoretical findings in the field of comparative politics suggest that regimes in communist countries should not be devoid of political participation by private citizens. Among them the most prominent one is, of course, modernization theory. Modernization theory holds that social and economic development in modern society is characterized by specialization. With the development of a society, many functions originally performed by the family, tribe, and other economic organizations shift to the political system. With the expansion of services and other regulatory activities, government gradually reaches previously untouched social groups. Government collects taxes, provides social programs and services, and makes rules and regulations that have far-reaching effects on the private lives of citizens. As the encounter between individuals and the state increases, the necessity for citizens to deal with government also increases. If taxes are collected, or regulations are imposed by the government, people will have incentives to bargain with the state to decrease their share of paying for public goods. Once the state becomes responsible for social welfare, people will want themselves or their family to reap such benefits. By increasing the scope of governmental activities, socioeconomic development generates the need for people to deal with political authority.

The increasing interaction between state and society accelerates people's participation in politics.[11] The experiences of many developing countries have repeatedly demonstrated that the level of participation in a society correlates highly with its economic development. One explanation postulates that the development process affects the processes of mobilization and socialization, which in turn change people's political attitudes and political behavior.[12] The process by which people shift from one set of attachments to another leads to new involvement in mass politics. Another explanation emphasizes the impact of modernization on people's social and economic status. Rapid social and economic development usually brings about dramatic status changes for many people, and status reversal can become a normal way of life in such societies. Dramatic declines in socioeconomic status create a sense of relative deprivation among people in societies experiencing rapid socioeconomic development, a sense that increases people's participation in both conventional and unconventional political activities.[13] A third explanation asserts that broadening the contacts between citizens and government will prompt people to participate in politics. No matter what the logical structure of the alleged correlations among economic development, modernization, and political participation, these theories imply that levels of participation in a society increase with an expansion in the role of government.[14]

Different from both industrializing and industrialized societies, governments in communist societies are not only involved in regulatory activities but also serve as direct suppliers, and sometimes the only supplier, of material and nonmaterial resources crucial for people's daily lives. Such a system design pushes the encounter between citizens and regimes to extremes. More important, communist societies usually have more limited resources than capitalist societies, so that competition for them is more intense than in other societies. In such a situation, modernization theory predicts that both the scope and the intensity of political competition in communist societies will be more intense than in other countries. Students of participation in communist societies usually assume that governments there are able to defend themselves against ever increasing demands of the general populace to participate in the political process to articulate their private interests by systematically suppressing any potential opposition. However, political suppression is not unique in communist countries. Suppression in some non-communist nations, such as South Africa, is even more systematic and more brutal than in China, but it failed to prevent an opposition movement from growing and eventually overthrowing the government. Why did the regime in China successfully do so before 1989? Why did the Chinese people refrain from organizing groups and from challenging their top leaders? Few scholars have tried to resolve this apparent tension between two of the most important theories in the field of comparative politics. Instead, they characterize communist countries as deviant cases in the study of the relationship between socioeconomic development and political participation.

As a result, some scholars reject the applicability of the notion of political participation to studies of communist societies. They argue that applying the term to communist countries can cause a "serious and unfortunate loss of precision."[15] For them, political participation assumes the existence of a pluralistic political system.[16] "Because political participation . . . is a concept that helps us define a particular kind of polity," writes Joseph La-Palombara, "it does not serve comparative analysis well to find the concept used to describe polities that are manifestly not democracies of any kind."[17] Since the existing institutions in communist countries can perform only specific functions—such as policy implementation and political socialization—other scholars argue that the "definition of political participation in the literature of political science is inadequate for the study of Communist systems."[18] They propose to redefine political participation to meet the political realities in those societies. For example, in his classic study of political participation in China, James Townsend redefines it as the "execution of party policies" and "popular political action support for a supreme, unified national interest as defined by the Communist Party," or "guided involvement in the implementation of political decisions."[19]

With the effort to encompass a larger geographic and temporal scope and to integrate the protests within democratic systems with more conventional participation patterns, a new image of political participation uncoupled from the concept of democracy gradually emerged in the 1970s. Under this new image, participation simply indicates the efforts of ordinary citizens in any type of political system to influence the actions of their rulers. In another major development, the unidimensional view of political participation that treats voting as the pivot and the only point where people may exert influence in the political process has been replaced by a multidimensional one. Studies by Sidney Verba and Norman Nie on participation in America and comparative studies by Verba, Nie, and Jae-on Kim on participation and political equality in seven nations discovered that in addition to voting and campaign activities, people may also use other methods, such as communal activities and personalized contacts, either to seek help from government officials or to communicate their own preferences to them. They found that participation is distinguished not only in terms of difficulty but also in terms of styles by which people attempt to relate to government and politics.[20]

These findings have great heuristic value for the study of participation in communist countries because they free us from two important assumptions dominating the study of political participation. The first assumption is that political participation requires a democratic polity, and the second is that the power to select their rulers is the necessary condition for ordinary citizens to effectively articulate their interests. These findings tell us that participation does not necessarily require democratic institutions and that the ability of citizens to articulate their interests is not necessarily linked to the opportunity for them to choose their rulers. Voting is obviously an important method but not *the* only method for citizens to communicate their policy preferences to governments and to affect public policy. As noted by these authors, both communal activities and citizen-initiated contacts are widely used in many different polities including the former Yugoslavia.[21]

If elections are not the necessary condition for people to effectively articulate their interests, do people in communist societies use other means to pursue their interests? Empirically, answers to this question are positive. Researches in the former Soviet Union have found that people there demonstrated a clear understanding of the workings of the political system in their society and that many citizens consciously and unconsciously adapted themselves to its political realities when pursuing their interests. Alex Inkeles and Raymond Bauer, for example, revealed that people in the Soviet Union clearly distinguished material matters from "abstract ideas and principles." They found that "Soviet citizens seem much less concerned with winning political rights and constitutional guarantees than with gaining more personal security and an improved standard of living."[22] Their research tells us that people in the Soviet Union did actively engage in various political acts to pursue their interests but that they deliberately avoided directly confronting their leaders in their private interest articulation.

This unique behavior pattern of people in communist societies is spelled out more clearly by Seweryn Bialer. In his study of the post-Stalin regime in the Soviet Union, Bialer makes a conceptual distinction between "high politics" and "low politics." High politics is alleged to involve the principal political issues of society, the abstract ideas and language of politics, and the decisions and actions of the political leadership. Low politics is alleged to involve decisions that directly touch on citizens' daily lives, communal matters, and conditions of the workplace.[23] Soviet citizens are apolitical, indifferent, and apathetic with regard to high politics but regularly involved to a high degree in low politics.[24] According to Bialer, "very seldom under Soviet conditions do the 'low' and 'high' dimensions of Soviet politics intersect. When they do, it is a matter of the objective *effects* of 'low politics' of mass political participation on 'high politics,' and not as a consequence of the conscious *actions* of citizens."[25]

At the same time, the more people participate in low politics, the more people become apolitical toward high politics. "The expanded participation of the Brezhnev era," Bialer argues, "goes hand in hand with the retention of one of the most characteristic features of major Soviet social groups— their high level of *apolitization*" (italics added).[26] Other scholars reveal that people in communist countries criticize governments or disagree with their policies but seldom *intend* to replace them.[27] During the democracy movement in Beijing in 1989, student demonstrators shouted such slogans as "support the Communist Party!" This phenomenon made certain scholars draw a conceptual distinction between political activities aimed at overthrowing governments and other political activities, to catch up with this rather "unique" psychological orientation of people in communist societies.[28] While Leonard Shapiro calls political activities not aimed at overthrowing governments in the former Soviet Union "dissent," which is fundamentally different from "opposition" in the West, Andrew Nathan calls the former acts in China "remonstration."[29]

Why do people in communist societies behave in such a way? Why do the low and high dimensions of politics in communist societies seldom intersect? Why does the expansion of participation in low politics go hand in hand with the retention of high levels of apolitization vis-à-vis higher politics in communist societies? A central question facing students of communist participation is, how are the political activities of ordinary people linked to the policy-making process in communist societies? In pluralist societies, the linkage is established either by elections or group-based activities. But meaningful elections that allow citizens to choose their rulers at the national level are not available in communist societies. It is true that there are interest groups in both the former Soviet Union and Communist China, but these "interest groups" are fundamentally different from those that students of political participation are familiar with. Jerry Hough, for example, clearly points out that the interest groups he is talking about are made up of those who "occupy elite positions within the political machine itself," whereas interest groups in the West are usually "associational interest groups which are autonomous vis-à-vis the government."[30] On the one hand, without proper institutions to bridge people's political acts with the policy process in communist societies, how can ordinary people make government officials listen to them? On the other hand, if participation in those societies constitutes only an isolated realm, tenuously linked to the policy-making chain, and cannot provide people with desired benefits from the authorities, as suggested by many students of communist participation, why do people bother to engage in politics at all?[31] Few scholars have ever tried to answer these puzzling questions.

Part of this neglect can be attributed to the inadequate usage of the comparative politics approach in studies of communist societies. As Gabriel Almond correctly points out, "comparing one political system with another can only begin when we describe their unique specialized structures." Preoccupied with comparing the functions of identical forms of political acts and identical political institutions in different societies, scholars may neglect the possibility that the same function may be performed by different institutions in different societies. More important, functions crucial to people's participation in one institutional setting may become unimportant or even irrelevant in another one. When the institutional setting changes, the articulative, aggregative, and communicative functions of participation may also change. "We may be misled if we follow structural lines in our comparative efforts."[32] Thus, an adequate analysis of political participation in different political systems requires us to identify, locate, and characterize all these functions in a political process, not simply those performed by specialized political structures.[33]

Suppose, as suggested by Almond, we put the problem facing us the other way around and ask different questions: How are private interests in communist societies articulated? What institutions are involved? What is the strategy for people there to articulate their interests? What resources are required? We would find that many functions performed by parties, interest groups, and elections in liberal democracies—such as interest articulation, interest aggregation, leadership recruitment, and political socialization—are performed by different political institutions in communist societies. We would also find that interest articulation in communist societies can operate at different levels of the government and at different stages of the policy process; that it may not require people to influence the selection of government personnel; and that the political power of ordinary people may not necessarily come from groups and group-based political activities. To understand this peculiar political process, careful examination of the institutional setting in Chinese society and its impact on people's political behavior is necessary.

Impact of Institutional Setting on Stage of the Policy Process People Participate In

As students of political science, we learned that politics is a process that produces decisions about the production and distribution of scarce material and nonmaterial resources. In this process, individuals and groups make competing demands or "inputs" on governments within political systems and states transfer those inputs into authoritative decisions and policies—that is, the "output" of the system. "In every political system, . . . individuals and groups seek to influence the state and thereby translate their interests into authoritative political decisions."[34] Groups are crucial in the process of transferring people's demands to government because effective interest articulation usually depends on certain political institutions to aggregate people's private interests. It should be pointed out, however, that group

and group-based activities may not be necessary for successful interest articulation in all societies. The new institutionalists remind us that political
struggles are mediated by the institutional settings in which they take place.
Such settings are alleged to be able to define the goals political actors pursue, allocate political resources among them, determine the strategies for
them to reach their goals, and circumscribe the outcomes of political struggles.[35] The means, strategies, and resources required for people to participate in politics cannot be exceptions to this rule. They must also be shaped
by institutional settings in the society.

To understand how institutional settings shape the way people participate in politics, a brief review of the decision-making process is in order.
For the purpose of simplification, the process can be roughly divided into
three stages: agenda setting, decision making, and policy implementation.
Social and political issues of course exist in all societies. But if no one in a
society raises the issues for the authorities to make decisions, they can
remain dormant for a long time without becoming salient. For example,
environmental problems existed in many societies for years before some
people realized their saliency and proposed that governments make rules
to regulate these problems. Once an issue is put on the agenda, it enters
into the policy formulation stage of the policy process. Different political
forces try to influence the decisions of government on issues to get the best
results for themselves. After decisions are made, the government also needs
to implement them to establish the link that allows the goals of public
policies to be realized as outcomes of government activities. Only when a
policy is successfully implemented by public authorities can the policy
process in a society be said to have been accomplished.

Theoretically, people may influence government policy at any of these
three stages of the policy process. They can influence agenda setting by
suggesting that decision makers act on certain issues concerning them.
They can also persuade decision makers to formulate policy in ways beneficial to themselves. If those in power refuse to listen, citizens in some
societies can manage to overthrow governments and replace them with
decision makers who may represent the people's interests. However, trying
to influence policy formulation is only *one* way, and not the only way, for
people to articulate their interests. Since decisions made by governments
have to be implemented to realize goals, formulating a policy begins but
does not complete the policy process. If political actors in a society fail to
make decision makers formulate government policy according to their preferences, they may also try to influence the way policy is implemented and
prevent the policy goals of the government from being achieved. Students

of public policy are familiar with the phenomenon whereby bureaucrats and interest groups continually influence decisions made by governments through bargaining at the policy implementation stage.[36]

Nonetheless, the ability of political actors to influence decisions of the authorities at the policy implementation stage varies from one society to another. In some societies, the social and political institutions are so designed that the system deliberately prevents people from articulating their interests at the policy implementation stage. In other societies, institutional arrangements make it much easier for people to pursue their goals at the policy implementation stage. Where in the decision-making process people in a society choose to exert influence is primarily determined, it seems to me, by the communication devices used by the authorities to transmit government decisions, by whether or not there exists a modern bureaucracy in a particular society, and by who serves as arbitrator when there are conflicts in policy interpretation.

Generally speaking, there are two major communication devices used by different polities in the world. One is law, which includes presidential orders, executive directives, formal government rules, and legal regulations. The other is documentation, which includes formal written documents, conference minutes, reports, and oral communications.[37] Law is characterized by precision in its language. Choosing law as a communication device requires government policy to be specific—it must clearly specify what bureaucrats can and cannot do regarding particular issues. Such a system design also assumes (1) the presence of an independent arbitrator to resolve conflicts in the interpretation of government policies, and (2) the existence of a legal-rational, impartial, and neutral bureaucratic corps. The purpose of such a bureaucracy is to carry out specialized administrative functions according to purely objective considerations and to serve as an instrument of *execution* of the authoritative decisions of the government. "Objective" refers to administration by calculable rules, "without regard for persons."[38] According to Max Weber, the birth of a modern bureaucracy requires a dehumanizing process to eliminate "love, hatred, and all purely personal, irrational, and emotional elements which escape calculation."[39]

> For the field of administrative activity proper, that is, for all state activities that fall outside the field of law creation and court procedure, one is accustomed to claiming the freedom and paramountcy of individual circumstances. General norms are held to play primarily a negative role as barriers to the official's positive and "creative" activity, which should never be regulated. The bearing of this thesis may be disregarded here. Yet the point that this "freely" creative administration (and possibly judicature) does not constitute a realm

of *free,* arbitrary actions, of mercy, and of *personally* motivated favor and valuations, as we shall find to be the case among pre-bureaucratic forms, is a very decisive point ... In the field of executive administration, especially where the "creative" arbitrariness of the official is most strongly built up, the specifically modern and strictly "objective" idea of "reasons of state" is upheld as the supreme and ultimate guiding start of the official's behavior.[40]

These arrangements have significant impacts on *where* in the policy process people can articulate their interests. The precision of language used in transmitting vehicles of government policies, an impartial modern bureaucracy, and the separation of the institutions responsible for policy implementation from the institutions responsible for policy interpretation have but one goal—making it difficult, if not impossible, for the general populace to influence government policy implementation to guarantee goals of public policies and outcomes of government activities in society. Using law to transfer government policies deprives bureaucrats of the possibility of interpreting policies according to their love, hatred, or personal, irrational, and other emotional elements at the policy implementation stage. As the law clearly states what can and cannot be done, it leaves little room for bureaucrats to maneuver. Knowing that bureaucrats can hardly make adjustments on government policy to adapt to the private needs of individuals, people in a society turn to three other ways to influence government decisions: entering into a legal proceeding to fight over bureaucrats' *interpretation* of the rules; simply breaking the rules; and trying to change the decisions made by the authorities.

Although people can fight bureaucrats over interpretations of public policy, using law as a communication device discourages such behavior. First of all, legal systems must have mechanisms to resolve conflict over interpretations of rules. When the battlefield moves from the political arena to the courtroom, the consequences of the struggle depend on legal expertise that specifies how to make arguments according to sets of rules. Second, the results of legal battles are usually hard to predict. There is no way for participants to predict how judges will decide their cases. Since political power can hardly be translated into legal victory in struggles over policy interpretation, people with political power often turn to other ways to influence government decisions.

Of course, there is another way for people to pursue their interests—they can simply break the law and ignore rules and regulations made by government. This behavior happens frequently in all societies. For example, people in the United States ignore traffic lights and exceed speed limits on highways daily. Some of them may also evade taxes or bribe government officials. To prevent such behavior from happening, all legal systems have enforcement mechanisms. The presence of enforcement mechanisms in modern administrations changes the payoff structure for offenders. For example, if caught, those who speed or ignore traffic lights will be fined and incur points on their driver's licenses. Tax evaders and government officials who accept bribes in New York City may end up in Rikers Island's prison "for a rest." The danger of being punished makes lawbreaking a less appealing alternative for participants in many societies. As long as the probability of being caught is high and the probability of escaping sanctions is low, breaking the law will be an unattractive alternative for participants.

Through these mechanisms, institutional settings in many societies make it difficult and less desirable for ordinary people to pursue their interests at the policy implementation stage. By depriving government officials of the ability to freely interpret rules and regulations made by the authorities, those structural arrangements free bureaucrats from political pressure from below over the way they implement government policies. By diluting the use of political power in struggles over interpretation of policy made by the authorities, by making the outcome of legal struggles in courtrooms unpredictable, and by dramatically increasing the risks of breaking rules and regulations made by the authorities, institutional arrangements in these societies divert political acts of people away from the policy implementation stage and force them to work either on agenda setting or on policy formulation to pursue their interests.

But not every society chooses law as a transmitting vehicle for government policies. The document is the quintessential communication device used in the People's Republic of China (PRC). By nature, documents are imprecise and vague in their language. The vague nature of documents enables bureaucrats in the PRC, to a large extent, to interpret policies made by the government according to their own preferences. The possibility for bureaucrats to freely interpret government policies is reinforced by other features of China's political system with regard to documents. First, different from law, documents are not required to be open to the general populace. Documents in China, moreover, even governing trivial matters, are usually kept semisecret. Only government agencies dealing with particular matters can get relevant documents. Ordinary people in society usually do not know the specifics of government policies, even for those regulations concerning issues in their daily lives. For example, government policy dealing with college graduates going abroad to study was handed down to each department in universities. Those documents have never been formally released to students. When students ask leaders about government policy on study abroad, leaders usually tell them the "spirit" rather than the exact wording of the policy. This arrangement allows government officials to freely interpret or even twist policy without being challenged by other political forces in society.

Second, the mechanism for conflict resolution remains the responsibility of the executive branch—there is no impartial third party to give authoritative readings of government policy. The bureaucratic corps in the society is responsible for both policy implementation and policy interpretation. Under such an institutional arrangement, political power is useful in the struggle over interpretation of government policy. Political actors can, at least in theory, fight bureaucrats over policy implementation and policy interpretation at each administrative level up to the highest stage.

It is true that there is an important mechanism—upward accountability—built into the system to induce compliance by bureaucrats. For example, in China bureaucrats at each level of administration are appointed by higher authorities rather than elected by the general populace from below. By making bureaucrats accountable to officials at higher levels of government rather than to ordinary citizens, institutional settings in China are designed to guarantee that bureaucrats will faithfully carry out policy made by the government. Unfortunately, the vague nature of the communication device, to a large extent, nullifies the effect. When the meaning of government policy reaching bureaucrats at each level of administration is subject to free interpretation, whether lower-echelon bureaucrats faithfully follow decisions made by higher authorities can be difficult, if not impossible, to judge.

If using documents as a communication device determines at which stage of the policy process people in a society participate in politics, the installation of the work unit in China creates incentives for bureaucrats to take care of local interests. As a mobilizational regime, the Chinese government worked hard in the past to stimulate the masses to carry out decisions of elites to transform the entire society. To ensure its control, the government developed a unique political structure—the work unit (*danwei*)—to help the authorities control the general populace in Chinese society. According to Martin Whyte and William Parish:

> Work units [in China] may run nurseries, clinics, canteens and recreational facilities; they convene employees to hear government decrees and for political study; they organize campaigns for birth control and to send down youths; they approve marriages and divorces and mediate disputes; they hold meetings to discuss crimes and misbehavior off the job by their members; they distribute rations and carry out cleanliness campaigns; they supervise untrustworthy employees and organize patrols to guard the area; and they may employ family members of employees in subsidiary small workshops or vegetable farms.[41]

One impact of such a system design on people's behavior has been noticed by many China scholars. The economic and political control of a work unit over its employees is alleged to be able to dramatically increase the ability of the state to control society. By making employees not only economically but also socially and politically dependent on their work units, the regime in China gains full control over employees' lives.[42] Since people in China lack cohesion and the organizational capability to pursue their interests on a collective basis, it is generally believed that citizens in urban China can hardly articulate their interests.

Political sociologists were the first to challenge this one-way relationship. Andrew Walder observed that, rather than simply representing the state to control society, work units in China possess a dual status and operate as economic or functional organizations. An important consequence of this arrangement is that leaders of work units are also responsible for material goods production, financial performance, and other functional activities as needed by these organizations. This situation requires work unit leaders to take care of the interests of their employees for the following reasons. First, material production and other functional activities of work units depend on employees to be completed. To fulfill the functional role of their organizations, bureaucrats at grassroots levels need cooperation from their subordinates. Second, until recently urban China had a lifetime employment system, which made it difficult for cadres to fire employees. Before the reforms gave bureaucrats this most important weapon to coerce their subordinates to cooperate, it was extremely difficult for bureaucrats to punish employees for simply refusing to work if they did not commit another "crime," especially a political one. Third, since leaders of work units in China do not own their enterprises but are simply political appointees, many of them may face legitimacy problems. It is true that the government in China can place whomever it likes in leadership positions, but such appointments do not guarantee that employees of an organization will cooperate with appointees. To win the support of their subordinates, political appointees usually need to demonstrate not only their competence to run organizations but also their capability and willingness to take care of the interests of employees in organizations. Many empirical studies demonstrate that leaders of Chinese organizations regularly make adjustments of government policies to represent local interests.[43] Thus, the major challenge facing bureaucrats in China is not simply representing the state to control society but keeping a proper balance between the two roles designated to them by the dual functions of the organization they represent. To satisfy higher authorities, bureaucrats need to stick to the rules and regulations made by the government. To fulfill their functional roles, they have no other choice but to co-opt their constituency.

Choosing documents as communication devices allows bureaucrats to interpret government decisions at the policy implementation stage according to personal elements. Installation of work units creates direct incentives for bureaucrats in urban China to do so. Since interest articulation at the policy implementation stage is usually situation-specific, involves less risks, and more important can save participants organizational costs, political competition under such institutional settings inevitably concentrates on the policy implementation stage.[44]

Impact of Institutional Setting on Primary Strategy for Participation

Most governmental functions in China, such as administrating welfare programs, distributing apartments, providing education, and even maintaining social order, are the responsibility of work units rather than of functional and residential systems as in many other societies. Among many functions performed by work units, an important one is representing the government in distributing scarce material and nonmaterial resources among employees.[45] This arrangement shifts the pivotal point of decision making for low politics from the central government to grassroots organizations. As the decision-making center descends to the grassroots level, people's strategy for pursuing their interests changes fundamentally.

The relationship between government officials and citizens in a society is a hierarchical one. To make government officials listen to the opinions of private citizens, the latter must find a way to alter the hierarchical relationship. The institutional arrangements in a society determine the way people can alter this relationship. If participants are forced to exert influence either on agenda setting or at the policy formulation stage, there are two ways for them to do so. One is through elections. Elections are an institution designed to periodically provide people with opportunities to alter the hierarchical relationships between themselves and government officials. If people are not satisfied with their rulers, they can wait for election time and replace them with other political leaders.

Another way to alter the relationship is through groups and group-based political activities. When institutional arrangements push people to work at the policy formulation stage to articulate their interests, government policy becomes collective in nature. Because governmental decisions affect so much of the population, many people compete for the attention of decision makers. The voice of a single person in such a setting can thus hardly reach decision makers. Even if an individual voice could reach decision makers, a single person acting on "critical centers" is unlikely to succeed. Among competing participants, groups usually have a stronger voice than a single person. Since interests of people with similar attributes are tied together, the institutional setting not only requires but also encourages people to lobby collectively.

Groups and group-based activities do not guarantee that participants will be able to alter the hierarchical relationship between themselves and government officials. No matter how many people get involved in the opposition, the government may still ignore their opinions. Tiananmen in 1989 is a prime example of this point. What makes group and group-based political activities effective is another political institution—elections. Because groups can mobilize support, energy, and resources to vote decision makers out of office, decision makers take groups and group-based opposition seriously. Individualized political acts such as communal activities and personalized contacts in many societies can be effective because they are backed by credible threats that if decision makers refuse to cooperate, the person concerned may mobilize others to vote them out of office in the next election.

Since Aristotle's time, political scientists have assumed that government decisions are collective in nature in their analysis of the policy-making process and in their study of political participation. With this attribute in mind, political scientists assign vital importance to group actions. To many scholars, group interests, group attitudes, and group pressures are the only things that matter. Many of them even neglect individual interests.[46] Nonetheless, as work units assume the responsibility of resource distribution, government policy outputs in China lose crucial attributes, specifically, *collective goods*. In making such an argument, I am not denying that certain basic goods and services provided by the government, such as defense, police protection, and courts, are still public goods in a society. They usually remain high-politics issues. I am arguing that by shifting most distributive and redistributive decisions to local bureaucrats or work units, institutional arrangements dramatically reduce the *scope* of high-politics issues in Chinese society. As work units in China are responsible for representing the government to provide a broad array of services to their employees, many resources and services provided by the PRC authorities are no longer public goods. As the nature of issues facing participants in China changes, actions, strategies, and resources required for people to assert influence over government must also change substantially.

We know that government policies—especially distributive and redistributive ones—are controlled by work units rather than functional government agencies in China. We also know that most material and non-material resources are appropriated to work units for distribution. A crucial but usually neglected consequence of such institutional arrangements is that as material and nonmaterial resources available for people to compete become limited in supply, one person in the organization getting desired resources clearly means that others in the same organization have less chance of receiving the same resource. As a result, the crucial assumption in modern political science—that government policy outputs are the in-feasibility of exclusion and the jointness of supply—no longer holds true in China. Down to the work unit level, exclusion becomes not only feasible but also necessary. Sometimes exclusion is even crucial for participants to get desired resources.

As many government policy outputs in China become selective goods, the primary strategy of interest articulation can no longer be organizing colleagues or people with similar attributes to lobby collectively to ask government to appropriate more resources to one's own group; rather, strategy is aimed at persuading leaders of one's organization to distribute the desired material and nonmaterial resources to oneself instead of to colleagues. Even if participants can manage to make higher authorities ap-propriate more resources to their organization, there is no guarantee that they can personally get the desired resources. Because government policy in China is usually vague in its language and leaves a lot of room for bu-reaucrats to maneuver, leaders of organizations can always give additional portions of material and nonmaterial resources to someone else in the same organization. Thus, under the institutional arrangements of the Chinese work unit, it is not rational for a person to sacrifice his or her time and take political risks to support collective action to demand that the govern-ment allocate more resources to his or her work unit when there is the alternative of dealing privately with leaders in the work unit for particular benefits.

Citizens in China usually rely on three methods to alter the hierarchical relationship between themselves and government officials. First, since gov-ernment policy is hardly monopolistic, there is always space for citizens to maneuver. People in China may find that certain government policies sup-port their own requests and ask government officials to "faithfully" imple-ment them. In doing so, they are actually borrowing "normative power" from government policies to change the balance of power between them-selves and local-echelon government officials.

Second, participants may "borrow" political power from someone else to change the balance of power between themselves and the bureaucrats they are dealing with. As pointed out by E. E. Schattschneider, outcomes of political conflict are determined not only by the balance of power of the parties involved but by the scope of conflict. "Every change in the number of participants, every increase or reduction in the number of participants affects the result."[47] If participants can make other political actors who are able to influence, change, and overrule the decisions of bureaucrats they are dealing with intervene on their behalf, they may force bureaucrats to make favorable decisions.

Finally, participants may also manage to turn the hierarchical relationship between themselves and bureaucrats into an exchange—they can use what they have in exchange for what they want from government officials. For example, Andrew Walder found that the institutional arrangements in Chinese enterprises shape a unique possibility—"patron-clientelism"—for people to pursue their interests. " 'Articulation' of interests is not the primary activity through which individual group members successfully pursue their interests" in Chinese enterprises.[48] "Individual members of subordinate social groups pursue their interests not by banding together for coordinated group actions, but by cultivating ties based on the exchange of loyalty and advantage with individuals of higher status and power."[49]

Having illustrated how institutional settings in China shape the *strategy* used by private citizens to pursue their interests, I now turn to the impact of institutional settings on resources required for people to articulate their interests.

Institutional Settings, Resources, and Political Participation in Beijing

Cross-national research on political participation has demonstrated that socioeconomic status is the most important factor in whether people participate in politics.[50] By exposing affiliated individuals to politically relevant stimuli, by "providing skills and expectations," and by controlling "the channels of political activity," parties and voluntary associations are found to be able to modify the conversion rates of socioeconomic resources into political activities either by mobilizing those who have institutional affiliations or by deterring those who have none from participation.[51] These institutions thus have an *"independent* effect on citizen participation *rates*—independent that is of the resources and motivation associated with citizen's socioeconomic level" (italics added).[52]

The finding that socioeconomic status is the most important resource for political participation and that party and voluntary associations can modify participation rates captures the political dynamics and political process under *certain* institutional settings. However, since this "standard model" is developed from studies of different societies with similar political pro-

cesses, researchers may neglect the possibility that institutional arrangements under which political struggle takes place can also influence the
relationship among status, political institutions, and political participation.
When both the process and the strategy of political struggle in a society
change, resources required for people to participate in politics may also
change.

Political processes from which the "standard model" of political participation is derived have the following common features: (1) most material
and nonmaterial resources are supplied and distributed by the market. The
government regulates rather than distributes resources related to people's
daily lives. As a result, politics is usually only indirectly linked to people's
lives. (2) As participation in such societies is pushed to the policy formulation stage by the particular structural arrangement in those states, participatory acts there have to go through a complicated conversion process to
produce desired benefits for participants. Those acts are only indirectly and
sometimes even remotely linked to the benefits they can bring participants.
In such settings, the ability of private citizens to reconstruct the linkages
between politics and their private lives as well as the linkages between their
participatory acts and the benefits those acts may bring them become the
most important resources for people to participate in politics. Socioeconomic status, especially education, is found to be able not only to help
participants link their political lives to their private interests and bridge
instrumental benefits with their participatory activities, but also to create
expressive benefits of participation by psychologically mobilizing people in
those societies. It thus becomes the most important resource in such a
political process.

Institutional settings in China are quite different: (1) most tangible goods
supplied by markets elsewhere are controlled and allocated directly by the
government. As the state penetrates into nearly every aspect of people's
lives and becomes directly responsible for resource allocation, citizens in
China are invited by the system design to deal with political authority on
a much broader basis. (2) As participation in China focuses on the policy
implementation stage, political acts can hardly produce results relevant to
the entire society or even to large segments of it. In other words, although
the scope of politics is much broader in China than in other societies, the
outcome of people's political activities is usually much narrower and more
directly linked to participants' private interests. Under such an arrangement, the ability of people to link politics to their private lives and to
participatory acts that benefit them will no longer be an important resource
for participation in politics. Most people would have no difficulty in estab-
lishing such linkage. Therefore, it is reasonable to expect that neither socio-

economic status nor psychological involvement in politics would be a crucial resource for people in China to get involved in low-politics issues.[53]

Moreover, without realizing the possibility that people effectively articulate their interests at the policy implementation stage, the standard model
assumes that interest aggregation is a necessary condition for people to
effectively articulate their interests and that group and group-based activities are major political resources in any society.[54] This argument neglects
the fact that this generalization holds true only when people are pushed to
the policy formulation stage to articulate their interests and when meaningful elections for people to choose their rulers are available in a society.
However, when people turn to the policy implementation stage to articulate
their interests and the game of resource competition changes from trying
to make the authorities allocate more resources to a particular segment of
people in a society to trying to obtain resources *already* allocated to that
segment, the political logic in that society requires that participants defeat
rather than collaborate with their colleagues or people with similar attributes. As a result, group and group-based activities may no longer be resources required for people to compete for material and nonmaterial goods
related to their daily lives in Chinese society.

The resources required for people in China to articulate their interests
must be determined by the strategy used by them to alter the hierarchical
relationship between themselves and government officials to defeat the latter. To be able to borrow "normative power" from government policies,
participants usually need to have detailed knowledge of government policy.
Information in this "game" is a crucial resource. Although information in
liberal democratic societies is also an important resource, the function of
information in different political processes can be fundamentally different.
While information in liberal democracies indirectly increases the probability that people will participate in politics by raising people's interest in
politics, the variable in China increases the chance for participants to get
what they want by providing them with ammunition against lower-echelon
government officials. To be able to "borrow" political power from someone
else to change the balance of power between themselves and bureaucrats,
participants in China must have access to government officials at higher
levels who are able and willing to överrule decisions made by lower-echelon
bureaucrats. Finally, to be able to turn the hierarchical relationship between
themselves and bureaucrats into an exchange, participants must have something, either in terms of material goods or services, to offer to decision
makers. Certain political skills are also required to strike deals.

By changing the strategy for people to participate in politics, institutional
arrangements not only change the resources required for people to par-

ticipate in politics but may also alter the causal link between resources and participation in a society. For example, since the publication in 1965 of Gabriel Almond and Sidney Verba's *Civic Culture*, scholars have tended to believe that people's psychological orientations, especially such feelings as efficacy and trust, can facilitate their participation in politics. However, under different institutional settings, psychological orientations may prevent people from engaging in certain acts to pursue their interests, even if they know such acts would bring them desired benefits. For example, it is hard to imagine that a person who believes that the government is responsive to his requests would either bribe officials or engage in regime-challenging political activities to express his opinions.

The finding that political institutions in a society not only determine the rate of participation but also shape the strategy and resources for people to participate in politics has important implications for the study of political participation. Research tells us that the relationship between resources and participation is dynamic, not static. When dealing with government, individuals choose political actions that can make the maximum utility of their political resources to pursue their interests. Since people lacking resources for certain political acts may possess resources useful for other political actions, rather than becoming "apathetic" and "ignorant," as is often assumed, they can turn to political acts requiring different resources to pursue their interests. In other words, since resource conversion in a society is a dynamic process, participants may be able to compensate for their lack of political resources required for certain political acts by choosing other political acts to pursue their goals.

Definition of Political Participation

Political participation in this study is defined as activities by private citizens aimed at influencing the actual results of governmental policy. I take this definition from Verba, Nie, and Kim's seven-nation comparative study, with two revisions. Their definition of political participation refers to "those legal acts by private citizens that are more or less directly aimed at influencing the selection of governmental personnel and/or the actions that they take."[55] First, I drop "legal" from my definition of political participation because many political activities frequently used by citizens in China, such as slow-downs on work sites, sending gifts, and using instrumental personal relationships (*guanxi*) in exchange for favors, are quasi-legal but nonetheless important forms for people to assert their interests. They are too important to be omitted from any study of political participation in Chinese society. Second, because people in China may be able to change the impact of government policy on them without changing the policies themselves, I use "influencing the results of governmental policy" instead of "influencing the selection of governmental personnel and/or the actions that they take" in my definition of political participation in the PRC.

Several other aspects of the definition of political participation should also be noted. First, a major difficulty in studying political participation in a country like China relates to the definition of the "sphere of politics" in the society. Most nonpeasants in China are employees of the state. Nearly every functional organization and enterprise is affiliated with the government in one way or another. Those organizations are responsible for many distributive and redistribution functions that clearly fall within the domain of governments in Western societies. Most political acts also take place in those organizations. But at the same time, those organizations have functional and economic roles. How can we differentiate political decisions from nonpolitical ones in such a society?

Political scientists usually distinguish political acts from nonpolitical ones by the locale in which the acts take place. Apparently, this method cannot be applied in China. On the one hand, we cannot categorize every decision made by work units as a political decision because many decisions of work units are managerial ones that have nothing to do with public policy. On the other hand, we cannot afford to leave acts within work units aimed at influencing government policy implementation untouched. To resolve this dilemma, I differentiate political participation from nonpolitical participation by the *type* of decisions participants are trying to influence rather than by the *locale* where the acts take place. No matter where they take place, participatory acts are political if people attempt to influence the selection of government personnel, the way bureaucrats or their agents implement government policies, and government policy itself. Even if participatory acts take place within work units, as long as participants are aiming at influencing government policy, they will be treated as political participation.

Second, in my study of political participation in China, I am concerned with acts aimed at influencing every stage of the decision-making process, including the policy implementation stage. As institutional arrangements in China not only allow people to exert influence over government decisions at the policy implementation stage but also enable them to alter the hierarchical relationship between themselves and bureaucrats to defeat the latter, I include acts in the policy implementation stage in my definition of political participation.

Third, participation at the policy implementation stage can take many forms. Some acts, such as trying to establish patron-client relationships to pursue one's interests, are unique to China; others are universal and can be found in many other societies. For example, contacts are used both in the United States and China. However, since the institutional arrangements in these two societies are different, the political dynamics of making contacts in the two societies are totally different. While contacting in the United States is backed by the threat to vote officials out of office if they refuse to cooperate, similar acts in China depend on the ability of participants to borrow power from someone else to persuade bureaucrats to make desired concessions. But can this kind of contacting be defined as *political participation*?

> Yes, if one means by political participation activities by which the individual tries to influence some allocational decision on the part of the government. These allocational decisions, furthermore, are often of crucial importance to the individual participant. Though any single allocation may have little effect on the shape of overall governmental policy, the sum of all such allocations represents a major way in which public resources are allocated.[56]

Finally, interest articulation occupies a central position in the definition of political participation.[57] Following this tradition, the kinds of participation I am interested in are flows of interests upward from the masses, rather than downward from the government. Participation refers to political acts aimed at influencing, rather than mere "involvement."[58] Purely ceremonial, mobilizational, or coercive types of "participation" are excluded from this definition. However, because China is now experiencing a dramatic political and economic transition, the nature of many political acts is also dramatically changing. Some important political acts now fall between these two categories.[59] For example, China offers opportunities for people to choose leaders of work units and deputies to people's congresses at the grassroots level through elections. The franchise in today's China is universalized and there are real contests for electoral office in many places. Nonetheless, structured competition among high-level officials in the governmental hierarchy still does not exist, nor do contests among political parties. Open campaign activities are not allowed, but people can persuade other voters how to vote privately. Does this mean we should exclude elections in China from the definition of political participation?

It seems to me that the Chinese government's ongoing attempt to control elections does not justify their exclusion. Elections in today's China do provide an opportunity for people to exert influence over the selection of government officials at the basic level. More important, as long as limited freedom is permitted, both masses and elites try to use the institutions provided by the regime to exert their influence over the political process in society. Elections in recent years have become more and more difficult for the government to control.[60] Many people choose to participate in these imperfect elections to facilitate desired changes in the election system itself, rather than wait for elections to become democratic to participate. Thus, including elections in this study will not only improve our understanding of this particular mode of political participation in China today but also help us to understand the dynamics of change under way in the political processes of the society.

Effectiveness of Participation

Judging the effectiveness of political participation is not an easy task in any society. Classical studies of political participation either try to indirectly infer the effectiveness of participation or avoid making such assessments altogether.[61] Scholars can ignore such issues partly because the effectiveness of participation in liberal democracies is usually self-explanatory. Elections in those societies provide people with opportunities to select government personnel, and citizens there do choose their rulers through elections. More important, political participation and its actual effectiveness are different analytical concepts. As Samuel Huntington and Joan Nelson point out, those who include only successful efforts under the heading of political participation actually "identify political participation with political power."[62]

Since this study attempts to reveal how ordinary people there exert influence over political authority in a communist society, although the full measurement of effectiveness of each participatory act is not necessary, I need to provide readers with at least some evidence to show that participants may be able to get what they want through the acts I describe.

As asking respondents to report whether they believe their political engagement can produce desired benefits directly is usually considered an inaccurate method to measure such a factor, I decided to approach the effectiveness of participation indirectly. To demonstrate the possible effectiveness of participation in Beijing, I asked respondents to identify the behavior of bureaucrats when local interests and government policies are in conflict. Specifically, I asked them to report whether their superiors bowed to pressure from above to sacrifice local interests or bowed to pressure from below to tailor government policy to individual circumstances when facing such a dilemma. Table 1.1 reports their responses. The answers reveal that less than one-third of the respondents are certain that their supervisors would carry out government policy if local interests conflicted with those of the central government. However, a quarter of the respondents believe that bureaucrats would either tailor government policies to private interests

Table 1.1   Perceived behavior of local officials toward "improper" policies
           ($N = 757$)

What respondents believe leaders have done	Percent
Carry out government instructions anyway	31.2
Modify them in implementation	23.1
Totally ignore government policy	1.7
Not applicable	13.2
Don't know	29.5
No answer	1.3

Note: Measured by the question, "When certain directives and instructions of higher
authorities do not take into consideration the concrete situation of your work unit, how do the
leaders in your work unit deal with it?"

or simply ignore such policies to protect local interests. A substantial number of respondents had personal experience with their superiors bowing to pressure from below to protect local interests under such circumstances.

Repeated practice creates a norm or even culture in a society that in turn influences people's behavior. Years of such practice produce a social norm corresponding to the common practice in the society whereby participants ask local officials to make adjustments of government policy at its implementation stage rather than trying to influence policy formulation. Therefore, another way to test the effectiveness of participation in Beijing would be to identify whether a norm has developed in Chinese society stipulating that bureaucrats *should* ignore government policy to protect local interests when necessary. I asked respondents whether they think leaders should modify government policy to protect local interests when government policy is harmful to local interests. Table 1.2 reports the results. It shows that more people (39.9 percent) in Beijing think local bureaucrats should modify policy than believe bureaucrats should carry out unpopular government policies anyway (34.2 percent). The data reveal that a parallel political culture has emerged in China that reinforces the choices of means for citizens to pursue their goals. If we believe that social norms can be produced only by repeated practice in a society, the existence of such unique norms in China can prove—although indirectly—the effectiveness of participation in Beijing.

Data

The population sampled in this study is the total of noninstitutionalized residents aged eighteen or older residing in family households and living

Table 1.2   People's attitudes toward modifying rules by government officials
(N = 757)

What respondents thought the leaders should do	Percent
Comply with rules and regulations	34.2
Modify rules and regulations	39.9
Don't know	24.6
No answer	1.3

Note: Measured by the question, "The leader of Mr. Wang and Mr. Zhang's work unit believes a certain policy does not take into consideration the concrete situation in his unit and is thus unfair and harmful to the interests of his people. After failing to persuade the higher authorities to change the policy, he decides to make appropriate adaptation in light of specific conditions in order to protect the interests of the local people. Mr. Zhang thinks the leader is right and Mr. Wang thinks the leader is wrong. Which point of view do you agree with, Mr. Wang's or Mr. Zhang's?"

in the eight urban districts of Beijing—the capital of the People's Republic of China. A stratified multistage sampling procedure with probabilities proportional to size measures (PPS) was employed to select the sample.[63] The primary sampling units were street offices (*jiedaobanshichu*). The secondary sampling units were neighborhood committees (*juweihui*). Family households were used at the third stage. After the households were selected, interviewers were instructed to use random tables developed by Leslie Kish to choose respondents within each family.

Students of the Department of Sociology and the Department of Statistics of the People's University of China and some staff members of neighborhood committees were used as interviewers. Before the interviews, I gave interviewers intensive week-long training in interview techniques based on the "General Social Survey" published by the Survey Research Center of the University of Michigan. Interviewers had to pass an oral examination to be dispatched for fieldwork.

The interviews were conducted face to face by students from the sociology and statistics departments of the People's University of China from December 12, 1988, to January 10, 1989. A total of 941 interviews were scheduled and 757 were completed, which represents a response rate of 80 percent.

The Validity of the Survey

The issue of validity of measurements used in a survey usually includes identification of random and nonrandom error. Random error refers to the situation in which answers given by respondents to some questions differ from one time to the next. As long as such differences are accidental rather than caused by deliberate misrepresentation, researchers can expect that accidentally reported errors would cancel each other out because the average of many such inaccurate answers would give researchers a true measure of the concept for a particular group of people. By contrast, nonrandom error refers to intentional, systematic error, which will distort the given measurement of a concept. Since the survey reported in this study was conducted in a communist society still under the control of a single party, there is every reason to suspect that some people in that society may want to hide certain political attitudes and behavior, especially political acts not authorized by the regime and attitudes not compatible with those advocated by the authorities. Nonrandom errors thus are likely to contaminate survey results.

Aware of possible political contamination of survey responses, I took several measures in the design of this study to avoid the problem. First, I took precautions against invalidity in construction of measurements. As a general rule, attitude questions are usually more sensitive and likely to worry respondents in China than behavior questions. People thus are more likely to give false answers to attitudinal questions than to behavioral ones. Since this work is designed to study people's political behavior, I tried to avoid attitudinal questions in the questionnaire. Because most participatory acts studied in this work are legitimate in China, at least in theory, behavioral questions used in this study are unlikely to make respondents give interviewers false answers. Moreover, my assessment indicates that people in Beijing did give interviewers frank and candid answers to behavioral questions, even sensitive ones. For example, when asking whether respondents have engaged in job slowdowns, a political act strictly prohibited by the current regime, nearly one-eighth of the respondents frankly told interviewers that they had engaged in such acts to express their opinions. In fact, even if the authorities could catch those who dared to engage in these unauthorized political activities, they could hardly punish them in today's China.

Second, the survey was scheduled during the most liberal period of the PRC in its forty-seven-year history. In late 1988 and early 1989, when the survey was carried out, political study sessions in China were canceled or stopped in most organizations, including governmental bodies. Students and professors in institutions of higher education talked freely about dropping political education classes from university curriculums. Some openly advocated that political cadres permanently withdraw from universities. Even government-sponsored newspapers published articles suggesting transferring political workers to other occupations. In this political atmosphere, I expected people to be more willing to tell the truth to interviewers than in any other period during the history of the regime.

Third, the survey was deliberately undertaken in the most outspoken region in the PRC. Because they live in the capital and have access to more varied information on governmental affairs than other Chinese, residents of Beijing are considered the most politically sophisticated and outspoken people in the country. As suggested by a Chinese saying, "Cantonese dare to eat whatever they can catch, Shanghainese dare to wear whatever they can find, and Beijingese dare to speak out about whatever they can think of." Having experienced various dramatic political upheavals, people in Beijing are less likely to be afraid of challenging the political authorities. In fact, a few months after the survey, millions and millions of people in Beijing took to the streets to protest.

Taking precautions in survey design may not necessarily eliminate non-random errors. We need to look carefully at the data to see if respondents gave candid answers to questions used in the survey, especially politically sensitive questions. Assessing the validity of survey data is never an easy task. Since all we can observe is the measurements, "we cannot know what the relationship between a concept and its measure is."[64] Lack of prior experience with surveys in China can only add to the difficulties of checking the validity of this survey. Nonetheless, there are tests we can conduct to *roughly* evaluate the validity of the data.

Since the major concern with the validity of the data comes from fears of political contamination, the following hypotheses can be developed to gauge the validity of the survey. If respondents felt they needed to hide from interviewers to protect themselves politically, they would have three choices: (1) refuse to be interviewed, (2) give interviewers "don't know" answers to questions they were reluctant to answer, and (3) give interviewers false answers. If we can rule out each of these possibilities, we should be able to conclude that nonrandom error due to political reasons is not a problem.

The first possible way for respondents in China to hide their opinions is the easiest to deal with. If people in China use survey nonresponses to hide their opinions, we should be able to find that survey nonresponses in China are higher than in other societies. Quite the contrary, many researchers found that survey nonresponses in China usually are extremely low—it is not uncommon for researchers to complete a survey in China with more than a 99 percent response rate.[65] Although the response rate of this survey is much lower than the usual 99 percent reported in other surveys, most nonresponses were due to interviewers failing to locate respondents at assigned addresses.[66] Only five respondents refused to be interviewed. Given that refusals reported both in this survey and in others are extremely low, we may safely conclude that survey nonresponses are not frequently used by people in China to hide their opinions for fear of political persecution.

The second way for respondents to hide their opinions is more complicated but not necessarily difficult to rule out. If people in Beijing answer "don't know" to hide their opinions for fear of political persecution, certain findings are likely.

1. Item nonresponse should be higher for politically sensitive questions than for abstract but nonsensitive political questions.

2. Because education increases people's ability to deal with complexity and abstract ideas, which in turn stimulates people to develop opinions independent from official ideology, item nonresponse should be higher among educated people, who are more likely to have something to hide from the authorities.

3. Since 1949, the Chinese Communist Party (CCP) has launched many campaigns to punish those who dared to express independent opinions.[67] Such experiences would not only make people deviate more from official ideology but also encourage them to resist revealing their views to strangers. Thus, we should find a positive correlation between people with experiences of political purges and "don't know" answers to sensitive political questions.

4. People in older generations, who spent most of their lives under intensive regime mobilization, would be more likely to refrain from telling interviewers their opinions than young people, who grew up in the relatively liberal period after the Cultural Revolution. We should find a correlation between age of respondent and "don't know" answers as well.

Of course, item nonresponses may also be given to interviewers because respondents do not have any opinions on questions. If that is the case, we should find that item nonresponse is higher for abstract but nonsensitive political questions than for tangible but politically sensitive questions. As education supposedly increases people's ability to deal with complexity, the less educated should be more likely to give "don't know" answers to survey questions. Nonresponses should also be negatively associated with respondents' access to information on economic, social, and political affairs. Finally, nonresponses should be negatively associated with respondents' interests in politics.

Analysis of item nonresponse to questions used in the survey shows that there is no clear association between the political sensitivity of questions and the frequency of respondents' giving interviewers "don't know" answers. On the contrary, item nonresponses are higher for questions regarding abstract subjects and questions not associated with respondents' daily lives. Moreover, education, media access, and an interest in politics are all negatively correlated with item nonresponse. Such results suggest that cognitive deficiency explains item nonresponse in Beijing better than the political persecution thesis common in the comparative politics literature.

The last strategy for people to conceal their ideas is much more difficult to test. However, simple observation of the answers to some sensitive political questions suggests that people in Beijing did give interviewers candid answers to sensitive political questions, even if their answers directly contradicted official doctrine and official ideology. For example, when asked with whom they don't want to talk about politics, quite a few respondents told interviewers that they don't want to discuss politics with either party secretaries or "activists" in their organizations. When asked about "grapevine rumors," which are prohibited by the regime, nearly half of the respondents confessed that they had listened to or even spread grapevine rumors on political, social, and economic affairs in society. Although simple observation does not allow us to rule out the possibility that respondents lied to interviewers, such observations do suggest that people in Beijing are quite receptive to giving their opinions to interviewers even on sensitive political questions.

Although respondents in Beijing are unlikely to lie to interviewers for fear of political persecution, there are still some other limitations of this study. Because the survey was conducted during the most liberal period in the history of the PRC and in the most politicized place in the country, we should be cautious when trying to make generalizations from the findings of this study across space and time. The timing of the survey can influence respondents' answers to survey questions *and* their behavior. When the political atmosphere in the society changes, as it did when the government tightened its control after 1989, people who are active in certain unauthorized political acts may refrain from engaging in them any more. Even if participants still choose to engage in unauthorized political activities, they may no longer want to reveal their behavior to interviewers.

Overview of the Book

I started my inquiry of people's political participation in Communist China by exploring the structural effects on people's political behavior. Chapter

2 identifies twenty-eight political acts used by people in Beijing to articulate their interests. I considered each of these political acts to answer such questions as, What purposes can participants achieve through these acts? What functions do these acts serve in the political process in China? How do political actors interact with one another? What are the political dynamics of these activities? Discussions of these issues are based both on my observations as a citizen living in China for thirty years and on intensive interviews conducted in Beijing from 1988 to 1989 with members of various organizations, including party and government bodies, research institutions, companies, and factories.

Chapter 3 presents an initial analysis of the survey results to see whether the respondents in Beijing actively engage in different forms of political activism or disengaged from the political process, as suggested by many students of communist participation.[68] I concentrate on questions such as, How widely do people in Beijing engage in these political activities? Specifically, do participants come from a broad segment of the population or from a small number of activists? I then explore the relationship between conventional and unconventional political activities in Beijing. Do people who get involved in conventional activities also choose unconventional acts to pursue their interests? Is there a threshold between conventional and unconventional political activism? Answers to these questions are important for us to understand the nature of various political activities in China.

Chapter 4 deals with questions raised by the differences among political acts found in Chapter 2. Some are encouraged by the authorities, while others are strictly prohibited by the regime. Some require a thorough knowledge of the political process, while others require few resources on the part of participants. Some involve substantial amounts of risk, while others are quite safe. How should we characterize these political activities? What are the dimensions behind them? How do these underlying dimensions influence one another and form alternative modes for people to pursue their goals? The analysis in Chapter 4 suggests that political acts in Beijing may be differentiated from one another by the initiative required, risks involved, and aspect of conflict. Different combinations of these three underlying dimensions cluster political acts in Beijing into seven participatory modes. They are voting, campaign activities, appeals, adversarial activities, cronyism, resistance, and election boycotts.

The focus of the study then shifts to the process by which people in Beijing become politicized and express their opinions through these alternative participatory modes. In analyzing the politicization process in Beijing, I pay special attention to the impact of institutional arrangements on the strategy employed and resources required for people to pursue their goals. Chapter 5 explores the process by which people in Beijing become politicized and vote in elections. Instead of mobilizing people to abstain from voting to protest, socioeconomic resources are found to mobilize people to go to the ballot booth on election days. The finding suggests that, rather than waiting for elections to become fully democratic to participate, people in Beijing vote in these not-so-perfect elections to pursue their interests.

Chapter 6 turns to other participatory activities associated with elections, that is, campaign activities and election boycotts. I consider the impact of recent changes in the electoral system itself as well as the impact of the regime's attitudes toward elections on people's political behavior. How do recent changes in the electoral system influence people's campaign behavior? the electoral system in China? Who in Beijing engages in campaign activities and election boycotts? What resources are required for them to get involved in these activities?

Appeals are the most frequently used political acts. Chapter 7 analyzes appeals in Beijing. I explore such questions as, For what purposes do people in Beijing make appeals to the authorities? What resources are required? How are these resources converted into appeals that help people get desired benefits? Examination of the causal links between various resources and appeals demonstrates that institutional arrangements can not only change the resources required for similar political acts in different societies but also shape unique ways in which resources are converted into political actions.

Chapter 8 deals with the remaining three participatory modes in Beijing: adversarial activities, resistance, and cronyism. Analysis of the process by which people in Beijing get involved in acts belonging to these modes shows that these participatory acts are another means for people to pursue their goals rather than acts utilized by people just to relieve their frustration. It also shows that engaging in these acts requires different political resources on the part of participants. This finding tells us that, rather than becoming "apathetic" and "ignorant," people lacking resources for certain political acts turn to political acts that require different resources to pursue their interests.

Chapter 9 summarizes the findings of this book and discusses their implications for future studies. The study demonstrates that the impact of institutional settings on people's political behavior is much more complicated than students of political participation have realized. Rather than simply blocking people from becoming involved in politics and effectively articulating their interests, institutional arrangements in China influence where in the decision-making process participation takes place, who participates, what strategies can be used by people, and what resources are required for people to participate. More important, when institutional settings in a society change, all four of these dimensions change.

2

Forms of Citizen Participation in Beijing

In this chapter, I answer some basic questions: Are there any ways for people in Beijing to participate in the political process to articulate their private interests? If so, what are the major ways? What resources do they have to influence the decisions of government officials at various levels? What are the political dynamics of these activities? Finally, do citizens in Beijing engage in these acts to articulate their interests, or is their political engagement mobilized and controlled by the government?

Elections

Two kinds of elections have been available to Chinese citizens in recent years. One is elections for deputies to local people's congresses, and the other is leadership elections for work units or villages. These two kinds of elections are different in the authority from which they are derived, the constituencies on which they are based, and their impact on individuals as well as on society.

ELECTIONS OF DEPUTIES TO LOCAL PEOPLE'S CONGRESSES

The system of people's congresses was first established in 1953–54 through a national election conducted by the CCP. The people's congress system in China has a hierarchical structure.[1] At the top of the structure is the National People's Congress (NPC). Below the NPC are the provincial people's congresses and people's congresses for special municipalities, that is, cities under the direct control of the central government. Below the provincial level are people's congresses in counties (*xian*) in rural areas and people's congresses in cities in urban areas. Since the special municipalities are considered provincial-level administrative organizations, people's congresses under special municipalities are held in districts (qu), which are equal to people's congresses in ordinary cities.

Counties in China are divided into townships (xiang), and cities are divided into districts. Districts in special municipalities are divided into neighborhoods (jiedao). People's congresses at the township level in rural areas and district level in urban areas are branches of the organization at the basic level. The right for ordinary citizens to vote was first codified by the election law passed in 1953 and confirmed in each subsequent PRC constitution. However, under the 1953 election law, not every Chinese had the right to vote. The landlord class and counterrevolutionary elements and those who were deprived of their political rights did not have the right to vote in elections.[2] The 1953 election law also provided for the direct election of basic-level people's congresses. Under the law, rural residents could vote for deputies to township-level people's congresses and urban residents could vote for district- or jiedao-level people's congresses in special municipalities. The deputies to the NPC and to other people's congresses were elected by the next lower level of deputies.

Elections for deputies to people's congresses were, however, suspended for thirteen years during the Cultural Revolution (1966–1979). In 1979 the authorities passed a new election law, which adopted some provisions from the Eastern European system before the collapse of the communist parties there. The 1979 election law stated that, first, the number of candidates in each precinct would be one and a half to two times the number of delegates to be elected rather than, as in the past, the same number. Second, all voting was to be by secret ballot, not by a show of hands.[3] Third, the new law limited disenfranchisement to those who "have been deprived of political rights according to law" and extended universal suffrage to all Chinese citizens.[4] Finally, the law raised the level of direct elections from the basic to the local level. Instead of voting for deputies to people's congresses at the township and district levels, people in China now vote for deputies to county-level people's congresses.[5] The elections from 1979 to 1981 under the new law were "the first nationwide elections based on universal suffrage for offices above the lowest level since China had become a republic in 1912."[6] Since then elections for deputies to local people's congresses have been held every four years all over the country.

Regime attitudes toward elections are mixed. On the one hand, the authorities use elections for regime legitimation, popular education, political socialization, and "subjecting local cadres to popular scrutiny."[7] On the other hand, the ruling elites are afraid of losing power through the very same elections. Unfortunately, these two goals obviously conflict with each other. To make citizens in the society accept the reality of being ruled by someone is one thing, but to make them accept that person as *a legitimate ruler* is a totally different matter. It is hard to imagine that people in any country would honor as legitimate rulers those who win offices in elections without candidate choice. Legitimation through elections requires both candidate choice and contestation among elites. Not only must the candidates be allowed to freely contest the elections but the masses should be allowed to make free choices. Over the past fifteen years the authorities in China have worked hard to keep a delicate balance between subjecting local cadres to popular scrutiny and political control.

The CCP is not always successful in its endeavors. At the national level, the NPC has begun to get out from under the party's control and play a more active role in Chinese politics. Unanimous voting has also become a thing of the past, and the deputies increasingly have expressed themselves openly and critically in some recent sessions. In 1987, a group of deputies to the NPC, in conjunction with members of the Chinese People's Political Consultative Conference, successfully blocked a project initiated by Premier Li Peng for construction of the Three Gorges (*Sanxia*) Dam on the Yangtze River. In May 1989, Hu Jiwei, a member of the Standing Committee of the NPC, successfully gathered thirty-eight legislators to sign a motion to convene a special session of the committee, hoping to revoke martial law and calling for the restoration of Zhao Ziyang as party general secretary.[8] This liberalizing trend was interrupted by the 1989 student movement for a short time but has resumed its strength in recent years.

At both the local and provincial levels, it is no longer news for candidates nominated by the authorities to lose elections. In 1986 Chen Yuan, son of Chen Yun and the chairman of Xicheng District in Beijing, was nominated by the CCP as a candidate for deputy mayor of Beijing, a position that required the confirmation of the People's Congress in Beijing Municipality. To be considered for the position, the candidate had to be a deputy to the People's Congress. Chen lost in the local election and thus was not eligible to be considered for deputy mayor. He was then transferred to another position. His case is not unique in today's China, and a growing number of similar cases have occurred in recent years. More important, deputies to people's congresses have also begun to nominate their own candidates for leadership positions. At the provincial-level people's congresses, a growing number of candidates without endorsement by the CCP are elected to leadership positions. Three candidates without the endorsement of the CCP were elected as deputy governors in the 1987–88 elections. The figure increased to five in the 1992 elections. The central government in Beijing finally endorsed the results of these elections.[9] Some candidates not nominated by the CCP have also joined electoral competition in local-level elections in China. For example, in Peking University's electoral district, a total of eighteen candidates, most of them dissidents, participated in the 1980 elections. Some of them were even elected deputies.

The fact that no alternative electoral platform is allowed in China does not necessarily mean that candidates cannot have their own agenda or advocate a platform different from that of the CCP. The way for them to do so is through the "game of interpretation." A single unified platform does not prevent candidates from interpreting such a platform in their own way. For example, promoting socialist democracy has always been in the party's platform. But what does socialist democracy mean? Since the CCP has never given a clear definition of it, candidates can feed constituencies with their own ideas. In the 1980 elections, some candidates advocated freedom of speech, while others produced a draft publication law to promote freedom of publication.[10] Even the separation of governmental powers, an independent press, and the breakup of the concentration of power in the CCP center were openly advocated "to support the party's platform to advance socialist democracy."[11] In these cases, the "interpretations" were so liberal that candidates actually provided their constituencies with a totally different platform, even in sensitive areas of high politics. The strategy is not a new one, and it has been widely used by political activists in China ever since the founding of the People's Republic in 1949. Mao Zedong himself condemned such tactics as "waving the red flag against the red flag."

Although both candidates and deputies have a certain freedom to maneuver, the impact of elections in China on national politics remains tenuous because most of these contests are still far removed from the highest levels. However, lacking direct impact on national politics and on government policies does not necessarily mean that elections for deputies cannot be used by people in China to articulate their interests. To fully understand the function of elections in the Chinese political process, an examination of the structural arrangement of the electoral districts and the mechanisms utilized by the regime to control elections is in order.

We know that the social and economic life of Chinese citizens is organized by work units. Work units are the primary source for satisfying people's needs in their daily lives, which are taken care of by local governments in many other countries.[12] People working in the same work unit tend to live in the same residential area built by that organization. Although electoral districts in Beijing are usually divided along geographic lines, the chances of their intersecting with work units are quite high. In places where electoral districts do not intersect with work units, deputy elections can hardly produce any tangible effects for the citizen. In places where electoral districts do intersect with work units, deputy elections can have a significant impact on voters, although the dynamic of this impact is significantly different from those in other societies.

We know the major issues facing local people's congresses are still low-politics ones related to people's daily lives. Work units in urban China remain the primary organization to which the government allocates resources. Such an arrangement makes interest in electoral districts homogeneous. Deputies elected from work units, if they overlap with electoral districts, must represent the interests of the units they came from rather than those of a particular group within the work unit. When dealing with the government, work units are in fact the most important organizational interest group in China.

The homogeneity of interests within Chinese urban electoral districts enables voters to pay little attention to the policy preferences of the candidates in determining whom to vote for. Voters know that no matter who gets elected, the policy preference of the person on issues that local people's congresses are capable of dealing with would be roughly the same. Given such a situation, the credentials of the candidate, his or her integrity, willingness to confront authorities in defending local interests, and even attitudes toward high-politics issues play a much more important role in voting decisions.

We know that the regime still tries to control elections in China. However, the changes in the election law in 1979 forced the authorities to change the mechanism for exercising that control. Rather than presenting people with elections without candidate choice, the regime now controls elections through monopolizing and manipulating the nomination process: authorities nominate people they trust to be candidates. Since the most trustworthy people are always their own people, the CCP usually nominates local cadres as candidates in deputy elections. Ironically, the efforts of the regime to control elections actually give citizens an opportunity to articulate their interests through deputy elections. The authorities can nominate whomever they trust to be candidates, but it is still up to the employees to vote for the candidates. Such a control mechanism actually puts party cadres under the scrutiny of ordinary citizens, and the way in which interests in China are organized enables citizens to ignore the policy consequences when making electoral choices.

For cadres who were nominated by the government as candidates, winning elections usually does not do them any good. They are expected to win anyway. But losing elections can be a disaster for them. Losing clearly exhibits to authorities their incompetence and usually blocks their way to further promotion. In many cases, the authorities transfer them to other leadership positions. Theoretically, transfers are supposed to be made among equal positions (*pingdiao*). In reality, the majority of losers are transferred to unimportant posts, and such transfers are actually demotions.[13] Many voters realize the workings of the system, and some of them have begun to use the opportunity to punish disliked leaders of work units.

To summarize, elections for deputies to people's congresses in today's China are still limited-choice elections. Different from plebiscitary elections, with one candidate per seat, limited-choice elections provide people with candidate choices.[14] Since votes are cast secretly, citizens in China can make free choices according to their will without worrying about potential punishment. At the same time, the government still works hard to control elections, and the influence of the deputies is still confined to low-politics issues. Despite institutional arrangements to prevent ordinary citizens from using elections to influence decisions made by the government on high politics, the control mechanism utilized by the authorities in China does produce compensatory effects—it enables some voters to use the opportunity to punish unpopular leaders in their work units.

ELECTIONS OF LEADERS OF WORK UNITS

The other kind of elections available to Beijing residents is elections of leaders of work units (*danwei lingdao*). Unlike elections for deputies to local people's congresses, elections for leaders of work units are prescribed neither by the constitution nor by electoral law. The 1982 constitution does require that elections be held for residents' and villagers' committees, but such elections have never been carried out seriously in urban residential areas. Members of residents' committees are usually appointed by higher authorities.

In recent years, more and more work unit leaders in Beijing have been chosen by elections. Several considerations motivate authorities to allow and encourage elections for leaders of work units. First, when elections for work unit leaders were introduced to the Chinese system in the late 1970s, economic considerations played a more important role than political questions. The regime hoped to identify competent individuals and put them in leadership positions through elections to increase the efficiency of these organizations. With nearly all factories in China owned by the state in one way or another and many, if not most, of them poorly managed, many people attributed the low efficiency of the enterprises to poor management and believed the leadership in these enterprises was the key to increased productivity. Yet, personnel officers at various levels of the government had difficulty in identifying the right people to be promoted. Even when personnel officers could identify capable people, their candidates were often unable to win the cooperation of the employees in the work units concerned, which was crucial for managerial success. To resolve these problems, some officials in the central government advocated direct elections for leaders of work units. They argued that elections were the only way for the authorities to identify individuals capable of increasing productivity and enjoying the support of their constituencies. Since the elections of work unit leaders are conducted at a low level, they argued, such elections could hardly create an immediate danger to the regime.[15]

The actual elections of leaders in work units were simultaneously initiated by factory workers in 1979. Workers in the Foreign Language Printing House took the initiative to organize such elections to choose all the heads of the workshop. The results of these elections seemed to confirm the expectations of the authorities.[16] In one report the Xinhua News Agency claimed that elections led to factories "fulfill[ing] state targets one month ahead of schedule" and that there was a "general rise in efficiency."[17] In another report, similar elections in other companies were alleged to have led to a "30 percent increase" in production.[18]

Second, with the economic reforms in China, legitimacy of leaders became an important political issue. In the Chinese system, the ownership of the means of production belongs to the state. At least in theory, the state has the power to appoint the leadership of various organizations to represent it and exercise control. With enterprises belonging to the state, each person working in them was known to enjoy the same rights as everyone else. However, with responsibility spread throughout the country after 1982, new managers and heads of organizations were no longer representing the state to run its enterprises or organizations. The question arose, why is A instead of B appointed as a new manager, or allowed to sign contracts with the state? Why should an incumbent manager give his or her power to a new one? The state needed to find a way to justify transfer of authority in such organizations. In addition, since the state was no longer responsible for any losses of enterprises or functional organizations after managers entered into agreements or signed contracts with the government, employees demanded that their voices be heard in leadership selection. This latent legitimacy crisis generated by the economic reforms forced the CCP to allow employees to choose their managers through elections.

Third, authorities in China also wanted to control corruption and the abuse of power by local cadres through elections. Students of Chinese politics are familiar with the way that China's social structure creates stable networks of loyal clients, who exchange their loyalty and support for preferences in career opportunities and other rewards.[19] Such networks are dysfunctional to the political system, and fighting against them has been a constant theme in Chinese politics since the founding of the PRC. Mao himself complained many times about their pervasiveness. His main mechanism for resolving these problems and "cleaning up" lower-echelon "corrupt" bureaucrats was the political campaign. On one occasion, he even claimed that political campaigns would be carried out every seven to eight years in order to fight against corrupt officials and "capitalist roaders."[20]

When Deng Xiaoping took over the leadership position in the early 1980s, he announced the abandonment of political campaigns permanently, without substituting another method for checking abuses of local power holders and bureaucrats at various levels of the government.[21] Deng's move helped to reduce tensions among the central authorities, lower-level bureaucrats, and the masses, but the regime neutralized its most effective means of controlling bureaucrats. Although the authorities can still control lower-level bureaucrats through appointments and promotions, this mechanism was actually eroded by the social networks and patron-client ties generated by the social structure in China over time.

With the economic reforms and decentralization under way, control over lower-echelon cadres became increasingly difficult. The authorities quickly realized the danger of abandoning political campaigns as a control mechanism without finding substitutes to engender regime support. Since the early 1980s, the government has tried in many ways to reclaim its control over local bureaucrats, and elections for leaders in work units is one of these ways. The authorities permitted elections for officials up to, but not above, the bureau chief level (sijuji). Under such an arrangement, many managers in factories, bureau chiefs in government organizations, and department chairs in universities are elected by the masses.

Finally, some officials support work unit elections because they believe these elections can be used by them in power struggles to get rid of lower-level government officials they dislike. Under the current system, once a person is in power, it is very hard for his or her superior to dismiss the person, unless he or she commits certain "unpardonable mistakes"—usually equal to crimes. Superiors may give subordinates a hard time, refuse them promotions, assign them to unwanted positions, but they cannot fire them. The introduction of work unit elections actually enabled unhappy superiors to take advantage of elections to get rid of disliked subordinates. As long as a superior predicts that the subordinate he does not like is going to lose, he will support an election. By the same token, political enemies of leaders within the work unit may also support elections to gain political power within the organization. Although cadres organize elections for various purposes, ordinary citizens in urban China have begun to use these elections to achieve their own goals. "Work unit elections offered significant scope both for participation and for interest articulation," observed Victor Falkenheim. "Unit leadership elections [in certain areas] elicited virtually total participation and considerable contention, including extensive lobbying efforts."[22]

Persuading Others to Attend Campaign or Briefing Meetings

In both elections, a series of meetings are organized by the authorities. In the meetings, the government presents voters with potential candidates to be scrutinized. Individuals presented by the authorities for discussion at this stage are still not the official candidates, and voters are encouraged to express their opinions about people proposed by the authorities in the meetings. The opinions of ordinary people expressed in these meetings can and do make a difference in the candidates' status. Voters can also nominate their own candidates at this stage. This process is called democratic consultation (*minzhu xieshang*). When the candidates are finalized, candidates can express their opinions on various issues at meetings.

Should attendance at such meetings be categorized as political participation? Judging by the current situation in China, I prefer not to categorize simple attendance at campaign meetings as participatory behavior. These meetings were the most important arena for people to communicate their evaluation of candidates to the authorities when elections were still plebiscites before and during the Cultural Revolution. Many voters used the opportunity to express their opinions on candidates selected by the authorities. But with the changes in the election system in China in recent years, especially with multiple candidates available and the introduction of secret ballots to replace shows of hands, voters in China prefer waiting until elections to express their opinion by secret ballot to speaking out publicly at meetings. Taking lifetime employment into account—people will live and work together in the same work unit for their entire lives—voters have every incentive to conceal their activities from their colleagues and from candidates they do not like. Even people chosen to lobby authorities to withdraw the nominations of certain candidates generally do so outside formal meetings. Covert actions are preferable to open confrontation at meetings since they can produce the same results and the risks involved are usually much lower for participants. To make the status of attendance at those meetings more ambiguous,

> some work units adopted compulsory attendance policies for public meetings, so that real variation occurred mainly in levels of "attentiveness." Under these circumstances, what was significant, in the words of one informant, was not

"who came to meetings, but who remained awake." Other work units encouraged attendance by awarding compensatory work points, particularly for
daylight meetings, thus introducing pecuniary incentives for participation.[23]

Even though attendance at campaign meetings can be characterized as a
participatory act most of the time, some people are mobilized by the authorities to participate in these meetings. To exclude mobilized participation from this study, I adopted a more stringent standard in judging
whether an activity should be characterized as participatory. Instead of
simply including attendance at campaign meetings, I treat acts to persuade
others to go to campaign meetings as participatory activities. Persuading
others to attend campaign or candidate briefing meetings is a far more
significant act—it requires more initiative by participants. Participants
must be actively engaged in such acts rather than passively engaged by the
authorities.

Two major groups of people in China usually engage in such activities,
although their purposes are usually different. Political activists engage in
such acts to help the authorities mobilize people to get involved in the
electoral process. "Troublemakers" may also engage in such acts to challenge incumbents. Even though activists engage in such acts to help the
government mobilize voters and troublemakers engage in such activities to
challenge candidates nominated by the authorities, both of them try to
mobilize other voters to support their own positions.

Campaigns for Candidates

As long as real competition is allowed among candidates, certain people in
society will try to influence the decisions of other voters. Scholars have
found that in certain elections in China, competition among candidates
became so rigorous that people actively involved in campaign activities
influenced the voting decisions of others.[24] Campaigns in China usually
take two forms: lobbying and persuasion. By "lobbying," I mean acts aimed
at influencing the decisions of authorities as to whether to put someone's
name on the ballot. Such acts usually begin before candidates have been
finalized by election committees. Campaigners can either lobby authorities
to include certain people on the ballot or exclude them from candidate
lists, or lobby other voters to support their own arguments. By "persuasion,"
I mean acts aimed at influencing the decisions of other voters. After the
authorities determine the candidates, campaigners shift their work from
the authorities to the masses and concentrate on persuading other voters
to vote for specific candidates.

Persuading Others to Boycott Unfair Elections

Even though the impact of elections on government policy is still limited in China, citizens have begun to use the opportunity provided to punish unpopular leaders in their localities. For bureaucrats, the stakes of today's elections are much higher than those of plebiscitary ones previously. As they realized that a lost election could cost them their job, many bureaucrats in China began to manipulate elections to increase the possibility for "victory." At the same time, changes in the Chinese electoral system also raised the expectations of ordinary citizens toward elections. If few expected plebiscitary elections in the past to be fair, more and more people have expectations of fairness today.

The manipulation of elections by bureaucrats and the rising expectations for elections have made more people dissatisfied with them. Dissatisfied individuals may choose to ignore elections or to protest them in several ways. With the declining ability of the government to mobilize people to vote, nonvoting can hardly bring unpleasant consequences for individuals. Some people no doubt abstain from voting or cast blank votes in elections to protest. The difficulty facing researchers is that people in China choose not to vote for various reasons. Some people choose not to vote because they are not interested in politics; others fail to vote owing to illness or physical absence; and still others don't vote to protest. Because more than one reason can prevent voters from casting ballots, it is extremely difficult, if not impossible, to differentiate apathy from protest behavior.

Fortunately, those who strongly object to the unfairness of elections not only boycott elections themselves but also persuade others to boycott elections in order to create trouble for bureaucrats. Even if it is difficult to determine why a person failed to vote, we can safely characterize the act of persuading others to boycott elections as protest behavior. Therefore, rather than categorizing simple nonvoting as protest activity, I made sure to ask respondents whether they had ever persuaded *others* to boycott elections both for deputies and for leaders of work units.

Personal Contacting

The authorities in China have long recognized that society is composed of complex interests and that private interests may indeed not be compatible with collective ones as defined by the CCP. Rather than broadly suppressing *any* kind of private interest articulation as suggested by totalitarian scholars, the CCP actually allows certain kinds of interest articulation. Chinese leaders accommodate private interest articulation if it does not challenge party control or damage CCP self-defined "collective interests." The regime not only allows citizens to pursue low-politics issues but also encourages officials at various levels of the government to address them as well.

The attitudes of the authorities toward private interest articulation were best illustrated by the mass line—"the correct leadership style"—in China. Mao Zedong identified the mass line as "from the masses, to the masses."[25] It required that leaders at various levels obtain information on what ordinary citizens were thinking and integrate it with government policy during the policy formation stage. After policies were made, the government was to brief people on the policies and resolve any doubts among them. Even though no one was allowed to challenge decisions after policies were made, bureaucrats were allowed and encouraged to make necessary policy adjustments during implementation to meet with the "concrete situation" of each locality. The mass line also required leaders to keep in close contact with the populace, and such contacts were in fact considered the major mechanism to prevent bureaucrats from abusing power.[26]

Since the definition of collective interests differs at different levels of governmental organization, and since bureaucrats in China are encouraged to make necessary adjustments when implementing government policy to adapt to the specific situation of localities, individuals in China do have some room to maneuver within this framework. Before policies are formalized, people can contact officials at various levels to express their opinions of them. When an unpopular policy is made by the government, rather than directly challenging it, citizens contact local officials to press them to use their discretionary power to protect local interests when implementing the policy. Citizens may also contact officials at higher levels to persuade them to overrule certain policies made by lower-echelon bureaucrats or report power abuses. The scope of issues involved in these contacts can be extremely broad, ranging from housing assignments to salary increases, power abuses, interpersonal conflicts, public transportation, public education, and children's employment.

Personal contact can entail officials at various levels of government. Some people choose to contact officials at the work unit level; others go to higher government organizations. Participants use various strategies when contacting government officials. Some people contact government officials in a conciliatory manner, to persuade government officials to make beneficiary decisions; others choose a confrontational style, to put pressure on the officials to induce desired changes. Still others contact government officials through patron-client ties, to turn the relationship from a hierarchical one into an exchange. Participants offer bureaucrats certain material goods or services they need in exchange for resources they control. Different forms of contacting require different resources and serve different purposes.

Contacting Leaders of Work Units

Since most aspects of people's lives in China are controlled by work units, citizens turn first to those organizations. People may contact leaders of their work units to voice demands, to express opinions, and to persuade or to press leaders to have their interests taken into consideration when making decisions. The issues involved in such contacts could be government policies per se or the discretion of the unit in implementing the policies made by higher authorities. Some people beg their leaders to "make adjustments" on policies deemed improper according to "concrete situations"; others challenge the legitimacy of policies according to certain principles; and still others choose to challenge the way in which leaders interpret policies.

Sometimes citizens persuade leaders of work units to support or even represent them when dealing with governmental agencies for issues related to their private lives. In such situations, representing interests of employees in dealing with government agencies can be justified as putting the mass line into practice. Work units as organizations possess more resources than individuals and are usually taken more seriously by various government agencies than private citizens would be. If a person can induce the leaders of a work unit to act on his or her behalf in dealing with other government agencies, the chances for successful intervention will be greatly enhanced as the bargaining will be conducted between two organizations (*zuzhi dui zuzhi*).

Given that the contacts I am discussing are done within the work unit and that many employees contact leaders for managerial purposes, the question arises whether we should characterize such acts as political participation. Calling certain contacting at Chinese work units political activities is one thing, but characterizing all such acts as political participation is another. I have included certain kinds of contacting at the work unit level in this study because the structural arrangements in Chinese society make work units represent the state to deal with private citizens on a daily basis and to carry out policies made by the authorities. If Chinese citizens want to influence authoritative resource allocation, the place for them to go is their work units rather than government agencies. Work units themselves should thus be considered government organizations.

Work units in China also play managerial functions. Many people contact their leaders at the work unit for managerial purposes on a regular basis. To exclude contacting for managerial purposes from this study, I created two scenarios to solicit personal contacting behavior at the work unit level in the questionnaire. First, I asked respondents whether they had contacted leaders of their work units when they "considered certain decisions of the work unit, such as salary raises, bonus distributions, apartment allotments and children taking over parents' positions as harmful and unjust." These issues are regulated by government policy and each work unit has certain autonomy in its actual implementation of such policies. If a person contacts the leaders of his unit for such issues, we know for sure that his or her act is political rather than managerial. Second, I asked if respondents had ever tried to persuade unit leaders to do something when they thought certain government policies were harmful. "When a policy or regulation of the government that you considered unjust or harmful was enacted," the question read, "have you ever gone to leaders in the work unit to seek help?" Such an act clearly has nothing to do with managerial decisions and should be considered a political action.

Various studies have found leaders in work units in urban China quite responsive to demands made by ordinary citizens. As Andrew Walder observes, "it is puzzling that in a political system where the organized expression of worker demands is discouraged so systematically, managers would be so sensitive to workers' needs, and so seemingly afraid of latent conflict."[27] Why do bureaucrats bother to listen to demands from below? We know that the bargaining leverage of people in liberal democracies comes from their votes in elections. We also know that elections are still not institutionalized in China. In such a system what, if any, bargaining leverage and resources do citizens have when dealing with government officials?

The official political culture in China does not prevent bureaucrats from listening to the opinions of the masses. According to the mass line, the correct working style requires government officials at various levels to listen to mass opinion. As long as the opinions and demands made by private citizens are not in conflict with the long-term interests of the state as defined by the CCP, the authorities in China encourage government officials at lower levels to accommodate those demands. Whether a demand is in conflict with the interests of the state is determined by bureaucrats rather than by participants, however; so the mass line cannot guarantee bureaucrats will listen to people. What the mass line in China does is provide a normative setting for individuals to contact officials of their work units. The key to the political power of ordinary citizens must be found in some of the specific institutional arrangements therein.

The lifetime employment system in China provides people with great bargaining leverage over bureaucrats. The right to work of the Chinese citizen is guaranteed by the constitution, and no one can infringe on such a basic right until quite recently.[28] Once hired, an employee cannot be dismissed unless the person "commits serious mistakes," meaning actual felonies.[29] Whereas once bureaucrats could punish people they didn't like for political reasons, after the Cultural Revolution, it became harder for them to do so. The lifetime employment system actually gives workers the same kind of protection provided by independent trade unions to their members in other societies. In addition, until recently, employees were free from the consequences of bankrupt enterprises. When enterprises went bankrupt, the government was responsible for finding employees new jobs. Although this lifetime employment system has begun to change in recent years, the "Iron Rice Bowl" still has not been broken for political reasons. Freed from the fear of being fired and losing jobs through bankruptcy, employees can easily become petty overlords if they know how to maneuver within the system.

Moreover, bureaucrats in China not only represent the state in controlling the society but are also held accountable for the performance of their work units. The evaluation and promotion of leaders is tied to their ability to fulfill the functional roles assigned to their organization, which depends on its employees. According to Walder, "one problem for which (the leaders) alone will always be held accountable is a decline in labor productivity."[30] Every employee in China knows this simple fact. To make things even worse for bureaucrats, unlike managers of enterprises in other countries, the managers of Chinese enterprises cannot freely decide on salaries of employees because the salary scale is regulated by the government. Within work units, the salary of employees is determined by a group consisting of leaders of the units as well as representatives of ordinary employees. Few leaders, if any, want to serve on this committee.

Although leaders have a certain amount of autonomy in distributing bonuses currently, their overall ability to influence the economic situation of their subordinates was rather limited at the time of this survey. Many arrangements are built into the Chinese system to make citizens dependent on work units, but leaders in China also depend on the cooperation of their inferiors to fulfill the functional role of their organizations. As the ability of leaders to punish noncooperative behavior and reward cooperation is limited, officials at the basic level generally need to seek and win the goodwill of their subordinates to carry out the functional role assigned to their organizations, a task crucial for their careers.

Several strategies can thus be used by employees to induce their leaders to accommodate their requests. Some people may use a conciliatory manner and "beg" bureaucrats for help. To get desired help from bureaucrats, participants usually need to have accumulated some "credit" with them for services done or help given beforehand. Those who do not have any credit with bureaucrats might choose to play the role of petty overlord when dealing with the officials.[31] They can contact the leaders with latent threats to refuse to cooperate in the future if their request is not satisfied. Tactics at their disposal range from work slowdowns and open insults to the harassment of leaders in their private lives.[32] As long as the acts are carefully kept within boundaries known to most people in Chinese society, it is hard for authorities to punish such behavior. For example, one laboratory worker told our interviewer:

> When I requested that the leader in our unit help me to put my daughter in a decent school nearby, he kept saying that the school refused to accept any more children because the classrooms were too small, the teachers were too few, and so on and so forth. I pointed out that he was able to help me if he really wanted to. But he claimed it was beyond his ability. I knew that discussions like this would lead us nowhere. I am a laboratory worker and all the products of the factory have to be examined before they can reach the market. If I abstain from the job, the whole production of my factory would be jeopardized. After several useless discussions with the leader, I told him that since he refused to help me, I had to work on the issue on my own. Therefore, I needed to ask for a leave of absence to deal with the school authorities by myself. He knew what that meant and quickly agreed to intervene. He picked up the phone and called the Education Bureau of the district government and lodged a complaint about the school authorities in our area and told them the behavior of the local school would have an impact on the production of our factory. The officials at the bureau agreed to investigate the case and my child got admission the next week.

A manufacturing worker told us another interesting and revealing story:

> Our factory built a residence and prepared to distribute housing among the workers. Of course, everyone wanted to get an apartment. My fellow workers were like "the Eight Immortals crossing the sea, each showing his or her special prowess [baxian guohai gexian shentong]." Some of them begged bureaucrats for help, others "bribed" acquaintances to lobby leaders on their behalf. Still others sent gifts to bribe leaders directly. Do you know how I got my apartment? I went to the manager of the factory and presented my case to him and asked for help. The manager simply refused to help and told me it was beyond his ability. I was very angry at his attitude and decided to give this bastard some "gifts." From that very day on, I went to his home twice a day, once at lunch time and the other at dinner. When I arrived at his apartment, I did not say anything but just waited for the meal and joined them. After the meal, I would find some topic to raise. I pretended to be very happy

and enjoyed being there. I deliberately did not even mention anything about the housing allocation in order to avoid being caught on a "vulnerable point" [*zhuabianzi*] by him during the whole period. He could not simply kick me out of his home. As you know, most people take a nap after lunch. The noon visits blocked him from taking a nap. When the time came for work, I went with him to the workshop and slept there. After the day was over, I went with him again to his home for dinner. After dinner, I stayed at his home watching TV until around eleven o'clock in the evening. He could stand this for a few days, but not longer. Two weeks later, he surrendered and told me that I was guaranteed to get an apartment in the unit's new building. I thanked him for helping me get the apartment and praised him as my "best friend." He had a wry smile and said nothing. After I got the apartment, I gave him some real gifts worth a couple of hundred yuan in order to repair our relationship, since I might need his help in the future.

The story may sound unusual to many outside observers. But similar stories come up again and again in Beijing. A clerk told one interviewer:

I know the leaders in my work unit. They are cowards. If they know you are simpleminded, you are in trouble. In this society, if you do not take care of yourself, no one will take care of you. A few years ago, the government decided to give salary increases to 60 percent of the employees in every work unit. Of course, everyone wanted to get salary increases. I knew the leaders would reward those people whom they liked and I was apparently not one of them. Therefore, I decided to act on my own. Do you know how I persuaded them to give me a salary increase? . . . First, I asked one leader if I would get a salary increase. The bastard dared to tell me he did not know. I knew that he was going to say that to me and took a bottle of DDT with me when I went to see him. When he told me he did not know, I pulled out the poison and told him that if I didn't get a salary increase, my wife would look down on me and give me a hard time. "Money is unimportant to me," I said, "but I cannot stand losing face like this in front of my wife." I told him I had no choice but to commit suicide in front of him. He was really frightened and stopped me from drinking the DDT by making a commitment to give me a salary increase immediately. At the same time, he begged me not to reveal his commitment to anyone else. Of course, I won't. Only fools would do that. If everyone else plays this trick, how can I become one of the 60 percent of people to get a salary increase? Do you believe I would drink that poison? Of course not. I enjoy life. I guessed that he knew my underlying threat—if I got mad, I might do something to him or his family members before I died. But he could not charge me with any wrongdoing, since I only told him I wanted to kill myself, which was not against any law. The risks for him and his family were thus so great that the best strategy for him was to give up.

These examples show how people in China can deal with officials in their work units. Making demands in a confrontational manner is a bargaining game. Depending on a person's power position, relationship with a particular official, and access to information, he or she can choose different strategies. Some invoke higher principles to build their arguments on normative grounds; others manipulate the vulnerability of leaders; and still others issue direct threats to push for desired concessions.

Appeals through the Bureaucratic Hierarchy

As mentioned before, Chinese authorities do recognize the diverse and sometimes conflicting interests among people as well as the necessity of providing some outlets for them. Grassroot expressions of discontent can be used to check and monitor the behavior of lower-echelon government officials. However, the authorities in China also clearly know that the actions of private interest articulation, if not properly managed, may create serious problems for the government. Facing this dilemma, the authorities, rather than simply preventing all private interest articulation, try to secure it under their own control. Both the CCP and the government have set up various channels for people to express their opinions and make complaints, and the authorities do in fact accommodate certain private interests through these channels.

Among the bottom-up channels available to private citizens to lodge their complaints, the most important ones are through the organizational hierarchy (*zuzhi qudao*). Every organization in China has a government agency supervising its operation. For example, an elementary school is supervised by the Bureau of Education of each district. The Bureau of Education of each district in the capital is supervised by the Bureau of Education of the Beijing Municipal Government, and the Bureau of Education of Beijing is supervised by the State Educational Commission. The responsibility of the supervising agencies ranges from mediating conflicts between leaders and employees at lower-level organizations to monitoring the performance of lower-level officials, redressing the evildoing of local cadres, and making necessary adjustments of government policies according to "concrete situations." If one is not satisfied with decisions made by the leaders of one's unit, has different opinions on certain government policies, or wants to report power abuses by local bureaucrats, the first place to go is usually the supervising agency of one's work unit.

Analytically, appeals made through the bureaucratic hierarchy can be divided into three kinds. The first are those taken *before* decisions of lower-level bureaucrats are made. Such appeals are usually aimed at influencing the formulation of rules and regulations to implement a particular government policy at lower levels. The second kind are those made *after* such decisions are taken; people appeal to higher authorities in order to change the decisions of lower levels. The third kind involves appeals aimed at influencing the appointment, promotion, and demotion of lower-echelon bureaucrats. Motivation for a participant to make this kind of appeal can be rather complicated. Some people make complaints about power abuses because they believe it is their civic duty to fight against "evil deeds and evildoers" (*yu huairen huaishi zuodouzheng*). Others want leaders they dislike dismissed or transferred to other institutions to improve their own condition, and still others may seek revenge for abuses they suffered.

These distinctions are made for analytical purposes and thus reflect ideal types only. Situations in real life are obviously more complicated. A person might start his initiative before deciding to specifically influence political issues. If he fails to get any satisfactory result from his initiative and chooses to continue his struggle, he may contact government officials at higher levels to persuade them to veto or change the decisions made by lower-level bureaucrats. If he fails and decides to continue, he might try to change the personnel of his work unit. Thus, appeals originally aimed at influencing a particular decision can be transformed into attempts to change personnel over time.

Whether participants can persuade officials at higher organizational levels to intervene on their behalf is determined by many factors. First, timing is crucial, especially when concerning issues related to resource distribution. For example, if a person wants to get an apartment from her unit but waits until all available apartments have been assigned to other people to make appeals to higher authorities to change the decision of lower-level organizations, even if officials at higher levels want to help, there is little they can do. Sophisticated interest articulators in China always try to influence resource allocation *before* decisions are made instead of trying to change them afterward. For nondistributive issues, intervention of officials at higher bureaucratic levels at this stage is also unlikely to cause resistance from lower bureaucrats.

Second, the nature of the issue influences the decisions of higher-level bureaucrats about whether to intervene or not. Facing complaints from below, one of the major concerns of higher bureaucrats is whether the decisions of lower bureaucrats violate government policies or if lower-level officials are abusing their power. If the decisions violate government policies or there is clear evidence of abuse of power, officials at higher levels are likely to intervene.

Third, the political skill of participants can make a significant difference. "Institutional design" in China puts a heavy burden on lower-echelon officials to balance different interests within organizations when implementing government policies. In this process, work units usually need to set up detailed rules and regulations. Those rules and regulations, called local policies (*tu zhengce*) by ordinary citizens, actually determine to a large extent the results of resource competition. When contacting officials at a higher level, participants can either argue that such local policies were unfair and contrary to certain government policies or that their own case is "exceptional" and requires special consideration. However, the best strategy for appealers in their endeavor is either to win the sympathy of government officials at a higher level or to make their argument on normative grounds. If skillfully managed, these arguments can succeed in getting officials at higher levels to intervene.

Fourth, the power balance between officials at lower levels and bureaucrats at higher levels to whom complaints are made affects the results of appeals. In China, each cadre has an official administrative grade (*jibie*). Depending on the nature of the appointment, those who work in higher-level government organizations may not possess higher administrative grades than those working at lower levels. For example, most principal leaders of lower-level organizations bear higher administrative grades than officials working in complaint bureaus at the immediate higher level of government offices.

The informal social and political network of officials involved also matters. As a general rule, if the official against whom the complaint is made is more powerful than the official to whom the complaint is made, the latter is unlikely to intervene. By the same token, if the official against whom the complaint is made is a client of a more powerful official—even if the former bears a lower administrative grade—the complaint bureau is unlikely to intervene. For the same reason, if the person to whom the complaint is made is associated with a political enemy of the official against whom the complaint is made, even if the former bears a lower administrative grade, the person may still intervene on behalf of the appealer. Since the power positions of particular government officials are determined by both formal criteria (the administrative grade of the person involved), and informal criteria (his social and political networks), it is difficult for participants to have an accurate appraisal of the power balance unless they actually make the complaint.

Complaints aimed at changing government personnel are much more difficult than complaints aimed at changing a particular decision. Personnel complaints aimed at removal of certain government officials require complicated strategic planning and a series of coherent activities. The first step is usually designed to damage the image of the official in the eyes of the supervising agency. People must make repeated contacts to achieve such a goal. The issues involved for each contact may be trivial, but repeated contacts can make officials at a higher level believe the charges, even if they are not true. Repeated contacts can also create an impression among officials at higher levels that the leader involved is incapable of balancing various interests in his or her unit. After the goal of damaging the reputation of the official involved has been accomplished, the attacker needs to find an opportunity to launch the decisive blow. Usually, the best time for the coup de grace is when the bureaucrat in question is up for promotion or a shuffling of bureaucrats within an organization is scheduled. A story told by an engineer in Beijing best illustrates how this strategy works:

> I hate the leader in my work unit. He is a person who always abuses power. In order to get him out of our unit, I made a plan to work for his removal. First, whenever there was a trivial mistake committed by that person, I myself or my friend would contact officials at a higher level to make reports. I know bureaucrats shield one another, but I also know that there are contradictions between them. The whole logic of making those reports was to erode his support base. Two years ago, I heard the news that he might be promoted to a position at the Bureau of Machinery of the Beijing Municipal Government. I knew it was time for me to launch a decisive attack. I began to make complaints to various organizations throughout the bureaucratic hierarchy about one minor case of power abuse. I know there must have been other people who were against his promotion, and the idea of making an appeal at the time was to provide "ammunition" for them to make a forceful argument. By choosing the right time to act, I successfully blocked his promotion. Some people told me I was used by another faction within the leadership group. It might be true. But so what? I would rather think officials in another faction were used by me. In fact, it is very hard to say who made use of whom. We actually used each other and I got what I wanted—to take out my revenge on him.[33]

To summarize, people make appeals through the bureaucratic hierarchy for different purposes. Some want to influence government policies or the detailed rules and regulations set up by their units to implement those polices; others want to punish leaders they dislike. While the vague nature of government policy in China makes it possible for officials to accommodate private interests during the policy implementation stage, the complicated power relationship among bureaucrats gives citizens an opportunity to play government officials in different positions off against one another. Of course, this does not guarantee participants that they will get what they want through their appeals. The actual result of an appeal depends on timing, the initiator's skills in making his or her argument, and power balances among the officials directly and indirectly involved.

Complaints through Political Organizations

People in China can also pursue their interests through political organizations, such as the Chinese Communist Party, the Communist Youth League (CYL), and the "democratic parties." Since the functions of these organizations differ from those in other societies, the dynamics of these organizations regarding private interest articulation also differ from those in other societies. In communist countries, unlike democratic polities, the major function of political parties is to mobilize the population for the predetermined goals of the regime, rather than aggregating private interests in the society. For the purposes of mobilization, the government in China installed branches of the CCP and CYL in every local unit. These branches, as instruments of the state, are primarily responsible for political and ideological work (*zhengzhi sixiang gongzuo*), that is, mass mobilization. During the Mao period from 1949 to 1977, the scope of political and ideological work was defined so broadly that everything was seen as having political implications under the jurisdiction of those organizations. The power of party secretaries was so expanded that many of them actively intervened in every decision of their organization. Thus, it was the party secretary rather than the administrative leader who was then considered the top man in an organization (*diyibashou*).

The emphasis on economic development and the separation of party and government in recent years have reduced the importance of political and ideological work. As the scope of politics grew narrower, the influence of party cadres was also reduced. However, although party secretaries are no longer the paramount leaders of work units, their powers have not been completely eliminated. Party organizations are still one of the major power centers within each organization. Many party cadres still have great influence on decisions over nonmanagerial issues in their units, especially distributive and personnel decisions. Party branches at higher administrative levels can also intervene in decisions of lower-level administrative organizations in today's China.

Since the functions of political organizations in China are different from those in liberal democracies, readers may wonder why CCP and CYL cadres would help non–party members rather than mobilizing them for predetermined party goals. An examination of the structure of the party apparatus in China and the sources of tension between the party apparatus and administrative cadres built into the structure of Chinese society will help answer this question.

First of all, the party apparatus in communist societies is never a monolithic group. As Jerry Hough points out, "even if we were to discover that officials of the party apparatus hold certain interests in common, the group approach would deny the possibility that they share many common interests."[34] In fact, the party apparatus in China is stratified into different levels. Similar to administrative cadres, party secretaries are divided into three categories and each of them bear certain administrative grades. Those who work at organizations equal to or higher than the bureau level (juji) are characterized as high-level cadres (gaoji ganbu). Those who work at organizations below the bureau level but higher than the section level (keji) are midlevel cadres (zhongji ganbu). And those who work at organizations equal to or below the section level are ordinary cadres (yiban ganbu). While high-level party officials are entitled to have four- to seven-room apartments and expensive cars with chauffeurs, low-level party cadres enjoy neither of these perks. Like ordinary citizens, they live on their salaries, stay in crowded apartments, and wait in line for scarce goods. The differences in privileges enjoyed by cadres holding different ranks are so great that most ordinary party cadres in China are considered part of the masses (laobaixing) rather than the elites.

More important, as noted above, work units in China are the primary organization around which the interests of society are organized. Under such an arrangement, resources and benefits for ordinary cadres come from the organization they are working for rather than independently from party organizations. This arrangement makes the interests of low-ranking officials at least partly identified with their own work units. If the work unit gets the desired resources, they may be able to acquire a share. By the same token, if their work unit fails in resource competition with other units, the possibility for them to get desired resources will also vanish. In contrast to high-ranking cadres, low-ranking officials in China, who live and work with ordinary people, know more about the daily lives and hardships of ordinary citizens in society. Such an environment plays an important role in shaping their attitudes toward both the state and the society. Since many of them are responsible for the functional role of their organizations, they need to co-opt employees to get their work done on a daily basis.

I do not mean to suggest that the party apparatus in China automatically identifies with the interests of ordinary people. Not only are cadres under constant pressure, coercion, and inducement from party organizations, but many of their interests are also identified with those of the party. What I am suggesting here is that since some of their interests are identical to those of ordinary people and they are also under constant pressure from below, the interests of the party apparatus lie neither in fully conforming with government policy nor in fully identifying with popular demands. They need to constantly keep a balance between the pressures from both sides.

Many cadres develop the skill of conforming symbolically to government policy but altering its effects in the course of its actual implementation to please both sides.

Finally, power struggles among different leaders of work units can also provide citizens with opportunities to pursue their goals. Office politics in enterprises and various organizations are not unique to China. What makes the Chinese experience different from those in other societies is that such power struggles are usually fought between administrative cadres and the party apparatus, and that it is a normal way of life in Chinese organizations. Once a power struggle begins, the parties involved will have strong incentives to establish allies. The political dynamic in such organizations can be quite similar to that in a bipolar or multipolar system in international relations, depending on the numbers of power centers involved and the intensity of the power struggle. In units where two factions are competing for power and the intensity of their struggle is high, the famous rule "if you are not my friend, you are my enemy" applies. Employees working in such organizations usually have to choose sides and line up with one power center or another. Once an employee determines which side to line up with, officials on that side need to take care of the employee's interests for the management of their allies. In such a situation, there is little room for independent actors to maneuver. In organizations where more than two factions exist, people are relatively free to decide whether to align themselves with any power center at all. If that is the case, people will have some space to maneuver in.

If a person in such a situation is not satisfied with a decision made by an administrative cadre, she may choose to go to the party apparatus to complain and ask officials there to intervene on her behalf and vice versa. The cadres the person turns to usually see it as an opportunity to recruit more clients to their own faction. Under such circumstances, the decision on whether to help the person is usually based on the status of the person in the organization; the potential contribution of the person to the faction; the potential damage the person can do to the faction if she decides to work with other factions; the possible reaction of the other faction, if that faction decided to intervene; and the nature of the issue involved. If the faction decides to intervene on her behalf, the person will be considered by everyone in the organization as a member of that particular faction, which may or may not work to her long-term interest. After the person is recruited as a client to a faction, the patron needs to continually provide her with services for managing the alliance, and any mistreatment of the individual will be considered a plot to destroy the authority of the faction. Such attempts must be deterred to maintain alliance solidarity. Since contradictions be-

tween the party apparatus and administrative cadres can be effectively ex-
ploited by people in an organization to articulate their interests, it is not
unusual for people in Chinese society to deliberately cultivate conflicts
between administrative cadres and the party apparatus and use such conflicts to pursue their interests.

Complaints through the Trade Unions

Trade unions in China are designed as the party's link to the masses as well
as a control mechanism over the general populace.[35] Their essential function is mobilizing people to implement party policies and, at the same time,
serving as a safety valve for popular complaints. Local union branches help
management carry on the production of enterprises, report any hardships
of employees to authorities, and mediate disputes over salaries, bonuses,
welfare, and so on. Membership in trade unions is compulsory and auto-
matic for most workers. Every employee, whether working in a state or
collective enterprise, government agency, school, or even a small shop, is
a union member.

To control trade unions, the authorities install their own cadres in leading positions within them at various levels. However, once installed in such
positions, many of those cadres begin to advocate the workers' interests.
The autonomy of trade unions can be traced back to the early days of the
People's Republic of China. For example, James Townsend found that even
in the period of intense regime mobilizations, "the trade unions have shown
tendencies toward greater representation of their members' interests."[36] But
in contrast to the situation in other societies, where unions and management usually fight each other, union cadres in China tended to work closely
with the management to fight against the state. To understand their behavior, we need to analyze the relevant institutional arrangements in China.

Union responsibilities in China include labor protection, welfare, and
professional education. Unlike market economies, where these issues are
determined by management in each enterprise, in China most benefits to
employees are decided by the government. Until quite recently, the funding
for those programs was still allocated by the government rather than by
individual enterprises. Enterprises merely represented the government in
distributing those resources. Under such an arrangement, there was really
no reason for management to oppose the efforts of union leaders to get
more benefits and better labor protection for employees. Union cadres and
management in China seldom oppose each other, even when dealing with
expensive welfare or labor protection programs within enterprises. Since
the money for such programs comes from the government's pocket, it is

the government that wants to limit the scope of workers' welfare. Therefore, it is not unusual to find union cadres and management in China joining together to oppose government agencies. As other bureaucrats do, union leaders participate in the power game primarily through "persuasion."[37]

Within enterprises, union officials often participate in many important decisions, such as salary increases, distribution of apartments and bonuses, job assignments, and benefits for retirees. The primary incentive for management in China to involve union cadres in such decisions is to shift responsibility for unpopular decisions. For example, when the government in China appropriates money for an enterprise for salary raises, it usually requires that enterprises raise the salary of a certain percentage of the employees. Management must decide who gets the raises and the decisions must be open to everyone in the organization.[38] Facing such opportunities, people press hard for management's help. If management refuses to help, there are many actions rebuffed employees can take. The most likely response is to withdraw cooperation in the future, for which management can do little to punish them. More dangerous is the spillover effect of such behavior. Noncooperative behavior can and usually does trigger more such actions in an organization. Since the cooperation of subordinates is crucial for management to carry on the functional role of the organization, management has every incentive to shift the responsibility of making any unpopular decision to someone else, a practice that gives union cadres in China important power within their organizations. People in Chinese organizations know what union cadres can do for them both within and beyond the primary union. Many people in fact go to union cadres for help on issues they believe the cadres can exert significant influence on.

Complaints through Deputies to the People's Congresses

Direct elections in China are still confined to local people's congresses, as noted above. The responsibilities of such organizations are limited to local issues, such as education, environment, crime control, and public transportation. No high-politics issues concerning national political life are debated and decided by people's congresses at this level. Although no one expects a local people's congress to be able to influence high-politics issues, some people expect to influence local issues by contacting their deputies. Such contacts are primarily aimed at communication rather than at conflict resolution. Some people contact deputies to local people's congresses to bring certain issues to the attention of higher authorities; others may even want to influence government decisions at higher levels through those deputies. Nonetheless, contacting deputies to local people's congresses is not an effective way to change decisions made by lower-echelon bureaucrats. Such acts are more likely to be effective in influencing agenda setting and policy formulation and less likely to be effective in influencing the policy implementation of local bureaucrats.

Deputies to local people's congresses are directly elected by citizens. When an electoral district overlaps with a work unit, access to those deputies is much easier for participants in China than for citizens in other societies. Many deputies are colleagues and thus are in daily contact with participants through their work. Such a system design greatly reduces the costs to citizens of contacting deputies in China.

Reports to Complaint Bureaus at Higher Levels

The history of people making complaints and expressing their opinions to higher authorities in China can be traced back to the Warring States Period.[39] For more than two thousand years, the willingness of the emperor to, at least in principle, accommodate such expression has been one of the most important indicators of the state of his "mandate" to rule the "central kingdom." The CCP inherited this time-honored tradition after assuming power in China in 1949. The 1982 constitution even codified "mak[ing] to relevant state organs complaints and charges against, or exposures of, any state organ or functionary for violation of the law or dereliction of duty" a constitutional right for citizens.[40] Reflecting this constitutional arrangement, every level of the Chinese government has a permanent office dealing with people's complaints. The agency at the district level is the Office of Letters and Visits (xinfang bangongshi). The agency of the Beijing Municipal Government is the Department of Letters and Visits (xinfang chu) of Beijing Municipality, and the agency at the central government level is the Letters and Visits Bureau of the State Council (guowuyuan xinfang ju). The major functions of these agencies are "helping responsible departments to resolve difficulties facing the masses to supervise [jiandu] local bureaucrats, to monitor the implementation of government policies, to collect information on the opinions of the masses on various issues, and to help higher authorities to understand the situation among the general populace."[41]

People approach complaint bureaus for different reasons: Some go to address personal grievances, especially to change decisions of bureaucrats at lower levels. If a participant can persuade officials at a complaint bureau to support him, he may be able to alter the balance of power between him and local bureaucrats to change their decisions. Others go to complaint bureaus to report local power abuses, and still others go to seek government resources or services. Although the reforms in recent years have begun to shift the supply of many necessities related to people's daily lives, such as electricity, coal, water, grain and vegetables, and services from the government to the market, the state in China is still the major supplier of these resources and services. When there is a shortage in their supply, complaint bureaus are usually the first place of recourse.

One high school teacher recalled that she contacted the Beijing Department of Letters and Visits about electrical power cuts in the residential area where she lived.

> I know about electrical power shortages in Beijing and I am prepared to accept the reality that each week we have to suffer at least a once-a-day power cut. However, we have had power cuts four times a week during the past two weeks and it is very hard for the government to justify such a pattern. I made a complaint to the Department of Letters and Visits of the Beijing Municipal Government and demanded the government take action. The officials there called people at the Bureau of Electricity and asked them to "reconsider the patterns of power cuts because of complaints by the masses." The officials at the Bureau of Electricity complied immediately with the suggestion and the problem was resolved immediately and there was at most one power cut per week during the entire winter season.[42]

Officials at complaint bureaus meet with complainers on a daily basis and have great freedom in determining whether to act and how to act on cases reported to them. Such decisions are determined by the nature of the issues and of the political power of the officials involved. The resources required for complaint bureaus to make independent investigations of cases also play an important role in their decisions. If officials decide to actively intervene, they can launch investigations, mediate the conflict between local bureaucrats and complainers, instruct local cadres to reconsider their decisions, and notify the organizations involved to change their policy.

Likewise, the responses of decision-making local bureaucrats to the active intervention of complaint bureaus are determined by many factors. As a general rule, local bureaucrats are more likely to ignore instructions from complaint bureaus after distributive decisions have been made than instructions given to them before they make any decisions. In making distributive decisions, no officials at basic-level organizations have an incentive to keep "strategic reserves" when distributing resources in their organizations because if those who failed to get resources in the competition find out there is still a strategic reserve left, they will join the second round of competition immediately and put even heavier pressure on bureaucrats. Strategic reserves are guaranteed to become strategic headaches for local bureaucrats;

thus few bureaucrats in China want to keep any at their disposal. With no resources left, even if local bureaucrats want to comply with instructions from above, there is no way for them to do so.

The power relationship between complaint bureaus and the officials or organizations about whom or which the complaints are made also influences the outcome. Positions in complaint bureaus in China are usually not desirable ones, and the rank of the cadres working in such bureaus is often not high. If the rank of the official responsible for the issue at the complaint bureau is lower than that of the leaders against whom the complaint is made, or if the organization involved belongs to a different government system from the complaint bureau, there will be little chance of action.

If officials at complaint bureaus decide to act passively, they simply transfer the case to the supervising agency that governs the unit where the dispute occurred, accompanied by a letter from the office asking officials therein to look into the case and resolve the issue and report back to the complaint bureau. People in China describe such behavior as "kicking people back and forth like a ball" (tipiqiu). However, transferring complaints to supervising agencies may not necessarily mean failure. The chance for someone in that agency to intervene is still quite high. For example, if leaders at a governing agency dislike the person against whom the complaint is made or are dissatisfied with the performance of the organization under investigation, they are very likely to intervene. In such a situation, the complaint may still produce results for the plaintiff even if officials at complaint bureaus adopt passive attitudes. However, if the cadre against whom the complaint is made is a client of the officials to whom the complaint is transferred, the plaintiff may have serious problems. The officials usually leak information about the plaintiff to the client against whom the complaint was made. Knowing who the plaintiff is, officials at lower levels almost definitely will seek revenge.

To summarize, government officials working at complaint agencies have some freedom to decide how to deal with citizens' demands. The nature of the issues involved, the nature of the relations between the government offices to which complaint bureaus belong and the organizations against which complaints are made, the balance of power between officials at complaint bureaus and officials against whom complaints are made, and factional struggles within the government play important roles in shaping the decisions of complaint bureaus. When the issue raised clearly violates government policies, and when the organization involved is under the direct jurisdiction of the government organization to which the complaint bureau belongs or the cadres involved belong to the opposing faction, officials at the complaint bureau are more likely to intervene positively. However, if the issue at hand is related to distributive decisions, the cadres approached are in the same faction as those attacked, and the organization involved is not under the jurisdiction of the government office to which the complaint bureau belongs, officials at the complaint bureau are usually reluctant to intervene. Even if they feel obligated to deal with the issue, they will choose to deal with it passively, transferring it to the relevant governing organization. Some people in Chinese society have learned from their own experience the working procedures of complaint bureaus and the usual rationale of decisions of officials working there. Through such experience, they have also learned how to selectively use this institution to effectively pursue their own interests.

Letter Writing to Government Officials

Complaint bureaus are also responsible for letters to government officials written by ordinary citizens. The bureaus deal with letters from the masses in the same fashion as they deal with visits. Officials at bureaus may decide to intervene personally, transfer letters to the supervising organization, or ignore them. Writing letters to government officials is more risky for participants than personal visits to complaint bureaus. If the letter gets transferred back to the work unit or to the officials against whom the complaint is made, the cadre there will have undeniable evidence of antagonistic behavior by the plaintiff. However, officials in complaint bureaus usually pay more attention to letters than to visits. As all letters received by complaint bureaus at various levels have to be registered, it is difficult for officials there to "kick people back and forth like a ball."

When writing letters to government officials, some people sign their names, while others remain anonymous. Among all letters received by complaint bureaus, 25 percent are anonymous. In some provinces, anonymous letters can reach 40 to 50 percent of letters received by complaint bureaus. There is no significant difference between anonymous letters and signed letters in terms of their accuracy. Statistics provided by the General Office of the Central Committee of the CCP and the General Office of the State Council show that while issues reported in 75 percent of the anonymous letters proved to be accurate, issues reported in 76 percent of the signed letters belonged to the same category. The authorities in China require complaint bureaus to give signed letters the same credit as anonymous ones but want complaint bureaus to make more thorough investigation before acting on issues reported in the anonymous letters.[43]

Individuals decide whether to sign letters on the basis of the nature of the issue, the position of the officials involved, the expected length of time for participants to achieve their goals, and the purpose and the timing of the letters. Moreover, their subjective evaluation of the risks involved plays a crucial role in such decisions. As a general rule, if a letter aims at acquiring particular material goods or services from the government, individuals must sign the letters. If a letter is designed as part of a long-term plan to destroy the reputation and credentials of an official, it is usually anonymous. Generally, letter writers must work a long time to achieve the desired results, and the process itself is extremely risky. Using anonymous letters can reduce the risk for participants greatly. Finally, the higher the position of the person against whom complaint is made, the more likely the letter will be anonymous. Among letters received by the Central Discipline Committee of the CCP from January to April 1986, 81 percent reporting cadre problems at the department level (juji) and 93 percent reporting problems at the ministerial level were anonymous.[44]

Letter Writing to Editors of Newspapers

People write not only to government agencies but also to newspapers, especially those attached to the CCP or to various government organizations. Those newspapers are seen by both the regime and the populace as branches of either the government or the party. Many of them are in fact administered directly by those bodies. For example, Renmin Ribao (People's Daily) is under the direct leadership of the CCP's Central Committee; Beijing Ribao (Beijing Daily) is run by the Party Committee of the Beijing Municipal Government; and Jingji Ribao (Economic Daily) is under the State Council.

According to official doctrine, the media in China perform two functions. They serve as the "mouthpiece of the party," which requires them to inform the masses of government and party decisions and to help the regime mobilize people to implement those decisions.[45] And they gather information, which requires them "to provide intelligence to the leaders on the public's feelings and behavior and the performance of lower-level cadres."[46] Reporters in China are required to provide decision makers with firsthand information about the populace so as to help them grasp current realities, and one source of such information comes from the letters of ordinary people.

The media in China receive numerous letters from the masses each day. For example, Renmin Ribao in 1979 alone handled over 800,000 letters.[47] All major newspapers affiliated with the government and the party as well as the Xinhua News Agency have a Masses Work Office (MWO) to handle such letters. According to Wu Guoguang, former senior commentator of *Renmin Ribao* and Zhao Ziyang's speech writer, more than forty regular staff members work at the MWO in his former paper. Some of them are new employees hired by the newspaper, while others are senior reporters who have assumed leadership positions.[48] Some are stationed at headquarters to process the letters, while others travel all over the country to investigate the issues raised by the letters and write reports to the head office. At *Renmin Ribao,* the office of the chief editor also has many permanent staff members to process those letters. There is no clear division of labor between the MWO and the office of the chief editor in handling letters from the masses. The general rule is that if the letter is addressed to the newspaper, or to a specific reporter, it goes to the MWO for processing. If the letter is addressed to the chief editor, it goes to his office directly.

After the newspaper receives the letters, the staff in the MWO sorts them into five categories. The first category is letters concerning major national policies. The second is suggestions to the government. The third is letters addressing special difficulties of a particular region in the country, such as shortages of certain basic production resources, electricity, food, and so on. The fourth category is letters exposing power abusers, and the fifth is letters expressing personal grievances. Letters dealing with issues in the first three categories (major national policies, special difficulties in a region, and suggestions to the government) are summarized by the staff of the MWO and routinely sent to the central authorities.

Xinhua and other major news organizations have daily internal publications to report the information provided by these letters to the authorities. The Xinhua News Agency publishes *Guonei Dongtai Xuanbian* (Collections of Recent Domestic Developments). It is a loose-leaf paper published on a daily basis, ranging from fifty to a couple of hundred pages per day depending on the contents. The publication is divided into two parts. One consists of investigative reporting concerning major issues facing the country done by special assignment reporters of the agency; the other is a summary of the issues included in the letters to the agency by ordinary citizens. *Guonei Dongtai Xuanbian* is a highly classified internal publication. Before 1987, only Politburo members and officials of the secretariat of the CCP Central Committee were entitled to read it. After 1987, each province was given two copies, one for the governor and another for the first CCP provincial secretary.[49]

Similarly, *Renmin Ribao* puts out *Qunzhong Laixin Zhaibian* (Collections of Letters from the Masses). When a special event occurs, the paper publishes *Qunzhong Laixing Zhaibian Tekan* (Special Issues of the Collections of Letters from the Masses). The office of the chief editor of the paper also publishes a daily report called *Qingkuang Fanying* (Reflections on the Situation), dealing with domestic questions. All these publications are also highly classified and only members of the CCP Central Committee and ministers in the central government have access to them. Although letters published in newspapers must fall within the guidelines of party policy, letters reported in internal publications have virtually no restraints.

When the MWO receives letters exposing power abuses and personal grievances, the staff may either send special assignment reporters to make independent investigations or transfer the letters back to the governing agencies of the organizations involved and ask the agencies themselves to conduct the investigation and report the results to the MWO. The results of an investigation may either be sent to higher authorities through internal channels or be transferred to the relevant department. For those who use such letters to redress personal grievances, their publication in newspapers is crucial. Given the limitations of the manpower of media to conduct investigations on such issues and, more important, the psychological attitude of the authorities in China against revealing dark aspects *(heianmian)* of society, only a limited number of letters addressing personal grievances or complaining of power abuses appear in newspapers for public consumption. Students of political participation in China are correct in pointing out that newspapers have difficulty in "gathering materials and checking facts," that "newspapers often could not get the necessary approval from higher-level authorities to print [letters]," and that even "if the letters were printed, there was no guarantee that any action would be taken."[50]

However, confining our inquiry of the effectiveness of letters to the editors of newspapers in the Chinese political process to counting the number of letters appearing in newspapers in a given period of time may be misleading. Such a method can lead us to ignore an important function performed by those letters in China—that is, communication. In fact, a large number of letters are used by people to express their opinions on government policies and to make suggestions to the government. For these purposes, publication in internal documents is as important as an appearance on the front pages of newspapers. According to a journalist in Xinhua, the classified daily publications are still one of the major sources of information for top-level authorities. "The importance of Xinhua's internal publications lies in the fact that those publications provide the central authorities with information about the *real* situation of the country through channels independent from their own cadres."[51] Therefore, letters to the editor are still an important way for people in China to participate in politics. Probably, they represent one of the few ways for PRC citizens to influence agenda setting and policy formulation in their country.

Guanxi and Gifts in Exchange for Help

Structural reasons for the emergence of patron-client relationships in many different societies have been documented by numerous scholars.[52] Instead of reiterating their arguments, I will concentrate my analysis on how and why the political and societal institutional design in China transforms the primary strategy for private citizens to articulate their interests from an "active-competitive orientation" to patron-client ties over time.

Compared to other former communist societies, China puts much more emphasis on positive sanctions, rewarding behavior encouraged by the authorities, than on negative sanctions, punishing behavior discouraged or prohibited by the authorities.[53] This system, according to Andrew Walder, induces people in urban China to adopt an "active-competitive orientation" to pursue their interests. Many Chinese workers therefore instrumentally adapt their behavior in exchange for desired benefits from the authorities.[54]

The active-competitive strategy might have been a good choice for individuals in the earlier mobilization period. However, when the game changed from a single play to repeated ones, the payoff structure for such "activists" changed fundamentally. We know that work units are responsible for resource distribution. Such an institutional arrangement turns most government policies into selective goods down to the work unit level. In each work unit, one person successfully getting authoritatively allocated resources usually means that the opportunities for others to get the same resources will be reduced. As resource competition at the basic level becomes a zero-sum game, the political logic for resource competition changes dramatically. By bringing the interests of citizens at basic-level organizations into conflict, the political system design in China not only forces employees in the same organization to compete with one another in a vigilant manner but also cripples group formation and group-based activities. Clearly, it takes time for citizens to understand how the system in China works—especially the mechanisms for authorities to reward activists. People learn about such mechanisms either from their own experiences or from the observation of the behavior of others. Of course, if they don't want to be penalized by the system, they have to join the competition in the way defined by the institutional design in China, that is, the active-competitive strategy. In this sense, the reason for the Chinese to be "a heap of loose sand" or in a state of disunity (yipansansha) has a logical structural basis.

As more people understand the workings of the system, more join the competition. As a result, escalation of competition among colleagues becomes a normal way of life in Chinese organizations. The escalation of competition is represented not only by an ever growing number of people getting involved but also by an ever increasing intensity of such competition within organizations. If one person behaves well, others have to emulate and outdo the person to become or to keep their status as activists. With an ever growing number of people joining competition and its ever growing intensity, one needs to put even more efforts into one's work, sacrifice more private time, and deny oneself more personal pleasures to retain the status of activist to enjoy the rewards of the leaders of the unit.

However, there are several limitations on the mode of competition within Chinese work units. The first one is, of course, the physical limitation on how much time one can work each day. Second, the ability of leaders to reward activists is limited by the resources available. With growing numbers of people realizing the workings of the system and adapting to its rules, more and more people in an organization try to become activists to join the competition. But the resources available for cadres to reward activities remain the same. As a result, the ever growing number of activists conflicts with the constant need to maintain resources for leaders to use as rewards. Facing this situation, leaders can reduce the value of rewards to each activist, reduce the number of activists to be rewarded, or increase the level of services and goods required for participants to get the desired rewards. No matter what they decide to do, the potential costs of the active-competitive strategy for an individual will sooner or later outpace the potential gains.

The third limitation can be described as the systemic constraint of Chinese politics.[55] According to Kenneth Waltz, theories that concentrate causes of behavior at the individual level are reductionist. "With [the] reductionist approach, the whole is understood by knowing the attributes and the interactions of its parts."[56] He reminds us that such an approach can only tell us part of the story because "the structure of the system affects the interacting units," which "in turn affect the structure."[57] Because the system design in China makes resource competition at basic-level organizations a zero-sum game, engagement in an active-competitive strategy will automatically threaten the interests of other people. Everyone knows that if a few people are allowed to achieve activist status, those people will be able to monopolize resources that are supposed to belong to everyone in the unit. For self-protection, nonactivists in a unit usually react to such activities strongly to block the efforts of activists. For each individual, the reaction is one of individualized acts aimed at self-protection. In the aggregate, these acts become "simultaneous political actions," which create "endur[ing] negative peer pressure from the rank and file and other psychic tensions."[58] Open antagonism and physical intimidation are not unusual in

Chinese organizations. Although "there are limits to the harassment of activists, . . . they do not come close to prohibiting it."[59] Such a reaction generated by the system's constraints forces many activists to abandon the above strategy by changing their payoff structure, especially when ideology grows less salient.

The limitations of the active-competitive strategy no doubt create incentives for people to seek alternative means to pursue their interests. An important way for people to do so is *guanxi*. The term means "relationships," or "connections," and refers to "an exchange relationship that mingles instrumental intentions with personal feelings."[60] Due to resource limitations, leaders in a unit, instead of distributing favors equally among activists, tend to selectively reward either those who are expected to be able to provide them with long-term or crucial support at times of crisis, or those having resources that are crucial for them to fulfill their administrative function, or those who have good relations with them. Purposefully cultivating good relationships with leaders thus becomes an "economic way" or shortcut for instrumental interest articulators in Chinese organizations to pursue their interests. The hostility of other actors helps to crystalize such relationships with unit leaders for purposes of self-protection.

Nonactivists in Chinese organizations also have great incentives to cultivate good relations with leaders. The essence of *guanxi* is, through a subtle form of reciprocation bordering on bribery or "instrumental-personal ties," to turn the hierarchical relationship between subordinates and officials into one of exchange. As long as people have something to offer, be it tangible or intangible, individuals in China may be able to seduce officials into deals—exchanges of material gains for favors. Since cultivating personal relationships with leaders requires different resources from being activists, those who are unable to become active for various reasons may choose this strategy to pursue their interests within their work units.

People who want to cultivate good *guanxi* with decision makers or establish instrumental-personal ties can either pursue these goals on their own or find some "power brokers" to represent them in dealing with government officials. For individuals, the goal of cultivating *guanxi* with government officials can be offensive or defensive. Some people cultivate good relationships with leaders for tangible or intangible benefits, while others avoid being left behind by other people. Using *guanxi* to pursue private interests is not limited to individuals. Many groups and organizations also rely on *guanxi* to pursue collective interests such as soliciting goods and services for higher government organizations. *Guanxi* may even be used by people in China to influence government policies. For example, some people rely on their *guanxi* with government officials at different levels to persuade officials to make policies beneficial to themselves or their reference group, while others persuade officials at higher levels to change decisions made by lower-echelon bureaucrats. Since using this tactic itself involves overstepping the boundary of legitimate authority, *guanxi* can seldom be used to check power abuses in the society.

Strikes and Slowdowns on the Job

Protected by the lifetime employment system, citizens in China generally have much more freedom than working-class citizens in other societies to express their dissatisfaction through withdrawals from work. Although the reforms in China have gradually reduced the scope of such activities, withdrawal from work is still one major form of leverage for people to bargain with their leaders in units where the lifetime employment protection system has still not been abolished. The bargaining power of employees in China comes from their control of resources crucial to their leaders. People in China know that immediate leaders are held accountable for the performance of their organization. To fulfill such a role, bureaucrats have to rely on the cooperation of the employees in their unit, which makes them care about the work performance of the employees under their control. Because the lifetime employment system impairs the ability of bureaucrats to punish those employees who refuse to cooperate, many local bureaucrats have to co-opt their subordinates.

If people decide to withdraw from work to protest or to create a bargaining situation with bureaucrats, they can either launch a strike or an individualized version of a strike—a job slowdown. The choice of the particular action is primarily determined by the issue involved. As a general rule, if people want resources from the government, a strike is more effective. However, if participants want resources already allocated to the organizations by the government, a slowdown is a better choice because it puts pressure on leaders of the work unit who already have resources under their direct control.

STRIKES

Before the Cultural Revolution, the views of CCP authorities on strikes could be divided largely into two groups. One was mainly represented by leaders who built up their political career in the labor movement under the Kuomintang regime. Such a background made those leaders extremely hostile toward organized labor and labor movements. Learning from their own experience of underground work, these leaders concluded that all strikes have agitators or "black hands" (heishou) manipulating them behind the scenes. They usually did not hesitate to suppress organized labor movements. Another group, represented by Mao Zedong, tended to regard strikes as the result of bureaucratism within the Communist Party. They tended to believe that bureaucrats within the Communist Party should be held responsible for strikes in socialist China.[61] The political struggle among Chinese leaders over this and other issues caused the attitudes of Chinese authorities toward strikes to fluctuate with the shifting of the power balance within the leadership group. Prior to the Cultural Revolution, the balance of power tilted toward the bureaucracy. During that time, the usual way for government to deal with strikes was to find "agitators behind the scenes." While ruthlessly punishing the agitators, the regime tried to educate "ordinary innocent people" involved in such activities. Mao, however, constantly blamed government officials for causing strikes and used such events to attack his political enemies.

The situation changed during the Cultural Revolution, when Mao dominated the political arena. During that period, Mao himself tried to mobilize workers to launch strikes against "capitalist roaders." To implement his own ideas, Mao even managed to codify the right to strike into the 1975 constitution.[62] The enthusiasm toward strikes quickly passed away with Mao after the Cultural Revolution. Soon after his death, the very right to strike was formally eliminated from the constitution. The Deng regime never made striking in China formally illegal, but the authorities adopted a hostile attitude toward the active organized labor movement.[63] Starting in the mid-1980s, a new group—trade union cadres—emerged to defend strikes in China. They also believed that the occurrence of strikes must be associated with bureaucratism within the party and government.

We do not hear many reports of strikes in Beijing. The only major one we know of was organized by employees of the public transportation system in 1987. Bus workers in China are underpaid and working conditions are very difficult. Many of them have to work irregular hours and their salary is lower than most other workers'. When the reforms and labor discipline were first enacted in Beijing, their hardships increased; freedom in the workplace was reduced, and the power of their leaders was greatly enhanced. Under these changes, leaders could not only determine workers' bonuses and work shifts on their own but also punish workers for violations of labor discipline at their discretion. At the same time, soaring inflation had shrunk the real incomes of ticket sellers and drivers in Beijing. Creating an even more serious psychological problem for public transportation workers, the municipal government began to introduce the responsibility system to the taxi industry in 1987. This measure greatly increased the income of taxi drivers in Beijing, and many of them soon began to earn at least ten times more than bus drivers.

Dissatisfaction over the income inequalities spread rapidly among public transportation workers, and most came to believe that they were entitled to a raise. They appealed to the authorities through various channels and on different occasions to the leaders of their units, but such moves failed to produce positive results—the decision had to be made by the municipal government and the unit leaders simply did not have the power to make it.

A group of radical young drivers and ticket sellers in fact wanted to confront the government, but they knew that without a good excuse, organized opposition could be extremely dangerous for the organizers as well as the participants. When a ticket checker was beaten by peasants as he asked them to show their tickets, these radical young drivers realized that their time had come. They formed an informal group to coordinate their plan among workers on a few bus routes and decided to demand immediate action by the authorities to locate and punish the assailants. At the same time, they contacted other drivers and ticket sellers on different routes as well as repairmen in their shop for help. Before the authorities had a chance to locate the assailants, they claimed that it was too risky for them to work and the "strike" began.

The movement bore "Chinese characteristics"—which could be described as action bordering between a strike and a slowdown. Throughout the entire period of the movement, drivers and ticket sellers went to work. In the workplace, however, some claimed that their buses needed repairs and the repairmen confirmed their claims. Others reported in sick and claimed that they could not drive—it was too dangerous for the passengers. Those who could not find any excuse drove but deliberately lagged behind schedule. Observers in Beijing described the buses as operating in those days like "sugarcoated haws on a stick" (tanghulu). Many buses did not come at all; those that came, bunched together. If a passenger missed one "bunch," he or she had to wait an hour or so for the next one, whereas the normal scheduled interval between buses is three to five minutes. The strike was so skillfully organized that during the whole period of the movement, the only people who made public appearances were the immediate colleagues of the ticket seller who was beaten by the peasants, and the only public demand was that the authorities promptly punish the assailants and guarantee the safety of public transportation workers in the future.

As usual, the regime initially responded by sending detectives to work with leaders on each route to locate the agitators or heishou. Unit leaders, however, also suffered from soaring inflation and low incomes, and most of them were thus sympathetic toward the acts of the drivers and ticket sellers. Many of them sought a delicate balance between the government and their subordinates and tried not to offend either side. The major strategy used by them was a "selective transmission of information." While faithfully transferring information on the dissatisfaction of the public transportation workers to the authorities, these cadres refused to help the regime to identify and locate the leading activists and agitators.

The cooperation of bureaucrats at the basic level was crucial for the consequences of the strike. Without their help, the ability of the government to control the situation was severely damaged. The detectives sent by the government could locate neither the agitators nor the coordinators of the movement. Without identifying the agitators, the government could not use its time-honored strategy of "killing the chicken to frighten the monkey" (shaji geihoukan) to demobilize the group. At the same time, with the help of local bureaucrats, transportation workers were able to transmit their demands to the authorities quickly and smoothly. The organizers of the movement clearly knew what the government would do next and thus could coordinate their response effectively. Their demands for salary increases and better labor protection kept coming to the municipal government through informal channels, which actually preserved a face-saving way for the government to retreat.

The strike surprisingly ended with a total victory for the public transportation workers. The Beijing Municipal Government bowed to the pressure of the bus drivers and ticket sellers. After the government announced that drivers, ticket sellers, and repairmen would get salary increases of three grades immediately, public transportation workers in Beijing ended the strike the next day.[64] The events in 1987 illustrate some interesting characteristics of strikes under the communist regime in China.

First, the hostility of the government in China toward strikes could not prevent this one from occurring, although it may have altered the form. Neither strike declarations nor formal demands to the authorities were made. Instead, strike leaders deliberately made it look like a spontaneous action. During the entire period of the strike, neither side officially recognized that there was a strike going on in Beijing. Demand making in Beijing was also different. Rather than clearly presenting their claims to decision makers, strike leaders used trivial matters to cover their real intentions in order to allow the government to save face when it retreated. The formal appeals were merely a pretext. The real demands were communicated only through informal channels.

Second, there was no formal bargaining process between the two parties.

No organizers wanted to bargain with the authorities. They knew that their presence in front of the bargaining table would provide the authorities with an opportunity to identify them. Once identified, they would face immediate punishment by the authorities. Because all strike leaders worked behind the scenes, the government had no opponents to negotiate with even if it had wanted to. Such a situation left the authorities with only two choices when dealing with the strike. They could be losers, and accept all the demands of the strikers, or winners, and reject them altogether. Compromise was extremely difficult, if not impossible.

Third, the nature of the issues involved and the nature of the transportation workers' jobs played a crucial role in mobilizing them to choose collective actions over an individualized version for their interest articulation. On each bus route, drivers are assigned to work on a specific bus. If one driver doesn't show up, another driver is expected to give up his spare time to replace the absent driver and guarantee that the entire bus route stays on schedule. Thus, instead of penalizing the government, slowdowns by individuals in this particular profession would only penalize the coworkers of participants. As individualized interest articulation was blocked, workers in this profession had to act collectively to pursue their interests.

SLOWDOWNS

In China, unlike in market economies, managers decide neither how many resources should be allocated for consumption for their units nor how their workers can be protected in labor programs. While the power of making distributive decisions lies with government organizations, lower-echelon bureaucrats usually have discretionary power over the distribution of resources already allocated to their unit. Such an arrangement makes the primary strategy for resource competition that of persuading bureaucrats to give desired resources to themselves rather than to someone else. In this kind of competition, collective action is hardly useful to help participants achieve their desired goals. In fact, the structural arrangement in China even makes slowdowns preferable to strikes when it comes to most issues related to people's lives.

Slowdowns can be performed in different fashions. At one end of the spectrum are slowdowns with explicit and antagonistic threats—open confrontational slowdowns. Participants clearly tell bureaucrats their demands and threaten noncooperation if they are not met. Bureaucrats consider open confrontational slowdowns a revolt against their authority. The most threatening part of open confrontational slowdowns is that they can produce spillover effects within organizations. Once a person begins to openly challenge the authority of official leadership, other people are likely to follow suit. For example, if one person tells her leader that if she doesn't get a salary increase, she is going to protest with a slowdown, people who hear the news are likely to do the same. Since it is hard for leaders to increase resources allocated to their organization, they will have a great incentive to resolve the conflict as quickly as possible, for if they allow it to continue, the situation might get out of hand.

To avoid such spillover effects, leaders often make deals with challengers secretly. Once the leader decides to compromise, informal negotiations usually occur. During negotiations, no one will mention the slowdowns. The leaders will express their concern over the difficulties of the employees and pretend to represent the CCP or the government in offering them a solution. The employees, in return, will thank the leaders, the party, and the government for their concern. The conversation and exchange of ideas are a formality. Both parties know that the solution arrived at is in reality the consequence of the slowdown.

Of course, not every slowdown has congenial results. Leaders may choose to mobilize other people in the unit to fight rebel employees or to ignore the slowdown if they are sure that those engaged in the slowdown cannot mobilize enough support. Precisely because the distribution of resources in a work unit is a zero-sum game, leaders might be able to play people under their control off against one another. As bonuses have been tied to the productivity of work units since the reforms of the 1980s, leaders have additional cards to play against slowdowners. If they believe the demands are absurd, leaders can manipulate other employees' fears of losing bonuses. Should leaders succeed in doing so, rebelling workers would be isolated and condemned as "unsuitable" members of the group. Therefore, before anyone decides to issue a threat to leaders, he must make sure that an alliance between leaders and other coworkers is unlikely to coalesce against him.

If employees are not sure whether they can block the formation of an alliance mobilized by leaders against them, or if they wish to avoid direct confrontation, they can choose to slow down without offering any reason or slow down and offer leaders some irrelevant excuse, such as "my child got sick so I am in a bad mood." Of course, the real issue is their dissatisfaction with a particular decision. This silent or passive slowdown widely occurs in China. When people get involved in silent slowdowns, they don't send any clear message to leaders, although many of the participants offer various hints about what they really want. It is up to the leaders to figure out what the issue is. Through silent or nonverbal communication, the leaders can gradually discern the problem and learn what they need to do to end the confrontation.

The advantage of using the silent slowdown is that employees can avoid open confrontation with leaders and leave leeway for both sides to retreat. Such acts are also unlikely to create spillover effects. If leaders decide to make concessions, other people can hardly follow suit. If the leader chooses not to compromise, there is leeway for the employee to quit the slowdown without being considered a coward or a pushover (laoshiren). Of course, such acts create less pressure than open confrontational slowdowns do and rarely produce the desired effects for the participants.

If passive slowdowns are unlikely to produce positive results for participants, one may wonder why people in China bother to engage in them. We should remember that an open confrontational slowdown often inflicts permanent damage on the relationship between participants and leaders. Even if participants win the battle, they may still be losers in the long run. Therefore, people choose open confrontational slowdowns only for issues they consider crucial to their fundamental interests. For issues not associated with fundamental interests but still important, or for which the expected return can hardly justify the risks associated with an open confrontational slowdown, participants may choose covert slowdowns instead.

Often enough, silent slowdowns are used by participants to deter leaders from categorizing them as pushovers. Students of Chinese politics are familiar with the way Chinese leaders systematically reward clients and "activists" to induce compliant behavior. However, many leaders in China appease troublemakers. With the lifetime employment system in place until recently, leaders could not easily punish employees and had to appease or co-opt them in order to keep organizations functioning properly. In a system that rewards both activists and troublemakers, pushovers or honest people get ignored. When the interests of those three kinds of people conflict, leaders will clearly sacrifice the interests of honest people, because they are unlikely to revolt. Therefore, being considered a pushover could be a disaster for an individual working in a Chinese organization.

To protect their interests, people need to show their leaders that they are *not* honest individuals. They need to demonstrate that they also know how to make trouble for leaders if they must in order to prevent the latter from sacrificing their interests in the future. An important way for people to do so in China is to initiate a covert slowdown, or to sulk (nao qingxu). Covert slowdowns in such situations usually last from a week to a few months, depending on the issue at stake. Even the loser of a particular power struggle would want to send an unmistakable message to the leaders that he or she is not someone who can be easily bullied and will not allow leaders to take advantage next time.

Free medical services in China are used by people to disguise slowdowns. Before the reforms, many employees enjoyed free medical services and sick leave with pay, features at the core of the lifetime employment system. Those who decided to engage in passive slowdowns usually saw doctors and told them they were "dizzy" or "had back pain." Since there is no way for a doctor to determine if a person really has such problems, doctors usually gave these "patients" a few days' sick leave. The patient then presented his leaders with proof of sick leave and stayed at home, hoping the leader would reconsider her decision or find a solution acceptable to both parties. People call these patients malingerers (paobinghao deren).

The health insurance system in China covers the full salary of a patient as long as sick leave does not exceed six months at one time. Many people thus take sick leaves for as long as five months and twenty-nine days, and then work for six months and one day, to avoid income cuts and take full advantage of the system. People call those who take advantage of the system to the extreme "5-2-9 and 6-0-1 cadres."

Most of the time, malingering is used to influence decisions of local officials, whereas "swaggering" is used to avoid being considered a pushover. Proof of sick leave provides both parties with an additional shield behind which to retreat in a face-saving way if they so desire. Although leaders in most organizations know that proofs of sick leave presented to them are usually invalid, it is hard for them to prove such suspicions. In many cases, it is even contrary to leaders' interests to find out the truth. If a leader confronts the patient by revealing that his sick leave is illegitimate, she cuts off her retreat and must bring the malingerer back to work and punish him for furnishing a false document. Unless the leader wants to confront the person directly and is able to bring the malingerer back to work, she will either bargain with the employee privately to resolve the conflict, or simply ignore the employee's demands and let the malingerer take sick leave for a certain period, especially if she can be sure that the worker won't be able to cause too much trouble for her or jeopardize the performance of her work unit.

Organizing Groups to Fight against Leaders

It is well known that communist regimes in all countries systematically suppress the collective opposition of private citizens. However, such an observation is only partially true in China. During the Cultural Revolution, the regime in China tolerated and even encouraged collective actions against its own bureaucrats when people from every walk of life were mobilized by Mao Zedong to struggle against "capitalist roaders" (*zouzipai*), those people in authority within the party who were taking the "capitalist road." Such experiences changed the perceptions of ordinary Chinese in many ways. The Cultural Revolution destroyed myths about communist leaders deliberately created by the propaganda department of the CCP. Before the Cultural Revolution, many people believed that the CCP worked only for the interests of the country, and that the party and its cadres had no special interests of their own. When people disagreed with government policies, they normally attributed such disagreements to their own problems rather than to those of the regime. Many of them would conduct self-criticism to reform themselves rather than criticize leaders and try to change policies. Any people attempting to oppose government policies would be considered by their peers as having political problems and thus be punished. The Cultural Revolution in China destroyed this myth by systemically revealing the corruption and power abuses of government and party officials during various stages of the campaign. The movement helped the general populace remove psychological barriers to opposing both cadres and policies of the Communist Party.

In addition, the experience of the Cultural Revolution helped many people draw a line in their minds between opposing the regime and opposing specific government or party officials. Before the Cultural Revolution, even attempting to oppose a local leader or leaders of one's unit might be labeled anti-party and counterrevolutionary. For example, many people were characterized as "rightists" simply because they criticized some leaders in their own work units in the anti-rightist movement in 1957. The then dominant political culture equated any criticism with opposing the party. People might be able to make appeals to leaders and explain to them what their problems were, but it was an extremely risky business for them to argue with leaders over policy issues. Such an attitude did not change until the Cultural Revolution, when Mao called on people to struggle against capitalist roaders and claimed that there were two headquarters within the Communist Party. Mao encouraged people to cast doubts on any policies issued by the government and to join the "proletarian headquarters" to fight against the "capitalist headquarters." During the entire period of the Cultural Revolution, people in China were free to oppose CCP officials up to the Politburo level. Such an experience successfully created a new political culture within China. Many ordinary people not only believed that they were allowed to launch a struggle against wrongdoings and wrongdoers on an individual basis or collectively, but also took the struggle as their civic duty.

After Mao opened this Pandora's box, it was difficult, if not impossible, for the regime to go back to the old ways and prevent people from opposing government officials or policies. After the Cultural Revolution, the government continued to tolerate certain organized political action at the basic level as long as such acts were targeted at local officials or at the policies of local government and had no "horizontal connections."[65] The regime tolerated collective actions at the basic level partly because it could not distinguish organized from spontaneous political action. There are many ways for people to conceal their mobilizational activities. Without expending tremendous resources, there is no way for bureaucrats to identify the nature of activities occurring in their organizations.

While the regime currently tolerates group-based activities at the basic level, bureaucrats are extremely antagonistic toward such acts, and the major risk to activists comes from potential revenge by lower-echelon government officials. Revenge usually takes the form known as "giving one tight shoes to wear" (chuan xiaoxie)—giving someone a hard time while avoiding the charge of abusing power. There are many forms of tight shoes in China, such as assigning difficult jobs to those leaders dislike; denying reasonable sick, emergency family or personal leaves; and refusing to give raises. To avoid such unhappy consequences, collective actions in Chinese organizations often start with secret contacts to mobilize support. Sometimes a single person initiates the whole chain of events, while on other occasions a small group of people work together to lobby their colleagues.

Persuading others to join group actions is usually done in three stages. First, organizers persuade their friends to join them. Then, coworkers who have also been harmed by the particular leaders or policies in question become the targets of persuasion. These ties may help to prevent them from betraying and reporting such activities to the authorities, even if they refuse to participate in the proposed action. If approached people refuse to participate, the action will stop at this point and the secret will be kept among them. But the fact that some people have already agreed to join can induce others to enlist in the proposed collective action. In the whole process, the agitators always carefully calculate the balance of power between the people they mobilize and the potential powers of opposition to the proposed action. How many people have decided to get involved in the action? What political resources do people in the group have? How unpopular is the leader involved or the policy concerned? If the scope of the conflict is to be broadened and the higher authorities decide to intervene, on whose side will the higher authorities line up? If the potential for the agitators' side to win is greater than the possibility of losing, or if the credentials of the leaders may be heavily damaged, then even if the agitators cannot claim an immediate victory, they may still choose to initiate the action and to fight against the leaders. Otherwise, after persuading people who share the same interests to join, the agitators may choose to begin the third stage of the mobilizational activities—drawing in the general populace of the unit whose interests are not directly harmed to join the struggle.

If the group decides to act at any point before mobilizing the unit's general populace, its members need to plan their actions carefully. They must gather information or "black materials" (*heicailiao*) about leaders—about their "misdeeds" in the past and evidence of "improper implementation of government policies." After gathering this information, they must schedule the timing of their attack, which can occur at study meetings, especially when leaders from higher authorities come down to visit the unit, or when the authorities decide to promote a particular person. The attack normally begins by revealing the misdeeds of the leaders, by claiming their implementation of government policies is improper, by charging leaders with abusing power, requiring higher authorities to make a special investigation, and by demanding leaders openly confess their mistakes or resign.

A well-organized attack usually has a clear division of labor. Some people initiate an attack at meetings, while others make appeals to higher authorities, and still others humiliate the leaders. A well-orchestrated collective action in China must appear to be spontaneous, as though no one is working behind the scenes.

Organized group opposition is one of the most effective ways for people in Chinese organizations to punish bureaucrats. If a group can attract enough people to join it, or is supported by a certain faction in higher-level government organizations, the chances for the group to achieve what it wants are reasonably high. It is not unusual for a targeted leader to bow to pressure from below and redress his own "misdeeds," or to adapt unpopular government policies to the "concrete situation" of the unit under pressure. The group may even be able to have unpopular leaders transferred to other organizations. Nonetheless, if the group fails, members of the group, especially the black hands or agitators, may be severely punished by the leaders. However, as the leaders can neither send people to the villages to be "reeducated" nor charge them with political evildoing in today's China, the ability of leaders to punish agitators is declining rapidly. Although the reforms in recent years have made it possible for leaders in many enterprises to lay off employees they don't like, the changes also provide a way for people to avoid the retaliation of local cadres, that is, to "exit" from the organization and find another job.

Whipping Up Public Opinion against Leaders

If a person calculates that there is little chance for her to change decisions made by a unit leader, she may choose to whip up public opinion against the leader to take revenge. She can complain about the leader to her colleagues, tell them what misdeeds the leader has committed, or make various accusations against the person. Some people do this subconsciously without any clear intentions. Others deliberately do so to erode evildoers' reputations. Still others intend to remove evildoers from their positions through such actions. The actions I am interested in are intended actions with a clear goal, that of eroding the legitimacy of particular leaders or organizations to jeopardize their leadership capabilities. Rumors and humor are the most important "weapons of the weak" in Chinese politics. According to a leader of the 1989 democracy movement, these weapons were skillfully used even by the student leaders in Beijing to mobilize political support.[66]

There are three major ways for people to incite public opinion against unpopular leaders. The first is to reveal wrongdoings. By spreading such information among the leaders' inferiors, agitators can mobilize public opinion against them. Exaggeration is a dependable weapon for participants to achieve such a goal. A worker told me the following story of how he managed to ruin the reputation of the party secretary of his factory:

> I learned that Mr. Zhang, party secretary of our factory, exchanged an apartment to be distributed to the workers of our factory for another apartment belonging to a neighboring factory with Mr. Wang, general manager of that factory. Don't you know why this happens? Both of them want to give their three-year-old son an apartment while they are still in power. If they distribute another apartment to themselves, it can hardly be justified. By making such an exchange, they hope to conceal their plot. I informed people in our factory about the exchange. I also told them, "Don't you know that Mr. Zhang was suspected of corruption ten years ago? That is the reason why the higher authorities transferred him to our unit."[67]

The most effective weapon against local leaders in China is to charge them with using public office for private gain (*jiagong jisi*). By spreading such information, agitators can easily mobilize their colleagues to oppose the leaders they are dissatisfied with.

The second way to whip up public opinion is to reveal evildoers' special weaknesses and deliberately exaggerate them to humiliate leaders. People may even exaggerate the weakness of leaders to such an extreme as to make them appear totally incompetent. The implication is that if leaders are so incompetent, they should not be in charge of a unit and everyone should feel free to disobey them. A Ph.D. candidate in the history department at Columbia University who used to live with workers of the Chongqing Steel and Iron Corporation told me how workers used this tactic:

> When I was a child, I lived in the resident quarters of the Chongqing Steel and Iron Corporation. I was deeply impressed by the innovative imagination of the workers and learned how they humiliated leaders they didn't like. The furnacemen hated their section chief. I still remember vividly that a furnaceman told a group of his colleagues that the section chief was so fond of women that whenever a woman passed by, the person drooled to the point that his shoes got wet. Everyone hearing the story laughed and laughed. Of course the leader didn't drool to the point that his shoes got wet, although he might have gazed at women passing by and tried to talk to them. Later on, whenever a woman passed by, everybody remembered the comment of the furnaceman and began to laugh at that poor guy. Such a story was very damaging to his reputation and, of course, his leadership ability. Can you imagine that people would obey the orders of a person who drools to the point that his shoes get wet whenever a woman passes by? Of course not. Half a year later, the person got transferred to another locality because no one under him took him seriously.[68]

The third way to incite public opinion against leaders is to dig out scandals about their family members. Confucian culture requires one to cultivate one's moral character (*xiushen*); rule the family (*qijia*); administer the kingdom (*zhiguo*); and then tranquilize the empire (*ping tianxia*). If a person cannot rule his family properly, how can he administer a kingdom and tranquilize the empire? The dominant political culture requires leaders in China, especially those working at the basic levels, to keep a high moral standard not only for themselves but also for their family members. This is not to say that leaders and their family members cannot commit any mistakes. However, certain kinds of problems would definitely exert a negative impact on their ability to govern. Such a cultural heritage provides people with an opportunity to make use of flaws in family members or relatives of local leaders to attack them. A worker told me the following story in an interview:

> You intellectuals have your way of doing things and we workers have ours. The chief of our workshop is a bastard. He always tries to give me a hard time and interprets government policies in a way that deprives me of my right to enjoy any privileges I am entitled to. Nonetheless, he has a very good relationship with the manager of the factory. It is beyond our capability to persuade higher authority to remove him by normal means. Do you know how we workers managed to punish him? His wife likes to carry on clandestine

love affairs with young men and this makes him a cuckold. We made use of his wife's love affairs and deliberately spread around the information about her. At the beginning, everyone believed it was merely a joke. However, the act turned out to be extremely damaging to his leadership ability. After people in the unit learned the facts, they had every incentive to use his wife's love affairs against him. In fact, three months after I began my scheme, when he tried to criticize a young worker, the worker shouted back to his face: "It is a shame for you to criticize me here while your wife has an affair with Xiao Zhang at your home! If you are a man, before you criticize me, you should run home to see what your wife is doing." The leader's face turned pale and looked listless. Since then, he has never dared to criticize any others in the workshop. A few months later, he asked the authorities to transfer him to another factory. Look, how my plot produced the desired result.[69]

The agitators in these cases manipulated the weaknesses of unpopular leaders to mobilize public opinion and to give other employees an excuse to challenge their leaders. They used any weapons available to humiliate their targets and erode their power base in the organization. As more people learned about the defamation of unpopular leaders, fewer people would pay them respect. With the gradual erosion of their legitimacy and the decay of their power base, leaders had a harder and harder time performing their roles properly. When someone reveals a leader's problems or claims that he is not qualified for the position in front of other employees, the turning point arrives. If this happens, the leader can no longer effectively control his inferiors. Since there are too many variables that may influence such political struggles, when and how they will happen, and what their results will be, are usually beyond an agitator's control. However, one thing is crystal clear—such schemes based on actual fact will sooner or later jeopardize leaders' legitimacy and will also usually induce noncompliance by other people in the same organization.

Going to Court

When other means have been exhausted, or when concrete evidence of misdeeds by government officials is available, people may choose to go to court to seek remedies.[70] The tradition of suing corrupt officials in court can be traced back to ancient Chinese society. The communist government inherited this tradition and tried to take advantage of it. A few years ago, the majority of cases brought to court concerned criminal offenses by government officials, such as graft and embezzlement.[71] With the economic reforms—especially the development of the responsibility system both in rural and urban areas—more and more disputes over contracts between citizens and representatives of the state, bureaucrats, are now brought to the courts for resolution.[72]

The effectiveness of using courts is difficult to judge, however. The regime does not recognize the separation of powers between the judicial and executive branches, and local officials commonly intrude on court decisions. This practice especially applies to cases dealing with corruption of government officials. The defendants, who often have well-established social networks, try every possible tactic and mobilize every resource available to influence judicial decisions. In fact, Chinese newspapers report many cases of plaintiffs being punished by defendants. However, it is also not unusual for plaintiffs to win legal battles against corrupt leaders. Courts in China have much more freedom in dealing with civil disputes involving governmental organizations and government officials, especially on economic issues. Although far from perfect, the court system is in the process of changing in today's China.

Big-Character Posters

Big-character posters, handwritten political posters usually voicing criticisms and complaints, were introduced into PRC politics during the antirightist movement in 1957, when Mao advocated "speaking out freely, airing views fully, holding great debates and writing big-character posters" (*daming dafang dabianlun dazibao*) to reveal the CCP's mistakes. In the short time before the anti-rightist movement, during the Hundred Flowers Campaign, many people in China also wrote big-character posters to criticize the party and to help it correct its mistakes. Unfortunately, the episode did not bring its participants a pleasant ending. After enduring serious criticism and fearing a loss of control, the CCP had *Renmin Ribao* publish a series of editorials criticizing "rightists' attacks on the party" and calling for an anti-rightist counterattack. After the campaign began, big-character posters were used by people mobilized by the regime to criticize the alleged political enemies of the society. Those who had previously answered the call of Mao himself to help the party were labeled "rightists" and their big-character posters were cited as evidence against them.

In 1966, in the early stage of the Cultural Revolution, people still remembered the painful experience of the anti-rightist movement and few, if any, dared express criticism of the CCP in big-character posters. Many of them wrote posters to support their leaders rather than criticizing and exposing the capitalist roaders around them, as Mao suggested. As the campaign progressed, people gradually realized that Mao was serious this time in mobilizing the general populace against the bureaucrats and that they could take advantage of the opportunity provided by Mao for their own purposes.[73] Freed from the fear that Mao's call for big-character posters was a trap, or a *yangmo,* many people rushed in to criticize government officials at the local level as well as certain government policies. They wrote big-character posters to criticize all leaders within the CCP except Mao himself, Zhou Enlai, and a few other key national figures, whose names changed from time to time depending on the political atmosphere. During the entire period of the Cultural Revolution, big-character posters were one of the most important means for people to participate in politics, and millions and millions of Chinese citizens wrote them almost on a daily basis. Toward the end of the Cultural Revolution, the right to write big-character posters was even codified in the 1975 constitution as one of the basic rights of Chinese citizens.[74]

Big-character posters remained an important form for Chinese citizens to participate in politics right after the Cultural Revolution. For example, in the first issue of the magazine *Zhongguo Qingnian* (China Youth) after it resumed publication in 1978, the editor published some poems and articles in memory of the demonstration in Tiananmen Square of 1976. Wang Dongxing, then director of the General Office of the CCP Central Committee, ordered that the issue be banned on the grounds that the Tiananmen demonstration was still considered counterrevolutionary. Not convinced by his reasoning, the editors and staff at the magazine plastered copies of the banned issue on a two-hundred-yard brick wall (soon to be known as Democracy Wall) surrounding a bus yard at the intersection of Changan Avenue and Xidan Street to protest his decision.[75]

This particular big-character poster in fact triggered a whole movement in Beijing. Within a short time, people put up numerous big-character posters at the same location to show their support of the magazine and to express their opinions on various key national issues. Some democrats like Wei Jingsheng joined the movement and wrote posters advocating a "fifth modernization, i.e., political democracy."[76] Coinciding with a crucial work conference of the Central Committee, many of the arguments on the wall were transmitted to the conference and used by reform leaders within the CCP, such as Hu Yaobang and Deng Xiaoping, to strengthen their positions. According to Ruan Ming, Hu's political assistant at that time, the big-character posters of Democracy Wall helped the reform leaders win a decisive battle over the conservatives in that conference.[77]

After winning the power struggle, however, the reform leaders realized that big-character posters were double-edged swords, which could be dangerous to their own authority. They decided to restrict people's rights to write them. The regime first confined the posters to Democracy Wall, then closed it down and moved the location to the more remote Moon Altar Park. Finally, under Deng Xiaoping's initiative, the constitutional right of writing big-character posters was formally abolished at a meeting of the Fifth National People's Congress in September 1980.[78]

Abolishing the constitutional right to create big-character posters greatly reduced their usage in Chinese politics, but the decree failed to eliminate big-character posters from political life in China altogether. Although they were seldom used to deal with low-politics issues after the Cultural Revolution, they are still a major weapon for influencing high politics. Nearly every major political event concerning high-politics issues in the 1980s started getting public attention with the use of big-character posters. For example, in the 1980–81 county-level elections candidates relied heavily on big-character posters to express their opinions and to promote democracy. Student demonstrations were accompanied by posters on the campus announcement boards in the Triangle Area at Peking University in 1987. Finally big-character posters emerged again as one of the most important weapons of political expression in the 1989 democracy movement used by activists to mobilize popular support in Beijing.

Demonstrations

Every constitution drawn up since the establishment of the People's Republic of China has granted the right of demonstration to Chinese citizens.[79] Nonetheless, the real attitude of the government toward demonstrations has undergone dramatic changes in the past forty-seven years. During the first twenty years of the PRC, the regime monopolized demonstrations and used them to serve its own purposes. The government made use of demonstrations to mobilize people for its own predetermined goals, to show popular support for the regime in times of crisis, to deter its opponents abroad, and to support revolutionary movements in Third World countries. Demonstrations during that period fostered mobilization rather than encouraged participatory political activities.

The situation began to change in the early period of the Cultural Revolution with Mao's support for demonstrations against the representatives of the capitalists within the CCP. To defend their political careers, many of these same people also tried to line up with mass organizations and encouraged people in those organizations to demonstrate on the street to defend themselves.[80]

As the Cultural Revolution continued, the power struggle quickly paralyzed the party, and the regime could no longer monopolize demonstrations. When the system of party control broke down in China with the intensification of the Cultural Revolution, more and more autonomous demonstrations occurred all over the country. Some of these demonstrations were aimed at local leaders, others at influencing the power struggle at the center. With the decline of CCP authority, spontaneous marches to express people's opinions gradually became a widespread phenomenon.[81]

In 1976, millions of Beijing residents went to Tiananmen Square to demonstrate against the Gang of Four. The event marked the birth of spontaneous demonstrations in Communist China, and Tiananmen Square became the most important locale for people in Chinese society to demonstrate to express their opinions on national affairs. Major demonstrations also took place in 1979, 1986, and 1989 in the square. Although all these demonstrations were somewhat related to the power struggle within the CCP and politicians in the central government tried to use them for their own purposes, none of them were mobilized by the authorities—demonstrators acted on their own to express their opinions on important issues facing the country.[82] Demonstrations in Beijing usually were supplemented by a chain of demonstrations all over China and resulted in changes of government personnel or government policies, although often not in the direction desired by the demonstrators. Strangely enough, since reformers supported by the demonstrators were generally the losers in those power struggles associated with demonstrations, reform leaders in China were more afraid of spontaneous demonstrations than the conservatives within the CCP.[83]

After the 1986 demonstrations, the Beijing Municipal People's Congress passed regulations limiting their use. The new rules required that the "organizers of demonstrations must submit written applications 5 days ahead of schedule to the concerned district or county public security organs." Except for a special showcase in 1987, the authorities in China have never approved any spontaneous demonstration.[84]

By delegating the power of approving demonstrations to the public security organs, the regulations made spontaneous demonstration in Beijing de facto illegal.[85] But the regulations did not stop people from going to the streets to demonstrate when they felt it necessary. The death of former General Party Secretary Hu Yaobang in 1989 triggered perhaps the largest spontaneous demonstration in Beijing and throughout China since the PRC's founding. From the beginning of the movement, demonstrators hinted obliquely at criticism of the leadership. In mourning Hu's passing, students in Beijing actually challenged the decisions of the veteran leaders to dismiss him in 1987. On April 27, they successfully organized the largest demonstration in the history of the PRC to protest a key editorial attacking them in the Renmin Ribao of the previous day. The target of the demonstrators was Deng Xiaoping himself. Students and people from other walks of life in fact continued marching on the streets of Beijing on a daily basis until June 4, 1989, when the regime brutally suppressed the movement.

Conclusion

Since social and political structures in China are fundamentally different from those in other societies, political acts may be quite different from those in other societies. They differ in terms of their functions, in the resources required for people to participate in them, the strategies needed for participants to bargain with government officials, and their impacts on participants, government officials, and the political system itself. For example, writing letters to editors of newspapers may not be an effective way for participants to achieve any tangible benefit. But if someone wants to communicate his or her policy preferences to the authorities, such an act can be an efficient way to do so. By the same token, when dealing with local bureaucrats, participants in urban China can always threaten to withdraw their support or imply noncooperation in their work to squeeze out desired concessions. When trying to make inferences about political participation in China or to make comparisons between similar activities in China and elsewhere, we must constantly keep these differences in mind.

The descriptions above of each of the possible ways for people in Beijing to articulate their private interests or to participate in politics lead to a series of new questions: Do citizens in Beijing actually use any of these tactics to articulate their interests in real life? If they do, how frequently do people in Beijing involve themselves in these activities and how widespread are they? Do large segments of people in Beijing in fact engage in these political activities or is it only a small group that chooses to do so? The next chapter addresses these questions.

3

The Extent of Citizen Participation

I turn to three specific issues in this chapter. First, how much participation is there in Beijing? Do people in Beijing widely engage in alternative political activism, or do only a few of them do so to articulate their interests? Second, how widespread is participation in Beijing: that is, do the participatory activities involve a broad segment of the population or only a small number of activists? Third, given the important distinction between conventional and unconventional political activism familiar to political scientists,[1] do those who choose conventional political activism also engage in unconventional acts to articulate their interests? In other words, is there a threshold between conventional and unconventional political activism in Beijing? And what is the relationship between conventional and unconventional political activities therein?

Methodology

The conventional method for studying political participation in survey research asks respondents if they have visited government agencies or offices of elected officials during certain time periods.[2] If a respondent reports that she has done so, she is seen to have engaged in politics. This method implicitly assumes all contacts made at government offices or with elected representatives in society are political activities. In societies where the distinction between the public and the private sectors is rather clear, scholars can distinguish political activities from nonpolitical ones either by the places where the activities occur or by the people those activities are aimed at, and the assumption is usually valid.

However, the situation in Chinese society is much more complicated.

Collective ownership of the means of production, in conjunction with regime efforts to exercise total control over its own people, has pushed the state to deeply penetrate into grassroot organizations. Moreover, the regime also delegates many governmental functions to basic-level organizations—the work units. Such an institutional design blurs the distinction between public and private organizations in the society. Most grassroot organizations in China not only represent the regime in controlling society but also represent the government in distributing authoritatively allocated resources; that is, they assume both economic and political functions. Such an institutional arrangement creates two major difficulties for survey researchers.

First, it is impossible for survey researchers to differentiate political activities from nonpolitical ones by locations where such actions occur. For example, researchers can neither exclude nor include acts at the work unit level from the study of people's political participation. Work units in China are responsible for implementing government policies, and the leaders usually have great autonomy when doing so. Some of them can even change the essence of policies at their own discretion. Nonetheless, work units in China can be enterprises that produce consumer products, retail shops that sell commodity goods, or research institutions that also perform other functions. While the function of policy implementation delegated to work units determines certain activities within them aimed at influencing the way government policies are implemented and should be included in this study, the managerial function of the organization determines many acts that are nonpolitical and thus should be excluded.

Second, institutional arrangements in Chinese society make it difficult for researchers to differentiate political activities from nonpolitical ones by the nature of the issues involved. Precisely because the public sphere in Chinese society is blurred with the private one, many issues belonging to the private sphere elsewhere are controlled and regulated by government policies. For example, issues related to salaries, bonuses, housing, and sometimes even products enterprises make may be regulated by official policies in China. Attempts to influence government decisions on such issues and the way in which related policies are implemented are clearly political behavior.

Given the difficulties of differentiating political activities from nonpolitical ones in communist societies, some scholars of China have suggested simply asking respondents if they have tried to influence government policies, letting them decide whether their activities are political or not. The difficulty of this approach is that with the government so intertwined with managerial functions, government and public affairs usually mean totally different things to different people. For some people, the work unit itself is a branch of the government, and decisions made by work unit leaders are governmental policies. For others, government means the central authorities in Zhongnanhai, where the state council is located. For those people, only the decisions made by the Politburo can be considered government policies. If we let people decide whether their acts are political or not, those adopting a broad definition of government would categorize any attempt to influence any decision of their work units, including managerial ones, in their definition of political participation. Those adopting a narrow definition of politics and government would only report attempts to influence decisions made by the central government and leave attempts to influence the way their work unit leaders implement government policies untouched.

Apparently, whether we categorize all initiatives of private citizens occurring at government agencies as political participation and disregard their acts at the work unit level, or codify all their efforts to influence decisions made by work units as political ones and include them in the study, more problems will be created than resolved. Nor is it proper to shift the burden to the respondents. What the researcher needs to do is to find a way to include efforts to influence decisions of work units on how to implement government policies and exclude efforts to influence managerial decisions *both* at their work unit level and at various government agencies.

Rather than using conventional survey instruments, I provided respondents with three scenarios to solicit their behavior both within and outside their work units to fight against corrupt officials and influence the way government policies were implemented. The first scenario was designed to explore respondents' efforts to fight against corrupt government officials. Using a "screener," a question to eliminate inappropriate respondents, I asked respondents if they had ever come across any leader who had abused power.[3] If the answer was positive, I presented respondents with a list of possible ways to fight against power abusers and asked if they had engaged in any of the specified activities. These acts, whether in the work unit or at government agencies, are usually aimed at influencing the appointment, promotion, and demotion of government officials, and thus can safely be characterized as political activities.

The second scenario was designed to explore acts that influence the decisions of work units to implement government policies. I asked respondents if they had made any efforts to change the decisions of their work unit leaders or local bureaucrats when not satisfied with the implementation of government policies on such issues as salaries, bonus distributions, apartment allotments, and children taking over parents' positions.[4]

Their attempts to influence the way government policies are implemented, whether occurring within the work unit, at government agencies at various levels, or through the news media also clearly fit our definition of political participation.

The third scenario was designed to solicit respondents' attempts to influence government policies per se without regard to where those acts took place. A series of questions were included in the questionnaire to determine if respondents had engaged in such activities to exert their influence when not satisfied with government policies.

There are two potential problems associated with this method. First, by providing various scenarios to help respondents identify their political behavior, the method may constrain people's recollections of their behavior to those contexts and prevent them from reporting their participatory acts in other situations. For example, asking respondents to report what they have done when not satisfied with government decisions regarding their salary may cause them to neglect acts with regard to government policies on housing allotments and lead us to lose some important information about people's political participation. Unfortunately, this problem cannot be resolved. No matter how many scenarios a survey researcher provides respondents with, there will always be residuals. The best we can do is make sure that the scenarios cover important issues facing Chinese citizens in their daily interactions with political authority as well as issues that are most likely to trigger citizen political actions.

Second, providing respondents with more than one scenario as a reference frame creates another methodological problem. Because the contexts are rather comprehensive, many respondents may not have come across all these situations. Some might have encountered them in one or two scenarios, and others not at all. The ideal way to analyze the data from the survey is, of course, to look at participants' behavior under different situations to study people's choices of political actions for various problems. Nonetheless, too many "not applicable" answers or missing values make it impossible to analyze the data in such a way.

Since the primary concern of this book is the way in which people in Beijing articulate their interests and the process of politicization of ordinary people in society, variations in political behavior under different situations are relatively unimportant. I therefore group the same forms of political activities together to create composite variables, regardless of the situation under which those political activities occurred. For example, if a person wrote to the news media in any of the above three scenarios, I mark his score for that particular form of political activity—writing letters to the media—as positive. While greatly reducing missing values, composite variables can provide us with information on the level of engagement in each form of political activity in Beijing. In the subsequent analysis, I therefore use composite variables when necessary.

How Much Participation Is There in Beijing?

Table 3.1 presents the proportion of respondents in Beijing who performed during the period 1983–1988 each of the twenty-eight participatory activities described in the previous chapter. The items are presented in descending order according to the proportion of respondents involved. Acts marked with asterisks in the table are composite variables. Items originally containing more than one category have been dichotomized.

The data show that voting for deputies to local people's congresses is the most widespread political activity in Beijing. In 1988 72.3 percent of respondents voted for deputies to local people's congresses.[5] Although the turnout rate in Beijing is similar to those in many other societies, the figure revealed here is more than 20 percent lower than that for the official records provided by Chinese authorities. This finding contradicts conventional wisdom on elections in communist societies, which holds that turnout rates in those states always exceed 95 percent.[6] Considering the fact that the population in Beijing is not only the most politically active but also the most tightly politically controlled in all of China, an explanation is in order.

The discrepancy between official records and figures reported by respondents in survey research on voting turnout is not new to students of political participation.[7] As Aage R. Clausen noted, "In the election studies conducted by the University of Michigan Survey Research Center (SRC) in every presidential election held during the period 1948 through 1960, a consistent pattern has emerged in the sample estimates of voter turnout and the partisan division of the vote. Estimates of turnout have consistently exceeded the population figure by about 12 to 13 percent."[8]

Students of participation found a similar phenomenon in the former Soviet Union. Theodore H. Friedgut, for example, in his classic study of political participation in the USSR reported that more than one million voters in Moscow—close to one-fifth of the eligible population—were absent in the 1970 elections, although official records showed that more than 95 percent voted in that election.[9] Studies based on emigrant informants also revealed that voting turnout in the former Soviet Union was lower than the widely proclaimed 99 percent.[10] Even "Soviet scholars now admit privately that the turnout data may have been exaggerated."[11] Information in China

Table 3.1   Percentage of people engaging in different acts of political participation (N = 757)

Political act	Percentage
1. Reported voting for deputies to local people's congresses in 1988	72.3
2. Reported voting for deputies to local people's congresses in 1984	62.4
3.* Contacted leaders of work unit	50.9
4.* Complained through the bureaucratic hierarchy	42.8
5. Reported voting for leaders in the work unit	34.7
6.* Used *guanxi* or connections	19.2
7.* Complained through the trade unions	18.8
8. Worked with others to attempt to solve social problems	16.1
9.* Complained through political organizations	14.9
10.* Slowed down on the job	12.5
11. Wrote letters to government officials	12.4
12.* Gave gifts in exchange for help	8.2
13. Persuaded others to go to campaign meetings for deputies	8.9
14.* Complained through deputies to the people's congresses	8.6
15. Persuaded others to go to campaign meetings or briefing meetings at the work unit	7.7
16.* Organized a group of people to fight against leaders	7.5
17.* Wrote letters to the editors of newspapers	6.7
18. Persuaded others to vote for certain leaders in work unit elections	6.1
19. Persuaded others to vote for certain deputies in elections to local people's congresses	5.2
20.* Whipped up public opinion in work units against leaders	5.0
21. Persuaded others to boycott unfair elections in work units	4.6
22.* Reported to complaint bureaus	4.0
23.* Applied for audience with higher authorities	3.8
24. Persuaded others to boycott unfair elections for deputies to local people's congresses	3.7
25. Brought cases to court	1.7
26. Wrote big-character posters	1.1
27. Participated in strikes	0.9
28. Participated in demonstrations	0.5

Note: Acts marked with an asterisk are composite variables. For each of them, the respondent was asked, "During the last five years, did you and/or your colleagues find any of your work supervisors abusing power?" Those answering in the affirmative were then asked whether they often, sometimes, rarely, or never did certain things. Then, they were asked whether they often, sometimes, rarely, or never did certain things when certain decisions of their work unit—regarding salary raises, bonus distributions, house allotments, and children taking over parents' positions—were considered harmful and unjust. Finally, respondents were asked whether they often, sometimes, rarely, or never did certain things when a policy or regulation of the government considered unjust or harmful was enacted during the past five years. Any affirmative answer to the three questions was considered a positive response.

also reveals that the high voter-turnout levels usually reported in the press are sometimes achieved with the assistance of poorly regulated proxy voting or are simply manufactured.[12]

Thus, although there exist discrepancies on voter turnout between official reports and estimates based on survey data in both communist societies and liberal democracies, the direction of discrepancy is different. While the official records of voting turnout are usually lower than the numbers acquired from survey research in liberal democracies, figures from official sources in communist societies are always higher than those obtained by other methods. The situation in Beijing is no exception to this rule.

The discrepancies between official records and data gathered by other methods can usually be attributed to sampling and response errors. However, the magnitude of the inconsistency suggests that the discrepancy found in Beijing cannot be attributed solely to sampling error. Instead, response error is more likely to be the reason behind it. Response error is closely associated with political institutions, structures, and cultures in a society. In liberal democratic societies, elections are designed to give citizens control over their government. Political culture in those societies treats voting in elections as a socially desirable behavior and a basic requirement for people to fulfill their civic duty. Research on voting behavior in such societies has found that absenteeism is considered a violation of this well-accepted social norm. When interviewers ask about people's voting behavior, they create psychological tension for nonvoters. To cope with the tension, those who do not vote (who fail to comply with socially desirable behavior) often lie to interviewers.

In researching the misreporting of voting behavior, scholars have developed the useful concept of "population at risk." In liberal democracies, since "it is nonvoters who risk being socially stigmatized by failing to conform to the social norm, it is nonvoters who are the appropriate population at risk for calculating the extent of vote misreporting."[13] As a result, a persistent pattern of overreporting of election-day turnouts in surveys is found in liberal democratic societies.[14]

If we apply the concept of population at risk to the study of voting behavior in Beijing, we should find that risk prompts Chinese citizens as well to overreport their turnout, although for different reasons. The regime in China tries hard to physically and psychologically mobilize ordinary citizens to vote in elections. It also tries to cultivate a political culture that sees voting as fulfilling civic duty, although the connotation of such "civic duty" might be different from that of liberal democracies. If, as suggested by mobilizational theorists, nonvoters in China are subject to possible regime retaliation and the regime has been successful in creating a dominant political culture in the society, then we would expect the population at risk in Communist China to be nonvoters. As elections turn from plebiscitary to limited-choice, voters now can pursue certain goals through elections. Many people even believe they should participate in not-so-perfect elections to facilitate further political change in the society. The new arrangement also makes people in Beijing think they should vote in elections, thus treating voting as a socially desirable behavior. Therefore, the population at risk in today's China must also be nonvoters.

The analysis leads us to predict that surveys in China, as elsewhere, under- rather than overestimate voting absenteeism. Apparently, response error cannot explain the discrepancy between official records and turnout rates reported by people to interviewers in surveys. Having demonstrated that the discrepancy in voter turnout between the survey data and official records is caused neither by sampling nor by response error, we should look at records provided by the government.

Turnout rates in each electoral district are considered not only the most important indicator of popular support for the regime but also an important indicator of popular support for local bureaucrats as well as the touchstone of their leadership capability. To guarantee the highest turnout, cadres at various levels of government usually assign work unit leaders to mobilize citizens to vote in various elections. Although these leaders are in constant contact with voters and have many ways to coerce them to vote, some people can still find excuses not to vote. Sickness and home absences are the most popular and legitimate excuses used by nonvoters.[15] To boost turnout, many leaders in China, rather than simply reporting such cases as absenteeism, use a loophole in the election laws to manipulate turnout rates.[16] Article 35 of the People's Congress Electoral Law makes it lawful to assign a proxy for a voter.[17] Since people using sickness or home absences as excuses for nonvoting never indicate that they are against voting in elections, local cadres usually deem it legitimate to assign them proxies. Such an arrangement satisfies the interests of all the parties involved—those who do not want to vote, unit leaders who want to achieve high official turnout rates, and officials at election committees who want to demonstrate their capability to higher authority.[18] When such practices become a "normal way of life" in China and are used by many people, official turnout rates must be systematically inflated.

The turnout rate for work unit elections seems quite low at first glance. As shown in Table 3.1, only 34.7 percent of Beijing residents reported that they had voted in elections for work unit leaders. However, since elections for work unit leaders are not mandatory in China, many work units may not have held any elections during the time period specified in the question.[19] The data show that only 46.5 percent of respondents in Beijing had a chance to vote for their work unit leaders. To get more accurate estimates of the turnout rates for work unit elections, I needed to exclude from the analysis those whose work units did not hold any elections. After eliminating them, the picture becomes quite different. As reported in Table 3.2, 82.4 percent of people who had a chance in the past five years to vote for the leaders of their work units chose to do so. The turnout rate for work unit elections is more than 10 percent higher than that for elections of deputies to people's congresses.

Higher turnout rates for work unit elections in Beijing may be attributed to the following reasons. First, the stakes of elections for work unit leaders are higher than those for deputies to people's congresses. Leaders of work units control many aspects of employees' lives and have great discretionary power to implement government policies. Changes of work unit leaders can dramatically change an employee's status. With the installation of the responsibility system in urban China in recent years, choices of leadership in work units now also have a significant impact on people's economic welfare.

Second, voters are in daily contact with candidates and usually know them well. Even without intensive campaign activities, voters are still able to make their choices. In addition, individuals are better able to influence the results of those elections. Since the poll is quite small, voters tend to know others' candidate choices. Such a situation not only makes bargaining among voters possible but also makes any cheating easily caught. As a result, strategic maneuvering by individuals to influence elections becomes possible.

Third, mobilization in work unit elections is usually quite intensive and hard to resist. Because elections determine the fate of incumbent officials, they tend to provoke power struggles among different factions in leadership groups. As power struggles intensify, not only do patrons actively mobilize their clients to vote, but many clients also actively engage in campaign activities to mobilize other voters to support certain candidates.[20] Since people's own interests are at stake, few of them can afford to ignore those

Table 3.2   Voting in elections for leaders of work units (N = 319)

Reporting voting in *danwei* elections	Percent
Did not vote	15.4
Voted	82.4
No answer	2.2

elections. For if a client allows the political enemy of her own faction to win an election, her privileged position in the work unit would disappear.

In addition to legitimating the regime, elections in China are used to demonstrate popular sovereignty and to select rulers at the grassroots level. How do people see these limited-choice elections? Do they take them seriously? Do they believe the elections really give them an opportunity to exercise popular sovereignty, or do they believe they have no choice and feel forced by the regime to vote?

To provide initial answers to these questions, I asked voters to report what motivated them to vote in various elections. Figure 3.1 presents the reasons reported by respondents for voting for deputies to people's congresses and for leaders in their work units.[21] The figure gives us a mixed picture. On the one hand, the data show that 16.1 percent of respondents voted in deputy elections because they were mobilized by their work unit leaders and 17.7 percent of people voted in work unit elections for the same reason. A remaining 6 to 7 percent of voters claimed that they had never thought about why they had voted in those elections. Judging from the fact that nearly 50 percent of people in Beijing failed to vote, were mobilized by the regime to vote, or cast their votes without thinking why they did so, we may conclude that the efforts of the Chinese government to mobilize and indoctrinate its own people are not as successful when it comes to the ballot booth as many China scholars have thought. However, judging from the fact that more than half of respondents believe they voted

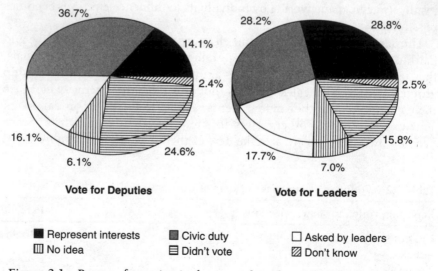

Figure 3.1   Reasons for voting in deputy and work unit leader elections

to help candidates representing their interests get elected or to fulfill their civic duty in both deputy and *danwei* elections, we may conclude that the change in the election system has begun to induce voters in China to change their behavior.

Another way to evaluate the impact of change on voting behavior is to compare the justifications people give for two kinds of elections. When asked about work unit elections—over which people have more autonomy to decide whether or not to vote and wherein the regime puts less efforts in socializing them to do so—28.8 percent voted to elect people who could represent their interests.

For elections that the regime intensively mobilized people to participate in but that were less relevant to people's daily lives—elections for deputies to people's congresses—less than one seventh (14.1 percent) of respondents voted for the same reason. If the mobilizational efforts of the regime had been successful, we would expect people to vote for instrumental benefits—to get those representing their interests elected in work unit elections—and to either vote for the same reason or join expressive benefit seekers in elections for deputies to people's congresses. Nonetheless, Figure 3.2 shows this is not the case in Beijing. Among instrumental voters for work unit elections who gave different reasons for participating in deputy elections, less than half (41.9 percent) declared that they voted to fulfill civic duties. More than one-quarter (27.9 percent) of them did not vote, and one-fourth of them (25.6 percent) could not give the reason why they voted in deputy elections. These results clearly indicate that the impacts

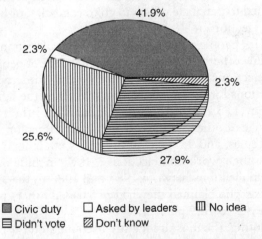

Figure 3.2 Reasons for voting in deputy elections reported by instrumental voters in work unit elections

of political education and regime mobilization are limited. Institutional change is more important in determining people's behavior.

It should be pointed out, however, that the efforts of the regime to regain its legitimacy through limited-choice elections were not a total failure. Regime efforts not only made some people believe they could get individuals representing their interests elected but also created a sense of civic duty among some people in Beijing, although the proportion of residents holding such views is not as great as in other societies.[22] Twenty-eight percent of respondents told the interviewers that they voted in work unit elections to elect people who could represent their interests, and slightly over 14 percent reported that they voted in deputy elections for the same reason. While more than 28 percent of respondents reported that they voted in work unit elections to fulfill civic duties to society and the state, 36.7 percent of people voted in deputy elections for the same reason. Given the differences in the electoral systems between China and other societies, more than one-third of Beijing respondents reported that they were motivated by civic duty to vote in elections, indicating that the efforts of the regime have been at least partially successful. To understand the dynamic of regime mobilization and its impact on people's attitudes, I will provide a more careful analysis of the data in Chapter 5.

Nearly 9 percent of respondents told interviewers that they tried to persuade others to go to campaign meetings for deputy elections, and 7.7 percent of respondents tried to persuade others to go to campaign meetings for work unit elections.[23] Excluding people who did not have a chance to vote for work unit leaders from the analysis increases the proportion of people who tried to persuade others to go to campaign or briefing meetings for work unit elections to 18.2 percent.

In elections for people's congresses, 5.2 percent of respondents attempted to influence how others voted. More than 6 percent of people did the same in work unit elections.[24] Again, if we include only those whose work units have held elections for leaders in the past five years, the figure becomes 6.7 percent. Moreover, 3.7 percent of respondents told the interviewers that they had persuaded others to boycott unfair elections for deputies to local people's congresses, and 4.6 percent of the respondents claimed that they had done so in their work unit elections.[25] If we include only those whose work units held elections between 1983 and 1988 in the analysis, the percentage of those who claimed they had persuaded others to boycott unfair elections increases to 10.9 percent.

Excepting voting, the most frequently used method for people in Beijing to articulate their interests was contacting leaders of work units when they were not satisfied either with government policies or with the way those policies were implemented. More than half of the population reported that they had contacted leaders of their work units at least once during the past five years.[26] All acts reported here were aimed at influencing government policies themselves, the way local bureaucrats implemented government policies, or the behavior of local bureaucrats. Contacting for managerial issues was deliberately excluded from this study.[27]

After contacting leaders of work units, people most often complained through the bureaucratic hierarchy. Nearly 43 percent of the respondents reported that they had gone through the bureaucratic hierarchy to make complaints, seek remedies, or register anger.[28] The intensive use of this activity reflects the success of the regime in channeling private interest articulation in society into officially sanctioned channels.[29]

From the early stages of the People's Republic, trade unions demonstrated a tendency toward greater representation of their members' interests; of course, all employees in China are automatically trade union members.[30] Reflecting such a reality was the willingness of respondents in Beijing to go to union cadres for help. The data show that trade unions are extensively used by people in Beijing to make complaints—18.8 percent of respondents have appealed to trade unions for help in the past five years.[31]

Roughly 15 percent of respondents reported having gone to various political organizations, such as the CCP, the CYL, and branches of democratic parties at various levels to seek help.[32] Deputies to local people's congresses are directly elected from various work units in urban China and they are usually in direct and constant contact with voters. When facing difficulties, 8.6 percent of respondents contacted deputies for help, the respondents reported.[33]

More than 12 percent of respondents had the experience of writing letters to government officials and 6.7 percent of them wrote to the news media to seek help.[34] Four percent of respondents reported having made reports to complaint bureaus at various levels of governmental organizations,[35] and 3.8 percent of them applied for audiences with higher authorities.[36]

Few people tried to seek remedies from the legal system in China. In the sample, only 1.7 percent of the respondents reported having had the experience of going to court to redress dissatisfaction with government policy or with bureaucrats.[37]

In addition to those conventional political activities, citizens in Beijing also actively engaged in various kinds of unconventional political activities to articulate their interests. Among those surveyed, 7.5 percent had the experience of organizing groups in their work units to fight against corrupt leaders, protest harmful government policies, or try to change the way in which their unit leaders implemented certain government policies.[38] Five percent of respondents confessed that they had had the experience of whipping up public opinion in their work units to demoralize or humiliate their leaders.[39] Slightly more than 1 percent reported having written big-character posters in the five years before the interview.[40] Even fewer—only 0.9 percent of the respondents in Beijing had participated in strikes,[41] and 0.5 percent of people had demonstrated on the streets during the same time period.[42]

Although strikes are not widely used by citizens in China to articulate their interests, 12.5 percent of people engaged in individualized versions—slowdowns on the job to express dissatisfaction.[43] Since slowdowns are not a socially acceptable way for people to express their opinions in Beijing, it is reasonable to expect that people may not be willing to tell interviewers about their engagements in such activities. To get a better estimate of the scope of slowdowns in China, I approached the issue from a different angle. I asked respondents to report if their coworkers had engaged in slowdowns to express their dissatisfaction.[44] Table 3.3 shows that more than 38 percent of respondents disclosed that their colleagues had engaged in slowdowns on their job to express their dissatisfaction. This figure is more than two times the percentage of respondents who admitted having engaged in slowdowns themselves as illustrated in Table 3.1.

I used two questions to examine how widely people in Beijing utilized patron-client ties to pursue their interests. One asked whether respondents had resorted to personal relationships to pursue their interests,[45] and the other whether they tried to turn relationships with their leaders from a hierarchical one to one of exchange to acquire desired resources.[46] It turns out that slightly over 19 percent of respondents in Beijing have resorted to personal relationships to solve difficulties facing them and a little more than 8 percent of respondents sent gifts to local bureaucrats in exchange for favors. Finally, 16.1 percent of respondents reported that they had worked with others to solve social problems.[47]

Table 3.3   Percentage of respondents who claim others in their work units have slowed down on the job (N = 753)

Reported slowdowns	Percent
Has not happened in their work unit	45.7
Happened in their work unit	38.2
Don't know	16.1

How Widespread Is Participation in Beijing?

Analysis of simple frequency distributions of various participatory acts can take us only so far. This kind of analysis, while providing us with an overall picture about people's political behavior, leaves many questions unanswered. For example, to understand the political process and people's behavior in Beijing, we need to know if participation there is confined to a small group of political activists or spread among different kinds of people. Participation in various political acts shown in Table 3.1 ranges from 0.5 percent to 72.3 percent. But what does that range mean? Does it mean that nearly 30 percent of residents in Beijing are totally apathetic and engage in no political activities to articulate their interests? If not, then what proportion of people in Beijing are totally apathetic? What proportion of them are somewhat active, and what proportion of them are extremely active in politics?

Figure 3.3 presents an analysis of how various participatory activities overlap. The numbers reported in the figure are the proportion of citizens who engaged in zero to thirteen different kinds of political activities from 1983 to 1988. Those who reported having engaged in more than thirteen

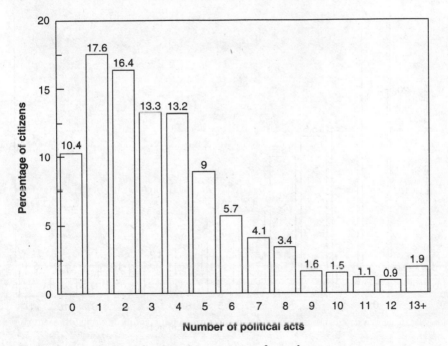

Figure 3.3   Number of political activities performed

kinds of political acts were grouped into category thirteen and above. Differing from a possible interpretation of the number reported in Table 3.1, that around one-third of people in Beijing never engaged in any political activity, the figure shows that only around 10 percent were totally apathetic. More than 17 percent of the respondents reported having engaged in at least one political activity, and more than two-thirds (72 percent) had engaged in two or more.

Among political activities presented in Table 3.1, voting is somewhat different from the others. As the regime sets the time and locale for elections, voting requires less initiative and is easier for people to engage in as compared to other activities. Some respondents are still mobilized by the authorities to vote. A more stringent test of the scope of people's political involvement in Beijing would exclude voting from the analysis and see how many people engaged in other activities. The result of this analysis is presented in Figure 3.4. The figure shows that even after excluding voting from the analysis, still more than 16 percent of respondents engaged in at least one participatory activity, and more than half of them (56.9 percent)

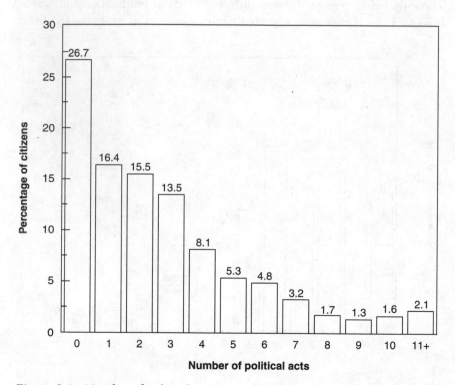

Figure 3.4   Number of political activities other than voting performed

engaged in two or more. Only around a quarter of respondents in Beijing have never engaged in any political activity other than voting in the five-year interval.

The previous inquiry of the scope of people's political engagement included political acts performed both within and outside respondents' work units. Political acts performed within a work unit are usually easier to do than those outside. Activities performed outside a work unit are more likely to have a direct impact on government policies as compared to those performed within the unit. Moreover, political acts outside the unit usually require participants to deal directly with government officials. Such activities are similar to political activities in other societies. To facilitate a comparison of people's political participation in China and elsewhere, it would be helpful to know the level and scope of people's engagement in political activities outside their work units.

Figure 3.5 shows the distribution of people's engagement in fifteen ac-

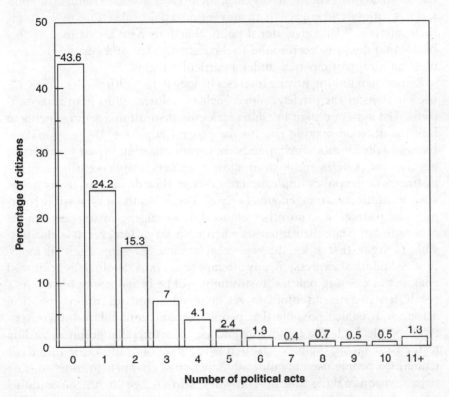

Figure 3.5 Number of political acts performed outside work units excluding voting

tivities outside their work units besides voting.[48] The figure shows that nearly a quarter of respondents in Beijing (24.2 percent) engaged in at least one political activity outside their work unit and slightly less than a third of them (32.2 percent) engaged in two or more. Together, more than half (56.4) of the population reported having engaged in at least one political act outside their work unit during the five-year interval. Even without taking people's political activities at their work unit into consideration, we can conclude that people in Beijing are quite active politically. Moreover, political engagement both within and outside people's work units is reasonably widespread among citizens in Beijing.

Students of political participation assert that as society develops and private interests diversify, existing political institutions may no longer be able to link the general populace to the political elite and thus decision-making elites may no longer be able to embody society's diversified interests. When the normal communication channels become blocked, citizens with particular demands will choose to organize themselves outside established political institutions and engage in unconventional political actions to articulate their interests.[49] Unconventional political actions here are defined as "behavior that does not correspond to the norms of law and custom that regulate political participation under a particular regime."[50]

Rather than linking private interests in society to political elites, the CCP tried to transfer the predetermined goals of political elites to ordinary citizens. The system design in China lacks the institutional arrangements to link the decision-making elite to the general populace. Decision-making elites usually do not care to embody private interests when formulating government policies and instead allow bureaucrats to make necessary adjustments at the policy implementation stage. How do citizens living under such institutional arrangements behave? Theoretically, it is possible to argue that people have no other choice but to engage in unconventional actions to articulate their interests when necessary. However, it is also possible to argue that since the regime systematically suppresses all unauthorized political expression, any attempt to act outside officially approved channels or existing political institutions will be brutally suppressed. As a result, few people can afford to get involved in unconventional political activities. It is also possible that people see conventional and unconventional political acts as a continuum and use them interchangeably according to the issue facing them. What then is the state of political life in today's China? Do people use only officially sanctioned channels to communicate with decision-making elites, or do they also engage in "unconventional political action" when necessary? Specifically, how many people in Beijing have engaged in unconventional political activities to articulate their interests? How widespread are unconventional political activities therein? Do unconventional acts come from a broad array of the populace or only from a small proportion of "anti-regime elements"? Answers to these questions can be placed within the contemporary debate concerning participation in communist societies.[51]

Figure 3.6 presents the distribution of the overall engagement in "unconventional" political activities in Beijing. Activities included in this analysis are using *guanxi* (19.2 percent), engaging in slowdowns (12.5 percent), organizing groups of people to fight against leaders (7.5 percent), sending gifts in exchange for help (8.2), whipping up public opinion in work units against leaders (5.0), persuading others to boycott elections for work unit leaders (4.6) and for people's congresses (3.7), writing big-character posters (1.1), and taking part in strikes (0.9) and demonstrations (0.5). More than 30 percent of the respondents reported having engaged in at least one unconventional political act within the five-year interval. The figure reveals that the level of unconventional political participation in Beijing is quite high. Taking into consideration that people may not be totally frank and

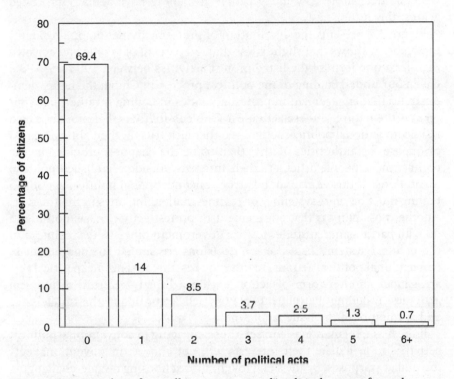

Figure 3.6   Number of overall "unconventional" political acts performed

open to questions about their engagement in unconventional political activities, actual participation may be even higher than the figures presented here.[52]

Analytically, acts reported in Figure 3.6 embody two rather different groups of unconventional political activities. One group of acts can be labeled as protest political activities. Acts included in this category are job slowdowns, organizing groups of people to fight against leaders, whipping up public opinion in work units against leaders, persuading others to boycott elections, and taking part in strikes and demonstrations. These actions, by and large, are prohibited by the authorities. Engagement in them may bring unpleasant consequences for participants. Another group of acts can be labeled as patron-client behavior associated with "traditional" society and the institutional design in China. Acts included in this category are using *guanxi* and sending gifts to government officials in exchange for favors. Participants in patron-client activities actually adapt themselves to the structural design of Chinese society in a creative way to pursue their interests. Having sorted out the two categories of unconventional activities, we must determine how many people in Beijing have actually protested against the authorities.

Figure 3.7 presents the distribution of protest activities among residents in Beijing. It shows that slightly less than 20 percent of people had engaged in at least one form of the listed protest activities between 1983 and 1988. Given our understanding of the political process in China, the figure demonstrates that engagement in protest activities in Beijing is rather high. But what is the nature of these activities? One possibility is that those engaged in unconventional political activities either lack trust in the political system or oppose the authorities. Rather than using the channels provided by the regime, these people articulate their interests outside established political institutions. If this explanation is true, unconventional political actions in Beijing must be "anti-systemic" or regime-challenging ones in their nature. Another possibility is that engagement in protest activities has nothing to do with participants' attitudes toward government officials, the regime, and the political system. Instead, such decisions are similar to engagement in conventional political actions. In other words, unconventional political acts are simply another form of action within a broad spectrum of political activities in Beijing. Participants choose acts according to their preference and the nature of the issue facing them.

If the first explanation is correct, those engaging in conventional political activities to articulate their interests will not choose unconventional acts for similar purposes. By the same token, those choosing regime-challenging activities to express their opinions will not get involved in conventional political activities to endorse the legitimacy of authority. If the second explanation is correct, there must be overlaps between people's engagement in conventional and unconventional political activities. Figure 3.8 presents a simple test of this competing hypothesis. It reveals that the proportion of people in Beijing who got involved in unconventional actions only was

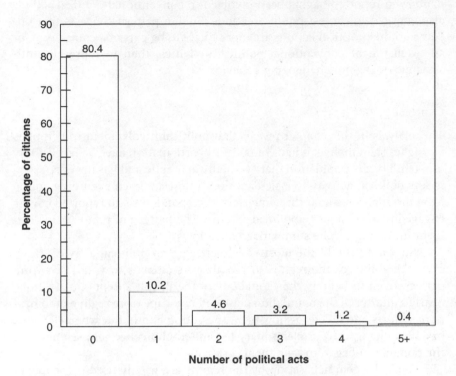

Figure 3.7   Number of protest political acts performed

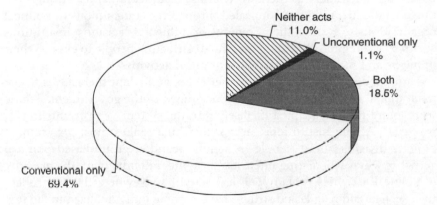

Figure 3.8   Overlap between conventional and unconventional political actions

extremely low. Only a little more than 1 percent of the respondents confined their actions to protest political activities. Instead, the figure clearly demonstrates that there is no threshold between conventional and unconventional political action in Beijing. More than 18 percent of the respondents who reported having been involved in conventional political actions also engaged in protest political actions. Such a pattern suggests that unconventional political actions are more likely to be part of a continuum, or an extension of conventional political activities, than to represent anti-systemic or regime-challenging behavior.

Conclusion

The analysis in this chapter reveals that political involvement in Beijing is far higher than many students of political participation have believed. Only one-tenth of the population there is totally apathetic and has never engaged in any political activity to articulate their interests. Even excluding voting from the analysis, about three-quarters of respondents still reported having engaged in at least some political actions. The pattern of political involvement in Beijing can be summarized as follows.

First, voting is still the most widely engaged in political activity. However, the ability of the regime to mobilize its citizens to vote is far from perfect. Even in Beijing, the capital city of the People's Republic of China, nearly a quarter of the population managed to escape from regime mobilizational efforts and failed to show up at the voting booth. But when elections in China changed from plebiscitary to limited-choice, certain segments of the population began to take them seriously.

Second, the channels set up by the regime are widely used by people to articulate their interests. The data reveal that more than half the population has contacted leaders at their work units, made complaints through the bureaucratic hierarchy, and appealed through the trade unions or political organizations to express their opinions or influence decisions. Institutions set up by the regime are thus successful in attracting people to express their opinions and in channeling people's political activities.

Third, people learn from their experiences and adapt themselves to the institutional designs of society when dealing with the government. People were found to have adapted themselves to the system's constraints in two ways. (1) As the institutional design in China makes most government policies divisible, most people in Beijing abandon group-based political activities when articulating interests, engaging individually in the majority of political activities.[53] Many political activities elsewhere that are collective, such as campaigns and strikes, have become individualized in Beijing.

Given the differences in the institutional design between China and other places, those political acts can be both individually based and effective. (2) As bureaucrats in China have great discretionary power to implement government policies, political institutions in China attract people to concentrate on individual bureaucrats to influence how they implement government policies rather than on the policy-making process itself. Such a design seduces participants into making long-term investments in individual bureaucrats to develop patron-client ties rather than making an investment in group formation and group-based political activities. People can also manage to turn the hierarchical relationship between themselves and government officials into one of exchange, sending gifts in exchange for favors. In this sense, corruption is built into the system design in China.

Fourth, although many people reported having engaged in protest political activities, regime-challenging political actions are rare. It is true that only around 5 percent reported either that they had whipped up public opinion against government officials or that they had persuaded others to boycott unfair elections. However, a majority of these activities occurred in respondents' work units, and the targets of those acts were usually work unit leaders rather than the political system itself. Moreover, those who chose unconventional political activities usually had no problem using conventional ones to articulate their interests, and there is also no threshold between conventional and unconventional political actions in Beijing. Such a finding suggests that unconventional political activities merely extend the continuum of conventional political actions. It indicates that unconventional political activities should not be simply interpreted as regime-challenging or anti-systemic political behavior.

Fifth, intensive involvement in political actions other than voting by ordinary citizens in Beijing suggests we ought to reassess a well-known myth of communist societies—that ordinary citizens are generally "apathetic and ignorant" toward politics. Although some people in Beijing may be apathetic and indifferent toward certain political activities—such as voting—most of them are actively engaged in various political activities to articulate their interests. This high level of engagement may be shaped by the society's political structure. Once most aspects of people's daily lives are controlled by the government, they can hardly afford to ignore the impact of politics and governmental affairs on their private lives. As one of our respondents explained, "even if you are not concerned with politics, politics in this country will get a hold of you." In this sense, many citizens in Chinese society are actually forced by its institutional design to *de facto* become involved in politics.

4

Modes of Political Participation in China

Mobilization theorists tend to evaluate political activities in communist countries in terms of the values and concerns of the political elite, thus considering them unidimensional phenomena. Political acts are treated as a whole, and citizens are divided into more or less political segments, which reflect the success or failure of regimes in manipulating or mobilizing their people. From the previous chapters it is clear that this view does not fit the political reality in Beijing. There are many forms of political activities therein. The authorities encourage some and prohibit others. Some require interpersonal communication skills and knowledge of the workings of government organizations, while others are related easily to job performance and need few resources. How should we characterize these political activities? What are the basic dimensions underlying each of them? How do these dimensions interact to form any alternative modes of political participation in Beijing?

Before discussing these questions, a brief review of other studies of participation in communist countries is in order. Studies have undergone dramatic changes over the past forty years. In the 1950s and 1960s, mobilization theorists evaluated political activities in communist countries according to the unidimensional view just described. Interestingly, this approach echoed the consensus among students of participation in the West. Participation studies in North America and Western Europe at the time concentrated on elections and differentiated political acts only by individual initiative.[1] Although scholars found more than one form of political activity in communist societies, most neglected the differences among them. For example, "a striking feature of the Chinese political system," wrote James Townsend, "is the degree to which a uniform style of participation pervades all popular political activities," and "the primary objective of all the acts through which the Chinese citizen participates in politics is execution of Party policies."[2]

Corresponding to the paradigmatic changes in the study of democratic participation in the 1970s, the unidimensional view of participation in communist societies also began to change. As students of democratic participation looked beyond elections and revealed more than one dimension of various forms of participatory activities in liberal democratic societies, students of communist participation looked beyond state-controlled elections and regime mobilization. Many of them revealed important differences among various forms of political activities in communist states.[3] For example, in his classic study of political participation in the USSR, Friedgut not only devoted a separate chapter to communal activities and the "revival of the Soviets" but also attributed theoretical importance to these acts.[4] On the China side, Falkenheim differentiated participation into formal participation, informal lobbying, and quasi-legal participation. Like Friedgut, Falkenheim believes that informal lobbying and quasi-legal acts often reap positive results for participants.[5]

The first systematic study of participation in a communist country was undertaken by Verba, Nie, and Kim as part of a comparative study of political participation in diverse political systems.[6] Yugoslavia, the only communist society accessible to Western scholars, was included in their study. Verba and his group found four participatory modes: communal activity, self-management, particularized contacts, and voting.[7] Other studies confirmed this group's finding that people have more than one way to articulate their interests, even in communist countries. For example, Wayne DiFranceisco and Zvi Gitelman identified three forms of participation in the former Soviet Union: "formal-ritualistic participation," "citizen-initiated contacts," and "contacts over implementation," based on emigrant interviews.[8] Donna Bahry and Brian Silver demonstrated that participation in the USSR could be arranged along a continuum of "unconventional political activism, compliant activism, social activism, and contacting" on the eve of political reform.[9]

Although scholars realize that political acts in communist societies differ by "how they relate the individual to his government,"[10] no consensus has yet been reached on how to characterize them. Analysis of dimensions and modes of participation can not only reveal the relationship among political acts but also enable us to understand the political process in Chinese society. To properly understand political participation in Beijing, an analysis of the dimensions of political activities is necessary before we can meaningfully examine alternative systems of political acts therein. In this chapter, I elaborate, first, the dimensions of political activities in Beijing and, second, how the different combinations of alternative dimensions creates different systems or modes for people in Beijing to participate in politics. I then subject the analytically deduced participatory modes to empirical tests.

Dimensions of Participation

INITIATIVE REQUIRED

Political acts in Beijing can be, first of all, arranged in hierarchical fashion. Some of them are difficult and require more initiative for participants; others are easier and require less. The initiative required for people to participate in politics is defined as "how difficult an activity is for individuals" and "how much resource expenditure it requires" from them.[11] It reflects a "common dimension [of political acts] that can be described as a propensity for political activity or a prime 'activeness' component" of the initiatives of private citizens.[12]

Political struggles are mediated by the institutional settings in which they take place. The strategies for political actors to reach their goals and the resources they have are shaped by political institutions.[13] Therefore, similar acts in different institutional settings may require different initiatives on the part of participants. In liberal democracies where politics is far removed from people's daily lives, engaging in political acts beyond voting not only requires time and energy from participants but also presumes knowledge of the government and an ability to deal with abstract ideas and complicated matters on the part of participants. Communal activities and personalized contacts in such societies thus are "difficult political activities," and a lot of initiative is required from participants to engage in them.

The "Chinese style [of political institution] emphasizes direct contact between cadres and masses as the surest means of eliciting popular participation and keeping political leaders in touch with popular demands."[14] Various institutions connected to citizens' work units have also been set up to facilitate such contacts. As government attempted to exercise total control over private citizens, politics in Chinese society became closely associated with people's daily lives. As a result, ordinary people not only understand the impact of government on their lives but also have no trouble locating government organizations. Making contacts becomes an easy political act in China, and little initiative is required for participants to engage in it.

Since the structure of political activity and its correlates differs among subgroups within a population, some scholars argue that initiative must be intimately related to the resources that a person brings to his or her participatory activities as well as the actual cost incurred in engaging in them. For example, contributing money to a campaign may be a costly and hence difficult activity for an impoverished person, whereas canvassing door to door might be less costly. But "for the wealthy executive with severe time demands, the relative difficulty of each activity might as well be reversed."[15] If we look more carefully at this example, we will find that whether a person contributes money or canvasses door to door during election time, the choices are still *among* different forms of campaign activities. Although initiatives required for wealthy executives or impoverished persons to engage in different forms of campaign activities obviously vary, campaigns still require more resources as compared to acts belonging to other participatory modes in the society.

In the subsequent analysis, I assume that the initiative required for people to engage in a particular participatory activity is a constant across different subgroups of the population. I would not deny that there is substantial variation in costs incurred by people in different subgroups of the population when engaging in a particular political activity. However, variation in the costs for each subgroup is usually not as important as variation for different participatory modes across the population.[16] For example, although it is more difficult for illiterate citizens to vote than for educated people, voting is still the easiest political act for both of them as compared to other political activities. For the purpose of categorizing various participatory modes, the differences between initiatives required for different systems of political acts are more important than the variance among subgroups of the population for political acts in the same participatory system or mode.

RISKS

From the early days of the People's Republic, the regime has been working hard to confine political activities within officially sanctioned channels. The CCP certainly does not hesitate to suppress unauthorized political expression. However, since the government controls most aspects of people's lives and monopolizes various kinds of resources, citizens in Chinese society are forced by institutional arrangements to deal with the government on a daily basis. Rather than passively complying and confining their acts to authorized channels, citizens in Beijing engage in a broad range of political acts to pursue their interests. As previously discussed, they make appeals to bureaucratic hierarchies, write to newspaper editors to register dissatisfaction, use job slowdowns to protest unfair treatment and *guanxi* in exchange for what they want from the regime, whip up public opinion against government officials, and even take to the streets to protest or write big-character posters to express their opinions. Some of their acts push the limits of what the authorities are willing to tolerate; others go clearly beyond such limits. At the same time, acts aimed at punishing unpopular bureaucrats can have undesirable consequences. Engaging in such acts would definitely attract retaliation by the regime or bureaucrats. This situation creates a unique dimension for political acts in Communist China—*risks associated with them.*

Risks associated with political activities in Beijing can be arranged along a high-low continuum. Some acts are very risky for citizens to engage in; others are less risky; and still others can be considered quite safe. Risks can also be differentiated by their sources. Such acts as writing big-character posters and even engaging in strikes and demonstrations are beyond what the current regime in China is willing to tolerate, and the authorities usually do not hesitate to take strong measures against those who dare to engage in them.[17] Even acts authorized by the regime may not necessarily be safe. To monitor bureaucrats, various channels have been set up in China for citizens to communicate with the authorities. Among them are offices in various newspapers to deal with letters to the editors, complaint bureaus, and other offices at various levels of the government. The regime in China encourages people to use these channels to report "evildoings" of local bureaucrats. Bureaucrats, of course, hold a totally different view, and many of them do not hesitate to use their power to prevent people from reporting their power abuses to the authorities. The tendency for bureaucrats to cover up their wrongdoings is not unique to China. In the United States, "even the most reasonable request, such as tracking down a lost Social Security check, may engender in the individual perception of conflict with authorities."[18] Still, there are certain important differences between the situation in China and that elsewhere. In China the ability of bureaucrats to harm their subordinates is vastly greater. As the political sphere in liberal democratic societies is separate from the economic, the power of bureaucrats over private citizens is confined to a specific aspect of their lives. Even if government officials in other societies want to retaliate against those who report their evildoings or dare to challenge their authority, the ability for them to impose damages on challengers is confined to a particular aspect of life. Moreover, many institutional arrangements in liberal democratic societies check and balance the power of government officials to curb such behavior. Not only is it more difficult for bureaucrats in democratic countries to retaliate against those participants, but if they do so, the chances of being caught and punished are much greater.

The dependency of people in Chinese society on the government for most of their livelihoods greatly increases the ability of bureaucrats to punish their subordinates. To make things worse, the lifetime employment system blocks the way for participants to leave and to escape retaliation by government officials. Without proper institutions to curb such behavior, retaliation from bureaucrats can inflict extremely severe damages on subordinates. Furthermore, the stakes for bureaucrats are also high. Without a fully developed electoral system, the most common way for bureaucrats to lose their power is to elicit antagonistic political actions by subordinates. To prevent such a nightmare from arising, bureaucrats in China need to impose the greatest pain on those who dare to challenge them. Even if they don't particularly want to take revenge against a challenger who has acted but failed to damage their careers, many of them may still feel it necessary to "kill chickens to frighten monkeys" (shajigeihoukan), that is, to punish someone in order to deter others from following suit. Thus, certain political acts in Beijing can be extremely risky for participants.

CONFLICT DIMENSIONS

Verba and his collaborators differentiate participatory activities by whether they generate or reconcile conflicts in a society. Although scholars agree that the conflict dimension plays an important role in determining people's choices of political actions, there are two problems in their conceptualization of its role. First, the conflict dimension operates as a macrolevel variable in their discussion. This macrolevel variable "may have very little to say about the obtained structure of participation."[19] When a participant makes choices among various political activities, whether an act generates or reconciles conflicts in the society may play a minor role in his or her decision to act. Second, there is also an apparent paradox in Verba and Nie's discussion of the dimensions and modes of political participation— more initiatives are required for less conflictual activities and vice versa. For example, campaigns are highly conflictual political acts, but only modest initiative is required. Particularized contacts in liberal democracies are usually considered nonconflictual political acts. Much initiative, however, is required for people to engage in them. Although subsequent factor analysis in the Verba and Nie study confirms the existence of four modes of participation based on three dimensions, including a conflictual one, these two problems in their discussion of the conflict dimension make Herbert Asher, Bradley Richardson, and Herbert Weisberg suspect that Verba and his group "may have gotten the right results for the wrong reasons."[20]

This is not to say that macrolevel variables do not influence people's political behavior. Nor is it to suggest that the conflict dimension does not influence people's choice of participatory acts to pursue their interests. Both macrolevel variables and the conflict dimension can significantly influence people's choices, but only in different ways. The decision of participants can only come from an individual perspective.[21] However, if we turn the issue around to examine whether political acts generate conflicts between participants and their colleagues, between participants and bureaucrats, and between participants and the state, we will find that the conflict dimension conveys much useful information.

First, the zero-sum nature of resource competition in Chinese society puts participants in certain acts in conflict with their colleagues, even if they do not intend to jeopardize each others' interests. For example, sending gifts to government officials in exchange for favors can generate severe conflicts between participants and their colleagues. When deciding to get involved in such acts, participants usually have to take the consequences of such conflict into consideration. Second, engaging in certain political activities in China may lock participants in a deadly struggle with government officials. Third, engaging in acts prohibited by the authorities generates conflicts between participants and the regime. Depending on participants' psychological orientation, such conflicts may either prompt or prevent them from engaging in prohibited activities. Participatory acts putting participants in conflict with bureaucrats or the regime are not necessarily risky. For example, slowdowns are prohibited by the authorities and engagement in such acts usually generates conflict between participants and the regime as well as bureaucrats. But since it is quite difficult for the authorities to catch those who engage in slowdowns, there is little risk associated with such a political activity in China.

The Dimensions and Modes of Activity

Different combinations of the three dimensions of political acts—initiative required, risks involved, and conflict—produce different sets of political activities by which citizens influence governmental decisions. Because the political process in China is quite different from those studied by Verba, Nie, and Kim, I anticipate different modes of participation will emerge from the discussion.[22]

VOTING

Studies of elections in communist countries often emphasize their differences from elections in liberal democracies. There is no alternative platform allowed for electoral competition. Voters' choices can, at best, be based on their evaluation of candidates' personalities and moral character, or on predictions about the abilities of candidates to serve in office. Candidates' preferences for certain government policies on various issues play little role in such elections. Since elections can hardly influence government policies per se, their outcome for society must be quite limited.

Even though elections are still limited-choice ones in China, voting therein has much in common with that in liberal democracies. It requires little initiative on the part of participants. As the regime sets the time and place for people to vote, "a voter does not choose the agenda; he doesn't choose the issues that divide the candidates, nor does he usually have much voice in choosing the candidates themselves."[23] And voting involves no conflict whatsoever between voters and their colleagues, local bureaucrats, or the regime. Finally, there are no risks associated with voting in China.

CAMPAIGN ACTIVITIES

People engaging in campaign activities may either have strong commitments to civic duty or strong preferences for particular candidates. Like the situation elsewhere, campaign activities in China are difficult political acts and considerable initiative is required on the part of participants.

The attitude of the regime toward autonomous campaign activities has changed over time. During the early stages of the PRC, the government held plebiscitary elections aimed at mobilizing popular support. Unauthorized campaigns at that time were considered a direct challenge to the regime and subject to severe punishment. As plebiscitary elections were gradually replaced by limited-choice elections in the late 1970s and early 1980s, the attitude of the authorities toward campaign activities gradually changed. Although the authorities are still quite hostile toward campaigns concentrating on high-politics issues, such as democracy and freedom of speech, the CCP began to tolerate campaigns focused on low-politics issues and on the behavior and qualifications of individual government officials. However, campaigners who focus on low-politics issues usually find themselves locked in a deadly struggle with incumbent local officials. If the candidates whom the participants campaign against have clients in the same unit, campaigners may also enter into conflicts with their colleagues. Therefore, I classify campaign activities as highly conflictual political acts in Beijing.

Although campaign activities can put participants into conflict with both the regime and local cadres, such acts may not be risky for participants. Unlike those in other societies, campaigners in China—especially those focused on local politics—usually persuade other voters privately. To reduce the risks associated with such acts, few of them openly confront their adversaries or challenge the qualifications of candidates they dislike publicly. Of course, if the major goal of a campaigner is to dramatically change the political system in China (is aimed at high-politics issues), the campaign would be an extremely risky political activity in Beijing.

APPEALS

Instead of thinking of contacting as a single mode of political participation, I divide it into three subgroups. The first subgroup, labeled appeals, refers to political acts whereby people communicate with the authorities in a conciliatory manner. Acts included in this mode are complaining through bureaucratic hierarchies; contacting leaders of work units; and complaining through political organizations, trade unions, and deputies to local people's congresses. These channels were set up by the regime for people to communicate with political elites and it is easy for people to engage in such activities to articulate their interests. Although appeals require more initiative than voting, they still require less than most other activities.

The channels for people to make appeals are located either at participants' work units or within their "spheres of influence." Because participants have to deal with their work unit leaders their whole lives, it may not pay for participants to damage their relationships with their leaders over noncrucial issues. The structural arrangements in China encourage participants to adopt a conciliatory manner when dealing with local bureaucrats about such issues. Appeals made in a conciliatory manner are also clearly easier for local bureaucrats to handle—they may be able to help their subordinates to resolve problems without losing prestige in front of subordinates. Although appeals seldom generate conflicts among participants, bureaucrats, and the regime, engagement in them can easily put participants in conflict with their colleagues, especially when the issues involved are distributive ones. There are, however, usually no risks associated with appeals generally.

ADVERSARIAL ACTIVITIES

If a participant fails to get what she wants from appeals and the issue involved is crucial, she might bring the issue to the attention of government officials at a higher level, inform the news media, or bring other political actors into the game to change the balance of power between herself and government officials. Activities belonging to this mode include letters to newspaper editors, letters to officials at various levels of government, appeals for audiences with higher authorities, and reports to complaint bureaus.

Similar to appeals, these channels of communication were set up by the authorities, and acts belonging to this mode are thus encouraged by the regime. However, there are also substantial differences between appeals and adversarial activities. Adversarial activities are more difficult than appeals. Complaint bureaus and newspapers are not immediately accessible to participants, and engaging in them presumes not only knowledge of the political system but also an ability to deal with such institutions on the part of participants. As more time, energy, and skills are required for people to engage in adversarial activities, more initiative is required for people to engage in adversarial activities as compared to appeals. Moreover, since the essence of adversarial activities is to borrow the power of other actors to overrule the decision of local bureaucrats, the latter must consider such acts extremely antagonistic. Thus, engaging in adversarial acts will likely put participants in direct conflict with local bureaucrats.

Such an outcome makes adversarial activities more risky than appeals. Although the authorities encourage people to "fight against unhealthy tendencies," bureaucrats in China usually do not hesitate to ruthlessly punish those who dare to engage in adversarial acts to pursue their goals. Ordinarily, since revenge-motivated bureaucrats can do more harm to participants than attacks from the regime, adversarial activities are quite risky for participants. As a result, people in Beijing choose this mode only after they have exhausted other means to achieve their goals and when the stakes of the issues involved are too high to abandon them. Once a participant engages in adversarial activities, his or her relationships with local officials will be permanently damaged.

CRONYISM

Another way for people in China to contact government officials is through the "subtle form of reciprocation bordering on bribery" to get particularized benefits.

This form, guanxi, needs to be carefully cultivated and nourished over time, and "bribery" must be properly managed for cadres to accept. If an individual explicitly implies that there exists an exchange relationship when sending gifts to cadres or cultivating personal relationships with them, he is very likely to fail. Few cadres in China are willing to risk their careers for gifts sent in such a flagrant manner. Gifts must be "separate from" rather than "linked with" favors for cadres to accept them and to produce tangible benefits. Even if a cadre agrees to enter a deal with participants, he or she will definitely deny the relationship between gifts and favors conferred on the participants. Participants must be highly motivated to engage in exchange acts, and both initiative and political skill are required to handle this delicate situation.

Cronyism, though a conciliatory political activity vis-à-vis bureaucrats in Chinese society, usually generates severe conflicts between participants and their colleagues. If one individual sends gifts to a leader to garner scarce resources, other people working in the same organization are usually forced to follow suit to prevent the first participant from getting ahead. However, since cronyism does not increase resources in the organization, the number of benefits at the disposal of local bureaucrats is a fixed value. More people sending gifts or providing services to government officials will make bureaucrats selectively reward those who provide them with more important services or more precious gifts and thus create competition among people in the same organization, which will make the situation for everyone in the organization worse. Therefore, cronyism is generally considered highly conflictual by initiators' colleagues, and such people can easily become the most hated in their organization. Many will in fact be severely punished by their coworkers.

Cronyism is also strongly opposed by the regime, which has outlawed all acts that belong to this mode. Starting in 1986, the CCP launched a series of unsuccessful campaigns to overcome such "unhealthy tendencies" (buzheng zhifeng). The attitude of the regime toward cronyism forces participants to confront the authorities. However, unlike other risky political activities, guanxi jeopardizes bureaucrats rather than citizens. Theoretically, both parties are culpable. If caught, though, the government officials bear the responsibility and punishment.

RESISTANCE

The remaining political activities belong to this category. Many resources and skills are required for participants to engage in them. The attitudes of the Chinese authorities toward these political expressions are vague and unclear. Attitudes toward some of them also change over time. For example, acts such as whipping up public opinion to fight against corrupt leaders, writing big-character posters, and engaging in strikes and demonstrations were allowed or even encouraged by the Chinese authorities, especially during the period of the Cultural Revolution, from 1966 to 1977. The constitution recognized demonstrations as a basic right of Chinese citizens until 1984, when a new version appeared. But even though the attitudes of the authorities toward these participatory acts changed, engagement in them has never been banned. Yet, other acts in this category, such as job slowdowns and persuading others to boycott elections, have never been permitted by Chinese authorities. Nonetheless, engaging in them has not been prohibited either.

Many people clearly know that the regime in China considers engagement in acts of resistance (though never banned) a challenge to its authority. To make matters worse, bureaucrats at various levels consider resisters extremely dangerous to their position and their authority. Many of them would not hesitate to take strong actions against people daring to engage in this behavior.[24] The consensus between the regime and bureaucrats against such political expression ensures that the risks associated with resistance are quite high.

The interaction of the three hypothetical dimensions of political activities in Beijing produces six modes or systems for people in Beijing to participate in politics. The characteristics of each mode in relation to the three dimensions of participation are summarized in Table 4.1. In the following sections, I undertake a step-by-step examination of the relationship among political acts in Beijing and the modes of political participation conceptually deduced above.

An Empirical Test of the Modes of Participation

I began the empirical test by exploring the nature of political acts in Beijing. According to Verba and Nie, political participation can be considered simultaneously as both a multidimensional and a unidimensional phenomenon. It is unidimensional because there is a common component—the "propensity of political activities" across all participatory acts in a society. Various political activities are simply different indicators of this prime "activeness" component.[25] Is there a single activeness component among var-

Table 4.1   Modes and dimensions of participation

| Modes | Initiatives | Risks involved | Conflict dimension | |
			Authorities	Others
Voting	Little	None	None	None
Campaign activities	Much	Little	High with regime High with leaders	Some
Appeals	Some	None	None with regime Possible with cadres	Some
Adversarial appeals	Much	High	None with regime High with cadres	None
Cronyism	Some	Some for cadres	Some with regime	High
Resistance	Much	High	High with regime High with cadres	None

ious political acts in Beijing? Are all political activities associated with this single activeness component? These questions are especially important for our understanding of political participation in China. Although few scholars will deny that adversarial activities and resistance in China are participatory acts, many of them would describe voting in Beijing as "political involvement" rather than a participatory activity. Exploring the relationship between various political acts and the activeness component in Beijing can help us to identify the nature of these political activities.

Principal component analysis serves the purpose well. The method is usually used prior to factor analysis to determine the dimensionality of common factor space. First, principal component analysis decomposes the total variance of the original variables and transforms them linearly into a small set of principal components that are orthogonal to one another. When focusing on explaining the total variation in the observed variables, the method maximizes the variance accounted for in the original variables. Since the first component accounts for most variation in the original variables, it represents an activeness component.[26] If results of the analysis indicate that any acts or modes are associated with this activeness component in a different way as compared to others, then the analysis tells us that the variable or mode differs in some crucial ways from other political activities. Although we may not be able to conclude that they are not participatory activities, such a finding certainly suggests that the status of such acts and modes should be subject to further scrutiny. By the same token, finding that a political act or mode is associated with this activeness component in a way similar to other participatory activities can certainly help us to confirm their status as *participatory acts* or *participatory modes* in Beijing.

Second, in the process of principal component transformation, a weight is assigned to each variable so as to maximize the variation of the linear composite of the component with the original variable. These weights are determined mathematically and assume no underlying statistical models about the observed variables. These components are located by theory-blind methods and can thus be used to explore the hypothetical dimension and test the validity of the participatory modes deduced from the abstract conceptual discussion.

Third, the component scores obtained from the analysis are exact mathematical transformations of the raw variables and thus exactly represent their combination. Using component scores enables researchers to reduce the number of dependent variables in the subsequent analysis. These component scores are continuous variables. Various useful and popular multivariant techniques, especially Ordinary Least Square (OLS) regression, can be used to analyze them to study the process of politicization. Compared to those of other multivariant techniques, results of OLS regression are not only more popular but also easier to interpret.

I exclude some political activities, however, from the following analysis. Variables with too few participants, such as bringing cases to court (1.7 percent), writing big-character posters (1.1 percent), engaging in strikes (0.9 percent), and engaging in demonstrations (0.5 percent), have been dropped because there is too little variance to explain. The "not applicable" answers—those who claimed that they had no problems to be solved—are recoded as nonparticipatory rather than missing values. What I am interested in is whether or not a respondent performs certain political acts to pursue his or her interests. Whatever the reason for nonparticipation, the consequence is the same—the person did not engage in that activity.

Table 4.2 presents the loading of various participatory variables in the principal component matrix. The first component has a strong correlation with nearly all political acts, and the loading accounts for more than 20 percent of variance across the board. It can be treated as an activeness component representing the "propensity of political activities." The only deviation to this component is voting. While voting in the 1984 election was negatively associated with this component, voting for work unit leaders and in the 1988 elections was found to be only weakly associated with this component. It is interesting to note that the relationship between voting and this activeness component changes with the change in the electoral system itself in Chinese society. The replacement of plebiscitary elections by limited choice ones is a gradual process. While 27.7 percent of respondents reported they were provided with choices of candidates in the 1984 elections, 41.8 percent told interviewers there were more candidates than seats in the 1988 election.[27] With more and more elections in China providing voters with candidate choice, the direction of association between voting and this activeness component changes over time. While voting in the 1984 deputy elections related negatively with this component (−.02), the relationship between voting in 1988 and this activeness component became positive although it is still weak (.04). Moreover, the relationship between this component and the most "meaningful" election in Beijing, that is, elections for work unit leaders, is not only positive but also the strongest (.18).

The analysis reveals that voting in Beijing is still not fully interchangeable with other political activities. Considering that voting is different from other participatory acts in the initiative required and that the regime is also working hard to get voters to the ballot booth, the deviation of voting variables in their relationship to this activeness component should not be

Table 4.2 Principal component loading matrix of participatory acts in Beijing

	Component						
Act	1	2	3	4	5	6	7
Wrote letters to newspaper editors	.73	−.24	−.01	.01	−.06	.33	−.21
Reported to complaint bureaus	.69	−.09	.02	.00	.02	.22	−.11
Used *guanxi*	.61	−.32	.16	−.16	−.15	.08	.47
Wrote letters to government officials	.60	−.13	−.22	−.03	−.16	.30	−.28
Applied for audience with higher authorities	.58	−.30	.09	.01	.05	.23	−.07
Complained through trade unions	.57	.10	−.35	−.02	.08	.02	.06
Complained through political organizations	.57	.22	−.36	−.14	−.24	−.10	.11
Organized a group of people to fight against work unit leaders	.54	−.41	.39	.34	.04	−.18	−.14
Gave gifts in exchange for help	.53	−.37	.21	−.17	−.15	.07	.53
Complained through the bureaucratic hierarchy	.51	.18	−.49	.03	−.17	−.35	−.16
Persuaded others to boycott unfair work unit elections	.49	.22	−.04	−.18	.61	−.07	.07
Slowed down on the job	.48	−.39	.33	.28	.17	−.22	−.04
Complained through deputies to people's congresses	.47	.18	−.33	−.07	−.17	−.01	.06
Contacted work unit leaders	.45	.10	−.42	.09	−.07	−.48	.13

Whipped up public opinion in work units against leaders	.40	−.28	.25	.50	.04	−.32	−.19
Persuaded others to boycott unfair deputy elections	.38	.33	−.01	−.21	.68	−.03	.10
Persuaded others to go to work unit campaign meetings	.34	.54	.39	−.11	−.17	−.01	−.12
Persuaded others to vote for certain leaders in work unit elections	.33	.56	.37	−.12	−.08	−.01	.04
Persuaded others to go to campaign meetings for deputies	.26	.57	.40	−.14	−.24	−.05	−.22
Persuaded others to vote for certain deputies in elections to people's congresses	.25	.57	.49	−.13	−.08	−.14	.07
Reported voting for work unit leaders	.18	.35	−.16	.47	.10	−.03	.01
Worked with others to attempt to solve social problems	.20	.07	−.14	−.23	.13	.26	−.31
Reported voting for deputies to local people's congresses in 1988	.04	.42	−.05	.67	.03	.30	.17
Reported voting for deputies to local people's congresses in 1984	−.02	.45	−.07	.61	−.04	.31	.24
Percentage of total variance	21.7	12.0	8.2	7.4	5.0	4.7	4.3
Eigenvalue	5.20	2.87	1.97	1.77	1.19	1.13	1.04

a surprise. However, the positive relationship between most voting variables and the activeness component suggests it may not be proper to characterize electoral participation in Beijing as political involvement, either. Voting in China is probably in the process of being transferred from political involvement to political participation.

The second component has both positive and negative correlations. Most officially sanctioned political acts—such as voting in elections; complaining through trade unions, political organizations, the bureaucratic hierarchy, and deputies to the people's congresses; contacting work unit leaders; and working with others to attempt to solve social problems—are positively associated with this component. Many political acts prohibited by the regime—such as organizing a group of people to fight against leaders, job slowdowns, using *guanxi*, and giving gifts in exchange for favors—are negatively correlated with this component. A careful examination demonstrates that all acts prohibited by the regime are not loaded negatively, and all political acts authorized by the regime are not loaded positively on this component. For example, persuading others to boycott unfair elections is prohibited by the authorities, but the variables loaded positively on this component. Writing letters to newspaper editors, reporting to complaint bureaus, writing letters to government officials, and applying for audiences with higher authorities are encouraged by the regime, but all of them are positively associated with this component. This pattern of association can be easily understood if we differentiate political acts by the risks associated with them, rather than by the attitudes of the regime. All "safe" political acts are positively correlated with this component, and all "risky" ones are negatively correlated with it. Although many political acts are approved and encouraged by the regime, lower-echelon bureaucrats may not be willing to tolerate their subordinates engaging in them and may feel obligated to fight back either for self-defense or to deter possible spillover effects. Since this component clearly distinguishes political acts by the risks associated with them, I label it the risk component.

Using the Kaiser Eigenvalue criterion, the data came up with seven, rather than six, components, as I had predicted. As components beyond the third usually become more and more difficult to interpret, a simplified solution is required. In addition to identifying modes of political participation, I am interested in common variance in the observed variables on the basis of a relatively few underlying factors rather than the total variance of all observed variables. For such purposes, I need to decompose the common variance of various participatory behaviors to illustrate how these variables combined to form common factors. Factor analysis suits these purposes better than principal component analysis does. Since I assume that various participatory modes are somewhat correlated with one another, oblique rotation, which does not arbitrarily assume factors are uncorrelated, is used in the analysis.

The Rotated-Factor Solution

The rotated-pattern matrix of factor analysis presented in Table 4.3 yields a clearer result, which is also easy to interpret. As expected, acts requiring more initiative are distinguished from acts requiring less. Risky acts and safe ones are clustered into different groups, and the conflict dimension makes important differences in forming different systems of participatory acts in Beijing.

Voting and campaign activities emerge as distinctive modes of participatory activities. Voting is an easy political act and little initiative is required for people to go to the ballot booth. Although electoral competition is a conflictual political activity at the macrolevel, voting as a political act can hardly generate conflicts among voters, bureaucrats, and the regime. Unlike voters, campaigners must be highly motivated. As campaigners always have opposition groups or candidates to fight against, campaign activities usually generate considerable conflicts. Since campaign activities in today's China are usually performed privately in a semisecret manner, the risks of engaging in campaign acts may still be limited.

The analysis shows that, unlike other societies where contacting is divided into communal and particularized contacts by the scope of outcome, in Beijing contacting is divided into appeals, adversarial activities, and cronyism based on their differences in the conflict dimension. Acts performed in a conciliatory manner with bureaucrats are clustered into appeals, and acts performed in a confrontational manner are clustered into adversarial activities.[28] Finally, acts that put participants in conflict with their colleagues emerge to form another mode of participation—cronyism.

Such clustering of the various ways people contact government officials clearly demonstrates how institutional arrangements shape the calculations of individuals in choosing their strategies to pursue their goals. As bureaucrats in China control most aspects of people's lives and participants have to deal with them on a lifelong basis, participants have to balance their long-term interests with short-term gains when choosing a political act to pursue their interests. Direct confrontation not only cuts off participants' freedom to maneuver but also seals the way for bureaucrats to retreat. Engaging in confrontational political acts indicates that the relationship between participants and bureaucrats has reached a point of no return. Although people may still use such a strategy to pursue their interests,

Table 4.3 Direct oblique rotated-pattern matrix for the twenty-four participation variables

Act	Appeal activities	Voting	Campaign	Resistance	Cronyism	Adversarial activities	Boycotts
Complained through bureaucratic hierarchy	.81	-.02	-.01	.04	-.06	.01	-.07
Contacted work unit leaders	.59	.06	-.06	.04	.12	.08	-.03
Complained through political organizations	.53	-.04	.12	.04	-.01	-.11	.04
Complained through trade unions	.53	.00	-.02	.00	.06	-.03	.14
Complained through deputies to the people's congresses	.33	.05	.03	.05	-.01	-.16	.09
Worked with others to attempt to solve social problems	.17	-.02	-.05	.05	.02	-.05	.03
Reported voting for deputies to local people's congresses in 1988	-.05	.79	.00	.04	-.01	-.01	-.04
Reported voting for deputies to local people's congresses in 1984	-.06	.68	-.01	-.05	.04	-.00	-.03
Reported voting for work unit leaders	.15	.38	.04	.06	-.08	.00	.09
Persuaded others to go to campaign meetings for deputies	.07	-.03	.71	-.00	-.06	-.03	-.13
Persuaded others to vote for certain deputies in elections to people's congresses	-.01	-.02	.70	.03	.02	.08	.00

	F1	F2	F3	F4	F5	F6	F7
Persuaded others to go to work unit campaign meetings	−.02	.05	.58	−.04	.08	−.02	.07
Persuaded others to vote for certain leaders in work unit elections	−.06	.06	.57	.00	.02	−.02	.19
Organized a group of people to fight against work unit leaders	−.04	.00	.02	.90	−.02	−.06	−.02
Whipped up public opinion in work units against leaders	.09	.06	.00	.69	.02	.05	−.02
Slowed down on the job	−.02	−.04	−.03	.66	.04	−.04	.03
Gave gifts in exchange for help	.01	−.03	.01	−.00	.88	.02	−.01
Used *guanxi*	.05	.01	.03	.04	.76	−.08	−.00
Wrote letters to newspaper editors	−.04	.06	−.01	.01	.02	−.89	−.03
Wrote letters to government officials	.19	.03	−.03	−.10	.03	−.62	−.06
Applied for audience with higher authorities	−.06	−.06	.00	.11	.03	−.51	.02
Reported to complaint bureaus	.05	−.03	.04	.09	.06	−.40	.14
Persuaded others to boycott unfair deputy elections	.02	−.01	−.07	.01	.04	−.00	.85
Persuaded others to boycott unfair work unit elections	.03	−.00	.11	−.01	−.03	.00	.44

many of them use it only as a last resort. Reflecting these constraints, acts that generate conflict with government officials and acts that do not generate conflict clearly cluster into different modes of political participation in Beijing.

Two patron-client political activities—using *guanxi* and sending gifts for favors—display high loading values for a unique factor and form another mode for people to contact government officials. These two political acts are actually interchangeable—those who make efforts to cultivate *guanxi* also send gifts in exchange for favors when necessary. Unlike participation in the modes already discussed, engaging in these acts not only undercuts the chances of participants' colleagues in resource competition but usually also forces them to enter into a competition in which everyone is doomed to lose. Although these acts seem to be conciliatory activities, they usually generate severe conflicts between participants and their colleagues.

Acts conceptually attributed to the mode of resistance clustered into two categories. Three of these political acts—job slowdowns, whipping up public opinion, and organizing groups of people to fight against leaders—are clustered together and display high loading with regard to the resistance mode as I have suggested. Another two election-related political acts—persuading others to boycott deputy elections and work unit elections—display a near-zero loading for the resistance mode and high loading for another factor. These patterns of factor loading indicate that political acts clustered around the first factor and the second belong to different modes of participation. My original hypothesis should thus be modified.

Careful examination shows that although activities in these two modes are similar in the initiative required and the risks associated with them, they are different on three accounts. First, the timing for participants to engage in acts belonging to these two modes is quite different. While persuading others to boycott unfair elections presumes the existence of the elections, resistance can be undertaken at any time as defined by the participants themselves. Second, the issues involved are also different. While the issues in election boycotts are related to elections, resistance can be used by participants for a much broader scope of issues. Finally, although both acts can generate conflict between participants and the regime and authorities, the risks associated with them are different. While resistance can hardly escape the attention of government officials, persuading others to boycott unfair elections can and is usually done privately, if not secretly, in China.

Therefore, based on the result of the rotated-pattern matrix of the factor analysis, I have revised the conceptualization of the modes of political participation in Beijing to incorporate a new participatory mode. Table 4.4 illustrates the results of this revision.

Confirmatory Factor Analysis

Although exploratory factor analysis is a useful tool to explore the modes of political participation in Beijing and allows cross-national comparisons,[29] there are some important deficiencies built into this model. Exploratory factor analysis assumes (1) all common factors are correlated, (2) all observed variables are directly affected by all common factors, (3) unique factors are uncorrelated with one another, (4) all observed variables are affected by a unique factor, and (5) the measurement error of observed variables is uncorrelated with latent factors.[30] Extracting the factors through the exploratory factor analysis model must be based on these assumptions regardless of their appropriateness. However, many of these assumptions are violated in real life. For example, although most students of political participation know that not all participatory variables are directly affected by all common factors, there is no way for them to impose constraints on the model in their analyses.

Table 4.4   Modes and dimensions of participation, a revision of the original model

| Modes | Initiatives | Risks involved | Conflict dimension | |
			Authorities	Others
Voting	Little	None	None	None
Campaign activities	Much	Little	High with regime High with leaders	Some
Appeals	Some	None	None with regime Possible with cadres	None
Adversarial activities	Much	High	None with regime High with cadres	None
Cronyism	Some	Some for cadres	Some with regime	High
Resistance	Much	High	High with regime High with cadres	None
Boycotts	Much	Some	High with regime High with cadres	Some

Fortunately, another statistical method—confirmatory factor analysis (LISREL)—allows researchers to impose substantively motivated constraints when examining their conceptually deduced models. Specifically, LISREL allows researchers to determine (1) which pairs of common factors are correlated, (2) which observed variables are affected by which common factors and which observed variables are affected by a unique factor, and (3) which pairs of unique factors are correlated. More important, after imposing the necessary constraints and specifying the relationship between observed variables and latent factors in the model, researchers can put a model to a statistical test to see if the data confirm or reject the conceptually deduced model.[31] In the following section, I use confirmatory factor analysis to test the revised model based on the result of exploratory factor analysis.

The results, illustrated in Table 4.5, provide strong support for the refined model.[32] In the process of testing, a variety of assumptions were made about possible correlations among observed variables and latent factors. None of them fits the data as well as the version presented in Table 4.5. In the revised model, each observed variable or participatory act is considered to be an indicator of only one latent factor, that is, one participatory mode. Following the results of exploratory factor analysis, the loading of participatory acts on the unobserved factors indicates that six items form a reliable scale for appeal; that four constitute a reliable scale for campaign activities; that three constitute a reliable scale for adversarial activities; and that two constitute a reliable scale for voting. The analysis also confirms that election boycotts separate from resistance to form a unique participatory mode in Beijing. Indicators of the goodness of fit for the model demonstrate that the model fits the data excellently, and we can conclude confidently that there are seven systems for Beijing citizens to participate in politics.

The Relationships among Factors

The principal component matrix clearly demonstrates that voting is not closely associated with the "prime-activity" component, a finding that raises questions about the relationship between other participatory modes and this component. In addition, many political activities in Beijing border on being both conventional and "unconventional." It is also more important for us to know if these unconventional participatory modes correlate with the prime-activity component the same way as the conventional ones do. Table 4.6 presents the correlation among seven principal components extracted from the exploratory factor analysis model as well as their loading on the "high-order" factor, which can be taken as the best measure of that which is common among the seven participatory modes in Beijing.[33] The findings can be summarized as follows.

First, excepting voting, all modes of participation load strongly on the high-order factor that can be treated as a "common core" of political participation. The loading of voting in the index is only .18, a sign that the relationship between voting and overall participation dimension is non-substantial. The correlation between voting and other modes of participation is not strong either. Such a finding indicates that voting in an election gives us a different indication of individuals' political commitment. What is the implication of this finding? One possible explanation is that voting in Beijing, as in other communist societies, is not a "real" participatory political act. The problem with this explanation is that the results of comparative studies of political participation suggest that the correlation between voting and the overall participation index in many other societies is also weak.[34] Unless we can demonstrate that the causes for the weak relationship between voting and the overall participatory index in Beijing are different from those found in other polities, this explanation cannot be confirmed.

Another explanation assumes that voters in Beijing are prompted by internalized motivation and that voting there also "measure[s] some underlying commitment to political activity."[35] The weak correlation between voting and the overall participation index is thus nothing more than a revelation of the simple fact that voting in Beijing is different from other "political" acts as it is in many other societies. Specifically, voting may be differentiated from other political acts in that it requires little initiative, has no associated risks, and does not put voters in conflict with either the authorities or other participants.

If the first explanation is correct, we would expect most voters in Beijing to tell interviewers that they voted because they were mobilized to do so. If the second explanation correctly represents political reality in China, people would tell interviewers that they voted either for instrumental or expressive benefits. Examination of respondents' answers to the question of their voting motivation, illustrated in Figure 3.1, suggests that both explanations have their merits although neither hypothesis fully captures the political reality of China. Fully understanding the nature of voting in Beijing requires a more rigorous test, which I deal with in the next chapter.

Second, the loadings of a participatory mode with a Chinese characteristic—cronyism on this high-order factor—are quite similar to those of other traditional or "real" modes of political participation, such as campaigning, election boycotts, adversarial activities, and resistance. The association between cronyism and the common core of political participation

Table 4.5 Confirmatory factor analysis (LISREL solution) of participatory activities in Beijing

Act	Appeals	Campaign activities	Resistance	Voting	Cronyism	Adversarial activities	Boycotts
Complained through political organizations	.59						
Complained through trade unions	.55						
Complained through the bureaucratic hierarchy	.54						
Complained through deputies to the people's congresses	.52						
Contacted work unit leaders	.42						
Worked with others to attempt to solve social problems	.26						
Persuaded others to vote for certain leaders in work unit elections		.63					
Persuaded others to go to work unit campaign meetings		.60					
Persuaded others to vote for certain deputies in elections to people's congresses		.57					
Persuaded others to go to campaign meetings for deputies		.56					

Organized a group of people to fight against work unit leaders	.70				
Whipped up public opinion in work units against leaders	.61				
Slowed down on the job	.60				
Reported voting for deputies to local people's congresses in 1988		.72			
Reported voting for deputies to local people's congresses in 1984		.53			
Used *guanxi*			.71		
Gave gifts in exchange for help			.65		
Wrote letters to newspaper editors				.66	
Reported to complaint bureaus				.63	
Applied for audience with higher authorities				.58	
Wrote letters to government officials				.55	
Persuaded others to boycott unfair work unit elections					.70
Persuaded others to boycott unfair deputy elections					.53

Note: Figures in this table are standardized estimates using LISREL (version 8.1) and the following goodness of fit indicators: chi-square = 394.3; degree of freedom = 209 (probability level = 0.00); goodness of fit index = 0.95; adjusted goodness of fit = 0.94.

Table 4.6 The correlations among seven modes of participation in Beijing

	Adversarial acts	Campaigns	Resistance	Voting	Boycotts	Appeals	Cronyism
Adversarial acts							
Campaigns	.10						
Resistance	.14	−.00					
Voting	−.04	.16	.05				
Boycotts	.23	.23	.06	.06			
Appeals	−.28	−.13	−.11	−.17	−.24		
Cronyism	.24	.07	.30	−.08	.11	−.16	
Overall index of participation	.64	.41	.43	.18	.58	−.63	.54

demonstrated by the loading suggests that cronyism has something important in common with other participatory acts in Beijing. Such a finding not only confirms that cronyism in China should be characterized as a participatory activity but also demonstrates how the institutional arrangements in Chinese society shape the political process therein. As the public sphere is still blurred with the private one, the policy formulation process is blurred with the policy implementation process; and as an impartial modern bureaucracy has failed to emerge, political acts belonging to traditional society remain an important way for people to articulate their interests in Chinese society.

Third, appeals are found to be negatively correlated with other participatory modes, although they load strongly on the overall participation index. The negative correlations between appeals and other participatory activities reveal that those who engage in appeals are unlikely to employ *all* other acts to pursue their interests. But why is this the case? Why are those who made appeals unlikely to get involved in other political activities? An examination of the impact of regime mobilization and the norms the authorities in China are trying to impose on its people will help answer these questions.

Rather than blindly forbidding private interest articulation, the CCP allows and even encourages it, subject to two conditions. First, if the interests of private citizens are in conflict with collective ones, private interests must be subordinated. Second, interest articulation can only go through the "proper organizational system" (*shidang zuzhixitong*). Extraorganizational system articulation is strictly prohibited in China. To help guarantee that people follow its will, the CCP works hard to socialize its own people to such norms.

Among all political activities found in Beijing, only acts belonging to the appeals mode fit this norm well. All channels belonging to appeals are officially sanctioned ones and thus fall clearly in the category of the proper organizational system as defined by the authorities. Making appeals requires participants to adopt conciliatory rather than confrontational strategies. Although many other channels of communication have also been established by the regime for private citizens to express opinions, their usage is usually opposed by bureaucrats. Acts belonging to the appeals mode are not only encouraged by the regime but also tolerated by lower-echelon government officials. The finding that people who have made appeals are less likely to engage in other political activities to articulate their interests suggests that some appealers would give up their interests voluntarily if they failed to get what they wanted from the authorities through appeals. Such a behavior pattern demonstrates that the norms imposed by the authorities in China are, at least partially, successful in shaping people's behavior. There are certain groups of people in Chinese society who choose to make appeals when they feel it necessary. However, if they fail to get what they want from the authorities, they will stop there and give up their interests to collective ones voluntarily rather than trying to engage in other political activities to pursue them any further. Appeals may thus be characterized as a "parochial participatory mode" with Chinese characteristics.

While the loading between most participatory modes and the overall index of participation is strong, the correlations among participatory modes are either weak or moderate. The weak correlations among various participatory modes indicate that they are independent of each other. Although those engaging in one act are likely to engage in another one in the same mode, they are unlikely to engage in acts belonging to another mode of political participation.

Conclusion

Unlike the situation suggested by mobilizational theorists, political participation in Beijing cannot be evaluated in terms of the values and concerns of political elites, and citizens cannot be divided by the success or failure of the regime in manipulating or mobilizing them. As demonstrated by the analysis in this chapter, there is more than one dimension underlying alternative participatory activities in Beijing. Different combinations of these alternative dimensions cluster political acts in Beijing into seven modes of participation: voting, campaign activities, appeals, adversarial appeals, cronyism, resistance, and election boycotts.

Two of the participatory modes identified in Beijing, voting and campaign activities, are similar to those identified by Verba and Nie in other countries.[36] Although the analysis shows that voting in Beijing is only weakly correlated with the overall participatory index, comparing data from Beijing with data from elsewhere shows that a similar pattern also exists in Austria, India, and Japan. While the weak correlation between voting and the overall participation index suggests that there might be some important differences between voting and other participatory modes in Beijing, the similarity of the pattern of relationships in cross-national comparisons argues against attempts to characterize voting in China today as a mobilizational rather than a participatory political activity.

The combination of the underlying dimensions of political acts in Beijing and the organization of the participatory mode highlights the impact of institutional arrangements on people's political behavior in society. For example, depending on the nature of the problems facing participants, the "breadth of referents," contacting in many other societies is divided into two modes: communal activities and particularized contacts.[37] The distinction between these two modes assumes that (1) institutional arrangements in these societies provide citizens with the opportunity to influence government decisions not only at the policy implementation stage but also at the policy formulation stage, allowing citizens to influence government decisions on issues with both broad and narrow scopes of outcome; (2) citizens have the right to assemble and to work together to put pressure on the government; (3) civic orientation makes large groups of citizens in the society concerned about community problems and problems not directly related to their lives. In a society like China, where participation can be both individualized and effective, few people would try to contact government officials to influence issues with a broad scope of consequences. It is reasonable to conclude that we cannot distinguish contacting by the nature of the issues involved. The differentiation between particularized contacts and communal activities thus will disappear.

In Chinese society, lower-echelon bureaucrats have great discretionary power and even the ability to change the essence of government decisions at the policy implementation stage. Such an arrangement fundamentally alters the basic strategies for people in Chinese society to articulate their interests. It is no longer necessary for people in China to change policy to get desired benefits from the government. As targets of political participation shift from policies to individual officials, private citizens will make their choice of political acts based on cost-benefit calculations. Risks associated with various political acts will emerge as the most important factor in determining their calculation. Analyzing the data acquired from Beijing confirms such expectations.

But what are the resources necessary for people to engage in these alternative modes of political activities to pursue their interests? What is the process of politicization of residents in Beijing? How active are different groups of people there? Do all the groups participate equally across all participatory modes? Is there any variation among different groups of people in their engagement in various political activities? If there is indeed variation, what is the process that leads some people to engage in each of the participatory systems illustrated in this chapter while it makes others remain inactive? It is to these questions that I now turn.

5

Understanding Voting in Beijing

The analysis in the previous chapter reveals that not all political acts in Beijing are "additive," in other words, that participation in one political act does not indicate that people will also participate in another. Specifically, while appeals are found to be negatively correlated with the overall participatory index, voting is only weakly correlated with it. This pattern suggests that it may be misleading for us to treat participation in Beijing as a whole because the way people get involved in the electoral process and appeals procedures is different from the way they take up other activities. Instead, alternative modes should be dealt with separately to reveal the different processes by which citizens in Beijing engage in politics. In this chapter, I examine how people get involved in the electoral process.

A common puzzle facing students of electoral politics in both liberal democracies and communist states is why, despite the apparent "irrationality" of voting in elections, people still bother to do so. For students of democratic participation, although outcomes of elections can and usually do lead to changes in government personnel or policies, the probability of any one person altering electoral outcomes with his or her vote is almost nil in a large electorate. The situation in communist societies is even more complicated. Even if voters in those societies can influence elections, the outcomes themselves can hardly lead to any policy changes. From this perspective, voting in both liberal democracies and communist societies seems irrational.

In liberal democracies where the voting behavior of private citizens has been intensively studied, various models have been developed to understand such "irrationality."[1] Among them, the most popular is the "rational voter model." According to this model, all human activities, including the decision to vote, can be explained in terms of cost-benefit analysis. As Anthony Downs postulates, "every rational man decides whether to vote just as he makes all other decisions; if the returns outweigh the costs, he votes; if not, he abstains."[2] "A major contribution of this approach is that it provides a more explicit, precise theoretical basis for voting decisions and for their analysis than do other approaches."[3]

Following the Downsian tradition of studying individual voting decisions in cost-benefit terms scholars went beyond election results and decomposed the benefits associated with voting into *instrumental* and *expressive benefits*. Instrumental benefits are those accruing from external sources. People voting to earn credits or money from organizations in machine politics and civil servants supporting their patrons are examples. Some people may vote in elections to resolve interpersonal pressures. For example, those living in a social environment where everyone votes in elections might be pressured to go to the polls to avoid being considered "deviant."[4] In addition to instrumental benefits, a more important benefit associated with voting is expressive. Expressive benefits include satisfying feelings of civic duty to society, to one's reference group and oneself, or the feeling of helping ensure the efficacy of the political system. Expressive benefits are usually believed to come from internal sources or the psychological orientations underlying voters' attitudes, beliefs, and value systems.[5] A major contribution of Downsian tradition is the theory revelation that even without changing governmental policies or personnel, voting can still provide voters with some important benefits.

When students of participation confront the irrationality of voting in communist states, they usually turn to theories of coercion or to political propaganda for explanations.[6] The mobilizational model tries to understand voting behavior in communist societies by exploring the rationality of voting. According to this model, people vote in elections to avoid regime retaliation. The problem with the mobilizational model is that the assumptions it is based on may be inappropriate in today's China. For example, the model assumes that the regime has the ability to coerce people to go to the ballot booth. However, the finding that only 72 percent of voters voted in the 1988 elections clearly indicates a dramatic decline in the ability of the regime to coerce its own citizens. In such a situation, why do people still bother to vote at all? Moreover, the theory can hardly accommodate recent changes in Chinese society. Apparently, we need a different explanation of the changes in electoral politics in China.

If we believe that people in communist China are rational actors and that they vote because of cost-benefit calculations, we will find that the rational voter model can be adopted to studying voting behavior in China. Several instrumental benefits can motivate voters there. Some choose to vote to avoid unpleasant consequences of nonvoting; others utilize the opportunities and turn elections into instruments for their own agenda—to get rid of leaders they detest. In organizations where patron-client social networks have crystallized, clients—like people in machine politics—may be motivated to vote to protect their own well-being and vested interests. Peer pressure and the benefits of not being considered deviant can also push some people to vote. People in China can be pushed further by expressive benefits—feelings of obligation to society. Finally, since 1979 democratic activists may have actively engaged in elections to facilitate desired democratic changes in Chinese society.[7]

In fact, 36.7 percent of voters in Beijing reported that they saw voting as their duty as Chinese citizens. Although respondents' explanations of their motivation to vote can provide us with useful information, I cannot use their explanations in the subsequent analysis for two reasons. One of them is universal and the other unique to the survey research of communist political systems.

A universal problem associated with self-reported motivation is that because of the apparent irrationality of voting, respondents may give researchers *post hoc* reasoning when asked about the motivation behind their voting behavior. Some people may not have thought of the problem until asked, while others may forget about the real reason that motivated them to vote, and still others may feel it necessary to lie to interviewers to divert alleged social pressure associated with the real reasons behind their voting decisions. Therefore, the reasons researchers acquire from voters may not be the real ones that motivated them to go to the ballot box on election day. In addition, in studying people's political attitudes in communist societies, there is the problem of the political risks associated with revealing people's real attitudes. As long as people can be punished for expressing nonorthodox political attitudes, researchers should be extremely cautious when interpreting attitudinal variables gathered from survey research. Because of these problems, students of participation usually do not rely solely on the answers of respondents in their analysis of voter motivation, even when studying voting behavior in liberal democracies. To avoid these pitfalls, scholars analyze the relationship between voting and various resources to infer the reasons people vote. Since such analyses rely more on objective behavioral variables than subjective attitudinal variables, they are considered more reliable.

Following this tradition, I examine the bivariate relationships between voter turnout and various socioeconomic variables to reveal the process through which people in Beijing become politicized and get involved in electoral politics. Since many independent variables, especially the socio-economic variables used in this study, correlate with one another, I also need to control the effects of other variables to single out the independent effects of each socioeconomic variable on people's voting behavior. I will demonstrate the step-by-step process in the analysis to show how final conclusions are reached.

The Effects of Socioeconomic Status on Voter Turnout

EDUCATION AND TURNOUT

Perhaps the best-known finding about voter turnout in liberal democracies is the strong positive relationship between rates of voting and levels of education.[8] However, such a relationship is never clearly manifested in communist countries. The empirical findings in communist societies are contradictory. On the one hand, Verba, Nie, and Kim found a strong correlation between respondents' socioeconomic status, for which education is the most important composite, and voting in the former Yugoslavia.[9] On the other hand, many other studies of political behavior in the former Soviet Union revealed a negative correlation between education and voter turnout.[10] Nonvoting in the former Soviet Union was found to be positively associated with respondents' educational achievements.[11]

In contrast to findings in other communist societies, the relationship between respondents' educational achievements and voting appears to be curvilinear in Beijing. As presented in Figure 5.1, 58.2 percent of people without formal education in Beijing voted in the 1988 elections. The turnout increased steadily with years of respondents' formal schooling for the first six years. In 1988, 73.3 percent of those who finished primary school voted in the deputy elections. Beyond primary school, increases in respondents' formal schooling did not increase the probability of voting until they entered college. The probability of voting for people with more than twelve years of formal schooling again increased simultaneously with the increase in educational level. More than 84 percent of people with twelve to fifteen years of formal schooling and 90.7 percent of people with sixteen to seventeen years of formal schooling voted in the 1988 elections. The most interesting aspect of this figure is that the turnout rate for people who have received more than eighteen years of formal education dropped sharply as compared to people in other categories, even people without formal education. Only 56.5 percent of people with more than eighteen years of schooling voted in the 1988 elections. The trend of voter turnout for the 1984 elections is identical to that of 1988, except that fewer people at each educational level reported voting in the 1984 elections.

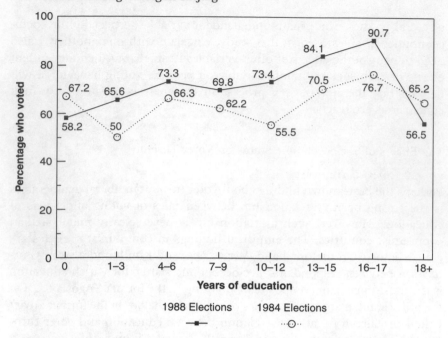

Figure 5.1   Educational level and voter turnout in the 1988 and 1984 elections

The dramatic reduction in the turnout rate for people with more than eighteen years of schooling deserves special attention. One consideration is that the suspension of formal schooling during much of the Cultural Revolution and continuous changes in the Chinese educational system caused discrepancies between respondents' formal years of schooling and their educational achievements.[12] Those who reported having more than eighteen years of formal schooling might have been graduate students, people whose specialization requires more than five years of college education, or alumni of special educational programs, such as party schools. Since different kinds of education can have different impacts on voting behavior, knowing the true education level of those respondents is necessary to address this issue.

To pinpoint the education level of people who reported more than eighteen years of formal schooling, I included a question asking about respondents' educational achievement in terms of the degree they had completed. Cross-tabulation of years of formal schooling and the diplomas respondents received revealed that all respondents who claimed to have received an equivalent of more than eighteen years of formal schooling, except one, had some graduate education. This result tells us that graduate school education in China plays an important role in shaping people's voting behavior. Once a person enters graduate school, the likelihood of his or her voting is greatly reduced.

When we classify people by length of formal education, we are actually measuring several different attributes. First, school in China is not only a place to transfer knowledge but also an important institution for political education and socialization. Starting from secondary school, pupils in China are required to take politics courses on a regular basis. Political education courses are also mandatory in Chinese colleges. In addition, courses in the humanities and social sciences, such as Chinese literature and Chinese and world history, have a lot of political content built into them. The entire educational system in China is actually designed to provide youngsters with civic orientation and to turn them into "new socialist men" as defined by the authorities. Direct and indirect political indoctrination, if successful, may help to internalize the norms the regime wants to impose on the Chinese people and create psychological pressure for people to express such values by voting in elections.

Second, education is alleged to increase "one's capacity for understanding and working with complex, abstract, and intangible subjects."[13] If it indeed increases people's interests in politics and prompts them to get involved in politics in liberal democracies, it must also be able to increase the ability of citizens in communist societies to understand and grasp opportunities provided by the regime to pursue their own interests. Specifically, the educated in China are more likely to have the skills and techniques to get maximum benefits from limited-choice elections and to turn them into "meaningful occasions" to articulate their interests. Moreover, such a capability can also help them to reduce risks associated with using limited-choice elections for their own purposes. In this sense, education can change the payoff structure for voters by increasing the benefits associated with voting and reducing the costs associated with it.

A third aspect of formal education relates specifically to the political history of the PRC. During its first thirty years, intellectuals and the educated in China were characterized as the "stinking ninth category" (chou laojiu). To deal with them, the CCP introduced a "redemption" (shumai) policy in the 1950s and early 1960s. Although the regime in China never fully trusted educated people, the government paid its elites higher than average salaries to "buy" their knowledge for "socialist construction," in exchange for their "departicipation."[14] To induce compliance, numerous political campaigns, such as "thought reform," the anti-rightist movement, and the Cultural Revolution were launched against those who dared to engage in anti-CCP politics. During these campaigns, the regime not only demonstrated its willingness to take strong action against those who dared to ignore its warnings, but also managed to create psychological pressure to remold people in society. The regime considered the educated the prime target of departicipation, deliberately discriminating against them and imposing much harsher punishment on them than on others for their intransigent behavior.

Over time, such policies may produce a subculture among the educated and make them extremely sensitive to the risks associated with their political behavior. To reduce potential risks and avoid punishment for noncompliant behavior, the educated might be more reluctant to openly confront the authorities. Although people like Andrei Sakharov in the Soviet Union and Chen Ziming and Wang Juntao in China dared to take risks to challenge the authorities, the majority of intellectuals in Chinese society may be captives of a subculture whose legacy survives even now that the purges of the intellectuals have begun to fade away. With this history in mind, it is easy to see how the benefits of avoiding punishment for nonvoting make the educated in Beijing go to the ballot box.

Nonetheless, the finding that people with graduate training had the lowest voting percentage in deputy elections raises serious questions about these arguments. On the one hand, if the political education theory is correct, or if historical experience matters, we would expect more graduate students to vote than college graduates, not only because they received more intensive political indoctrination through their education, but also because the educated are the people the regime in China most wanted to departicipate in the past. If a political subculture exists among the "stinking ninth category," it should dominate the behavior of people with a graduate education. On the other hand, if we believe that education increases one's ability to deal with complexity, people with graduate-level education should be the most sophisticated people in Chinese society and thus the most likely candidates to use limited-choice elections for their own agendas. All the explanations suggest that the educated should vote more than other groups, but the data analysis shows exactly the opposite.

The difficulties in explaining the reasons why fewer people with graduate education voted in Beijing suggest that the relationship between education and voter turnout might be spurious. Both increases in voter turnout with respondents' education before the graduate level and decreases beyond it may be the product of some other variable. To learn more about the relationship between education and turnout, we need to isolate the effects of education from other variables to see if the pattern revealed in the bivariate analysis still exists. I take up this challenge in the next section when doing multivariant analysis.

ECONOMIC STATUS AND TURNOUT

Income has also been found to be positively correlated with voter turnout in many Western democracies, although such a relationship exists neither in Japan nor in the former Soviet Union.[15] Two major theories have been developed by students of political participation to explain the relationship between economic status and participation in liberal democracies. One emphasizes the spiritual and the other the materialistic aspects of the relationship. Since affluent people have more stake in the system, the first theory argues, they are more likely to develop attitudes and beliefs encouraging them to sustain the system by participating in it. The other theory suggests that poor people are too preoccupied with the struggle to fulfill their subsistence needs to participate in politics. Active citizenship is a sort of luxury that the poor cannot "afford."[16]

Examination of the relationship between income and voting turnout in Beijing reveals that there is no significant correlation between the two variables. Many students of communist participation would explain this absence by invoking mobilization theory in conjunction with Verba, Nie, and Kim's findings that "the less a political act depends on individual-level motivation and resources, the greater will be the effect of institutional constraint."[17] The Chinese regime has worked hard to reduce the costs and increase the benefits associated with political participation. Specifically, the authorities have set up ballot booths at workplaces, launched propaganda campaigns during election time, and even reduced the size of electoral districts to "make personal acquaintance with deputies likely, thereby enhancing the public-recognition element in office-holding and encouraging the election of candidates who hold some degree of natural group support."[18] Such efforts may be able to equalize the effects of socioeconomic resource levels (SERL) on voting by reducing the costs of voting for the poor.[19] Since there is usually no extra time and energy required for people to vote, poor people—who may be otherwise kept from voting by the daily "struggle to keep body and soul together"—can be easily included in the process.[20]

Probably more important to this "equalization" argument is the institutional setting in China, which increases the benefits associated with voting for the poor. Danwei leaders in China have the power to distribute various resources to people in the organization as well as subsidies to the poor.[21] Since members of election committees in Beijing are usually danwei leaders, following their directives helps individuals create a positive image of those officials and thus enhances the possibility for them to obtain the desired resources and subsidies, which are crucial to poor people. By linking instrumental benefits to turnout in elections, the institutional arrangement

in China seems to have its greatest impact on those who dearly need resources from the government—the poor in Beijing.

Before testing this theory, the validity of the measurement itself must be
verified. We know that income is used by scholars as indicators of respondents' economic status as well as their stakes in the system elsewhere. The
question facing us is whether income can represent both dimensions in
China. This issue has two aspects. One is whether money can be transferred
into better living conditions and vice versa in China as elsewhere. Another
is whether more affluent people in China have more stakes in the system.
Careful examination suggests that neither assumption is true.

At the time of my survey, it was not clear whether higher monetary
income in Beijing was bringing people a better life. People making more
money in Beijing include newly emerged small entrepreneurs, contract
workers, and cadres. Although the income of small entrepreneurs is usually
much higher than others, they seldom enjoy any benefits provided by the
government, such as medical insurance, good education for their children
and, most important, prime housing allotments. The same is also true for
contract workers. Most newly hired workers in Beijing enter into the labor
market under fixed-term contracts. Although all of them earn higher salaries than permanent workers, none of them enjoy any benefits or receive
any kind of social welfare from the state.

At the other end of the spectrum are the middle- and high-level cadres.[22]
Although the salary of cadres is usually higher than ordinary people's, it is
still less than many contract workers', not to mention that of entrepreneurs.
Nonetheless, the "content of gold" (hanjinliang) of their salary is much
higher than that of contract workers and entrepreneurs. For example, cadres usually enjoy such privileges as spacious apartments, automobiles, tel-
ephones, and even government-paid housekeepers. Many of them eat frequently in first-class restaurants at public expense and bring home various
"gifts" from their subordinates. All these privileges are legal. These observations suggest that people's real economic status can hardly be measured
simply in pure monetary terms in China.

Moreover, people's income hardly represents their stake in the system in
China. For example, newly emerged entrepreneurs, perhaps the most affluent people, are discriminated against by the current establishment. They
have yet to claim any political power and their proper socioeconomic position within the system. Rather than sustaining the system, many entrepreneurs may in fact want to change it. Meanwhile, a less affluent group
in Chinese society—cadres—have the greatest stake in the system. To guarantee the functional compatibility of people's economic status in China
with those found elsewhere, we need to find a better measurement

to gauge not only people's economic status but also their stakes in the political system.

People's subjective evaluation of their relative economic situation serves this purpose better than income measured in money terms. Figure 5.2 presents the relationship between this measurement and voter turnout for both the 1984 and 1988 elections.[23] The figure shows that turnout in Beijing increases with respondents' subjective evaluation of their economic status. In both elections those considering their economic status far below average were least likely to vote, and those considering their economic status far above average were most likely to vote. More interesting is the finding that economic status had the greatest impact on the poor.[24] As in the United States, those believing their own economic status was far below average had a substantially lower turnout than people believing their own economic status was below average. Beyond below-average levels, the impact of economic status on voter turnout was found to be rather limited, and increases in respondents' economic status did not significantly change the likelihood of an individual's voting.

Comparing the data of the two elections reveals another interesting phe-

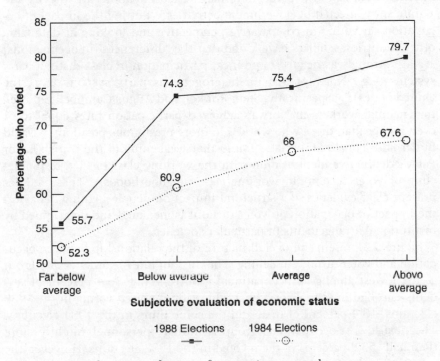

Figure 5.2   Subjective evaluation of economic status and voter turnout

nomenon—the impact of voters' economic status on turnout increased for the poor over time. In 1984, the gap in election turnout for people believing their economic status was far below average and those believing their economic status was below average was around 8 percent. However, the same gap jumped to nearly 20 percent for the 1988 elections. This finding tells us that the developments over the four-year interval kept poor people further away from the polls. Taking into consideration the price reforms and double-digit inflation between 1984 and 1988, the fact that fewer people of lower economic status voted indicates that the importance of economic status for turnout has increased dramatically with the recent reforms in Chinese society.

OCCUPATION AND TURNOUT

The impact of occupation on voter turnout has been found to be distinctive in different societies. For example, voters from several occupational categories in the United States tend to be more active in electoral participation than people from other occupational groups. The higher turnout rates among voters in these occupations are generally attributed to instrumental benefits—that is, to the perception that these occupations are directly and significantly affected by government activities.[25] Putting the impact of occupation on voting in comparative perspective and looking at data from other countries, scholars have found that the "differences [in occupations] are less strongly associated to political participation in class-distinct party systems (e.g., Norway) than in heterogeneous party systems (e.g., the United States)."[26] Specifically, Stein Rokken and Angus Campbell reported that manual workers in Norway achieved participation rates equal to or even higher than those who worked in more prestigious positions.[27] David Butler and Donald Stokes also found that weakening of the British Labor Party's distinctive identification with the working class has led to the decline of voter turnout in working-class neighborhoods.[28] These studies present clear evidence of a structural impact on people's voting behavior: the impact of occupation on voter turnout is mediated and determined by institutional arrangements in particular societies.

Figure 5.3 presents an overall picture of the relationship between occupation and voter turnout in Beijing. The turnout rate of students stands out as the lowest among all occupational groups. While 36.4 percent of students enrolled in schools of higher education reported voting in the 1988 elections, 18.2 percent of them did the same thing in the 1984 elections. The next-lowest occupational group is military personnel. Slightly more than half (53.8 percent) of them voted in the 1988 elections. However, the relationship between occupation and turnout for these two occupational

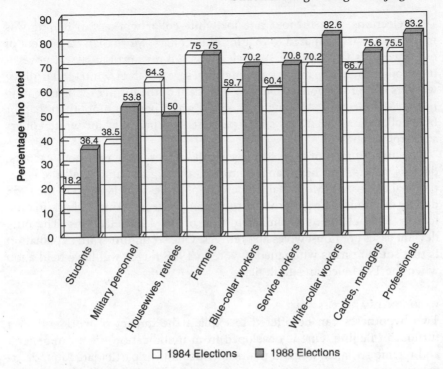

Figure 5.3 Occupation and voter turnout

groups in Beijing might be spurious. Students might have failed to vote because they had not reached eighteen years of age and become qualified voters by the time of the elections. Meanwhile, elections in the People's Liberation Army (PLA) are not only held under totally different rules and regulations but also kept completely separate from those of civilians. More important, they usually take place at different times from those held for civilians.[29]

By contrast, the findings of lower turnout rates for housewives and retirees in Beijing are not beyond expectations (only 50 percent of them voted in the 1988 elections). Following mobilization theory, we can attribute lower turnout rates for housewives and retirees to the difficulties the regime has in mobilizing them. Using a rational voter model, we may argue that the benefits associated with voting for housewives and retirees are extremely low, and costs for them to vote are usually higher as compared to those for other people.

Turnout rates for blue-collar and service workers were quite similar. Slightly more than 70 percent of those in both occupations voted in the

1988 elections. The turnout rate for white-collar workers in Beijing was much higher as compared to that for blue collars. More than 82 percent of office workers voted in the 1988 elections. To my surprise, fewer government officials and managers of enterprises voted than white-collar office workers and professionals. Only 75.6 percent of the former reported voting in the 1988 election. Although this figure was 5 percent more than that for blue-collar workers, it was still 7 percent less than that for white collars and professionals.

The turnout rate for professionals, including researchers, schoolteachers, doctors, actors, and newspaper editors, is the highest among all the occupational categories. More than 83 percent of professionals voted in the 1988 deputy elections. The pattern of association between voting and occupation for the 1984 elections is similar to that of the 1988 elections. The only deviant cases are housewives and retirees. One straightforward explanation is that some retirees who failed to vote in 1988 might still have held a job when the 1984 elections took place.

WORK UNITS AND TURNOUT

Two hypotheses can be offered to explain the impact of work units on turnout in Beijing. One is developed from mobilization theory in general and regime socialization and political education in particular. Another attributes the impact of *danwei* on voting to the political skills of employees acquired from their working experience.

The work unit in China is not only a place where employees earn their living but also a political organization utilized by the authorities to mobilize people to carry on the predetermined goals of the regime and to socialize them into official norms. However, the willingness and the ability of the regime to control different types of work units in China is not a constant, and employees in different types or levels of *danwei* receive very different "political treatment" (*zhengzhi daiyu*). For example, political study sessions are held once every other week in collective enterprises but every week in state enterprises. Employees working at government organizations or government institutions are exposed even more frequently to political education. They must attend more political study sessions, but they have more access to various internal reports and instructions from leading government and party bodies.

Political education in Chinese society can also push voters to the polls by imposing certain norms on private citizens and thus helping to develop expressive benefits—the "feeling that one has done one's duty to society, to a reference group, and to oneself"—among certain citizens.[30] Even though elections in today's China provide people with only limited choices, some people may have been indoctrinated via political education and believe these elections provide them with an opportunity to control the government. Thus, they may feel it is their responsibility to vote in these elections.

Alternatively, the impact of work units on voting can be attributed to the differences in employees' political skills, acquired from their working experiences at different *danwei*. As illustrated in previous chapters, elections for deputies to people's congresses in China can be used by employees in a *danwei* to get rid of unpopular leaders. However, if such "schemes" fail and participants become known to leaders of work units, those who dare to engage in them are guaranteed punishment by leaders. Therefore, participants need to have a thorough understanding of the workings of the political process, correct calculations of power balances between different factions, and prepared escape routes to reduce the risks associated with such actions. These skills can be learned only from personal experiences of encounters with political authorities and the bureaucracy. People working at higher-status organizations are usually more exposed to such complicated and delicate situations. They are thus more likely to be imperceptibly influenced, through their work experiences, by what they constantly see and hear and get to know about the art of maneuvering within the regime regularly.

Figure 5.4 reveals a strong and linear relationship between types of work units and voter turnout. In 1988, whereas 43.5 percent of people who did not belong to any work unit voted, 63.3 percent of employees of *sanzi qiye*, or foreign enterprises, joint ventures, and enterprises leased to foreigners, voted. The turnout rates for those who worked in *jiti qiye*, or collective enterprises, and *gouying qiye*, or state-owned enterprises, were nearly identical: 73.1 percent for the former, and 74.4 percent for the latter. The turnout rate for people working in *guojia jiguan*, or government organizations, was highest among all work units: 81.1 percent of them voted in the 1988 elections, and 73.2 percent reported voting in the 1984 elections.

Although the analyses in previous sections provide us with an overview of the impact of various socioeconomic characteristics on turnout in Beijing, analysis can only serve as a prologue to our understanding of the process by which people become politicized. Since all variables examined in these sections are interrelated, the bivariate relationships revealed may not be real. Unless we can control the effects of other variables to isolate the impact of a specific one, we can never be confident about the relationship between these variables and turnout. In the next section, I explore

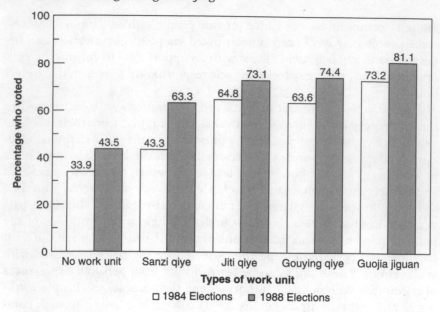

Figure 5.4 Types of work unit and voting behavior

trivariate relationships to see if the various indicators of respondents' socioeconomic status examined in this section have independent effects on voting.

Isolating the Effects of Socioeconomic Status and *Danwei* on Voter Turnout

EDUCATION, *DANWEI*, AND TURNOUT

As in many other societies, different types of work units require different educational levels from their employees to properly handle their jobs. For example, employees in government organizations and state organs must have the abilities and skills to deal with complicated bureaucratic procedures; thus the average educational levels of the employees in those organizations must be higher than those working in other work units. Because the educational achievement of respondents and the *danwei* in which they work are interrelated, if we find that these two variables correlate with voting turnout, there will be four possible ways that education or *danwei* influence voting turnout in Beijing.

1. The relationship between *danwei* and voter turnout is caused by the higher educational level of employees in work units. *Danwei* is but a confounding variable.

2. By the same token, the linkage between education and turnout can be a spurious one. It may be that the *danwei* a respondent works at makes the difference.

3. Both education and *danwei* have independent effects on the probability of respondents voting.

4. There can be an interaction between the two variables. This explanation suggests that *danwei* and educational backgrounds can produce joint effects on the probability of respondents' voting and that such effects are "additive." The higher the educational level *and* the status of the *danwei* in which a respondent works, the greater the possibility of his or her voting. The impact of work units thus depends on respondents' educational levels, and vice versa.

Unless I can control the effects of *danwei* and education to single out their respective effects on voting, the effects of socioeconomic status on voter turnout in Beijing can never be fully understood. In the next step of the analysis, I am going to examine the impacts of particular socioeconomic variables on voting by controlling the impact of yet another variable. The dependent variable used in the analysis is a unit weight scale of voting taking into account respondents' voting behavior in both the 1984 and 1988 deputy elections. The unit weight scale is a three-category ordinal variable—those who never voted in any election, those who voted in one election, and those who voted in both elections.

Because the dependent variable is not a continuous one, the estimate produced by the Ordinary Least Square model will be biased. I have chosen to use the logistic regression model to manipulate the data in the following analysis. Conceptually, the coefficients in logistic regression are similar to regression coefficients in the OLS model.[31] While the regression coefficient in the OLS model represents the amount of change in the dependent variable for one unit change in the independent variable, estimated coefficients in logistic regression represent the change of log odds for one unit change in the independent variable. The odds ratio in logistic regression is the ratio of the probability that an event will occur to the probability that it will not.[32]

Table 5.1 examines the relationship between *danwei* and voter turnout with the impact for education held constant. By holding a variable constant, I can examine the behavior of respondents who are similar in one aspect of their socioeconomic status but different in another one to see if there is a difference in their behavior. Specifically, by holding education constant, I can compare the behavior of those who have received the same level of education but work at different *danwei* to see if they voted differently. If

Table 5.1   Effects of education and *danwei* on voter turnout

Variable	Estimated coefficient	Probability > chi-square	Odds ratio
Intercept 1	−0.95	0.00	
Intercept 2	0.15	0.60	
Danwei[a]			
Joint ventures	0.74	0.09	1.09
Collective enterprises	1.51	0.00	4.52
State enterprises	1.52	0.00	4.55
State organizations	1.76	0.00	5.80
Education			
1–3 years	−0.73	0.09	0.48
4–6 years	−0.07	0.84	
7–9 years	−0.35	0.25	
10–12 years	−0.35	0.22	
13–17 years	0.28	0.40	
More than 18 years	−0.73	0.15	

Note: −2 log likelihood = 55.44; $p = 0.0001$.
[a]Private enterprises are used as base category.

people with the same level of education working at different types of work units did vote differently, I may attribute the difference to their *danwei* experience.

In the equation presented in Table 5.1, *danwei* types are recoded into four design variables. People without any work unit affiliation are used as a reference group.[33] The two intercepts in the model are intercepts for voting in one election and for voting in both elections. Education was first entered into the equation as a continuous variable. The result showed that the variable has no significant impact on the odds of voter turnout in Beijing. Considering that the bivariate relationship between education and voter turnout is a curvilinear one as shown in the previous analysis, I recoded education into six design variables, using nonschooled voters as a reference group.[34] The odds ratio presented in the model is the probability that respondents will not vote to the probability that respondents will vote in two deputy elections.

The model reveals that the *danwei* has a significant impact on voting even when the effect of education is controlled. People with the same level of education working at different *danwei* behave differently when voting.

Slightly more of those working in private enterprises or joint ventures voted than those without work units or retirees, while working at a collective or state enterprise greatly increased the probability of employees' voting (4.52 and 4.55, respectively), even when the effects of education were controlled. Working experiences in governmental organizations and state institutions have the greatest impact on the probability of an individual's voting. The odds ratio for employees of state organizations and state institutes voting is 5.8 as compared to unaffiliated people. The model clearly demonstrates that the odds of voting increase with the increase in status of one's *danwei*.

This equation can also be interpreted as controlling the effects of *danwei* to isolate the impact of education on voter turnout in Beijing. By doing so, we actually compare the voting behavior of people working in the same *danwei* who received disparate education. The equation presented in Table 5.1 shows that when the impact of the *danwei* is controlled, respondents' educational levels *do not* have any significant effect on voter turnout. For people at the same type of *danwei*, greater educational levels did not increase the probability of their voting.

DANWEI, OCCUPATION, AND TURNOUT

Work units in China have been characterized as small societies (*xiaoshehui*). Many of them embody a broad array of functions that are the responsibility of governments in other societies. For example, many *danwei* have their own kindergartens and primary, secondary, and even high schools. Some *danwei* have their own staff hospitals, private shops, and internal restaurants; others own fleets of cars and buses to transport their employees from home to work. With these arrangements employees in a *danwei* can range from government officials, to white-collar workers, schoolteachers, and blue-collar and service workers. In China, where people in different occupations work in the same *danwei*, researchers have an excellent opportunity to test whether the higher voter turnout in some *danwei* comes from respondents' working experiences or from their organizational affiliations. If we find that occupation has a significant impact on turnout after the effects of the *danwei* are controlled, we can conclude that it is job status that made the difference. But if we find that different occupational groups voted similarly in the same *danwei*, we can conclude that the difference in voter turnout comes from employees' organizational affiliations.

Table 5.2 shows the partial effects of *danwei* and occupation on voter turnout. Housewives and retirees are used as the reference category in the model.[35] The analysis shows that once the impact of the *danwei* is controlled, variations in occupation do not have any significant effect on voter turnout.[36] Comparing the model with occupations in the equation to one

Table 5.2   Effects of *danwei* on voter turnout, controlling for occupation

Variable	Estimated coefficient	Probability > chi-square	Odds ratio
Intercept 1	−0.22	0.66	
Intercept 2	0.91	0.07	
Danwei[a]			
Joint ventures	0.38	0.52	
Collective enterprises	1.29	0.00	3.63
State enterprises	1.25	0.00	3.51
State organizations	1.38	0.00	3.96
Occupation			
Blue collar	−0.86	0.18	
Service worker	−0.77	0.24	
White collar	−0.41	0.54	
Cadre	−0.70	0.32	
Professional	−0.13	0.85	

Note: −2 log likelihood = 32.06; $p = 0.0002$.
[a]Private enterprises are used as base category.

without (not shown), we find that the two models are significantly different.[37] Since there are different variables in the model, we cannot simply compare the changes of −2 log likelihood to evaluate the overall fit for each model. Akaike Information Criterion (AIC) statistics adjust the −2 log likelihood statistic for the number of terms in the equation and thus serve this purpose well. The lower AIC values usually indicate a more desirable model. The AIC statistics for the model with and without occupation in the equation are 1352.9 and 1440.6, respectively. Such a result indicates that the model with occupation included in the equation is better than the model without that variable in the equation.

Thus we have a paradox here—although occupation does not have any independent impact on voting when the effects of the *danwei* are controlled, the model with occupation in it fits the situation in Beijing better. This result alerts us to the possibility that only people in certain occupational groups voted differently from people belonging to other occupational groups in each *danwei*. If that is the case, the choice of the reference group would influence the results of the analysis. To examine this possibility, I can choose another occupational group—blue-collar workers—as a reference group for the analysis. Table 5.3 presents the results of this choice

Table 5.3   Effects of *danwei* and occupation on voter turnout in Beijing

Variable	Estimated coefficient	Probability > chi-square	Odds ratio
Intercept 1	−1.08	0.01	
Intercept 2	0.05	0.89	
Danwei[a]			
Joint ventures	0.38	0.52	
Collective enterprises	1.29	0.00	3.63
State enterprises	1.25	0.00	3.51
State organizations	1.38	0.00	3.96
Occupation			
Housewife	0.86	0.18	
Service worker	0.09	0.69	
White collar	0.45	0.05	1.57
Cadre	0.16	0.64	
Professional	0.73	0.01	2.07

Note: −2 log likelihood = 32.06; $p = 0.0002$.

[a]Private enterprises are used as base category.

and demonstrates that while cadres, managers, service and blue-collar workers, housewives, and retirees in each *danwei* voted nearly identically, more white-collar workers and professionals voted in these elections. The analysis tells us that when the impact of the *danwei* is controlled, being white collar and professional does increase the possibility that a person will vote. Based on these findings, the impact of *danwei* and occupations on voting can be explained in the following ways.

First, employees in a higher-status work unit, no matter what their occupation, generally receive better political treatment and more economic benefits from the state than those working at lower-status *danwei*. It is not unusual for a plumber working in government organizations to have more access to internal documents than a party secretary in a collective enterprise. The difference in *danwei* is manifested not only in the political treatment of its employees but also in the social and economic benefits received by them. As a general rule, employees of state organizations get higher salaries than those of state enterprises. People working at state enterprises get higher pay than employees at collective enterprises. More important, people working in higher-status *danwei* also get better housing allotments and their children can attend better schools. Thus it is not unusual for a cleaning lady working at a government organization to live in a better apartment than a top manager in a collective enterprise. Since a person's social status in urban China is based more heavily on the *danwei* he or she belongs to than on occupation, the *danwei* in Beijing may be considered the primary indicator of a person's socioeconomic status. If that is true, the finding that more employees of higher-status *danwei* voted is compatible with the finding in many other societies that higher socioeconomic status leads to a higher level of voter turnout.

We should be aware that there is a competing and equally plausible interpretation—that the ability for the higher-status *danwei* to mobilize its citizens to vote is better than that of lower-status *danwei* in Beijing. This explanation attributes higher turnout among people in higher-status work units to a special kind of instrumental benefit—avoiding possible unpleasant consequences of nonvoting. The differences in voter turnout among people in different *danwei* may simply represent the differences in the ability of different types of work units to mobilize their employees to vote.

Mobilization requires mobilizers. Cadres and managers are the most likely candidates to play that role in Chinese society. If mobilizational theory is correct, we should find the turnout of cadres and managers in each *danwei* to be higher than that of others. Unless we can prove that *danwei* cadres and managers are not the mobilizers and find replacements in each work unit, or that mobilization can take place without mobilizers in China, the finding that no more cadres and managers voted than employees in other occupational groups in Beijing argues against the explanation based on mobilization theory.

The finding that more professionals and white-collar workers voted in each *danwei* also contradicts mobilizational theory. An implicit assumption of mobilization theory is that people in communist societies are dissatisfied with the authorities and that their political involvement in elections can be mobilized only by the regime. Since professionals and white-collar workers are not only more likely to understand the "nature" of elections controlled by the CCP but also more likely to have their own independent judgments, they should be the groups most difficult for the regime to mobilize to vote. If the survey was conducted during the Cultural Revolution, I might be able to argue that the fear of punishment for nonvoting compelled professionals to go to the ballot booth. However, such an argument can hardly be valid in today's China. Specifically, the reforms from 1977 to early 1989 and the changing emphasis in society from political campaigns to economic development dramatically increased the political status of professionals and white-collar workers in each *danwei* as well as their autonomy. As fear of punishment no longer plays a major role in their decisions to vote, the finding that more members of these two occupational groups voted than other people suggests that mobilization theory in its traditional form cannot be used to explain the relationship between *danwei* and voting in Beijing.

The puzzle can be understood by looking at the changes in the electoral system. Given the fact that limited-choice elections in today's China have certain impacts on *danwei* affairs, the higher voter turnout rate for professional and white-collar workers can easily be explained. Professionals and white collars are more likely to have access to information on the functioning of their own *danwei*. Through frequent interaction with cadres and managers, white-collar workers can generate various ideas and opinions on how to manage the organization. More important, they have not only the ability to forecast the consequences of "bad decisions" related to their *danwei*'s affairs but also the skill to utilize limited-choice elections for their own agenda, that is, to get rid of incompetent or corrupt leaders. Moreover, there usually exists considerable internal and external pressure for them to exercise their social responsibility (*shehui zeren*) and to be concerned about the public affairs of their own *danwei*, if not those of the whole country.

Finally, because professionals and white-collar workers in various *danwei* usually occupy strategic positions in their units, cadres engaging in power struggles triggered by elections also would like to incorporate them into their own factions. Power contenders usually do not hesitate to offer them various tangible and intangible benefits to win their support. To keep their influence over *danwei* issues and avoid being abandoned by both parties—which could be a nightmare—white-collar workers and professionals usually have to line up with one faction or another. To guarantee the continuing flow of benefits and to keep their influence over *danwei* affairs, many of them also need to show up at the polls to help their patrons.

ECONOMIC STATUS, *DANWEI,* AND TURNOUT

Using respondents' subjective evaluations of their own economic status as an indicator, I examined the effects of economic status on voter turnout by holding constant the effects of *danwei*. Table 5.4 shows that respondents' subjective evaluations have an independent effect on the probability of their voting even when the impact of the *danwei* is controlled. People who believe their economic status is higher than others are more likely to vote in deputy elections, no matter what kind of *danwei* they work at.

Respondents' subjective evaluations of their economic situation reveal their perceptions of their stakes in the system as well as their economic status. People who succeed materially in China generally understand the workings of the system better than others and are often the clients of leaders or "activists." Elections provide them with opportunities to get what they

Table 5.4   Effects of *danwei* and subjective evaluation of economic status on voter turnout

Variable	Estimated coefficient	Probability > chi-square	Odds ratio
Intercept 1	−1.58	0.00	
Intercept 2	−0.48	0.11	
Danwei[a]			
Joint ventures	0.55	0.20	
Collective enterprises	1.33	0.00	3.80
State enterprises	1.37	0.00	3.94
State organizations	1.68	0.00	5.35
Economic status			
Below average	0.53	0.03	1.69
Average	0.67	0.00	1.96
Above average	0.93	0.00	2.53

Note: −2 log likelihood = 50.87; p = 0.0001.
[a]Private enterprises are used as base category.

want from their patrons, or to pay for the material benefits received from their leaders and to demonstrate their loyalty to them. Such perceived stakes in the system may also facilitate attitudes encouraging them to participate in the political process in order to sustain it. Since there are greater instrumental and expressive benefits associated with voting for leaders they know, economically better-off people in Beijing are highly motivated to show up at the polls and make "appropriate" choices on election day.

Party Affiliation and Voter Turnout

Party affiliation has been found to be one of the fundamental explanatory variables for not only the levels but also the directions of electoral participation in the competitive democracies.[38] Studies in many societies reveal the connection between citizens' ties to political parties and variations of levels of participation for different social groups. As Verba and Nie observe, "at all levels of education or income, those who are strong partisans are more active than the weak partisans or the independents" in the United States.[39] In another comparative study of participation, Verba, Nie, and Kim further demonstrate that political parties can "both mobilize the affiliated and restrict the unaffiliated" in elections.[40]

The relationship between party affiliation and voter turnout in communist societies, however, has never been clearly spelled out by students of
political participation. For example, Verba, Nie, and Kim examined data
gathered from the former Yugoslavia, the only communist country included
in their comparative study of political participation, and found that party
affiliation therein was a "neither necessary nor sufficient" condition for
people to vote.[41] A more recent study of participation in the former Soviet
Union extends Verba, Nie, and Kim's findings.[42] The question facing us
now is whether the findings in the former Yugoslavia and the former Soviet
Union before liberalization can be applied to communist regimes in general
and China in particular?

Figure 5.5 presents the bivariate relationship between respondents' party
affiliation and voter turnout. People are divided into four categories—politically unaffiliated, Communist Youth League members, those who have
applied for CCP membership, and CCP members. The CCP selectively re-
cruits its membership and not everyone who wants to join can become a
member. It is not unusual for people to apply for CCP membership all their
lives but still not be admitted. Since I expect that the political behavior of
those who applied for party membership may be different from people
without political affiliation, I decided to place them in a separate category.

In the 1988 elections, 67.7 percent of politically unaffiliated people
showed up at the polls. Substantially more Communist Party members
voted than politically unaffiliated: more than 81 percent of party members
voted in the elections. The turnout rate for those who had applied for CCP
membership—79.3 percent—was substantially higher than that for the politically unaffiliated and nearly matched that of party members. Moreover,
I found that more CCP applicants than CCP members voted in the 1984
elections. Bivariate analysis clearly demonstrates that being a party member
in China, or even having applied for CCP membership, can greatly increase
the likelihood of a person's voting.

By contrast, CYL members in China were found to have the lowest turnout rate in the 1988 elections. Their rate (63.6 percent) was lower than
that for the politically unaffiliated or the ordinary masses. Unlike the CCP,
the CYL in China is a mass organization. Nearly 95 percent of young people
aged fifteen to twenty-six in urban China are CYL members, if they are
affiliated with a danwei or attending school. Therefore, CYL membership
tells us little about the political orientation of individuals.

Although the bivariate relationship between voting and party identification provides us with interesting information, it is more important to
know if more party members in each danwei voted than other people when
the effects of respondents' socioeconomic status are controlled, because

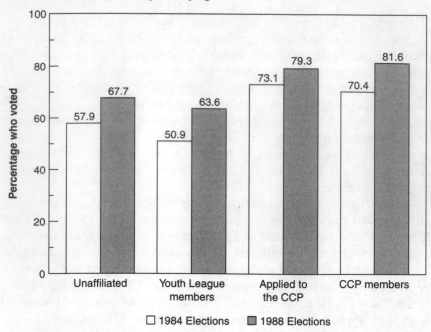

Figure 5.5 Party identification and voter turnout

such analysis can help us further evaluate the nature of the electoral system in Chinese society. We have ruled out the possibility that two groups of people—cadres and managers—act as mobilizers for the regime. Other potential mobilizers are of course CCP members. If we find that substantially more CCP members in China voted than other people in each *danwei*, we may still be able to use mobilizational theory to explain voting behavior in China. If, however, we find that party members in each *danwei* voted at similar rates to those of other people when the impacts of socioeconomic variables are controlled, we will be able to conclude with additional confidence that mobilization theory is no longer useful in studying voting behavior in today's China.

Table 5.5 controls for the effects of *danwei* and other indicators of respondents' socioeconomic status to see if party affiliation has an independent impact on voting.[43] The result shows that being a party member in China slightly increases the probability that a respondent will vote in elections, and being a CYL member reduces that probability when the effects of other variables are controlled. The equation presented in Table 5.5 could not allow us to fully refute the mobilization model in explaining people's

Table 5.5   Effects of party affiliation, controlling for socioeconomic status

Variable	Estimated coefficient	Probability > chi-square	Odds ratio
Intercept 1	−1.51	0.00	
Intercept 2	−0.39	0.20	
Danwei[a]			
Joint ventures	0.23	0.52	
Collective enterprises	1.23	0.00	3.42
State enterprises	1.22	0.00	3.38
State organizations	1.42	0.00	4.15
Economic status			
Below average	0.52	0.03	1.68
Average	0.69	0.00	1.99
Above average	1.02	0.00	2.77
Party affiliation			
Applied to the CCP	0.29	0.17	
CYL member	−0.37	0.09	0.69
CCP member	0.36	0.09	1.43

Note: −2 log likelihood = 62.00; p = 0.0001.
[a]Private enterprises are used as base category.

voting behavior in Beijing. The implications of this finding will be discussed later in this chapter.

Age, Gender, and Turnout

Studies of political participation have found that turnout in many societies "increases steadily with age until it reaches a peak in middle years, and then gradually declines with old age."[44] In the early years of people's life cycles, residential and occupational mobility as well as specific legal obstacles to enfranchisement may prevent some from voting in elections. Old age and retirement from active employment usually bring sociological withdrawal. Physical infirmities and fatigue can also lower the rate of political activism for the old.[45] Students of voting behavior describe these phenomena as "start-up" and "slow-down" effects.[46]

Figure 5.6 presents the bivariate relationship between age and voter turn-

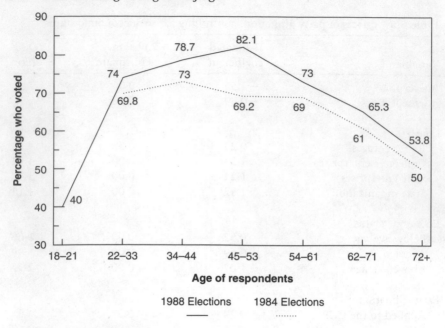

Figure 5.6   Age and voter turnout

out. As in other societies, the relationship between age and voter turnout in Beijing is a curvilinear one. Starting at a low level, turnout increases sharply with age and reaches its peak among those in their late forties and early fifties. Turnout then declines steadily with the aging process.

When we categorize people by age, we are using three possible determinants. The first is the effect of a person's position in the life cycle, which can be labeled the life-cycle effect. This determinant tells us the impact of physical conditions and biological features of different age strata on voter turnout.

The second one tells us the impact of the socioeconomic status of respondents on voting, which can be labeled a sociological determinant. "The increase in age will be accompanied by movement through various stages of a sociological life cycle."[47] For example, when the impact of voters' socioeconomic status is controlled, aging by itself is found to produce "not a decline but an increase" in turnout in the United States.[48] In Beijing, two important determinants of turnout—respondents' economic situation and *danwei*—are closely interrelated with age. Youngsters in urban China may not necessarily find a job right after graduation from school and thus some of them may not have any *danwei* affiliation. Moreover, men in Beijing retire from work at the age of sixty and women at age fifty-five. Without a job, the economic status of the young and the old can hardly be favorable. Thus, the relationship between age and turnout revealed here may simply represent a variation of voters' socioeconomic characteristics.

The third possible determinant is respondents' historical experiences, which can be labeled generational effects. Not only can different life experiences shape different political attitudes and political behavior for respondents, but "the timing of the same experiences having occurred at different points in their life cycles [may produce] varying results."[49] People in their sixties were socialized during the last period of Kuomintang rule and experienced intensive thought reform in their twenties. People in their fifties grew up with the birth of the People's Republic and were socialized during the period of intense political mobilization. Both groups have experienced intensive political campaigns at various stages of their lives. People in their forties, the so-called lost generation, were socialized during the period of the Cultural Revolution. Many of them joined the Red Guards to revolt against "capitalist roaders" and had the experience of being sent down to the villages to be "reeducated" by the peasants. The younger generation, which grew up after the Cultural Revolution, was socialized under the environment of the market economy and has little experience with regime mobilization. These dramatic differences in the experiences of different age groups may not only shape different political orientations but also result in different political behavior.

Given the varied meanings of age, differentiating three possible effects of age on turnout is not only desirable but also crucial for us to understand people's voting behavior in China. Isolating effects of socioeconomic factors from that of the life cycle is relatively easy. The effects of education, *danwei*, and economic status can be controlled to single out the effects of age. Unfortunately, distinguishing effects of aging from those of generational experience requires longitudinal data, which is still a luxury for students of Chinese politics. With only cross-sectional data available, I have to ignore the differences between generational and life-cycle effects in the following analysis.

Since the impacts of gender on voting may also be intertwined with those of age, I need to examine gender effects before disentangling various determinants of age on voting.[50] As impacts of the "traditional division of labor which assigns political roles to men rather than women has not vanished," more men than women are found to vote in most societies.[51] In Beijing, however, more women than men are found to vote (74.8 versus 70.8).[52]

Figure 5.7 presents the partial effects of age on turnout for the two gen-

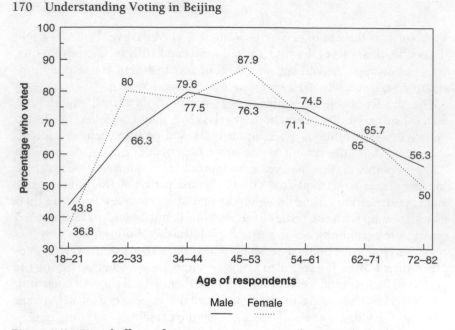

Figure 5.7   Partial effects of age on voter turnout in the 1988 election by sex of respondent

ders. The figure shows that while the curve between age and turnout for men is an upside-down V shape, the curve for women is an M-shaped one with two plateaus. Younger women start at a less active level than do men. The turnout for women quickly rises to the first plateau for those in their late twenties and early thirties and exceeds that of men. While the turnout for men reaches its peak among those in their late thirties and early forties, the turnout for women in the same age group drops to a valley. The level of men's electoral participation begins to drop among those aged forty-four, yet the record for women in the same age group climbs to the second plateau and reaches a peak. Among people in their late forties and early fifties, the women's rate is 11.6 percentage points higher than the men's. Electoral participation among women drops to that of the men between the ages of fifty-four and sixty-one, and such a trend continues with the aging process. Among the oldest age group in Beijing, fewer women than men voted.

Careful examination of the figure shows that turnout among women starts at a lower rate in their early adulthood and ends at a lower level in their old age. Although the falloff in the turnout rate among women comes ten years later than that among men, the women's is more rapid than the men's. The relationships among age, gender, and turnout revealed in Figure 5.7 raise some interesting questions: Why does voting behavior among women in Beijing deviate from that among other women in the world but resemble that among women in Argentina and the former Soviet Union? Why is the relationship between age and turnout for men different from that for women?

Cross-national comparisons have found that male-female gaps vary with the developmental levels of nations. The gap is greatest in developing countries and smallest in the developed countries.[53] Intrastate comparisons of voter turnouts within one country reveal that more advanced areas have higher voting turnouts among women than less modernized regions.[54] Since economic and social modernization in Beijing is not only higher than in other areas within China but also higher than that in many developing countries, the higher level of female electoral participation may be attributed to the developmental factor. The difference between men and women can also be attributed to the legacy of the traditional division of labor.

To fully understand the effects of age and gender, I need to control the effects of *danwei* and economic status to single out their impact on voting. The results shown in Table 5.6 demonstrate that nearly all impacts of age on turnout can be accounted for by *danwei* and respondents' economic status. When the impact of socioeconomic status is controlled, the only impact of age on voting appears for the youngest age groups, with fewer among them than among other groups in Chinese society voting. But the impact of gender on voting is much more persistent. Even after the effects of *danwei,* age, and respondents' economic status are controlled, more women than men are found to vote in Beijing.

Figure 5.7 revealed that age has a significant impact on voting among both men and women in Beijing. And from Table 5.6 we can conclude that when the gender difference of respondents is controlled, the impact of age on voting vanishes. Such a pattern suggests the possibility that men and women in Beijing might undergo different politicization processes. In the next step of my analysis, I compare the impacts of four major determinants on voter turnout among men and women—*danwei*, economic status, age, and party identification—to explore such a possibility. The findings, presented in Table 5.7, can be summarized as follows.

First, the impact of socioeconomic variables on voting among men is quite different from that among women. The most important variable measuring people's socioeconomic status in China—the *danwei*—is found to have different effects on men's and women's voting behavior. While *danwei*

Table 5.6   Effects of sex, *danwei*, age, and economic status on voter turnout

Variable	Estimated coefficient	Probability > chi-square	Odds ratio
Intercept 1	−1.55	0.00	
Intercept 2	−0.38	0.43	
Danwei[a]			
Joint ventures	0.13	0.78	
Collective enterprises	0.89	0.01	2.43
State enterprises	0.87	0.01	2.40
State organizations	1.21	0.00	3.34
Economic status			
Below average	0.51	0.03	1.66
Average	0.76	0.00	2.14
Above average	1.28	0.00	3.58
Age			
18–21	−1.99	0.00	0.14
22–33	−0.34	0.15	
34–44	0.16	0.54	
45–61	−0.09	0.76	
62–71	−0.39	0.20	
72–82	−0.66	0.12	
Sex[b]	0.38	0.01	1.47

Note: −2 log likelihood = 75.89; p = 0.0001.

[a] Private enterprises are used as base category.

[b] Coded as 1 if male, 2 if female.

affiliation has little impact on the likelihood that men will vote, experiences of working at state institutions and state organizations can substantially increase the likelihood that women in Beijing will vote.

Second, the impact of respondents' economic status also clearly demonstrates a gender difference in voting. Subjective evaluation of respondents' economic status is found to have a significant effect on the likelihood that women in Beijing will vote, but the variable has only limited effects on men. While every improvement in women's evaluation of their economic status increases the probability that they will vote, only those men who believe their economic status is above average are more likely to vote in Beijing.

Table 5.7 Effects of *danwei*, age, economic status, and party identification on voting among men and women

Variable	Male[a]		Female[b]	
	Estimated coefficient	Odds ratio	Estimated coefficient	Odds ratio
Intercept 1	0.99		−0.34	
Danwei[c]				
Joint ventures	−1.52*	0.22	1.02	
Collective enterprises	−0.35		1.19**	3.28
State enterprises	−0.46		1.17**	3.22
State organizations	−0.52		1.52***	4.59
Economic status				
Below average	0.59		0.96**	2.62
Average	0.48		1.06**	2.89
Above average	1.08**	2.93	1.53**	4.60
Age				
18–21	−1.20		−1.56**	0.21
22–33	−0.14		−0.26	
34–44	0.23		−0.56	
45–61	−0.03		−0.87	
62–71	−0.62		−0.73	
72–82	−0.85		−0.05	
Party affiliation				
Youth league member	−0.39		−0.01	
Applied for CCP	0.05		0.54	
CCP member	0.41		1.21**	3.36

[a] $N = 369$; -2 log likelihood $= 24.29$; $p = 0.08$.
[b] $N = 370$; -2 log likelihood $= 55.17$; $p = 0.001$.
[c] Private enterprises are used as base category.
*$p < 0.1$ **$p < 0.05$ ***$p < 0.01$.

Third, the impact of party affiliation on turnout among men substantially differs from that among women. Party affiliation in Beijing hardly has any impact on voting behavior among men. No matter what their political status—CCP member, CYL member, applicant for CCP membership, or politically unaffiliated—men vote in a roughly similar way. Being a Communist Party member, however, can significantly increase the likelihood that women will vote, even after the impacts of other socioeconomic variables are controlled.

Fourth, as in other societies, when impacts of respondents' socioeconomic status are controlled, slow-down effects disappear for both men and women.[55] This result confirms the conclusion reached by Verba and Nie, and also Wolfinger and Rosenstone, that "slow-down has been exaggerated by failure to consider the relationship of age to the educational composition of the populace."[56] Moreover, surprisingly similar to the situation in the United States, the start-up effect in Beijing is also concentrated among women. Fewer women below twenty-one years of age than other people are found to vote in Beijing, but the same comparison does not hold true for men of that age group.

The differences in the effects of socioeconomic status on voter turnout for men and women revealed in this analysis suggest that the process by which men in Beijing become politicized is different from that of women. The best-known finding in the study of political participation—that citizens of higher social and economic status have a higher turnout rate in elections—holds true only for women in Beijing. While *danwei* experience, subjective evaluation of economic status, and Communist Party affiliation in Beijing increase the probability that women will vote, voting behavior among men is influenced only by their subjective evaluation of their economic status.

Why are the processes of politicization for men and women different in Beijing? One possible explanation is actually a variation of mobilization theory. It attributes the fact that certain women have higher turnout rates in elections to the different roles assigned to women in Chinese society by traditional culture, which makes them easier to mobilize. While men are expected to be independent and politically competent, women in Chinese society are assumed to be dependent politically. It is true that the CCP has been trying hard to raise women's positions, with some success in urban areas, but the efforts cannot be quickly realized and have not changed the deep-rooted psychological orientations of Chinese women. Under the influence of traditional culture, women in Chinese society are more obedient than men. They are more likely to follow official directions and less able to resist peer pressure. As the ability of higher-status *danwei* to mobilize employees to vote might be greater than that of lower-status *danwei*, women in the former organizations are more likely to be mobilized by the authorities.

Nonetheless, there are two major difficulties with this line of argument. First, if the gender difference in people's voting behavior can be explained only by the influence of traditional culture and regime mobilization, those who are more heavily influenced by the traditional culture should show higher turnout rates than those who are less influenced by the culture. Since older people in China were socialized before the communists took over in 1949, we should expect older women, who must be more heavily influenced by cultural heritage, to be more easily mobilized by the authorities. Unfortunately, the data analysis does not support this argument. Rather, fewer older women than other people in Chinese society are found to have voted. As illustrated previously, the second difficulty with this argument is that we cannot identify any mobilizers in Chinese society. All possible mobilizers in China, be they political cadres, managers, or male party members, are found to have the same turnout rates as other groups or strata do.

Another explanation also relates the gender differences in voting to regime mobilization, but in a different way. The theory attributes higher turnout rates for women to the dramatic change in their status under CCP rule and to the change in their psychological orientation brought about by the change in their social status. Before the reforms started in 1979, the regime tried to politically mobilize the largely apolitical population of Chinese women and to boost their social status in society. This process intentionally destroyed the traditional cultural heritage, and the authorities propagated such ideas as "women hold up half the sky" (funü nengding banbiantian) and "Chinese girls should love martial attire rather than gay feminine costumes" to change women's orientation toward politics. More important, the regime also makes substantial efforts to lift the social status of women. The authorities set up quotas for women entering universities, working in higher-status work units, such as state institutions and the government, and assuming leadership positions. To guarantee the success of the policy, the authorities also tried to increase the economic independence of women and tried to make equal work in Chinese society pay equally regardless of the employee's gender. If successful, this policy should have raised a previously inferior group's status in society and encouraged the group's participation in the electoral process, either to sustain the system or to repay the emancipators by following their directives.

Although the nature of the data prevents me from vigorously testing this hypothesis, two propositions can be developed to examine its validity. If this hypothesis is valid, we should find, first, that women benefiting most under the current regime—those working in organizations previously inaccessible to them—are more likely to vote in elections. Second, women who achieved an economic status previously impossible for them should also be more likely to vote in elections. The equation presented in Table

5.7 confirms both expectations. Not only are women working at higher-status units found to be more likely to vote, but the turnout for women also increases with every positive change in their economic status.

Finally, there is a substantial difference in voting behavior between women having experienced regime mobilization and those not having done so. The behavior of the only group of women who have not experienced regime mobilization—the youngest females in the sample—is similar to that of women in other societies rather than to women in other age groups in China. Resuming their traditional nature, the youngest women in China have become the least politically active group among all age groups when the impacts of other socioeconomic variables are controlled, and there is clearly a start-up process for them. Without panel data, which would enable me to compare the behavior of people who have experienced regime mobilization with the behavior of people without such an experience when the impacts of other socioeconomic variables are controlled, any results of the analysis can be only preliminary, but the finding does add some weight to the above explanation.

Conclusion

It is well known that plebiscitary elections in many other communist societies, especially in the former Soviet Union, alienated traditional voters. Because the sole function of state-controlled elections was regime legitimation and such elections never provided people with the opportunity to select their rulers, traditional participants (people of higher socioeconomic status) in communist societies tended to abstain from voting to protest. Empirical research confirms this argument and reveals that socioeconomic status in communist societies has usually negatively correlated with voting.

Since 1979, plebiscitary elections in China have been replaced by limited-choice elections. The shifts in election procedures have forced the regime to alter the way it controls elections. In today's China, presenting people with elections without candidate choice is difficult, if not impossible. Government officials now manipulate the nomination process, nominating people they trust and putting their names on candidate lists. Since the most trustworthy people are their own cadres, the CCP usually nominates leaders at the grassroots level as candidates for deputies to people's congresses. An important, although unintended, consequence of this control mechanism is that it puts the nominated officials under public scrutiny and provides people with an opportunity to show their displeasure with candidates to the higher authorities.

The changes in the electoral system in China have actually brought both instrumental and expressive benefits to voters. Properly managed, voters are able to utilize these elections to get rid of or humiliate officials they dislike. Democratic activists and dissidents in China have also chosen to grasp the opportunity to facilitate desired changes in Chinese politics.[57] How do people respond to changes in the electoral system? What resources are required for people to vote in limited-choice elections? How do resources connect to voting? The shift in the electoral system in China provides us with a rare opportunity to study the impacts of institutional change on people's voting behavior.

As elections began to provide voters with candidate choice and the regime ceased to coercively mobilize people to vote, voting in China resumed its traditional nature—benefits derived from the act are now indirectly associated with people's daily lives. Under this new arrangement, the ability of people to realize the relationship between voting and their own interests and to link voting in imperfect elections to their long-term goals should reemerge as a major determinant in their decision to vote. Since this ability is closely associated with respondents' socioeconomic status, I expect status to play a crucial role in mobilizing people to go to the ballot booth in today's China.

Analysis of voting behavior in Beijing confirms that changes in the electoral system have fundamentally altered the relationship between resources and participation. Unlike the situation in the former Soviet Union, in China people of higher socioeconomic status tend to vote rather than abstain from voting. Decomposition of the effects of socioeconomic status reveals that the *danwei* respondents affiliate with, their subjective evaluation of their economic status, and their gender have positive effects on voter turnout in Beijing.

In earlier scholarship, the interpretation of the impact of *danwei* on participation followed two models. One, the mobilization model, treats the *danwei* as a political institution designed and used by the regime to control and mobilize citizens. More employees in higher-status *danwei* vote, because they are efficiently and effectively mobilized by the authorities through political education or explicit coercion. Another interpretation sees the *danwei* as a determinant of its members' political, social, and economic status. Those who work at higher-status *danwei* enjoy better political, economic, and social treatment than people working at lower-status organizations, and the former are generally more likely to be respected. This model concludes that *danwei* boost voter turnout because people in higher-status work units are either more sophisticated, and can better understand how the change in election procedures gives them an opportunity to pursue their interests, or have more at stake in the political system, and thus participate to support it.

The empirical findings in Beijing call the mobilization model into question. If mobilization theory can be properly used to interpret electoral participation in Beijing, we would expect more mobilizers in each *danwei* to vote than others in the same organization. However, once the effects of *danwei* are controlled we find that potential mobilizers (cadres and managers) voted in no greater numbers than ordinary people in each organization. Party members in each *danwei* did not have significantly higher turnouts than others. Unless we believe that the Chinese authorities use only female party members as mobilizers, or that mobilization in China can be done without mobilizers, or that mobilizers coerce others to vote but not themselves, mobilization theory may not be used to explain the correlation between *danwei* and turnout.

A remaining difficulty with this argument is why education has no independent effect on turnout in today's China. In discussion of the bivariate relationship between education and turnout, I suggested several ways that education might influence voters: (1) it can be used as a vehicle for the regime to carry out political education and mobilization; (2) it increases the ability of people to deal with complexity and helps them to realize the implication of the change in election procedures, in turn inspiring them to get involved in imperfect elections to articulate their interests; and (3) discrimination against intellectuals in the history of the PRC might leave some educated people with a legacy that prevents them from participating in electoral politics. Perhaps the lack of a coherent relationship between education and turnout reflects the complexity of the connection between education and turnout in today's China. As elections themselves are still in a transitional stage, all these factors play a role in shaping people's voting decisions. Because these effects cancel each other out, they produce the puzzling result that there is no relationship between education and voter turnout, even though other measurements of socioeconomic status are found to be closely associated with voting. To support this argument, I remind readers that although education in today's China still does not have an independent positive effect on voting, it no longer encourages people to abstain from voting as it did in the former Soviet Union.

The finding that traditionally politically active people in Beijing are more likely to vote than abstain from voting tells us that nonvoting should no longer be considered a political activity, as suggested by many scholars of communist participation based on their experiences in studying voting behavior in the former Soviet Union. Rather than waiting for elections to become fully democratic to participate, people in Beijing choose to vote in imperfect elections to pursue their interests. The finding tells us that we should take limited-choice elections more seriously and closely monitor the changes in people's participatory behavior to understand the political dynamics of Communist China.

Another interesting but puzzling finding of this chapter is that men and women undergo different politicization processes. Many socioeconomic resources work for females. For example, *danwei* affiliation and Communist Party membership increase the probability that women will vote but have no such effect on men. Why does there exist such a difference between women and men? What makes the politicization process for men different from that for women? Is this a phenomenon unique to people in Beijing, or can the finding also be applied to the entire country? Even if this phenomenon is unique to Beijing, we need to extensively study people's voting behavior there to fully understand the political process. Unfortunately, the nature of the data does not allow me to explore the issue any further.

6

Campaign Activities and Election Boycotts

Clearly, elections in Communist China have undergone a dramatic change. The advent of limited-choice elections has fundamentally altered people's voting behavior as well as the calculation of voters in making voting decisions. Citizens choose to actively participate in the electoral process and vote in elections. Some of them are pushed to the ballot booth by their willingness to remove unpopular leaders in grassroots organizations, others by civic orientation imposed by communist political propaganda, and still others by their burning desire to promote Chinese democracy. In any case, people in Chinese society now participate in the not-so-perfect elections either to articulate their private interests or to facilitate desired changes in the political system rather than waiting for the elections to become fully democratic before participating.

But what are the impacts of the changes in the Chinese electoral system on campaign activities? Who in today's China chooses to engage in campaign activities or boycotts unfair elections? What motivates people to participate in these political activities? Do campaigners in China try to help the authorities coerce people into voting or promote candidates they want to get elected? Who chooses to persuade others to boycott unfair elections? Finally, what resources are required for people in Beijing to get involved in these political actions?

Although the regime introduced limited-choice elections, both it and incumbent officials strongly oppose unauthorized campaign activities and election boycotts, but for different reasons. From the authorities' point of view, campaigners engage in elections either to help candidates they like to get elected or to introduce "bourgeois democracy" into China, that is, to challenge the monopolistic control of the CCP and even "overthrow the government." While campaign activities aimed at influencing the selection of government officials, which are limited to the local level, are tolerated, campaign activities aimed at influencing the overall political system and challenging the monopolistic control of the CCP are strictly prohibited and brutally suppressed.[1]

The attitudes of incumbent officials toward election campaigns in China are somewhat different. In China today incumbent officials still try to control candidate nominations in local elections. Whereas the regime allows campaign activities initiated by private citizens aimed at influencing voters' choices of candidates, which are usually aimed at unseating incumbent officials and their heirs, few local government officials tolerate such challenges to their careers or hesitate to punish those who dare to engage in such political actions. Campaign activities aimed at defeating incumbent officials in Chinese organizations often attract the attention of authorities at higher levels. The presence of such campaigns indicates that people at lower levels are not satisfied with the current leadership. Even if campaigners cannot defeat incumbent officials in elections, the existence of such campaigns in organizations actually sends clear messages to the authorities that the bureaucrats at lower levels may not have the ability to control their organizations. These messages can severely damage the confidence of higher authorities in the leaders of those organizations.

Election boycotts are also strongly opposed by both the regime and bureaucrats in Chinese society. Even though the capability of the regime to mobilize people to vote has dramatically declined in recent years and toleration of nonvoting in various elections has begun, few incumbent officials, if any, are willing to tolerate people under their control maneuvering to organize other voters to protest by boycotting elections. As with campaign activities, election boycotts in an organization can cause higher-level officials to suspect the ability and integrity of local bureaucrats. To the general populace in an organization, protest activities signify that bureaucrats are in trouble and often end up attracting more people to engage in other incumbent-challenging political acts to further challenge them. Officials thus see such acts as a direct challenge to their authority, and few neglect to punish any troublemakers they can identify.

The attitude of the "regime" toward election boycotts is more complicated. Changes in the electoral system in today's China require that limited-choice elections be held in a "fair" way to achieve their designed effects, and the nature of the electoral arrangement argues that people should be allowed to protest if local bureaucrats manipulate elections. Thus, if participants do have evidence that certain local government officials or work unit leaders have manipulated elections, the regime is usually willing to punish the manipulators and annul the election. However, if the regime believes that participants want to use the opportunity to challenge the legitimacy of communist control, it will back its officials and turn the gun on participants and severely punish them. These observations tell us that there are important distinctions between the regime and incumbent government officials in their attitudes toward antagonistic political acts. The distinctions can be used by both participants in China to pursue their interests and incumbent officials to safeguard their own positions.

Campaign Activities

Students of Chinese politics tend to treat campaign activities in China in one of two ways. Those subscribing to the totalitarian model in their study of micropolitics believe the major functions of campaigns are the "raising of mass political consciousness, increasing production, and strengthening unity and democratic education for the masses and cadres."[2] To them, campaigners in China work *for* the regime to mobilize people to go to the ballot boxes regardless of who the candidates are, rather than trying to influence people's choices of candidates on election day. Such acts can only be mobilizational rather than participatory.

Other scholars have noticed that with the changes in the electoral system of the 1980s, some "serious" campaign activities emerged in Chinese organizations. For example, Andrew Nathan reports on the changes in the behavior of candidates and their staffs in the county-level elections of 1979 to 1981 in *Chinese Democracy*. According to his account, democratic activists all over China seriously engaged in campaign activities in the 1979–1981 elections. He also notes that democratic activists participated in the elections not because they believed elections had become democratic, but because they wanted to promote Chinese democracy through their participation in these processes.[3] Bruce Jacobs further demonstrates that people in China can and do exert influence on elections organized by the CCP. He believes that people in China can influence not only the candidate choices on election days but also the nomination of candidates in those elections.[4]

Although the nature of the electoral system in China has changed in recent years, elections there are still far from democratic by Western standards. Are there "serious" campaign activities associated with these not so democratic elections? If so, what is the minimal requirement for people to pursue their interests through serious campaigns in imperfect elections? I argue that serious campaigns do not presume the existence of fully democratic elections. As long as candidate choice is available, some voters will try to help one candidate or another to get elected for various reasons. Since elections in today's China must have more candidates than there are seats, the minimal requirement for people to engage in campaign activities to pursue their interests has been achieved.

However, although recent changes in the electoral system provide people in China with both incentives and opportunities to influence the decisions of other voters on election days, some people still have strong incentives to support officially sponsored candidates in various elections either because they are socialized to do so or because they want to use their support to bargain for certain tangible benefits. Thus, two kinds of campaign activities may exist in today's China. The first, voluntary acts aimed at influencing voters' candidate choices on election day, reflects self-motivation. Campaigners belonging to this category are motivated by their own preferences to campaign for their preferred candidates. Of course, campaigners supporting candidates sponsored by the government may also be included in this category. As long as they are motivated by their own preferences, whether the candidate is sponsored by the regime or not does not influence the nature of their activities. For example, if the authorities nominate a person belonging to faction A as a candidate and people in the faction campaign for the person because they believe they will receive benefits if he gets elected, their campaign should be characterized as self-motivational because they are motivated by their own interests rather than by the regime's decision.

The second kind of campaign activity is mobilizational. Rather than pursuing their own interests, the primary goal of campaigners in this group is to mobilize people to go to the ballot booth on election day, either to guarantee the well-known 99 percent turnout rate desired by the regime or to help candidates nominated by the authorities to get elected. To campaigners in this category, whose names appear on the ballot is not important. What is important is that the authorities have nominated and support the candidate. As long as the candidate is endorsed by the authorities, they will campaign for that person. Such campaigns embody mobilizational, rather than participatory, political behavior, with the campaigners serving as mobilizers for the regime.

Two hypotheses can be deduced conceptually to test the nature of campaign activities in today's China. First, if campaign activities are voluntary acts aimed at influencing decisions of the authorities on candidate nominations or of the voters on candidate choices on election day, the availability of candidate choice should play a crucial role in prompting people to engage in campaign activities. People in Beijing should be more actively engaged in campaign activities when elections provide voters with candidate choices. Only when choices exist can campaigners in China exert influence over other voters' selections on election day. But if campaigns in China are still mobilizational activities, elections providing voters with candidate choice may or may not make any difference in the probability that people will get involved in campaign activities, since their goal is simply to coerce people to go to the polls on election day.

Second, if the mobilization thesis is correct, we should find that people having vested interests in the political system and enjoying privileges in the society are more likely to engage in campaign activities. Individuals such as CCP and CYL members, those applying for CCP membership, work unit leaders, and government officials are usually believed to have more at stake in the political system and to be regime mobilizers. We would also expect them to campaign more actively to mobilize people to vote. But if campaigners try to help candidates they like get elected, rather than helping the regime to mobilize people to vote, we should find that those who have more at stake in the political system are no more active than others, as campaigns in today's China are primarily aimed at challenging candidates sponsored by the authorities.

Table 6.1 presents the results of regression analysis of campaign activities in Beijing. The results are striking because some crucial variables are found to play no role in mobilizing people in China to get involved in campaign activities. They are missing from the equation. Those not in the equation may be as important, if not more so, than variables found in the equation in helping us to identify the nature of campaign activities. First and most important, socioeconomic status is found to have no impact on the probability that people will engage in campaign activities. None of the traditional measurements of people's socioeconomic status—such as education, occupation, and economic conditions, measured in both objective and subjective terms—have any impact on the probability of engagement. The analysis shows that none of the potential mobilizers in Chinese society—CCP and CYL members, party and government officials—campaign more than the general populace in Beijing. These findings clearly show that people's stakes in the political system do not increase the likelihood of their campaigning, as the mobilizational theory predicts.

On the contrary, the nature of the elections plays a crucial role in making people in Beijing get involved in campaign activities. People are clearly more likely to campaign in competitive elections than in single-candidate plebiscitary elections. Even when the impacts of other resources are controlled, the nature of the elections is still found to have the most significant

Table 6.1 Multiple regression on campaign activities

Independent variables	Unstandardized coefficients[a]
Kind of elections[b]	.41***
Sex[c]	−.16**
Evaluation of influence of local government[d]	.20***
Desire to participate in political study[e]	.12**
Grapevine rumors	.15*
Criticism in political study session[f]	.09**

Note: N = 616; constant = −.09; adjusted R^2 = .10.

[a] The dependent variable is the principal component transformation of the four participatory variables belonging to this mode.

[b] Election with choice of candidates coded as 1, others coded as 0.

[c] Coded as 1 if male, 0 if female.

[d] Measured by the question, "Let's now discuss the local government. How much effect do you think its activities have on your day-to-day life? Do they have a great effect, some effect, or none?" Answers were coded from 1 (no effect) to 3 (great effect).

[e] Measured by the question, "Generally speaking, do you like to participate in political studies? Do you like them very much, somewhat enjoy them, not like them so much, or not like them at all?" Answers were coded from 1 ("not like them at all") to 4 ("like them very much").

[f] Measured by the question, "During political study sessions, have you ever offered any criticism to the authorities? Did you often, sometimes, rarely, or never offer any suggestions?" Answers were coded from 1 (never) to 4 (often).

*p < 0.1 **p < 0.05 ***p < 0.01.

effect on the probability that people in Beijing will get involved in campaign activities. Although the finding is merely common sense to many political scientists, it reveals important information about the nature of campaign activities as well as the goal of campaigners in today's China. These findings—that people are more likely to engage in campaign activities if there is a choice of candidates and that potential mobilizers in Chinese society are not more active—suggest that campaign activities there are more likely to be voluntary political acts aimed at influencing voters' choices than mobilizational activities aimed at involving people in the political process designed by the regime to implement the predetermined goals of the authorities.

As I anticipated, access to "grapevine" rumors increases the possibility that people will get involved in campaign activities in Beijing. Among various pieces of information from unofficial channels, those leaked by members of the nominating committee play a crucial role in mobilizing people to engage in campaign activities. The causal link between unofficial information and campaign activities can be understood only by examining the institutional arrangements of the Chinese election system, especially the nomination process of elections in China. As mentioned previously, changes in leadership can make significant differences for people working at grassroots organizations. Since Chinese society is usually organized so that "vertical networks of personal followings . . . are in conflict with other such networks,"[5] and since the welfare of each faction can be highly dependent on the results of elections, elections there can and usually do trigger factional politics. Even though elections in today's China provide people with only the possibility of selecting cadres at the grassroots level, and even though the results of such contests can hardly have any direct impact on government policies, political competition around elections can be and usually is quite vigorous.

Although campaigns in an open and confrontational manner aimed at high-politics issues are not permitted, ordinary citizens are allowed and even encouraged to have input in the process, even to exert influence on the candidate nomination stage. Article 26 of the 1986 Electoral Law codifies two methods of nomination—political parties or mass associations can make nominations, or ten or more voters can jointly nominate a candidate.[6] Case studies of elections confirm that electoral competition in China usually starts at the nomination stage.[7] Because the stakes in local elections can be quite high for government officials, they have every incentive to neglect the regulations specified in Chinese election law and to try to monopolize candidate nomination to guarantee their choices for reelection. To prevent voters from destroying their plans and influencing the electoral process, many local leaders deliberately withhold information on decisions of candidate nomination from voters as long as possible in order to reduce voters' response time. For the same reason, people excluded from the nomination process want to use every possible opportunity to empower their own favored people in leadership positions who would be eager to get information on candidate selection. To join electoral competition, power contenders need crucial information early, and the only place for them to acquire such information is from unofficial channels.

Information on nominees from grapevine rumors can not only mobilize opponents of candidates nominated by the authorities but also provide them with precious time to coordinate their strategy to influence voter decisions.[8] An interesting example concerns Deng Liqun's candidacy for membership in the Politburo at the CCP's Thirteenth Party Congress. According to a decision of the organizational department of the CCP, Deng was to be promoted to the Politburo at the Thirteenth Party Congress. However, his political enemies in the organizational department leaked this information to deputies to the party congress as soon as they arrived in

Beijing. This information quickly mobilized liberals among the deputies. Since candidates for the Politburo must be members of the Central Committee, they designed a strategy to launch an attack on Deng and block his election as a member of the Central Committee to prevent him from becoming a Politburo member.

The liberals picked up an old scandal about Deng Liqun and spread it among the deputies. More than forty years earlier, Deng had seduced the wife of Li Chang, an influential member of the Central Committee who was under investigation by the party. To protect her husband, the woman had no choice but to bow to pressure from Deng. In traditional Chinese culture, taking advantage of others when they are having difficulties is considered among the most obscene behavior. Since constant political campaigns in PRC history made many middle-level cadres suffer betrayal by their colleagues, such acts also became hated behavior among CCP cadres. Like negative campaigns elsewhere, the strategy designed by the liberals worked well. The story agitated and mobilized many deputies to the party congress. Even deputies not opposed to Deng's political views did not want to vote for him to become a member of the Central Committee. Failing to be elected a member of the Central Committee, Deng was, of course, not eligible for candidacy in the Politburo.[9] The information leaked by people in the organizational department gave Deng Liqun's enemies plenty of reaction time and allowed them to carefully calculate the timing of their "surprise attack" to achieve the maximum effect.

A general rule in politics is that it is always easier to influence a decision in its formulation stage than to change it after the decision has been made. If a campaigner wants to help the candidate he or she likes, the most effective method is to influence the decisions of the nomination committee to put the person's name on the ballot. For the same reason, if a campaigner wants to defeat a potential enemy, the most efficient way is to persuade the nomination committee not to nominate the person. Past experience shows that opinions over the qualification of candidates expressed in the nomination stage may be considered seriously by the committee. Otherwise, "unhappy voters will refuse to go to the polls or will cast invalid ballots."[10] Since the decision-making process of the nomination committee is not open to the public until a consensus has been reached by its members, the only way for people to get information is through grapevine rumors.

After the nomination committee makes its decision, there is another stage in the election process called democratic consultation. In this stage, the committee solicits people's opinions on the candidates. Based on suggestions from below, the committee makes final recommendations on candidates whose names should appear on the ballot.[11] This consultation period provides campaigners in Beijing with another opportunity to exert their influence over candidate selection. If they can persuade electoral officials to add or drop someone from the ballot, they can effectively influence the consequences of elections. For campaigners to effectively exert their influence, they must know of committee decisions prior to public announcement and must be aware of the major considerations behind such decisions. The only way for people in Beijing to get information on the decision-making process of the electoral committee is again from grapevine rumors.

As with voting, I found that women are more active in campaign activities than men. The cognitive dimension—knowledge of local governmental output—is also positively associated with campaign activities. Given the political reality in today's China that direct elections are limited to people's congresses at the basic level, the association between the perceived impacts of local government and campaign activities should not be a surprise. Because people's congresses at the basic level are political institutions designed to supervise the work of government at the same level, those who have confidence in their understanding of major issues of local government are more likely to engage in political acts aimed at influencing local politics than others.

People's attitudes toward political study are reflected in their campaign activities. There is no doubt that political study in China is a mobilizational mechanism designed by the regime to persuade people to carry out its goals and to socialize them into official political culture. However, such mechanisms may not achieve their intended goals. In fact, when classifying respondents by their attitudes toward political study, we are actually measuring several attributes. As political study is designed to increase people's political consciousness, it may help people to develop a sense of "civic duty." Those who have a strong sense of civic duty will take limited-choice elections seriously. Thus, if they think a candidate is not suitable for the position, the "sense of civic duty" imposed by the regime would make them act as "masters of the country" to exercise their "democratic right." One way for them to do so is to persuade others not to vote for the unsuitable candidates regardless of what unhappy consequences such acts might bring them. For the same reason, if they believe a candidate is a proper choice, they should be more likely to persuade others to vote for that person. Thus the association between respondents' attitudes toward political study and their campaign activities highlights the impact of that sense of civic duty on campaign activities. Rather than making people in Beijing blindly follow the instructions of the authorities, the sense of civic duty created by the regime can make participants in China take those limited-choice elections offered by the regime seriously to exercise their democratic rights even if such acts require them to challenge the authority of individual government officials.

Political study can also make people pay more attention to *danwei* politics. Political study in China is generally divided into activities oriented toward high politics, such as communicating specific instructions from higher levels to the general populace, studying documents and other materials, and providing people with a forum to show their attitudes on major political issues facing the country to the authorities, and activities oriented toward low politics, such as *danwei* politics. Thus, in addition to regime socialization, political study can also help people understand and get involved in *danwei* politics. The discussion of issues facing *danwei* in political study sessions and the exchange of information acquired from both official and unofficial channels with others in those meetings could generate people's interests in *danwei* politics. "The more sense one can make of the political world, the more likely one is to pay attention to it."[12] Engagement in *danwei* politics in China is no exception to this rule. People's interests and understanding of *danwei* politics acquired from political study sessions can make them engage in the political process and exert their influence whenever they have opportunities to do so. Since the primary function of elections of deputies to people's congresses in today's China is to influence *danwei* politics through the selection of officials, those who are psychologically involved in *danwei* politics and those who understand *danwei* politics better should be more likely to engage in campaign activities to influence the results of those elections.

Yet, there may be another connection between political study and campaign activities. Although political study is designed by the regime to mobilize people, many Chinese also utilize the opportunity to pursue their own interests according to the rules of the game in Chinese politics. As observed by Victor Falkenheim, even in the late 1970s and early 1980s, "important economic and planning meetings were well attended" in China, and "factory workers generally commented on economic supplements and decisions on bonuses; while villagers focused on questions of work points, work grades, rations, outside work and the like."[13] Many Western Sinologists are familiar with scenes of people taking naps, playing poker, making dirty jokes, and talking "nonsense" in political study sessions. But people in China also use the sessions to challenge the decisions of local cadres, criticizing government policies, making suggestions, embarrassing leaders they don't like, and even humiliating them.

The skills acquired from political study sessions enable people to utilize opportunities provided by the regime for their own purposes. In other words, the experience acquired from political study sessions teaches them how to use the mobilization institution set up by the regime to pursue their own interests. On one occasion, a group of workers in Beijing helped nominate a leader they didn't like as a candidate and then mobilized voters in their work unit to defeat him in the election in order to demonstrate to higher authorities how unpopular the leader was.[14] Of course, people can also use the skills acquired from political study sessions to campaign for leaders they like or to campaign against leaders they don't like to pursue their interests. As elections in today's China provide people with opportunities to influence the selection of *danwei* personnel, it is reasonable to expect that those who are psychologically involved in *danwei* affairs and those who acquire the political skill to find a way to exert their influence within the framework of current political institutions from political study sessions are more likely than others to engage in campaign activities to influence elections in today's China.

This analysis of the process of involvement in campaign activities suggests that changes in the election system in China have brought fundamental changes in campaign activities in Beijing. As plebiscitary elections were replaced by limited-choice ones, campaign activities changed from regime-directed mobilizational activity to voluntary acts initiated by private citizens. The finding that the type of elections in China plays a crucial role in making people engage in campaign activities provides clear evidence that campaigners try to influence people's *choice of candidates*, rather than help the regime to coerce people to show up at the ballot box on election day. Moreover, the finding that all possible mobilizers in the mobilizational period—political activists, government and party officials, and CCP members—are no more active in campaign activities than the general populace suggests that campaigners in today's China are unlikely to be mobilizers working for the regime. Finally, the finding that better understanding of the impact of local government on their daily lives, more active involvement in political study sessions, and having more information from unofficial channels are important political resources for people to engage in campaigns indicates that campaigners are more likely prompted to such acts by their own interests.

Election Boycotts

"By Western democratic standards, Chinese elections have many faults."[15] First of all, people are provided with a choice of candidates but not of political platforms. Thus choice for voters is only "one between personalities and not between policies."[16] Second, "the 'consultation' and 'fomentation' processes provide numerous opportunities for the Party leadership to exert its will in both direct and indirect state elections and in Party elections [thus creating] dissatisfaction in China."[17] Third, because the stakes of the elections for lower officials are extremely high, bureaucrats have every incentive to manipulate them. Such a situation has convinced students of communist participation that those realizing the faults of elections in communist countries develop *fundamental* disagreement with the electoral arrangements in these societies and either oppose elections through "covert actions," such as withdrawal from the electoral process to protest,[18] or become "apathetic, alienated, and beset with anomie."[19]

From previous analyses of voting and campaign activities, we learn that most people in China no longer fundamentally reject elections and withdraw from the electoral process to protest. Although they still cannot influence government policies through their votes, people begin to engage in the electoral process to influence the selection of local government officials. But the question facing us here is, when participants find that local officials manipulate elections, or that candidates they believe are not qualified are going to be elected, what do they do? Do they attribute the problem of the elections to the regime or to the political system and become apathetic and alienated? Or do they attribute the problem to individual officials and actively seek remedy for power abuse by local officials from higher authorities and even try to change the results of elections? Hypothetically, people can have three possible reactions when discovering that some government officials manipulate elections and believing them to be unfair. Some people think that the problem of elections is built into the political system in China and that it is unrealistic to believe anyone affiliated with the system can resolve the problem. The most likely reaction of such people is to withdraw from voting so as to avoid endorsing the elections. Other people put the blame on individual officials rather than on the political system itself. They choose either to report events to higher authorities to seek remedies, or to take actions of self-defense such as organizing their colleagues to boycott "unfair elections." Persuading others to boycott unfair elections does "not necessarily assume antiregime properties; rather, it may form one element of an expanded repertory of political action."[20] Still others, organizers of election boycotts, may want to attract the attention of officials at higher levels and make them intervene on their behalf. Both instrumental and expressive benefits can motivate participants to organize their colleagues to boycott unfair elections.

Table 6.2 reports the results of regression analysis of election boycotts in Beijing. Data manipulation shows that the existence of *danwei* elections is a very important variable in predicting people's involvement in election boycotts. Since political lives are organized around *danwei*, elections for

Table 6.2   Multiple regression on boycotts

Independent variables	Unstandardized coefficients[a]
Danwei elections	.36***
Grapevine discussions[b]	.17**
Income[c]	.00004**
Perceived influence of neighborhood committees[d]	.11*
Expectation of equal treatment by the government[e]	−.17**
Father's education[f]	−.02**

Note: $N = 649$; constant $= -.43***$; adjusted $R^2 = .06$.

[a]The dependent variable is the principal component transformation of the two participatory variables belonging to this mode.

[b]Measured by the question, "How often do you talk about unofficial news concerning the political, social, and economic situation in our country with other people? Do you do that nearly every day, a few times a week, about once a week, from time to time, or never?" Answers were coded from 1 (never) to 4 (nearly every day).

[c]Yearly income by yuan.

[d]Measured by the question, "Let's now discuss neighborhood committees. How much effect do you think their activities have on your day-to-day life? Do they have a great effect, some effect, or none at all?" Answers were coded as 1 if no influence, 0 if other.

[e]Measured by the question, "Suppose there was some issue that you had to take to a government office. Do you think you would be given equal treatment? I mean, would you be treated as well as anyone else?" Answers were coded as 1 if affirmative, 0 if not.

[f]By years of formal schooling.

*p < 0.1   **p < 0.05   ***p < 0.01.

danwei leaders in China usually have a more significant impact on voters than elections for deputies to people's congresses. Although *danwei* elections have no significant impact on government policies whatsoever, changes of leadership in work organizations can fundamentally alter people's status. Because of their importance, citizens usually take *danwei* elections more seriously than elections for deputies to people's congresses. For such reasons, if they find anyone manipulating *danwei* elections, they are more likely to either demonstrate their dissatisfaction or try to induce officials at higher levels to intervene on their behalf.

Moreover, although the stakes in *danwei* elections for both voters and leaders of organizations are higher than the stakes in elections for deputies to people's congresses, *danwei* elections are less institutionalized and thus more likely to be subject to manipulation by lower-echelon bureaucrats. Unlike elections for deputies to people's congresses, *danwei* elections have no independent organization providing supervision. Incumbent officials usually organize those elections to which many of them or their presumptive heirs are candidates. Because of the higher stakes for incumbent officials in those elections, the temptation for them to engage in manipulation is also higher. Therefore, *danwei* elections are more likely to be unfair compared to deputy elections, a tendency that also helps us to understand why people in Beijing are more likely to boycott *danwei* elections.

Grapevine rumors again emerge as an important resource for motivating people to boycott unfair elections. There are two possible explanations for the causal link between access to grapevine rumors and election boycotts. First, election boycotts presume that elections are unfair. For participants to identify an election as unfair, they must know what happened in the electoral process. However, any incumbent leader who wants to manipulate the election must do it in a "covert" way. Given the government's monopolistic control of the news media in China, information on election manipulation can only come from informal channels, that is, grapevine rumors. Moreover, if campaigners in China want to defeat candidates they don't like, they will also use grapevine rumors as a political weapon to "throw mud" on candidates to mobilize other voters.

Second, the association between grapevine rumors and election boycotts may be related to the risks associated with this particular political act in China. Owing to constant changes in government policy, the timing of the engagement in elite-challenging political activities in China usually determines the consequences of such activities. It is not unusual in China for acts that bring participants the desired consequences at one time to bring them severe punishment and disaster at another. For the same reason, acts usually escaping the attention of government officials at higher levels at one time may attract their intervention at another time and help participants defeat leaders they don't like. Since grapevine rumors are the most important source for participants in Beijing to acquire information on possible policy changes as well as on the political atmosphere in society, politically sophisticated people test the temperature of the water before jumping in not only to minimize the risks but also to maximize possible gains from their engagement in such acts.

Awareness of the impact of neighborhood committees on people's lives is positively associated with election boycotts. This particular association can be easily attributed to the impact of "output cognition" on people's behavior.[1] Direct elections in today's China are still limited to deputies to people's congresses at the basic level. Since the functions of local government and people's congresses at the district level are parallel and compatible to those of the neighborhood committees, those who attribute significance to the influence of neighborhood committees on their lives take elections for deputies to local people's congresses more seriously. If they find elections for deputies to district-level people's congresses unfair, they are more likely to take the initiative and try to seek remedies.

The data analysis demonstrates that the probability of people in Beijing persuading others to boycott elections increases with their income. The more a person earns, the more likely he or she is to boycott unfair elections. To understand the causal relationship between people's income and election boycotts, we need to find out who in China earns more money than others as well as the status of the well-paid in society. With the economic reforms of recent years, private enterprises have flourished. People have became involved in businesses either on a full- or part-time basis, and newly emerged entrepreneurs usually earn substantial amounts of money. Those whose incomes are higher than others are very likely to come from this group.

Although people in this group earn more than others, their real living standard may not necessarily be higher than other people's since the living standard urban residents in Beijing enjoy does not solely depend on monetary income. Most people in China get government subsidies one way or another. These subsidies range from housing, medical insurance, and private cars, to servants paid by the government based on their administrative rank. Although people's income may not differ significantly in monetary terms, the "content of gold" of their wages may cause fundamental disparities when we take into consideration this government redistribution function. At the time of the survey, higher income did not necessarily bring Chinese people better lives.

This difference in people's status in the redistribution network in China can have a significant effect not only on people's living standards but also on their psychological orientation, especially their attitudes toward the political system. For example, the newly emerged entrepreneurs in China make a lot of money but few of them enjoy any government subsidies. In other words, most of them are excluded from the redistribution network in the society. Since housing in Beijing is allocated primarily through people's work units, most of the newly emerged entrepreneurs, lacking *danwei* connections, cannot find a decent place to live. To make things worse, it is exactly because they are not eligible for many of the benefits redistributed by the system that few of them enjoy the respect of other people in society, not to mention the prestige of entrepreneurs in other societies. As a result, one entrepreneur laments: "we are so poor in society that we have nothing but money."[22]

What we have here is a unique social stratum. On the one hand, people have benefited from the reforms in recent years and have great economic stakes in the system. On the other hand, although they pay a lot of taxes to the state and have to make substantial amounts of donations (*juan*) to support the system, none of them enjoy any resources controlled by the regime for redistribution. They are excluded from the redistribution system in society and do not have any political rights. The existence of this unique social stratum provides us with a good opportunity to examine the impact of economic development on people's political behavior in a developing society. If the newly emerged wealthy people are satisfied with their economic gains, they should be more likely to identify with the system and thus be more likely to engage in political acts to sustain and to support the regime. The analysis of voting behavior in Beijing shows that this is apparently not the case in China. However, if their exclusion from the redistribution system in society creates resentment and disillusionment with the political system, they should become apathetic and ignorant and thus abstain from any political activities. This is not the case in Beijing either. But there exists a third possibility: if those people use their newly acquired economic resources to fight for a fair share in the system, we would expect them to engage in incumbent-challenging, rather than regime-challenging, political activities.

The analysis shows that people who benefited from the recent reforms are more likely to engage in a particular incumbent-challenging political activity—election boycotts. They need to pay taxes, whereas most Chinese have never even heard of such a thing as taxes, and the amount of payment is usually determined arbitrarily by officials of the taxation bureau. They need to deal with various inspection groups composed of officials from the district public security and sanitation bureaus. Many of them also need to please officials at the grassroots level as well as "footbinding policewomen"[23] from neighborhood committees. Although those officials can hardly provide new entrepreneurs with help, the ability for them to punish the entrepreneurs, to exact revenge against them and to destroy their businesses, can never be ignored. In other words, the newly wealthy usually need to deal with local government officials on a much more frequent basis than others.

Since such people generally do not have any *danwei* affiliation, there is no intermediate organization to represent their interests and serve as a buffer zone to absorb conflicts between the authorities and this particular stratum. Nor do they have much bargaining leverage over local cadres. As a result, local elections become the major and probably the sole opportunity for them to punish unpopular government officials and to voice their dissatisfaction. Because their stakes in those elections are higher, as is their desire to exert influence in the political process, if they find someone trying to manipulate elections, they take the behavior more seriously than other groups of people in Beijing. They cannot afford to stand idly by and let the opportunity pass. Since they have yet to possess the political power to defeat lower-government officials, many of them seek to use such acts to make their voices heard and to drag other political actors into the struggle to change the balance of power between themselves and lower bureaucrats. Election boycotts, if successful, definitely attract the attention of government officials at higher levels. Their intervention may lead to the dismissal or transfer of unpopular leaders.

Finally, the analysis shows that the likelihood of a person's boycotting elections is reduced with the increase of the respondent's father's education. Explanations of this unique relationship lie in the political history of the PRC. For a long time, the authorities believed that the more educated a person was, the more anti-revolutionary he or she would be (*zhishi yueduo yue fandong*). The regime thus purged not only intellectuals but also their descendants. Children of intellectual origin were criticized by their peers and systemically discriminated against by the authorities in education, jobs, and career paths. Such experiences no doubt created deep-rooted hostility toward social injustices in society. When facing unfair elections, these descendants tend to act either to protest or to seek proper remedies.

Conclusion

The analysis of campaign activities and election boycotts in this chapter demonstrates the impact of changes in the electoral system on the political process in Chinese society. Although people's right to campaign is not only deliberately omitted from the constitution but also practically prohibited by the authorities, and although elections still do not have any significant impact on government policies, the fact that elections enable voters to influence the appointment of local officials prompts people in Beijing to campaign for candidates they like or against candidates they dislike. No matter what the attitudes of the regime and government officials toward such political actions are, no matter how risky it is to engage in them, as long as campaign activities can bring people in Chinese society certain benefits, citizens will engage in them to pursue their interests.

Moreover, when people find local officials manipulating the imperfect elections, rather than developing a fundamental disagreement with the regime or with the election system, as suggested by mobilizational theorists, many citizens in Beijing choose to fight against manipulators. An important way to do so is to persuade others to join them in boycotting "unfair elections." As long as people can mobilize many others in their locale to protest with them, election boycotts may attract the attention of government officials at higher levels. Their intervention may even lead to the punishment of offenders. The analysis shows that people who have access to unofficial information, who believe acts of local government have significant impacts on their lives, and who do not expect equal treatment by the government are more likely to organize people to boycott unfair elections to take revenge against their oppressors.

The analysis in this chapter again demonstrates that people in Beijing choose to participate in the imperfect political process in Chinese society to facilitate desired changes, rather than wait for political institutions in society to improve. Such a finding indicates that the changes in the electoral system introduced by the regime in Communist China could have their own momentum, which might lead to further change of that very political system.

Electoral participation is but one way for people in Beijing to participate in politics. People there also engage in other political activities to articulate their interests. Since the process of politicization is situation-specific (determined by the nature of the particular political activity in the society), the process by which people get involved in political acts other than electoral ones may be quite different from the one revealed in this chapter.

7

Appeal Activities in Beijing

Appeals involve citizen meetings with government officials at various levels or with *danwei* leaders. People in Beijing frequently engage in these acts. As demonstrated in Table 7.1, more than half of the respondents reported having contacted leaders of their work units at least once during the five years preceding the survey. Nearly 43 percent of them reported having made complaints through the bureaucratic hierarchy. The least frequently used activity in the appeals mode is complaints through deputies to local people's congresses. Only 8.9 percent of people contacted deputies during the five-year period.

Although making appeals in Beijing seems to be similar to making contacts in non-communist societies, there are substantial differences between the two activities. First, the scope of acts embodied in appeals is much more limited compared to political acts under the umbrella of "contacting" in other societies. Some important political activities that take the form of meeting with government officials in China are clustered around two other participatory modes—adversarial activities and *guanxi*.[1]

Table 7.1 Frequency distribution of appeal activities ($N = 757$)

Political activities	Percentage
Contacting work unit leaders	50.9
Appeals through the bureaucratic hierarchy	42.8
Complaints through trade unions	18.8
Complaints through political organizations	14.9
Complaints through deputies to people's congresses	8.9

Second, because channels for appeals to government officials are usually immediately accessible to people, appeals in China are generally easier than contacts elsewhere. Therefore, the initiative required for people in Beijing to make appeals should be lower than that required for people to contact government officials in other societies.

Third, while contacting governments in other societies is considered the basic right of private citizens, acts of appeal in China are approved, encouraged, and manipulated both by authorities at the top and cadres at the bottom for different reasons. Authorities believe that appeals by ordinary citizens serve the interests of the regime in two respects. Appeals transmit the opinions and grievances of ordinary citizens to party officials. According to the mass line, "scattered and unsystematic views of the masses are to be collected by Party organizations, carefully studied and coordinated, and then turned into statements of Party policy." Corruption of government officials and bureaucratism may also be controlled through close contacts between the state and society.[2] The regime uses appeals to identify "persons who lag behind" (luohou fenzi) and educate them about the rationale of CCP decisions based on "the long-run collective interests of the people."[3] Although bureaucrats in China are required to "resolve" problems for people appealing to them, resolving problems in the vocabulary of the CCP does not necessarily mean that officials bow to the pressure of popular demands. They may choose to use appeals as opportunities to "educate" appealers and even to criticize them. By exposing their ideas to the authorities, appealers in China provide government officials with an *opportunity* to persuade them to subordinate their private interests to collective ones as defined by the party.

Lower-echelon bureaucrats make different calculations when dealing with appeals since they understand that "the outcome of every conflict is determined by the extent to which the audience becomes involved in it. That is, the outcome of all conflicts is determined by the *scope* of its contagion."[4] To prevent subordinates' grievances from damaging their careers, lower-echelon cadres in China prefer that their subordinates lodge complaints with them rather than with other officials. The actual response of government officials to appeals depends on many factors, such as government policy governing the issues involved, the prevalent political atmosphere when the appeals reach them, the balance of power between the parties involved, and the expected consequences if they refuse to help.

For the same reason, the motivation of participants in China may also be somewhat different from participants elsewhere. Three kinds of benefits—instrumental, expressive, and "satisfying"—motivate citizens in Chinese society to make appeals. Instrumental appeal makers may want to change the impact of government policies on themselves, on their families, and sometimes on their reference group. Or they may want to influence the selection of unit leaders and government officials at the local level. It is well known that appointments, promotions, and demotions of bureaucrats depend on the preferences of higher-level government officials rather than on electoral competition. This is not to suggest that ordinary citizens in Chinese society cannot influence the selection of lower-echelon government officials. However, the way for people to exert such influence should be different from ones we are familiar with. Under such arrangements lower-echelon bureaucrats try to keep a positive image in front of their superiors to maintain their positions, while power contenders work hard to destroy that image. The political game in China thus becomes an "image competition." Digging up others' faults and denouncing them can have enormous effects on political struggles. By repeatedly reporting misdeeds of lower-level officials, citizens in Beijing can severely damage the power bases of bureaucrats they don't like and sometimes even force them from office.

As with voting, there can be expressive benefits associated with appeals. During the past forty years, the CCP has constantly advocated that the people, as the "masters of society," consciously fight against unhealthy tendencies and report any evildoings of corrupt officials to the authorities. If the efforts of the regime have been at least partially successful, we should find that certain people in Beijing, motivated by the sense of civic orientation, are concerned with issues with potentially broad outcomes though not directly related to their personal interests. For example, during the Cultural Revolution, millions of people joined the Red Guards in attacking "capitalist roaders."[5] After the Cultural Revolution many people complained that they were "cheated," or "manipulated," by the CCP and by Mao. Such complaints in fact tell us that many "blind followers" joined the Red Guards because they believed they were doing their civic duty for society. Since the impact of indoctrination can last even after the regime ends its efforts to mobilize citizens, we can expect to find some people who are motivated by the legacy of regime mobilization to make appeals even in today's China to fulfill their duty to society.

Theoretically, people in Beijing may also make appeals to government officials in order to achieve emotional balance. Since the publication of Ted Robert Gurr's *Why Men Rebel,* students of political science have been aware of the relationship between psychological tension and aggression, but little attention has been paid to the transformation of such tension into oral attacks, such as defamation of officials, to satisfy people's psychological needs.[6] Herbert Simon has argued that people usually do not maximize but satisfy.[7] When the environment becomes complex, people may choose not the best alternative but a "satisfactory" one.[8] Albert Hirschman criticizes political scientists who confine their attention to situations in which the only alternative to articulation is acquiescence.[9] He notes that between articulation and "desertion," there are two other choices—"voice and exit."[10] The angered in a society may voice their dissatisfaction even though they know expression may not bring them tangible benefits. Therefore, it is reasonable to assume that some people in China make appeals to higher authorities simply to achieve psychological balance by attacking the chief culprit responsible for their personal grievances. Unlike instrumental appealers, the people in this group aim not to "maximize," to change specific decisions made by bureaucrats, but to satisfy their anger.[11]

The differences illustrated above between making appeals in China and contacting government officials elsewhere derive from the institutional arrangements in Chinese society. Under altered institutional arrangements, the decision of participants on whether to make appeals, their choice of strategy to persuade government officials, the resources required for them to make appeals, and finally the way those resources are converted to political action may be fundamentally different from the ones we are familiar with. To understand appeals in Beijing, we need to examine the political process in Chinese society. Thus, the analysis in this chapter is divided into three parts. First, I examine the impacts of the institutional arrangements of Chinese society on appeal making in Beijing. Second, I treat appeals as a whole and identify resources required for people to engage in this participatory mode and how these resources are converted into appeal activities. The analysis in this section compares the process of appealing with that of voting, to illustrate the impacts of the structural arrangements on the political dynamics in Chinese society. Finally, I decompose political acts belonging to this mode into different kinds of appeals to examine the impacts of certain crucial variables on the political dynamic of appeals in Beijing as well as the resources required for people to engage in them.

State, Society, and Appeal Making in China

Because the structural arrangements in communist societies make the authorities the sole source of many resources crucial to people's daily lives and the planned economy blocks their way to seek alternative sources of supply, citizens in China are forced to deal with the government on a broader scope of issues than in Western countries. As Friedgut points out with regard to the former USSR, the "political system is so structured that the citizen must almost surely turn at some time to local officials or political figures for their help."[12] Whether they are interested in politics or not, citizens in Chinese society are more likely to be motivated by tangible benefits that concern private citizens to make appeals to government officials.

Structural arrangements in Chinese society also fundamentally change the way participants pursue their goals. The challenge facing participants in every society is to find a way to alter the hierarchical relationship between themselves and government officials. When electoral competition is available for citizens to choose government officials, the major way citizens meet this challenge is by forming a group to put pressure on bureaucrats. Behind such group-based activities is an implicit threat—if you do not help, we will drive you out of office in the next election.

As responsibility for resource distribution in China is assigned to local organizations or work units rather than managed directly by government agencies, the structural arrangement in Chinese society encourages participants to compete for resources already allocated to the organization they belong to rather than to get more resources from the government. Everyone eligible for the resource knows that if someone in his or her organization gets the resource, his or her own chance of getting the same would be reduced. In contrast to the situation in other societies, resource competition in China on low-politics issues is usually a zero-sum game. It requires participants to "steal" or "sell" interests of their colleagues to make the desired but limited resources go to themselves rather than to someone else. Group and group-based political activities familiar to students of participation thus become largely irrelevant to the pursuit of interests related to people's daily lives.

With most aspects of people's lives controlled by the government and many necessities of life in Chinese society provided to citizens only by government agencies, citizens do not need too many cognitive skills to establish a linkage between desired benefits and required political actions. As long as the person knows who or what organization is responsible for the issue involved, the minimal requirement for him to make appeals is achieved. The crucial resource for people to participate in politics elsewhere—socioeconomic status—may not have direct effect on the probability that people in Chinese society will pursue their particularized interests through appeal making.

Studies of participation across different cultures and political systems have found that participation correlates with certain cultural variables under a broad rubric of civic orientation, such as political attitudes, beliefs, and value orientations of people in a society.[13] There are two approaches to studying the impacts of these cultural variables on people's political behavior. One concerns macrolevel issues—the impact of political culture on political development and change in a society. The research question raised by scholars concerning such issues makes them seek, a priori, differences rather than similarities in people's political attitudes in different societies.[14] According to them, there exist three different versions of political culture in communist societies: an official political culture, which represents official norms or the culture the regime wishes to impose on private citizens; a dominant political culture accepted by most people in real life; and an elite political culture. The interaction of these three versions of political culture determines political developments in those societies.[15]

Another approach concerns microlevel issues—the impacts of political culture on political behavior of individuals in the society. The research question raised by scholars in this area makes them seek, a priori, similar beliefs, attitudes, and psychological orientations among citizens in different societies.[16] Political culture in this tradition is treated as a "black box" between stimuli and response.[17] Many scholars argue that people's psychological orientation is associated with their socioeconomic status and that "those who have a greater psychological involvement in politics will be more active politically."[18] For example, Verba, Nie, and Kim developed a "standard model" of political participation that found "civic orientation" to be a crucial intervening variable produced by people's socioeconomic status and prompting them to participate in politics.

However, certain crucial but unspoken assumptions underlie the proposed causal links among socioeconomic status, civic orientation, and political participation in this standard model. First, the model assumes that there are no structural causes forcing citizens in society to be "concerned" about politics or to deal with government. People in society are free to choose whether to get involved in politics and they are free to stay away from politics and public life if they so choose. Second, the model assumes that political processes in society are so designed that dealing with government on an individual basis can hardly produce desired results for participants. As interest articulation at the policy implementation stage is blocked, citizens are pushed to the policy formulation stage to influence government policy. Such a structural design breaks the linkage between people's participatory acts and the benefits that those acts might bring them. Third, the model assumes that the institutional arrangements give people an opportunity to choose government officials through electoral competition and such an opportunity is the foundation of all political activities in the society. When people contact a government official or representative, they tacitly threaten to vote the official out of office if he or she won't help. Only when these prerequisites hold true in a society can the causal link between respondents' psychological involvement in politics and political participation specified in the standard model of political participation be valid.

Examination of the political process in China shows that none of these assumptions hold true. Citizen involvement in politics often results from necessity at the time of the survey. Although economic reforms have introduced market mechanisms into Chinese society, people continue to rely on the government to provide most resources crucial to their personal lives. Moreover, although the ability of the Chinese regime to mobilize citizens to get involved in various political activities has been greatly reduced in recent years, few people can afford not to pay attention to politics and governmental affairs in order to survive. As stated in a popular proverb, "even if you don't concern yourself with politics, politics will concern you" (*ni buguanxin zhengzhi, zhengzhi guanxin ni*). Attending political study sessions is still mandatory in many work units in today's China, as is expressing views compatible with those advocated by the regime in those meetings. To survive in Chinese society, paying lip service to official positions is still absolutely necessary. Many people read newspapers, listen to radio, and watch TV regularly to learn official viewpoints on political issues. Rather than representing people's psychological involvement in politics, these kinds of "interest" in politics simply represent a survival technique. Thus we cannot expect people's interests in politics to bridge socioeconomic resources with participation in Chinese society.

Although some scholars have noticed that the "rules of the game" can influence people's political behavior, their inquiries into structural effects on people's political behavior assume that people have little choice but to passively respond to regime mobilization efforts. For example, Townsend suggests that "there can be little incentive to participate when one believes that all the conventional political phrases and practices are simply a disguise for dictatorial rule by a small group of men."[19] Friedgut observes that "conformity rather than initiative still guides the Soviet citizen. Administrative *raison d'état* is served before community self-determination, and preserves its primacy through control of both the form and content of the participatory structures of the community."[20] This tradition of scholarship ignores the possibility that citizens can creatively respond to structural constraints.

Research on the impacts of the change in the rules of the game in communist societies on the relationship between people's psychological orientation and their political behavior is even more confusing. On the one hand, Wayne DiFranceisco and Zvi Gitelman report that those who are most alienated from the regime and most distrustful of others are most likely to contact public officials and to seek informal channels for interest articulation and the satisfaction of demands.[21] On the other hand, Donna Bahry and Brian Silver demonstrate that both an interest in politics and a sense of efficacy are positively correlated with levels of participation in the former USSR, even after the impacts of socioeconomic variables have been controlled.[22]

Such conflicting findings on the impact of psychological orientation on people's participation in communist societies are in part caused by a measurement problem: under differing structural arrangements, similar psychological orientations may require different measurements for detection. Measurements of people's psychological orientations may not be used in communist societies without adapting to the social and political structures therein.[23] Still more important, the findings in the previous chapters suggest that when participation through conventional means is blocked, most people in Chinese society will find other ways to articulate, rather than give up, their private interests. In other words, the authorities in China can only change the way people articulate their interests, not prevent them from doing so. If the assumption that people in communist societies only passively respond to regime mobilization does not hold, then the whole political dynamic in those societies changes, as does the relationship between people's psychological orientation and their political participation.

For example, if a society gives people no way to articulate their interests, apathy and ignorance will dominate their psychological orientation. However, if people can respond to the structural constraints of the society creatively, they may not lack feelings of efficacy. Although such feelings may not prompt people to use paths blocked by the regime to articulate their interests, efficacious people may identify and use other methods to articulate their interests.

In addition, the regime may try to impose some unique dimension of people's psychological orientation that can also influence their political behavior. For example, the authorities in China have tried to impose norms on their citizens according to which people should always follow party and government instructions even if they do not understand the rationale behind those decisions (lijie de yaozhixing, bulijie de yeyao zhixing). If such political indoctrination has been at least partially successful, we should find that the doctrine has become a norm of "communist political culture" in people's minds and influences their behavior.

Table 7.2 shows that there does exists such a cultural orientation among some people in Beijing. More than 10 percent of Beijing residents still be-

Table 7.2   Responses to the question, Should people be allowed to disagree with government policies?

Answer	N	Percentage
No	92	12.2
Yes	562	74.2
Don't know	94	12.4
No answer	9	1.2

lieve that citizens should not be allowed to disagree with government policies even though the ability of the authorities to mobilize people has dramatically declined in recent years. This orientation can be categorized as subject culture in China, which may be an important obstacle to people's pursuing their interests.[24] When conflict arises between their private interests and the collective one, as defined by the regime, people subscribing to such attitudes would wage psychological warfare in their minds against their own interests rather than trying to change decisions made by the government. Breaking away from such psychological shackles may be an important precondition for people in Chinese society to articulate their interests. Such an analysis tells us that understanding the political process in a society requires examining not only the impact of people's psychological orientation on their participatory behavior as specified in the standard model but, more important, the impact of institutional arrangements on the political culture and the cultural impacts on the political dynamics in the society. "If the concept of political culture is to be effectively utilized, it needs to be supplemented with structural analysis."[25]

The structural arrangements in Chinese society create a political process that differs from those in other societies. For example, people working under a power abuser would be more likely to contact government officials than those who faithfully implement government policy. Moreover, those whose work units have additional resources to distribute would be more likely to engage in resource competition than those whose work units lack available resources. When stimuli reach them, the perceived consequences of their acts would play an important role in shaping people's decisions to engage in various political acts. Since the consequences of appeals depend on the ability of supplicants to temporarily alter the hierarchical relationship between participants and government officials, anything increasing such abilities can be a political resource in Chinese society.

There are several ways for people in China to temporarily alter the hierarchical relationship between themselves and government officials to articulate their interests, and I deal with two in this chapter. First, people can borrow "normative power" from existing government policies to press government officials. In doing so, participants in China can ask bureaucrats to "faithfully" implement government policy. Since government policies are hardly monopolistic, there is usually space for citizens to maneuver. Nonetheless, the semisecret status of government policies is a major obstacle for participants gathering information. Thus, the ability of a private citizen to break such barriers to acquire desired information in China is one of the most important required political resources.

Second, participants in China can also borrow someone else's power to change the balance of power between themselves and lower-echelon bureaucrats. In so doing, they manage to drag political actors who have the power to influence, change, and overrule decisions of local bureaucrats into conflicts and make them intervene on their behalf to force bureaucrats at lower levels to make favorable decisions or to change unfavorable ones. Articulating their interests in such a way requires that participants understand the dynamics of the political system in China and have access to officials with such political power. Access is an especially important resource in today's China.

People can alter power balances if they have the ability to properly present their arguments to government officials and make appeals. The communication skills required for people to make successful appeals may be different from that for academic debates. While successful appeals require participants either to make government officials sympathetic to participants' positions or to threaten officials with unhappy consequences if they do not satisfy participants' demands, academic debate requires scholars to present their arguments clearly and unequivocally, without considering whether such presentations offend anyone. Although appeals skills require a certain level of education, too much education can be counterproductive in shaping such skills. The experience of a university professor perfectly illustrates this point:

> This happened ten years ago when I was in the May Seventh Cadre School of the Ministry of Foreign Trade in Henan province. One day, I received a telegram from my wife telling me that she was hospitalized for high blood pressure. I wanted to go back to Beijing to see her. To me, I had a perfect reason to ask for leave and the whole thing was quite simple. I went to see a leader of my platoon, who was an uneducated veteran and appointed to the leadership position based on his contribution to the revolution during the Yanan period. I presented him with the telegram and asked him to give me a permit to go back to Beijing for half a month to take care of my wife. To my surprise, he refused my request for the reasons that it was too busy in the school and

someone else had already left for Beijing. He asked me to wait till after the other employee came back. I simply could not see any relationship between my case and the absence of other people. I began to reason with him and we ending up quarreling but got nowhere. I was frustrated and vowed that I would never talk to any uneducated leader again. When I went back to the dormitory, I told the story to my roommate, who always had successful experiences in his encounters with the leaders, and asked for help. After carefully listening to my story and getting to know the context, he told me that my major mistake was taking permission for a leave of absence for granted. He said, "You intellectuals are fond of seeing things as either black or white. However, in real life, things are not that simple. It depends on him to give you permission. He may choose to offer you help, or he may choose to make a decision according to standard operating procedure [*gongshi gongban*]. And it is always very easy for him to find a plausible reason to reject your demands. If I were you, I would make him feel important and show my appreciation for his help in advance. I would make him know that if I got permission for leave, I would give him all the credit. Your strategy of making appeals is wrong from the start." I learned a good lesson from this experience. I confess that compared to those workers, we intellectuals have yet to learn how to handle these delicate situations.[26]

As the political dynamics in society shift, the way resources are transferred to political actions also changes. For example, as the scope of the outcome of appeals in Beijing is usually limited to participants themselves or their immediate families, participants do not need to be interested in politics or have a sense of civic duty to make appeals. Not only will civic orientation no longer have any direct effect on appeals in China, but the most important determinant of people's civic orientation—socioeconomic status—will also have no indirect effect on appeals. Since institutional arrangements encourage people to compete for resources through individualized rather than collective action, group-based activities are no longer a necessary condition for them to articulate their interests. Instead, politically sophisticated people in China try to defeat their colleagues rather than cooperate with them. Resources that benefit groups and group formation may no longer be important for appeals. Resources in different societies may be the same, but the way those resources are used may be totally different.

Multivariate Analysis of Appeals

The estimates presented in Table 7.3 form the regression analysis of the appeals mode in Beijing. The dependent variable in the equation is the principal component transformation of five participatory acts belonging to the appeals mode.[27]

Table 7.3 Multiple regression of appeals by age, education, party affiliation, access to information, and political efficacy

Factor	Estimate
Age	
22–33	.29*
34–44	.49***
45–53	.58***
54–61	.52***
62–71	.19
72–82	.52**
Education (years)	
1–3	−.18
4–6	.18
7–9	.24
10–12	.48***
13–15	.30
16–17	−.16
Over 18	.19
Party membership[a]	.21**
Sex[b]	−.18**
Talking about political affairs[c]	.08**
Grapevine rumors[d]	.23***
Confidence in own ability to influence *danwei* decisions[e]	.26***
Understanding of important issues of the locality[f]	.13***
Opinion on the role of the CCP for democracy in China[g]	.10***
Opinion on the role of the people for democracy in China[h]	.05*
Ideas of disagreement with government policies	.20**

Note: $N = 719$; constant $= -1.97***$; adjusted $R^2 = .17$.

[a] Coded as 1 if CCP member, 0 if not.

[b] Coded as 1 if male, 0 if female.

[c] Measured by the question, "What about talking about public affairs in our country with other people? Do you do that nearly every day, once a week, from time to time, or never?" Answers were coded from 1 (never) to 4 (nearly every day).

[d] Measured by the question, "Last month, did you happen to hear anything on the grapevine [*xiaodao xiaoxi*] concerning the political, social, and economic situation in our country?" Answers were coded as 1 if yes, 0 if no.

[e] Measured by the question, "If you believe your supervisor is wrong, is there anything you can do?" Answers were coded as 1 if yes, 0 if no.

[f] Measured by the question, "How about local issues in this town or area of the country? How well do you understand them? Do you understand them very well, understand them well, understand them not too well, or understand them not at all?" Answers were coded from 1 (not at all) to 4 (very well).

[g] Measured by the question, "Do you strongly agree, agree, disagree, or strongly disagree with the statement: Democracy can only be achieved under the leadership of the CCP?" Answers were coded from 1 (strongly disagree) to 4 (strongly agree).

[h] Measured by the question, "Do you strongly agree, agree, disagree, or strongly disagree with the statement: Democracy can only be achieved through the struggles of the people?" Answers were coded from 1 (strongly disagree) to 4 (strongly agree).

$*p < 0.1$ $**p < 0.05$ $***p < 0.01$.

I demonstrated in the previous chapter that the relationship between respondents' age and voting behavior is curvilinear. Age is found to have similar effects on appeals. People aged eighteen to twenty-two are least likely to make appeals to government officials. Beyond that threshold, the frequency of appeals increases with age. Appeals reach their peak among respondents between the ages of forty-five and fifty-three and remain high for virtually the rest of people's lives.[28]

Why do fewer members of the youngest age group appeal than members of most other age groups in Beijing? There are two possible but competing explanations. The first one argues that citizens need to be familiar with the working procedures of the government as well as the division of labor within the political system to make appeals. Such knowledge and skill can only be developed from people's encounters with authorities. Youth in China usually have limited experience in such encounters and they have yet to develop such skills. This explanation is similar to the start-up theory developed in the study of voting behavior, which attributes lower turnout rates among young people to their marginal integration into their community.[29]

The second explanation suggests that the relationship between age and appeals revealed here is a confounding one. Unlike voting, in which the agenda, issues involved, and timing are all set up by someone else, appeals are initiated by the participants themselves, who determine the timing and agenda of their appeals. While the outside stimuli for people to vote are the same for everyone in a society, the stimuli for people to make appeals must vary. We know that the work unit is still the primary place to satisfy most needs related to employees' daily lives. Problems such as public security, the environment, public transportation, and even family planning are still under the jurisdiction of the *danwei*. To resolve these issues, the proper place for people in China to make appeals is, of course, their responsible organization, the work unit. At the same time, the work unit is the primary provider of housing in urban China. As youngsters in urban China usually do not have their own residences, most of them live with their parents. If any problem related to their daily lives arises, they would probably ask their parents to appeal to the responsible agency on their behalf to get the problem resolved. Thus, younger people in urban China are less likely to make appeals either because the stimuli for them to do so are fewer or because they can usually find someone to act on their behalf who can get the job done more effectively.

Testing between these two hypotheses requires knowledge of the places of people's residence, whether respondents live with their parents, and how long they have held their jobs. If the first explanation is correct, we should find that appeals reflect people's job experience, especially the length of time people have held jobs. If the second explanation is correct, we should find that those living with their parents are less likely to make appeals. Unfortunately, neither piece of information is available in the data set, so we cannot test these two hypotheses directly. However, if we can reasonably assume that most young people in Beijing live with their parents before marriage but move to their own residences after getting married, we can compare the behavior of those married to that of unmarried people in each age group to isolate the influence of marriage on appeals. If the effect of age disappears when respondents' marital status is controlled, we may conclude that the place of residence makes a difference in the probability that people will make appeals indirectly. Of course, if the relationship between age and appeals remains the same after controlling for respondents' marital status, we will be able to reject this hypothesis.

Table 7.4 shows the multiple regression of appeals, controlling for respondents' marital status. The result demonstrates that respondents' marital status does have a clear and significant impact on the probability that people will make appeals. When the impact of respondents' marital status is controlled, the impact of age on appeals vanishes. Before accepting the family residence model, we should be aware of another possible explanation of the causal link between marriage and appeals: marriage itself could have a significant impact on people's willingness to take risks. Given the fact that many participatory activities in Communist China have certain risks associated with them, it is possible that the risks associated with appeals deter young married couples from making appeals to leaders. I tend to reject this explanation. All acts embodied in appeals are not only approved but also encouraged both by the Chinese regime and by local bureaucrats. Appeals are actually one of the few "safe" political activities in Communist China. Across the spectrum of participatory activities, only voting is "safer" than appeals. If people need to deal with government leaders and want to avoid political risks, they will choose appeals rather than other political activities.

However, when respondents' marital status is controlled, another age group—those from forty-five to fifty-three—are found to be more active in appeals making. Why are people belonging to this group more active than others? The generational effect may provide us with an answer.[30] People of this generation were from six to thirteen years old when the Communist Party took power in China in 1949. The most important part of their socialization process—adolescence—was not only accomplished under communist control but also during a period of intense regime mobilization. If political education, thought reform, and various methods designed and

Table 7.4   Multiple regression of appeals by age, education, marital status, party affiliation, access to information, and political efficacy

Factor	Estimate
Age	
22–33	.13
34–44	.30
45–53	.39*
54–61	.35
62–71	.03
72–82	.41
Education	
1–3 years	−.18
4–6 years	.16
7–9 years	.20
10–12 years	.45***
13–15 years	.28
16–17 years	−.19
Over 18 years	.14
Marital status[a]	.21**
Party membership	.19**
Sex	−.18***
Talking about political affairs	.08***
Grapevine rumors	.23***
Confidence in own ability to influence decisions	.26***
Understanding of important issues of the locality	.12***
Opinion on the role of the CCP for democracy in China	.09***
Opinion on the role of the people for democracy in China	.05*
Ideas of disagreement with government policies	.20**

Note: $N = 719$; constant $= -1.91$***; adjusted $R^2 = .18$.
[a]Coded as 1 if married, 0 if single. See Table 7.3 for description of other factors.
*$p < 0.1$ **$p < 0.05$ ***$p < 0.01$.

used by the CCP to transform people in Chinese society into "new socialist men" could produce any effects on the psychological orientation of private citizens, this age group would be the one most likely to be successfully indoctrinated. Since political education by the CCP encourages citizens to report "unhealthy tendencies" to the authorities, people in this age group would be most likely to develop a sense of civic duty. They are more likely than any other people in Chinese society to be prompted by such expressive benefits to contact the authorities.

Before I go on with the analysis of the resources required for people in Beijing to make appeals, I want to point out that neither of the two most important indicators of socioeconomic status in Beijing—the type of *danwei* respondents work in and their subjective evaluation of their economic status—are found to have significant impact on the probability that people will make appeals. The relationship between appeals and another indicator of socioeconomic status—education—is also unique. The data show that among all educational groups only people with ten to twelve years of education are more likely to make appeals. It is relatively easy to understand why they are more likely to do so than people with less education. The political skills required for people to make appeals—to communicate one's demands to government officials, to press for concessions and at the same time avoid offending them, to borrow power from somewhere else to change the balance of power between themselves and bureaucrats—must be associated with people's ability to deal with complexity. And this ability requires at least some education.

But a more difficult question facing us is why college graduates are less active in appeals than high school graduates in Beijing. Part of the answer may be found in traditional Chinese culture, which specifies that the educated should remain aloof from politics and engage in material pursuits for their *private* benefits. "A gentleman should plan and worry ahead of the people, and enjoy the fruits after the people," wrote Fang Zhongyan, a literati politician living in the Song Dynasty.[31] Although this tradition supposes that the educated avoid being preoccupied with pursuing their private interests, it encourages them to be concerned and get involved in politics for public interest. As most appeals are aimed at private interests, attitudes inherited from traditional culture can be a psychological obstacle preventing the educated from engaging in such political acts.

Moreover, the huge gap in the educational level of intellectuals and government officials may be another barrier. When the communists took over in 1949, Mao advocated that "nonprofessionals lead professionals in socialist China." Appointments of work unit leaders and government officials for a long time were based either on candidates' contributions to the communist revolution or their loyalty to the regime. Many illiterate revolutionary veterans were appointed to leadership positions, especially in grassroots organizations. As a result, the educational level of *danwei* leaders and government officials is usually substantially lower than that of intellectuals working under them. To many bureaucrats, intellectuals are aggressive, difficult to understand, prone to playing tricks, and dangerous to deal with. This stereotypical image of intellectuals makes bureaucrats tend to respond unfavorably to demands or requests made by intellectuals, to deter them from making further trouble. Intellectuals also consider their dealings with government officials a painful experience. The analytical skills acquired from school training can hardly have any use in such contacts. Their reasoning, based on the merits of issues, can easily be defeated by bureaucrats who simply invoke policies stating the opposite. Frustrated by such painful experiences, intellectuals usually blame bureaucrats as unqualified for their jobs (*meiyoushuiping*), and many of them simply give up and turn away from officials.

The analysis shows that party members are more active in making appeals in Beijing. The relationship between party membership and appeals can be understood in the following ways. First, CCP membership can be an important political resource. CCP members usually have more opportunities to access government officials at higher levels than other citizens. Although their interactions with government organizations and officials mostly concern public affairs, party members can develop better knowledge of the division of labor within the government and of its working procedures, which allows them to locate "responsible persons or responsible organizations" when they need to make appeals. Intimate relationships can also be developed from such interactions, which make it easier for them to borrow power in their conflicts with lower-echelon bureaucrats. Party members in China also have more opportunities to read "relayed reports" and "internal" briefings on government policies. This information gives them normative power when dealing with bureaucrats and makes them more aware of their own rights under existing government policies, an awareness that can encourage them to make appeals to authorities.

Second, although political reforms and decentralization in recent years may have reduced the power of the CCP, the reforms may have reinforced the power of individual CCP members in grassroots organizations. The major administrators in most Chinese organizations are still party officials. Their status in organizations usually reflects their position in the party. Political reform in recent years has made elections with candidate choice via secret ballot mandatory for leadership positions of the CCP at the grassroots level. Nearly half of the respondents in Beijing also reported having a chance to vote for *danwei* leaders. These changes make the support of ordinary party members crucial to leaders at basic-level organizations seeking to be nominated as candidates for various leadership positions in grassroots organizations. As more and more leaders have realized that losing party elections will lead to their loss of administrative positions, many leaders have begun to co-opt party members in their organizations. This is not to say that party officials do not need to please their superiors anymore. However, appeasing or co-opting party members also becomes important for them to survive. They need to balance the pressures both from above and below. In such a situation, appeals made by party members, their primary constituency, are considered more seriously and responded to more favorably, which in turn attracts party members to engage in appeal activities more aggressively to protect their interests.

Third, close interactions nurtured during the application process usually create dependence of party members on *danwei* leaders. Applicants to the Communist Party must go through a long and painful process to become party members. During the application process, especially during the nurturing period (*peiyang jieduan*), frequent interaction between applicants and representatives assigned by the CCP is established.[32] The goal of such a mechanism is to provide applicants with an opportunity to access power in exchange for their cooperation. Party cadres are usually very helpful and willing to assist applicants in resolving any problems. These experiences motivate applicants to make appeals to government officials whenever they come across difficulties. Moreover, such interaction has its own momentum, which can lead to the establishment of patron-client ties between cadres and party members, an important political resource for members. Although their beliefs in the propaganda of the CCP and even their attitudes toward the party itself may change over time, the behavior patterns created, nurtured, and encouraged by the authorities can continue.

In many societies information is a crucial resource for people seeking to participate in politics. In China, however, traditional measurements of people's access to information—newspaper reading, radio listening, and TV watching—are found to have no direct effects on appeals. As suggested before, in a society where politics is closely associated with people's lives, information may serve a totally different function from that scholars have found in other societies. Rather than inspiring people to become interested in politics, it provides citizens with normative power or "ammunition" in their dealings with bureaucrats, which can increase the possibility of their getting desired concessions. If this hypothesis is true, having ammunition—from grapevine rumors or "back street gossip" (*xiaodao xiaoxi*)—will increase the probability that people will make appeals, since the government monopoly on information on its policies makes ammunition obtainable only from unofficial channels. The analysis confirms this expectation. Although access to unofficial information does not increase people's interests in politics (correlation .07, not shown in the table), it does have independent and significant effects on the probability that people in Beijing will make appeals even after the impacts of other variables are controlled. This outcome also clearly demonstrates that the causal link between information and appeals in Beijing is different from that found elsewhere.

In contrast to DiFranceisco and Gitelman's findings in the former Soviet Union,[33] but comparable to those reported by Bahry and Silver,[34] I found that people who are confident about their ability to influence decisions made by *danwei* leaders and about understanding issues in their locality are more active in making appeals, although confidence in their understanding of political issues at the national level does not increase the likelihood of their making appeals (not shown in the table). This finding supports Seweryn Bialer's conclusion that "a major distinction has to be made between 'high politics' and 'low politics' " in studying communist societies. Although citizens in those societies may be apolitical, indifferent, or apathetic with regard to high politics, many are involved in low politics.[35] As appeals in Beijing are primarily aimed at low-politics issues concerning participants themselves and their immediate family members, rather than at changing government policy at the national level, it is easy to understand why local efficacy can make a difference in people's political behavior.

Not surprisingly, appeals in Beijing also positively correlate with regime-based trust and civic competence. Both people who believe "democracy in China depends on the CCP" and those who believe "democracy depends on the struggle of ordinary people" are found to be more active in making appeals. Moreover, breaking away from the psychological shackles imposed on people in Chinese society also increases the likelihood of appeals. Those who believe ordinary people should be allowed to disagree with government policies are found to more actively pursue their interests through appeals than those who do not think so.

In the previous chapter, I reported that the processes by which men and women come to engage in voting are quite different. Not only do some important socioeconomic factors work differently on men and women, but the politicization processes for the two genders differ significantly. To examine the resources required for men and women in Beijing to make appeals and the processes for these resources to be converted into appeal actions, I ran a separate regression analysis. Table 7.5 reports the results.

The analysis shows that there are both similarities and differences in the resources required for men and women to make appeals in Beijing. Not surprisingly, the most important resource for both is access to information (ammunition from unofficial channels). Grapevine rumors—the major source of information on various government policies and the general political atmosphere of Beijing society—can substantially increase the probability that both men and women in Beijing will make appeals. Regime-based trust also makes a difference. People of both sexes believing that the CCP can bring democracy to China are more likely to make appeals to authorities. This finding suggests that regime-based trust can shape people's

Table 7.5 Multiple regression of appeals for different sexes

Factor	Male[a]	Female[b]
Age		
22–33	.17	.02
34–44	.12	.38
45–53	−.00	.79**
54–61	.05	.66**
62–71	−.25	.33
72–82	−.00	.84*
Education		
1–3 years	−.12	−.43
4–6 years	−.06	.25
7–9 years	−.20	.60**
10–12 years	−.02	.94***
13–15 years	−.20	.82***
16–17 years	−.21	−.26
Over 18 years	−.21	.58
Marital status[c]	.33**	.12
Party membership	.24**	.02
Talking about political affairs	.13***	.01
Grapevine rumors	.26***	.22**
Confidence in own ability to influence *danwei* decisions	.32***	.17
Understanding of important issues of the locality	.10	.15**
Opinion on the role of the CCP for democracy in China	.07*	.11**
Opinion on the role of the people for democracy in China	.00	.10**
Ideas of disagreement with government policies	.17	.23*

[a]N = 354; constant = −1.04**; adjusted R^2 = .20.
[b]N = 365; constant = −1.67***; adjusted R^2 = .19.
[c]See Table 7.3 for description of factors.
*$p < 0.1$ **$p < 0.05$ ***$p < 0.01$.

choices of political acts to pursue their interests. Those who trust the regime are more likely to choose channels encouraged by the authorities.

Aside from these two variables, the resources needed for men and women to make appeals are different. CCP membership, interest in politics, marital status, and confidence in their ability to influence decisions made by work unit leaders increase the chance that men will make appeals. Education, civic competence (measured by their understanding of local issues), age, frequency of discussions of political affairs, and legacy of regime mobilization have no such impact. The resources for women are completely re-versed. While education, legacy of regime mobilization, and civic compe-tence increase the chance that women will make appeals, marital status, CCP membership, and efficacious feeling are found to have no impact on women's rates of appeals in Beijing.

Some of the differences revealed in Table 7.5 have simple explanations. For example, we can easily understand why marriage in China is positively associated with appeals for men but not for women. The division of labor in Chinese culture assigns wives the primary responsibility for dealing with domestic affairs, while all the issues outside the home are the responsibility of husbands (*nuzhunei, nanzhuwai*). If a family needs to contact government officials, it is the responsibility of the husband to do so. This legacy is reinforced by the housing allotment system in urban China. To prevent couples working at different *danwei* from acquiring two apartments, the system in China makes only the husband of the family eligible for a housing allotment from his work unit if husband and wife work in different *danwei*. Because a family lives in the residence assigned by the work unit of the husband, it is natural for the husband to make appeals to his work unit when the family needs to contact the government.

The other three variables associated with appeals for men—party affili-ation, frequency of discussing political affairs, and confidence in their abil-ity to influence decisions made by work unit leaders—suggest that men are more likely to aim appeals at certain instrumental benefits. Political dis-cussion can bring a person information on various government policies. Being a party member not only increases people's access to information but also allows them to meet government officials at various levels and develop skills to deal with complex situations. These experiences are important resources for participants to defeat bureaucrats and get what they want from them. Of course, efficacious feelings can make participants believe that they can get what they want from authorities through appeals, an outlook that in turn increases the likelihood they will engage in such ac-tivities.

The situation for women is more puzzling and difficult to explain. The analysis reveals that middle-aged and elderly women in China are more active in making appeals to authorities. Such an association can hardly be explained by life-cycle effects and can only be the consequence of genera-tional effects. Traditionally, women in China were not supposed to perform any political role. However, after the communists took over in 1949, Mao considered women to be an important political resource for the CCP. He repeatedly told cadres that they should pay attention to their "half of the sky" (banbiantian) and mobilize women for socialist construction. The regime worked hard to raise women's political consciousness and encourage them to participate in the political process. It is quite possible that women are more responsive to regime mobilization than men. I expect such mobilization to influence the political behavior of women in Chinese society in two ways. First, it makes women choose only officially approved channels to articulate their interests. Second, it creates a sense of obligation or civic duty, which prompts them to report any "unhealthy tendencies" to the authorities. Once mobilization successfully reshaped their belief system or attitudes, women's political orientation and attitudes remained relatively stable over time.

The finding that women aged seventy-two to eighty-two are more active in making appeals deserves special attention. Understanding their behavior also depends on understanding PRC history. During the early days of the People's Republic, the regime recruited many unemployed women to form neighborhood committees in the cities and used them as arms for the state to penetrate society. These "footbinding policewomen" (xiaojiao jingcha) began to work in residential areas on a voluntary basis or for small compensation as crime watchers. As the authorities in China increasingly stressed class struggle, their power expanded dramatically. Many were recruited into street revolutionary committees (jiedao geming weiyuanhui) as paid government employees during the Cultural Revolution. Changing from unemployed middle-aged women without any skills, whose lives depended on their husbands and semigovernment officials, into women with vocations and some control over their lives, they experienced a dramatic boost in their social status. It is reasonable to assume that such changes made them loyal to their "emancipator" and that they tended to do what the regime wanted them to do, that is, to report on unhealthy tendencies in society.

This cohort experienced a status reversal after 1979. As the emphasis shifted from class struggle to economic development, their power base was shaken and their social status was concomitantly downgraded dramatically. Many of them lost their power over people in their neighborhoods and were even forced to retire when they reached the age of sixty. These changes no doubt created a "perception of discrepancy between their value expectations and their value capabilities."[36] Human beings are alleged to have four general response patterns to such discrepancy and frustration: submission, dependence, avoidance, and aggression.[37] Two of them, dependence and aggression, can increase their interaction with government officials. For example, memory of the past would tell women that they had to "depend" on the CCP to search for glory in society. Thus to reclaim their lost status, they would turn to government officials to save their political lives and recover the glory of their past.

Another possible response, of course, is aggression. With their anger aroused by frustration, women might find that whenever they encounter an external cue—an object or person associated with the source of frustration—an aggressive response usually follows. In contrast to goal-directed behavior, frustration-instigated behavior tends to be satisfying in itself, and the original goal to relieve frustration may become irrelevant to further behavior.[38] Such anger often leads to political violence. However, both the political environment in Chinese society and the age of the frustrated women make physical assault impossible. As a result, defamation of the object or person associated with their perceived source of frustration and reporting "improper behavior" of enemies to higher authorities become logical substitutes for collective violence.

The comparison of resources required for men to make appeals with those for women reveals that while men's decisions to make appeals are primarily influenced by tangible resources that can increase the probability of their getting what they want from such activities, women's decisions are primarily influenced by the psychological orientation deliberately created by the authorities. This finding actually suggests that men in Beijing are likely to be motivated to appeal by certain particularized benefits for themselves or their immediate family members, whereas women are more likely to be prompted by expressive benefits, that is, perceived obligations to the society. This finding also tells us that regime mobilization is more likely to produce effects on women than on men in China.

Confrontational versus Conciliatory Appeals

In Chapter 2, I suggested that people in Beijing may choose either a confrontational or a conciliatory strategy when dealing with leaders of work units or government officials. The choice of strategy is determined, primarily, by the nature of the issue involved. If participants are not satisfied with policy made by government officials, rather than trying to persuade them to make certain adjustments during the policy implementation stage, they must confront the decision makers. For the same reason, if a person wants to influence the selection of government officials, his or her appeals must be confrontational if the nature of the issue involved demands such an approach. When making appeals in a confrontational manner, participants in Beijing usually demand from officials what they believe they are entitled to or charge them with wrong implementation of government policies. Some appealers may even threaten to make trouble for officials or physically harass them. Confrontational appeals are similar to political acts in other societies in many aspects. People engaging in such appeals know their rights, dare to confront the authorities, and are concerned about issues with a broad scope of outcome. Those people are more likely to be citizens rather than mere subjects.

Appeals made in a conciliatory manner are different. Rather than challenging decisions of the authorities, participants try to persuade government officials to make certain adjustments during the policy implementation stage according to the "concrete situation" or based on a precedent in which other leaders did so. Even if conciliatory appeals are successful, the results of the actions can hardly go beyond the welfare of the participants and their immediate family members. The participants in conciliatory appeals, rather than believing that they have certain rights to make demands on the government, hope that the good will of individual officials can help them. In this sense, conciliatory appealers are more likely to be subjects rather than citizens. Of course, this is only a conceptual distinction developed for analytical purposes. In daily life, people may blend the two strategies in various combinations to pursue their interests. In the analysis of appeals so far, I have combined the two different types together. In the next section, I separate appeals made in a confrontational manner from those made in a conciliatory manner to see if the resources and the processes for people in Beijing to become engaged in these two types are the same.

CONFRONTATIONAL APPEALS

The regression analysis of confrontational appeals in Beijing is presented in Table 7.6. The most important finding of this analysis is that the resources required for people to make confrontational appeals are quite similar to those required for people to get involved in politics in many other societies. Both respondents' socioeconomic status and their psychological involvement in politics are found to increase the likelihood that people in Beijing will make appeals in a confrontational manner.

Respondents' levels of educational achievement can increase the frequency of their appeals, although the relationship between confrontational appeals and education is a curvilinear one. As with voting, the uneducated and the poorly educated are least active. Four years of formal schooling is an important threshold. Once respondents pass that threshold, the frequency of their confrontational appeals increases with increases in their formal schooling. The likelihood that respondents will make confrontational appeals reaches its peak when their educational achievement reaches high school level but declines with further increases in education, although

Table 7.6   Multiple regression of confrontational appeals

Independent variables	Unstandardized coefficients[a]
Reporting issues needing to be resolved[b]	.99***
Education	
1–3 years	.01
4–6 years	.30*
7–9 years	.41***
10–12 years	.53***
13–15 years	.41**
16–17 years	.11
Over 18 years	.22
Talking about political affairs	.10***
Grapevine rumors	.20**
Confidence in own ability to influence *danwei* decisions	.25***
Student status at beginning of the Cultural Revolution[c]	.20**
Opinion on the role of the people in influencing democracy in China	.08**
Ideas on ignoring government policies[d]	.17**

Note: N = 717; constant = 1.06***; adjusted R^2 = .23.

[a]The dependent variable is a composite variable made of two questions. The first question was, "During the past five years, did you and/or your colleagues find any of your work supervisors abusing power?" Respondents answering positively were asked, "Did you often, sometimes, rarely, or never tell him personally that he was wrong?" The second question was, "In the past five years, when certain decisions of your work unit were made regarding salary raises, bonus distributions, dwelling house allotments, and children taking over parents' positions that you considered harmful and unjust, did you often, sometimes, rarely, or never demand equal treatment in front of leaders?" Responses to all the questions were coded according to the highest positive category.

[b]In the survey, I provided different scenarios to respondents and asked their probable behavior in each situation. Some respondents simply told our interviewers that they had not come across the scenarios provided. I created this variable by coding the "not applicable" answer as 0 and the other answers as 1. The data presented in the table represent the behavior of those who reported having come across any of the given scenarios. See Table 7.3 for description of factors not explained below.

[c]Anyone who was a student at the beginning of the Cultural Revolution was coded as 1. Others were coded as 0.

[d]Measured by the question, "Were you going to school when the Cultural Revolution began?" Answers were coded as 1 if yes, 0 if no.

*p < 0.1   **p < 0.05   ***p < 0.01.

college graduates are still more likely to make confrontational appeals than many other people. Access to information and talking about political affairs also make important differences. Those who have access to unofficial information and discuss political affairs are more likely to make confrontational appeals.

Contradicting findings regarding the former USSR, a sense of personal influence in China does increase the likelihood of confrontational appeals. By contrast, in the former Soviet Union "subjective personal influence had no effects on" contacting the authorities, according to Bahry and Silver.[39] They attribute the lack of association between subjective personal influence and contacting to the observation that "people who felt influential had other, less formal ways of getting things done, such as relying on connections to handle problems and complaints."[40] Such an interpretation makes sense only if we believe that contacting leaders in those societies is totally useless for people seeking to articulate their interests, which is apparently not true in China.

One possible reason for such a discrepancy might be associated with the battery used to gauge subjective personal influences in those societies. As I have demonstrated, if the primary way people in Communist China influence governmental decisions is at the policy implementation rather than the policy-making stage, asking respondents to assess the possibility for them to change government policy cannot provide us with adequate information on their feelings of efficacy. Even if a person in Beijing believes he cannot influence government policy formulation, he may still be extremely confident in his ability to influence government decisions at the policy implementation stage through appeals to his *danwei* leaders. For the same reason, a person believing he has no influence on national politics may have a strong belief in his ability to influence politics in his locality or his *danwei*, which are far more relevant to him. In other words, the situation in China is quite different from that in countries where "local competence and national competence, are, as one would expect, fairly closely related."[41]

Local competence and national competence in communist countries may be separate from each other. A person without national competence can have strong feelings of local competence. If that is the case, proper measurement of political efficacy in Chinese society should include not only a battery to measure people's assessments of their ability to influence the decisions of national government, but also a battery to measure people's evaluation of their ability to influence the decisions of government organizations at the grassroots level. The association identified here actually tells us that local competence in China can increase the probability that people will make appeals. Replacing the battery gauging local competence with a battery for national competence would give us the same results revealed in the Soviet Union—that the sense of "personal influence" does not increase appeals.

Respondents' experiences of the Cultural Revolution can significantly increase the likelihood of their confronting government officials. Those who were students at the beginning of the Cultural Revolution are found to be more active in confrontational appeals than other people in the society. The harsh days of the Cultural Revolution made certain people become disillusioned with government officials. Disillusionment can make people lose respect for all officials and turn to fighting for their interests even if that means they have to actually confront authority. Many of them also had the experience of being sent "up to the mountains and down to the villages" to be reeducated by workers, peasants, and soldiers. This experience not only made them tougher and more determined to get what they want, but also provided them with a rich background in terms of dealing with bureaucrats at different levels.[42]

Finally, respondents' evaluation of how government officials should deal with improper policies made by higher authorities is found to be related to confrontational appeals. The stronger the belief that unfair government policies should be ignored by local bureaucrats in the policy implementation process, the more frequently respondents contacted government officials in a confrontational manner, even when the impacts of other variables were controlled.

CONCILIATORY APPEALS

Table 7.7 presents the results of multiple regression analysis of appeals made in a conciliatory manner. Not surprisingly, both the resources required and the processes for people to get involved in conciliatory appeals differ from those necessary for people to engage in confrontational appeals. While the process of engagement in confrontational appeals is somewhat similar to that of politicization in other societies, the resources required for people to get involved in conciliatory appeals are found to be closely associated with the ability of participants to successfully persuade officials to make desired concessions.

Information is clearly a crucial resource for people making conciliatory appeals. Both grapevine rumors and talking about political affairs are found to increase the possibility of appeals. Participants' status in society also makes a significant difference. While major leaders in *danwei* are least active in making conciliatory appeals, midlevel cadres are most active, which leaves ordinary people somewhere in between. The position of the major leaders in *danwei* makes them seldom need to appeal to resolve their prob-

Table 7.7 Multiple regression of conciliatory appeals

Independent variables	Unstandardized coefficients[a]
Reporting issues needing to be resolved	.70***
Job status[b]	
Administrative and managerial personnel	.51***
Noncadres	.34***
Talking about political affairs	.06**
Grapevine rumors	.21***
Ideas on ignoring government policies	.17***

Note: $N = 729$; constant $= 1.07***$; adjusted $R^2 = .13$.

[a] The dependent variable is a composite variable made of two questions. The first question was, "During the past five years, when a policy or regulation of the government that you considered unjust or harmful was enacted, did you often, sometimes, rarely, or never talk about the matter to the leaders in your work unit and persuade them to make a concrete analysis of the conditions and make certain adjustments of the regulations according to concrete conditions?" The second question was, "In the past five years, when certain policies jeopardized your interests, have you ever gone to the leaders of your unit and tried to persuade them to make your case an exception? Do you often, sometimes, from time to time, or never do that?" Responses were coded according to the highest positive category. See Table 7.3 for description of factors not explained below.

[b] The base categories are major leaders (diyibashou) in party, government, or other administrative positions, including party secretaries at factories. The ordinary cadre category includes those who do administrative jobs in party and government organizations but only work at the second level, that is, have bosses supervising them in the same organization in which they are working. All others were coded as ordinary people.

*$p < 0.1$ **$p < 0.05$ ***$p < 0.01$.

lems. Even if they want to make appeals, there is rarely any person or organization for them to appeal to. Taking into consideration the great discretionary power they usually have when implementing government policy and the many resources at their command, their inaction in appeals making can be easily understood.

Although midlevel cadres are also part of the bureaucratic establishment, their position in society is quite different from major leaders. Occupying positions where the state meets society, midlevel cadres in China suffer constant pressure from above and below. While the regime relies on them to carry out decisions made by the government, the masses put constant pressure on them to make necessary adjustments on policy during the implementation stage to protect local interests. Under pressure from both sides, they try to keep a delicate balance to please both in order to survive. Many of them have to mollify government officials at higher levels and appease the masses below them, which often requires making appeals to higher authorities on behalf of their subordinates. Of course, such appeals can only be made in a conciliatory manner. Therefore, their position in society forces them to represent the interests of subordinates to deal with higher authorities.

APPEALS THROUGH THE BUREAUCRATIC HIERARCHY

Appeals through the bureaucratic hierarchy are distinct from contacts with lower-level government officials or *danwei* leaders. Since the channels for such contacts are generally far removed from people's daily lives, it is more difficult for people to locate and access them as compared to contacting work unit leaders. Moreover, while appeals to local government officials are usually made in a conciliatory manner, appeals through the bureaucratic hierarchy usually produce serious conflicts between work unit leaders and local government officials on the one hand and participants on the other. People make complaints through the bureaucratic hierarchy to challenge decisions made by lower-echelon bureaucrats or work unit leaders. Participants try to enlarge the scope of conflict and bring other actors into the game to defeat local bureaucrats. Officials at lower levels do, of course, consider these appeals antagonistic and extremely dangerous to their careers. Many cadres deliberately punish those who dare to make appeals through the bureaucratic hierarchy in order to deter others under their jurisdiction from engaging in such activities in the future. Therefore, appeals through the bureaucratic hierarchy are more difficult, riskier, and likelier to create severe conflicts between participants and bureaucrats.

Analysis of appeals through the bureaucratic hierarchy is presented in Table 7.8. It shows that engagement in such acts does not require traditional socioeconomic resources. Neither education nor income increases the possibility of appeal through the bureaucratic hierarchy. Again, access to information emerges as the crucial resource for people to participate in this type of action. In addition, those who have reasonable confidence in their understanding of local political issues, a stronger sense of personal influence, and greater faith in people as a vehicle for Chinese democracy are also able to push people in Beijing to appeal through the bureaucratic hierarchy.

The analysis also reveals that People's Liberation Army experience can significantly increase the possibility of appeals through the bureaucratic hierarchy. The impact of army experience on people's political participation may be understood with reference to studies of the impact of the modernization process in Third World countries, especially work associated with Alex Inkeles and David Smith. For people living in industrialized nations,

Table 7.8 Multiple regression on complaints through the bureaucratic hierarchy

Independent variables	Unstandardized coefficients[a]
Reporting issues needing to be resolved	.90***
Job status	
Administrative and managerial personnel	.36**
Mass	−.12
Marital status	.20**
CCP membership	.26**
PLA experience[b]	.25***
Talking about political affairs	.08***
Grapevine rumors	.16**
Confidence in own ability to influence *danwei* decisions	.34***
Understanding of important issues of the locality	.14***
Opinion on the role of the people in influencing democracy in China	.09**

Note: $N = 721$; constant $= .53$**; adjusted $R^2 = .23$.

[a]The dependent variable is a composite variable composed of two questions. The first question was, "In the past five years, when certain decisions of your work unit were made regarding salary raises, bonus distributions, dwelling house allotments, and children taking over parents' positions that you considered harmful and unjust, did you often, sometimes, rarely, or never demand equal treatment in front of leaders?" The second question was, "In the past five years, when certain policies jeopardized your interests, have you ever gone to the leaders of your unit and tried to persuade them to make your case an exception? Do you often, sometimes, from time to time, or never do that?" Responses were coded according to the highest positive category. See Table 7.3 for description of factors not explained below.

[b]Measured by the question, "Have you ever been on active duty in military service?" Answers were coded as 1 if yes, 0 if no.

*p < 0.1 **p < 0.05 ***p < 0.01.

school is found to be the major institution providing people with the necessary skills to become involved in politics and socializing them into the participatory culture that will in turn boost their participation. However, studies of the modernization process in Third World countries reveal that when the impacts of other social attributes are controlled, the influence of education on people's political participation breaks down in many developing countries.[43] Nonetheless, other institutions associated with the modernization process in such societies emerge to replace the role of education in determining people's "modernity" in general and level of participation in particular. For example, Inkeles and Smith report that factory experience can make people in developing countries become "modern."[44] This observation raises the possibility that other political institutions may also replace schools to provide people with the necessary skills to participate in politics.

The PLA is one such institution in the PRC. Many people from rural areas are recruited into the army, serve a few years, and are then sent back to their home regions to become local leaders. The PLA pays special attention to providing its members with the skills to deal with complicated bureaucratic procedures. These skills enable PLA veterans to participate in local politics. Some people may argue that military organizations usually emphasize discipline and obeying orders and that such training can become an obstacle to their participation in politics. However, although training to obey rules and discipline in an army can effectively confine interest articulation of members to officially approved channels, it is never designed to prevent them from articulating interests for the people, if not for themselves. Given that one of the most important and "proper" channels for such articulation is making complaints through the bureaucratic hierarchy, it is reasonable to find that army veterans are more likely to do so.

PLA veterans usually enjoy better "political treatment" in their locality than ordinary citizens. They have better access to official documents and listen to more internal reports. Their exposure not only enables them to identify problems with decisions made by local bureaucrats but also provides them with normative power when challenging those decisions. Knowing exactly what government policy is as well as the spirit of that policy, they do not hesitate to enlarge the scope of conflict and try to bring other actors to their aid when they fail in encounters with local bureaucrats. Normative power thus increases their confidence in their chances of success.

The PLA has been trying to create a sense of duty in its members through various educational programs. A good example of such efforts is the "learn from Lei Feng" campaign. Many students of Chinese politics are familiar with one aspect of Lei Feng's spirit—self-sacrifice. But there is a more important dimension of his spirit that requires people to bravely engage in struggles against "evildoers and misdeeds." Lei Feng has been praised for "treating comrades as warmly as spring weather" but also for "treating enemies as ruthlessly as the winds of winter." If integrated into actual behavior, these teachings will push veterans to launch struggles against evildoers rather than stand idly by when facing them.

PLA experiences may also exemplify political efficacy for its members, to borrow Inkeles's phrase.[45] For quite a long time in the history of the PRC, especially during the Cultural Revolution, the PLA was heavily involved in domestic politics. Its members were assigned to local governments as well as functional organizations all over the country to "support the left" (*zhizuo*). Many army officers assumed leadership positions in these organizations. Both involvement in political affairs by the army and calls by Mao for people in China to "learn from" the PLA probably helped create a strong sense of efficacy among its members. Even those who were not personally involved in supporting the left might have found that watching their comrades-in-arms returning from such assignments increased their confidence in their own ability and pride in the organization. The lessons learned from the Cultural Revolution can be extended to other life situations for veterans.[46] Mao's practice of assigning PLA veterans to assume leadership responsibility in civilian organizations after their retirement reinforced the sense of efficacy. Even those not appointed to such positions found their social status in various *danwei* higher than other employees'. Leaders at various levels tended to treat them as "activists" and consult with them on various issues.

Another possible effect of PLA experience is associated with veterans' positions in various organizations in Chinese society. For quite a long time, veterans were considered major candidates for leadership positions in various organizations. Without formal electoral competition in the Chinese political system, contenders learned to attempt to remove competitors from leadership positions by revealing their incompetence and reporting their evildoings to higher authorities. This tactic would show a contender to be concerned about public affairs, capable of identifying local problems, and willing to struggle against evildoing in society. If successful, these reports may have even knocked incumbents out of offices the appealers were competing for.

Conclusion

Analyzing the appeals mode in general and three different forms of appeals specifically demonstrates the diversity and complexity of the political behavior of Chinese citizens. People in Beijing make appeals for various reasons, which can be associated with four major purposes. The first one is to change the impact of government policies on themselves and their families. Appeals for this purpose usually address issues oriented toward instrumental benefits. The second is related to the "mass supervision" of government (*qunzhong jiandu*) as advocated by the CCP. Citizens make appeals to report evil deeds or power abuses of lower-level officials. Both expressive and instrumental benefits can motivate people to make such reports. Some people want higher authorities to overrule the decisions of lower-echelon bureaucrats; others make appeals simply out of a sense of civic obligation to

society. The third goal is to influence the selection of lower-level governmental and work unit leaders. Because the appointment and promotion of
bureaucrats still depends on the evaluation of higher authorities rather than
on electoral competition, making reports of evil deeds or power abuses by
lower-echelon bureaucrats is a major means of political struggle in Chinese
society. Finally, people may use appeals to express their anger. By attacking
targets whom they believe to be the source of their frustration, people are
able to release psychological tensions.

Owing to differences in political structure and institutions, traditional
political resources—as measured by people's socioeconomic status—are
found to have little effect on appeals in Beijing. The deep penetration of
the state into society and the lack of independent sources for many daily
necessities change the function of the state in China from regulator to sole
provider of those resources. Such arrangements make contacting government officials a necessity in people's daily lives. The regime also makes
channels for such contacts immediately accessible to ordinary citizens.
These arrangements fundamentally change the resources required for people in China to make appeals. With contacting government officials a necessity and the cost of engaging in contacts minimal, people do not need
to be interested in politics to make appeals. Instead, the decision to make
appeals in Beijing depends on (1) the ability of participants to temporarily
alter the hierarchical relationship between themselves and involved government officials, (2) predictions of potential gains from the acts, and (3)
their sense of duty to society.

The analysis shows that appeals relate to people's ability to alter the
hierarchical relationship between themselves and government officials. Information on government policies can provide participants with normative
power to defeat bureaucrats. Information is thus one of the most important
political resources available in China. Party members in Beijing have more
access than others to both government officials at higher levels and information on government policies. They are also more active in making appeals than ordinary citizens. People's experiences during the Cultural Revolution, which destroyed the myths of righteousness of political authorities,
and their subsequent experiences of "up to the mountains and down to the
villages," which forced "sent-down youth" to deal with complicated situations in order to return to Beijing, are found to be very important political
resources in China. Certain age groups—those in their late forties and early
fifties—are also more active in appealing than others. The intensive mobilizational efforts of the authorities during their adolescence not only increased their sense of civic duty but also shaped their judgment on the
proper way to articulate their interests. Many of them thus concentrate on

channels approved and encouraged by the authorities to articulate their interests.

The most interesting and puzzling finding in the analysis of appeals again concerns the role of gender. Except for the most important political resource in society—information gathered through grapevine rumors—the resources required for men in Beijing to make appeals are substantially different from those for women. While appeals for men are associated with resources that increase the probability they will acquire desired benefits, appeals for women are more likely to be motivated by their psychological orientation. Such a finding actually suggests that while men are more likely to be motivated by instrumental benefits to make appeals, women are more likely to be motivated by expressive benefits to do so.

More important, the analysis in this chapter demonstrates that when the nature of political acts becomes differentiated, both resources required for people to engage in such activities and the way in which various resources are converted to political acts vary tremendously. Examination of appeals made in a confrontational manner shows that when the benefits of political acts go beyond participants themselves or their immediate families and the scope of outcome of the acts becomes broader, both socioeconomic status and the civic orientation of participants reemerge as crucial political resources. Although education and civic orientation have no impact on the likelihood of appeals in general, people with higher levels of educational achievement, a strong sense of personal influence, and a positive belief in the people's role in Chinese society are more likely to make appeals for issues not directly related to their own families. Moreover, regarding acts with a broad range of outcomes, not only respondents' socioeconomic status and civic orientation reemerge as political resources, but the causal links between these resources and participation are also found to be similar to that found in many other societies. Such a finding demonstrates that different institutional arrangements can alter the resources required for people to participate in politics and the process by which various resources are converted to political actions in Chinese society.

Finally, the analysis tells us that other institutions in Chinese society can replace formal school education to socialize people into the political process. The PLA is one such important agent used by the regime. The PLA experience not only provides people with knowledge about how to deal with bureaucratic procedures but also creates a sense of civic duty and efficacy in its members. The government's time-honored practice of promoting veterans to leadership positions tends to boost their political ambition and encourage them to erode the power base of the incumbent leadership by reporting misconduct to higher authorities in order to increase their chances of replacing existing leaders. The channels provided by the regime for people to articulate their own interests and for the authorities to monitor lower-level bureaucrats could subsequently be transformed into a battlefield for actual power struggles and used by PLA veterans to further their own political ambitions.

8

Adversarial Activities, Resistance, and Cronyism

In this chapter, I analyze the remaining three participatory modes in Beijing. As it turns out, the attitudes of the regime in the abstract sense and those of individual government officials toward people's engagement in acts belonging to these modes usually contradict each other. For example, people's engagement in adversarial activities is encouraged by the regime but strongly opposed by participants' supervisors or lower-echelon government officials. Cronyism, by contrast, is strongly opposed by the regime but tolerated and sometimes even encouraged by individual officials. Acts of resistance are strongly opposed by both the authorities and individual government officials at the present time, although using those acts to express personal opinions had been encouraged by radical leaders of the CCP in the past. How do the attitudes of the authorities toward these participatory modes shape people's behavior? Who chooses to engage in them? Why do they choose these activities? Do they engage in these political acts to articulate their interests or to protest? What resources are required for people to engage in them? Are the resources required for people to engage in these political acts the same as those required for people to engage in political activities studied previously? Examining these issues will definitely increase our understanding of political dynamics in Beijing, especially the impact of institutional arrangements on people's political behavior.

Adversarial Activities

The mode of adversarial activities includes four participatory acts—writing to government officials, writing to newspaper editors, reporting to complaint bureaus, and seeking audiences with higher authorities. These channels of communication have been established by the regime to gather information on popular responses to government policies and to monitor the behavior of lower-echelon bureaucrats. Such a design requires the regime per se to encourage citizens in China to utilize these channels to report "unhealthy tendencies" to the authorities.

But the regime is made of people. It is because the regime uses these channels to control its own people—bureaucrats—that citizen's engagement in this participatory mode can and sometimes does lead to certain unhappy and even serious consequences for bureaucrats at grassroots levels. As a result, lower-echelon bureaucrats generally have extremely antagonistic attitudes toward people's engagement in these political acts. Few would hesitate to punish those who challenge their authority. Although the most important political resource urban residents in China have to defend themselves against arbitrary retribution of local bureaucrats—the lifetime employment system—provides participants with a certain kind of protection against unauthorized retaliation of local officials, by forbidding officials from firing participants from their organizations, the system at the same time gives bureaucrats the power to block the way for dissatisfied people to "exit" from their organization and escape unauthorized retaliation, by transferring to another organization or quitting their job if they so desire. At the time of this survey, resigning from a job still entailed the consent of work unit leaders.

Bureaucrats in China prefer keeping challengers under their control to getting rid of them. Most bureaucrats know that allowing such participants to quit will hurt their interests. If they allow their challengers to quit without being punished, not only other power contenders in the same organization but also those who simply want to leave the job will follow the precedent of challenging their authority, and the situation in the organization will quickly get out of their control. Thus, lower-echelon bureaucrats in China commonly deal with their challengers by keeping them in the organization and gradually "broiling" (kao) them, that is, maltreating them, to demonstrate to other people how serious the consequences of challenging their authority could be. Given the possibility of being punished for engagement in such political activities, why do people in Beijing still do so? What are the motivations of participants in Beijing when they decide to engage in these political acts? And what resources are required for people to defend themselves against unauthorized retaliation and get involved in these political activities?

Although bureaucrats in China usually do not hesitate to punish those who dare to engage in these political activities, punishment is never authorized by the regime. The regime actually encourages people to utilize these channels of communication to report the wrongdoings of bureaucrats to the authorities. The regime considers most participants responsible citizens following the proper organizational principle and procedures to express their opinions to the authorities. They are fulfilling their civic duty to society. The attitude of the regime provides participants with normative grounds to sustain their engagement in these political acts. Facing the possibility of unauthorized retaliation, some people may focus on the regime's attitude and ignore the danger of unauthorized retaliation by local bureaucrats. In other words, the discrepancy between the attitude of the regime per se and the actions of individual government officials provides participants with important "breathing space." Rather than simply preventing people from engaging in adversarial activities, unauthorized retaliation presents risks that shape people's behavior in the following ways.

First, the risks associated with adversarial activities and the attitudes of local bureaucrats toward participants tend to confine the goals participants pursue through these political actions. Given the risks, participants will not choose these acts for issues unrelated to their own interests. This is not to suggest that people won't choose adversarial acts to pursue interests beyond those of themselves and their immediate family members. Some people do so, even for expressive benefits. But these benefits must be closely related to certain instrumental benefits deemed important for participants and their immediate family members for people to engage in adversarial activities. Moreover, unless a person has exhausted other political acts in trying to resolve the problem, he or she is unlikely to choose adversarial activities.

Second, the discrepancy in the attitudes of the authorities toward adversarial activities determines who tends to choose these acts to pursue their own interests. Two groups of people are the most likely candidates of adversarial activities in Beijing. The first group are the young, who have less experience in society (shehui jingyan). The possible unauthorized retaliation of government officials against participants in these acts can never be learned in school. People learn this social reality only from their personal experiences and observations of the experiences of other people. Youngsters with little life experience tend to naively believe what the regime wants them to know, which is usually far removed from the political realities of society. Without realizing there are substantial dangers associated with these political acts, or hoping the authorities will come to their aid if local bureaucrats dare to make unauthorized retaliation for their engagement in political acts encouraged by the authorities, youngsters face expected costs quite different from those facing other people. The second group are people having little to lose even if bureaucrats take revenge against them. There are two potential candidates for people in this category.

This group includes those who have bad class-origin labels and those who have been purged politically in the past.

From 1949 to 1979, a person's worth and trustworthiness in China were "measured . . . by the yardstick of class origin."[1] Those from bad class origins were systematically discriminated against in job assignments, school admissions, promotions, and so on. Few, if any, people in China would want even to marry people with bad class origins because these labels would automatically be transferred to their children.[2] Although this notorious *chushen* system was formally abolished in 1981, a long history of systematic discrimination makes the condition of people with bad class origins worse than others.

Similarly ostracized are those considered to have "historical" or other political problems. Starting in 1949, the CCP launched numerous political campaigns in which people with certain backgrounds were labeled as having political problems. Some of them were discriminated against, others were sent to rural areas to be reeducated by peasants, and still others were sent to labor camps. They were purged mercilessly by the regime. Although most of them were rehabilitated after 1979 and some have even received monetary compensation from the regime, there could hardly be sufficient compensation for their lost opportunities. The housing conditions, salary, administrative rankings, and technical or professional titles of many of them still rank below those of other people in the same age group with the same level of education and seniority.

Since their rehabilitation, most of the people in these two groups have had to stay in the original *danwei*, where the officials responsible for their miserable past are not only still in charge of but also responsible for "implementing the rehabilitation policy of the party and the government." Although they had no choice but to implement government policy to rehabilitate those whom they had purged years before, most officials still believe their decisions to purge their victims were basically correct. Under their direction, rehabilitation can hardly be satisfactory to those previously purged. To make things even worse, many officials continually discriminate against their victims. Facing these unsolved problems and continued discrimination by their persecutors, people in this category are eager to seek faithful implementation of party policies (*luoshi zhengce*) to change the status quo.

Logically, such experiences should lead to two possible attitudes toward the existing political order in general and the risks associated with political acts in particular. Having been politically purged would alienate people from the regime. Some might feel that no political act could bring any desired benefits to them until the regime is overthrown. Others, knowing how helpless a citizen could be in front of the state apparatus, might be reluctant to offend government officials any further. In either case, previously purged individuals should be unlikely participants in adversarial activities.

However, political purges may have impacts on people's political behavior unlike those anticipated. Having been mistreated and deprived of all benefits they are entitled to, the previously purged can become even more determined than other people in the society to pursue their legitimate interests. Moreover, having experienced the worst days of their lives, they might conclude that there is no difficulty they cannot cope with and they have little to fear. As suggested in a Chinese proverb, "dead pigs are never afraid of being scalded by boiling water" (sizhu bupa kaishuitang). Thus, their ability to sustain political risks in pursuing their goals is actually higher than that of others in the society for the following reasons. (1) Compared to other people, the previously purged have less to lose and more to gain from adversarial activities. Already at the bottom of society and their own danwei, they face limited punishments from bureaucrats. Retaliation of lower-echelon bureaucrats cannot bring them more pain than what they have already suffered. However, if they succeed in persuading a higher authority to intervene on their behalf, their situation can change dramatically. (2) Their resentment of bureaucrats responsible for their miserable past adds other incentives to their engagement in adversarial activities—possible revenge against those officials responsible for their purges. Even if officials at higher levels refuse to come to their aid regarding the specific issues they are agitating for, adversarial activities may still bring them the important benefit of eroding the image of the officials involved. (3) Political skills learned during the period when they were purged may help them deal with complicated situations and reduce risks associated with adversarial activities. Thus, survival techniques acquired in the past may help them defeat unauthorized retaliation by local bureaucrats.

Since participants in adversarial activities rely on the regime in an abstract sense to defend themselves against possible unauthorized retaliation by lower-echelon bureaucrats, people's psychological orientation, especially their attitudes toward the political authorities, should play an important role in making people choose adversarial activities to express their opinions. Even if people know they will suffer unauthorized retaliation by local bureaucrats, those who expect the regime to come to their aid and those who believe that "justice will prevail eventually" would be more likely to engage in these acts as compared to people without such expectations. Specifically, I expect three sets of psychological variables to influence people's decisions to engage in adversarial activities to pursue their interests:

knowledge of the impact of the government on their daily lives (the "knowledge of government output"),[3] awareness and exposure to government policies ("output cognition"),[4] and a sense of political efficacy.

Given the differences between the political process in China and elsewhere, especially the distinction between high politics and low politics, we should be sensitive to the impact of such distinctions on the cognitive map of Chinese citizens.[5] Although people cannot influence decisions made by the central government, or high-politics issues, many of them can exert effective influences over low-politics issues, or decisions made by local government officials. As the structural arrangement in Chinese society separates low and high politics, the psychological orientation of citizens in society may reflect this structural arrangement and also be divided along such lines.

We should be able to differentiate people's knowledge of the impacts of government policies along the lines of high and low politics. Since adversarial activities are primarily aimed at influencing decisions made by government organizations at the grassroots level, participants' knowledge of the impact of local government on their lives may be an important resource for people in Beijing who engage in these political activities, while knowledge of the impact of the central government becomes not so important, or even irrelevant.

Although we may not be able to differentiate people's exposure to government policies in China along the lines of high and low politics, we do need to use different instruments to measure output cognition in Chinese society. People's exposure to government policies is usually measured by respondents' access to the news media elsewhere.[6] However, since the media in China is controlled by the government and its major function is still "cheerleading" for the CCP, those who follow accounts of politics through these channels can get only information that the government wants them to know. Those people are more likely to be "communist subjects" than independent citizens in Chinese society. Instead, those who understand the political dynamics in Chinese society and those who really want to get information on government policy outputs manage to acquire such information from unofficial channels. Thus, output cognition in China should be measured by people's access to unofficial rather than official channels of information in Chinese society.

"Political efficacy is the feeling . . . that a person believes that he can influence government officials or public issues."[7] Such a feeling is usually seen as having two dimensions—one is internal and the other external. Internal efficacy refers to "beliefs about one's own competence to understand and to participate effectively in politics." External efficacy refers to beliefs about the responsiveness of governmental authorities and institutions to citizen demands.[8] The structural arrangement and the political process in the PRC may create an additional dimension of efficacious feeling in Chinese society. Political efficacy in China may also be divided along the lines of high and low politics and be differentiated by central and local efficacy. Those who do not think they have the ability to influence the decisions of the central government in China may be confident in their ability to influence the decisions of local government officials and *danwei* leaders. I expect those who are confident in their ability to get involved in local politics and those who believe that local government officials are responsive to people's requests to be more active in adversarial activities.

Table 8.1 presents the regression analysis of adversarial activities in Beijing. As expected, the analysis shows that participants' psychological orientation plays an important role in prompting people to engage in adversarial activities to express their opinion in Beijing. Those who believe local government has great influence on their lives, those who actively gather information on government policies from unofficial channels, and those who are confident in their ability to understand local politics are found to be more active in adversarial activities. Contrary to my expectations, external efficacy does not increase the possibility that people will engage in adversarial activities. During the process of data manipulation, I put several variables measuring both the central and local external efficacy of respondents in the equation. None of them yielded any effects on the probability of adversarial activities.

The finding that external efficacy does not increase the probability of adversarial activities suggests that the major goal of participants might be punishing bureaucrats they dislike. As the goal changes from acquiring specific benefits from the government to damaging the image of local government officials in the eyes of higher authorities, the expected responsiveness of the political authorities toward people's requests will become relatively unimportant in shaping their decisions to get involved in such activities. As long as complaints can reach officials at higher levels, the major goals of participants will have been achieved.

Workers are found to be less active than people in other professions in their engagement in adversarial activities. Four possible reasons can be offered to explain this finding. First, workers in enterprises usually need to meet "hard" production quotas. But managers can easily manipulate quotas to punish workers they don't like. For example, management can assign workers more difficult jobs and require them to meet the original production quota. Although all employees know what management is doing, it is hard for anyone in an organization to prove that bureaucrats are actually

Table 8.1   Multiple regression on adversarial appeals

Independent variables	Unstandardized coefficients[a]
Sex[b]	−.16**
Occupation[c]	−.28***
Evaluation of influences of local government[d]	.13**
Grapevine rumors	.31***
Understanding of important issues of the locality[e]	.11**
Membership in voluntary associations[f]	.44***
History of political problems[g]	−.63***
Living conditions as compared to others[h]	.04
Relationship with colleagues[i]	−.06
Interaction term[j]	.13***

Note: $N = 665$; constant $= -1.05$; adjusted $R^2 = .11$.

[a] The dependent variable is the principal component transformation of the four participatory variables that belong to this mode.

[b] Coded as 1 if male, 0 if female.

[c] Coded as 1 if worker, 0 if member of other occupation.

[d] Measured by the question, "Let's now discuss the local government. How much effect do you think its activities have on your day-to-day life? Do they have a great effect, some effect, or none?" Answers were coded from 1 (none) to 3 (great effect).

[e] Answers were coded from 1 (understand not at all) to 4 (understand quite well).

[f] Measured by the question, "Are you a member of any social organization?" Answers were coded as 1 if not a member of any social organization, 2 if an ordinary member, and 3 if a cadre of such an organization.

[g] This is a composite variable. Any positive answers to one of the following questions were coded as 1; negative responses were coded as 0. "Have you ever been investigated, criticized, or denounced at a public meeting? Toppled from your position? Searched? Has any property been confiscated? Have you ever been sentenced to reform through labor?"

[h] Measured by the question, "Compared to houses/apartments in the city, would you say your house was far above average, above average, average, below average, or far below average?" Answers were coded from 1 (far above average) to 5 (far below average).

[i] Measured by the question, "How well do you get along with your fellow workers/other people in your neighborhood? Do you have very pleasant relations with them, a somewhat pleasant relationship with them, an ordinary relationship with them, relatively bad relationships with them, or very bad relationships with them?" Answers were coded from 1 (very unpleasant) to 5 (very pleasant).

[j] This term is created by the multiplication of three variables: respondent's history of political problems, housing situation, and relationship with colleagues.

*$p < 0.1$ **$p < 0.05$ ***$p < 0.01$.

engaging in unauthorized retaliation against victims. Such behavior is described as "making someone wear small shoes" *(chuan xiaoxie).* It is true that similar kinds of punishment can occur in other organizations in Chinese society. However, without a production standard, leaders in other organizations have a harder time covering up their behavior if they take revenge against their subordinates. Compared to employees in other organizations, workers in China have more difficulty protecting themselves against unauthorized retaliation owing to the nature of their job.

Second, recent reforms in the Chinese factory, especially *youhuazuhe,* which gave management the power of hiring and firing, deprived workers of their lifetime employment guarantee, their best defense against unauthorized retaliation from local bureaucrats. Workers have become extremely vulnerable to management. Although they can now "exit" from enterprises to escape retaliation from local bureaucrats, without a developed labor market, they are forced to join the "industrial reserve army" and suffer the consequences.

Third, the introduction of the "factory manager responsibility system" also provides managers with important and useful weapons to defend themselves against intervention by government officials in their decisions. The responsibility system not only specifies how much in profits enterprise management is responsible for each year but also provides management with autonomy to make decisions on *danwei* affairs. Under the responsibility system, if certain government officials want to intervene in the decisions of management on behalf of workers, management can easily defend its decisions by arguing they are necessary for meeting the production quotas established by the authorities. If any official insists on challenging a manager's decision, the manager will usually threaten to shift the burden of meeting the production quota to the official. Such a strategy is extremely useful in preventing outsiders from intervening in decisions made by management since outside officials are not in a position to take responsibility for production. Even if a worker can successfully drag high-level officials into the conflict and make them intervene on his behalf, such threats can easily make government officials withdraw their intervention. When workers learn that they cannot rely on officials to defend themselves against unauthorized retaliation by local bureaucrats (because of the introduction of the responsibility system), they doubtless refrain from choosing these acts to express their opinions.

The fourth reason has to do with a well-established theme—working-class authoritarianism.[9] Studies of the behavior of the working class have revealed that "low education, . . . little reading, isolated occupations, economic insecurity, and authoritarian family patterns" are some of the most important elements shaping working-class authoritarianism.[10] According to Genevieve Knupfer, having an "economic underprivilege is psychological underprivilege: habits of submission, little access to sources of information, lack of verbal facility . . . appear to produce a lack of self-confidence which increases the unwillingness of the low-status person to participate in many phases of our predominantly middle-class culture."[11] Because they are less educated and ill informed about political affairs, workers are found to be less tolerant than employees in other occupations.[12]

Institutional arrangements in Chinese society reinforce the intolerance of the working class. As Andrew Walder points out, "China's factories are especially prone to factionalism within the official clientelist network: whenever factory officials are seriously at odds with one another, they may head separate personal followings and engage in what . . . may border on open conflict."[13] Antagonisms between two distinctive groups in the work force thus become a normal phenomenon in Chinese enterprises. The polarization of the shop floor in Chinese enterprises makes the political dynamic there resemble a tight bipolar system in international relations. There is usually a clear tendency for both sides to punish "immoral neutralists."[14] Since neither faction tolerates these neutralists, workers are forced to line up with one faction or another. As all workers become affiliated with one faction or another, those who dare to challenge a particular leader in the organization are seen by people affiliated with that leader as threatening their welfare, an offense that must be answered forcefully. Thus, challengers in Chinese enterprises are usually humiliated, harassed, or even physically attacked by people from other factions.[15] Although such a behavior pattern can also be found in other Chinese organizations, the attacks launched by intolerant workers are generally much more humiliating, more harmful, and even more violent. Given the widespread "vertical ties which divide the work force socially and politically," further accelerating the authoritarianism of the working class in China, "deviant" behavior in such an environment is usually more costly for participants.

In most societies, men are more active than women in unconventional, elite-challenging political activities.[16] Scholars have been debating whether "men are innately more aggressive than are women" or "simply more likely to be socialized into adopting aggressive roles and a more belligerent outlook," which make them more active in protest political actions.[17] Unlike the situation in other societies, women in Beijing are found to be more active than men in adversarial activities. I attribute this "deviation" to the impacts of regime socialization. As revealed in the analysis of voting behavior in China, women tend to believe statements made by the authorities, even if the statements contradict the political reality in the society. Such a tendency would make women in China more likely to follow the directions from the authorities to vote in elections and to follow directions to report wrongdoing by bureaucrats. It would also make women more confident that the authorities would come to their aid if any officials dared to punish them for their engagement in acts encouraged by the authorities. In other words, the tendency to believe the promises made by the authorities can greatly reduce the perceived costs associated with adversarial activities and increase the desire to comply with the perceived wishes of the regime.

The relationship between membership in voluntary associations and political activism is not new to students of political participation.[18] Political parties and voluntary associations are believed to be able to "mobilize citizens to a level of activity above that which would be predicted by their socioeconomic resource level," and institutions are seen to "inhibit political activity so that it is at a level below that which one would predict on the basis of socioeconomic characteristics."[19] So far, I have not found any significant relationship between organizational membership and any other political act in Beijing. Why does associational membership increase the probability that people will get involved in adversarial activities, but not in other modes of participation?

When trying to explain the relationship between membership in voluntary associations and adversarial activities in Beijing, we should keep in mind important differences between the political process in China and those elsewhere. In different political processes the same relationship may represent a totally different political dynamic. The logic structure of the relationship between membership in voluntary associations and adversarial activities in China is quite different from the relationship between associational membership and the level of participation in other societies for the following reasons. First, voluntary associations in China have different functions from those in other societies. As Townsend notes, "the distinction between state organs and nongovernmental organizations in China is not the same as that between 'public' and 'private' government in the West. There is no 'private' government in China, in any real sense, as all nongovernmental organizations perform some 'public' functions and are controlled, in varying degrees, by the state and Party hierarchy . . . [they are] the primary mechanism for transmitting Party policies to the people and mobilizing them for the execution of those policies."[20] Although it becomes harder and harder for the regime to use "voluntary" organizations to mobilize people to carry out its predetermined goals, the CCP still tries to use them as a transmission belt to control society. Such a system design leaves members of voluntary associations in China better informed about government policies. As repeatedly demonstrated throughout this book, knowledge of government policy is one of the most important political resources in Communist China.

Second, since the regime intends to use these voluntary associations to control its own people, the authorities are still heavily involved in various activities of these organizations. Party and government officials regularly visit the associations and receive their members. This practice provides members of the associations with additional opportunities to access officials at higher levels and even to establish personal contacts with them. Although no one wants to use such contacts for minor issues, few would hesitate to contact officials at higher levels and persuade them to intervene on their behalf if local government officials launched unauthorized retaliation against them. Knowing members of associations have the ability to enlarge the scope of conflicts and drag other actors in to change the balance of power to defeat them, bureaucrats at lower levels are usually reluctant to retaliate against them. With such important political resources in their hands, these people may perceive substantially lower risks in adversarial activities than ordinary people in the society do.

Third, although voluntary associations are still under the control of the CCP, special organizational interests deviating from those of the regime can develop. When members of these associations come into conflict with officials in their own organization, leaders of the associations may be prompted by organizational interests to intervene on behalf of their members. Most leaders of voluntary associations are appointed by the government; in fact, they are often retired government officials. Many of them bear administrative grades higher than those of officials at the grassroots level. The intervention of those leaders can deter bureaucrats from retaliating against members of their organizations for participating in adversarial activities. Knowing that intervention by association leaders can prevent local bureaucrats from retaliating against them for challenging the authorities, members of associational groups further downplay the risks associated with these political activities.

Contrary to my expectations, the family origin (*chushen*) of participants does not have any significant impact on the probability of adversarial activities.[21] As expected, people's political history is found to have a significant impact on their involvement in adversarial activities although the effects of such experience on people's political behavior are much more complicated than I had predicted. In and of itself, the experience of being purged politically reduces the likelihood that people in Beijing will choose adversarial activities to articulate their interests. Further data manipulation reveals that the impact of political purges is heavily influenced by the current economic situation of those purged. In fact, I found that the behavior patterns of previously purged people can be divided into two categories. The first category is for those who were purged but fully rehabilitated in the early 1980s. They resumed their salary, prestige, and even status in the society. People belonging to this category now have vested interests to protect. Preoccupied with preserving the status quo, they tend to keep away from dangerous adversarial activities and avoid antagonizing bureaucrats.

However, not every previously purged person has been fully rehabilitated. The calculations of those in this second category, who have been purged but whose current economic conditions are still inferior to others', are fundamentally different from those in the first. Although people's economic situation does not have any independent effect on their decision to engage in adversarial activities to express their opinions, and although the experience of having been purged has a negative effect, the joint effects of these two factors reverse the trend and increase the probability that people will choose adversarial activities to pursue their interests. Already at the bottom of society, people in the second category have little to lose even if local bureaucrats decide to retaliate against them for their engagement in adversarial activities, but they can have substantial potential gains if they can defeat those officials.

Resistance

Scholars have found that participation in most societies "springs from two fundamentally different processes, one being an older elite-directed mode of political participation, the other a newer elite-challenging mode."[22] While elite-directed modes of participation take place within the framework of the established political order, elite-challenging acts take place outside the established order. Different from elite-directed political activities, elite-challenging modes of political participation are usually issue-oriented and issue-specific. Resistance in China includes three participatory acts—slowing down on the job, whipping up public opinion against leaders, and organizing groups of people to fight against leaders. These acts are clearly elite-challenging political activities.

The attitudes of the regime toward people's engagement in these elite-challenging political activities have changed over time. During the Cultural Revolution, these political acts were considered legitimate ways for people to fight against a corrupted bureaucracy. Radical leaders in the CCP even openly advocated that people use these political acts to fight against capitalist roaders. When Deng Xiaoping resumed power after the Cultural Revolution, however, these political activities became the "pernicious vestige" of the Gang of Four (the Politburo members who led the ultraleft faction of the CCP during the Cultural Revolution), and engagement in them was explicitly prohibited by the authorities. Given the attitudes of the current political authorities toward political acts included in resistance, why do some people still choose to engage in such acts?

Study of elite-challenging or unconventional political behavior is guided primarily by variation in the deprivation and the resource models. The deprivation model alleges that people's engagement in elite-challenging political acts is based on feelings of frustration and dissatisfaction. Frustration is defined as an interference with goal-directed behavior. The existence of frustration usually leads to some form of aggression. When people's discontent and frustration is politicized, unconventional and even violent political action often follows.[23] Although this model denies that the "revolutionaries or conspirators are deviants, fools, or maladjusted," it does imply that people's involvement in elite-challenging political acts is irrational and deviant political behavior.[24]

The resource model, by contrast, treats unconventional political activities as an alternative political resource by which people pursue their goals through challenges to the political establishment.[25] Instead of viewing people's engagement in unconventional political acts as emotional outcries of frustration or as "irrational deviant acts," this tradition sees people's engagement in elite-challenging political activities as a normal part of the political process in a society.[26]

Although the data do not allow me to rigorously test these two models, several hypotheses can be developed to explore whether the deprivation or the resource model can better explain resistance in Beijing. According to the deprivation model, dissatisfaction and alienation should be major predictors of people's engagement in unconventional political activities. If this model is correct, we would expect people of lower socioeconomic status to be more likely to engage in elite-challenging political activities to express their opinions. Lacking communication skills and the ability to understand complicated issues, people in this group tend to "view politics as black and white, good and evil."[27] Lacking imagination, they usually have difficulties in abstracting from past experience.[28] The psychological disposition of lower-status people also makes them seek easy solutions to social and political problems facing them. Since easy solutions rarely exist, people from lower strata are more likely to be alienated and choose elite-challenging political activities to express their opinions. "This theory suggests that unconventional political activity should be more common among lower-status individuals, minorities, and other groups who have reasons to feel deprived or dissatisfied."[29]

The resource model assumes that participants in elite-challenging political activities are pursuing certain specific goals rather than merely expressing frustration. Elite-challenging or unconventional political acts in this tradition are simply another means for people to participate in politics.

If this model is correct, we should be able to find, first of all, that efficacious feelings rather than simple frustration and alienation make people participate in elite-challenging political activities.[30] The relationship between socioeconomic status and elite-challenging political activities should also be reversed from that predicted by the deprivation model. Since participants in elite-challenging political acts are pursuing specific goals, various resources, such as an understanding of political processes in the society, information on government policy output, and communication and organizational skills, are required to facilitate their participation. These resources, of course, usually belong to higher-status people. "The phenomenon of protest amidst affluence has become well-known" in liberal democracies.[31] If the resource model is correct, we should also be able to find that higher-status people in Beijing are more likely to get involved in elite-challenging political activities. Finally, since the model holds that the elite-challenging mode is another way for people to express their opinions, people perceiving important differences between their own goals and those pursued by elites in power and expecting that such differences cannot be resolved through existing channels of communication should choose elite-challenging political acts to pursue their goals. The model actually expects that "an individual's value priorities play a crucial role in determining whether or not one engages in unconventional political activities."[32]

Examination of historical records of elite-challenging political acts in Beijing after 1979 reveals evidence supporting both models. On the one hand, nearly every salient protest that occurred in Beijing from the Democracy Wall Movement in 1979 to the democracy movements of 1989 was dominated by students in schools of higher education. The value priority of those participants clearly differs from that of elites, and such differences can hardly be resolved through existing channels of communication. On the other hand, the observation that upper-socioeconomic-status people are more active in elite-challenging political activities is true only for certain kinds of elite-challenging political activities but not others. There is also evidence that lower-status people in Beijing are more active in certain other elite-challenging political activities. For example, bus drivers and ticket sellers of the public transportation system in Beijing dominated a large-scale slowdown, or latent strike, in 1984.

Table 8.2 presents a multiple regression analysis on resistance in Beijing. The findings revealed in the equation can be summarized as follows. Respondents' status, as measured by education, economic status, or occupation, is found to have no impact on the probability of elite-challenging political activities. In the process of data manipulation, I tried every pos-

Table 8.2   Multiple regression on resistance

Independent variables	Unstandardized coefficients[a]
Age	− .01***
Grapevine discussion[b]	.11***
Attitudes toward the Gang of Four[c]	.34***
Mother's occupation[d]	.57***
Father's education[e]	− .02**

Note: $N = 641$; constant $= 1.05$; adjusted $R^2 = .10$.

[a]The dependent variable is the principal component transformation of the four participatory variables belonging to this mode.

[b]Measured by the question, "How often do you talk about unofficial news concerning the political, social, and economic situation in our country with other people? Do you do that nearly every day, a few times a week, about once a week, from time to time, or never?" Answers were coded from 1 (never) to 5 (nearly every day).

[c]Measured by the question, "There are always some people whose ideas are considered bad or dangerous by other people, for instance, those sympathetic to the policies of the Gang of Four. If some writers want to publish a book on this subject, would you allow their book to be published?" Answers were coded 0 if not allowed, 1 if allowed.

[d]Coded as 1 if white-collar office worker, 0 if member of other occupation.

[e]By years of formal schooling.

*p < 0.1   **p < 0.05   ***p < 0.01.

sible combination of socioeconomic variable and status respondents' *danwei* in the equation and none of them either increased or decreased the probability that people would get involved in this particular participatory mode.

Although the traditional measurement of people's status does not have any impact on the likelihood that people in Beijing will get involved in resistance, respondents' father's education was found to be negatively related to this elite-challenging mode of participation. A father's educational achievement can have significant impacts on his children's value priorities and their attitudes toward political authorities. The policy of the regime to systemically discriminate against children from educated families would reinforce such an impact. From 1949 through the late 1970s, the regime systematically discriminated against children from educated families in Communist China. Few of them could acquire a decent job, let alone any promotion. During the early period of the Cultural Revolution, children from educated families were barred from getting a high school education, not to mention going to college. As already mentioned, most of them were sent to the villages to be reeducated by peasants. The systematic discrimination against children from educated families cruelly deprived them of the opportunity to receive a proper education. Under the influence of Chinese culture, people with such family backgrounds usually value education above all else. Such a policy must have had a devastating impact on their psychological disposition toward the regime. Even if they can forgive the regime for their physical suffering in the past, few of them can pardon the authorities for depriving them of educational opportunities. As their value priorities are usually substantially different from those pursued by elites in power, children from educated families tend to choose elite-challenging political acts to express their opinions.

The analysis also reveals that children of female white-collar office workers are more active in resistance than other people. The nature of office jobs gives white-collar employees access to various pieces of information on government policies and even encourages them to establish personal contacts with officials at higher levels. Both information and personal contacts are important resources in China for people to participate in politics. While information on government policies can provide participants with normative power in their dealings with bureaucrats, personal contacts with government officials enable participants to borrow power from them to defend themselves against unauthorized retaliation by local bureaucrats. Under the current social structure in China, resources possessed by one generation can be transferred to another generation. Since most people in urban China still live in extended families, resource transfer between generations is relatively easy and usually occurs naturally. For example, if a child suffers from unauthorized retaliation by bureaucrats for their engagement in certain political acts, other family members would come to the child's aid if possible. This scenario would change the cost-benefit calculation of children from resourceful families when making decisions on whether to engage in such risky political activities.

The remaining difficulty with this argument is why children of white-collar mothers, but not the children of white-collar fathers, are more likely to engage in resistance than other people. Specifically, why are resources possessed by mothers more easily transferred to children than those possessed by fathers? I believe the pattern of relationships in the Chinese family can help us explain this phenomenon. As William Parish and Martin Whyte note, children in China are usually "distant from, and even somewhat fearful of, their fathers."[33] Although their relationship with their fathers can relax somewhat as children mature, these relationships "never become really close."[34] The lack of an intimate relationship with their children enables fathers to stick to the principles advocated by the authorities and prevents them from compromising principles for their children.

Unlike their relationship with their fathers, children's relationship with their mothers is intimate and close. This connection makes it more difficult for mothers in China to resist the temptation to offer their children desired help when necessary. When children are in danger, instinctively mothers mobilize all the resources they have to rescue their children. While lack of communication between fathers and children in China blocks the way for fathers to transfer their resources to their children, the intimate relationship between mothers and children in China facilitates such a transformation of political resources within the family.

Moreover, as in other societies, age is negatively correlated with resistance in Beijing. Students of political participation usually attribute the impacts of age on people's political behavior either to life-cycle effects or generational effects. The life-cycle effect model has two variations. One explanation attributes the activeness of younger people in elite-challenging political activities to their physical energy. According to Alan Marsh and Max Kaase, young people "enjoy the physical vigor, the freedom from day-to-day responsibilities of career and family."[35] These physical characteristics push them to pursue "the energetic kinds of political activities implied by a high protest potential."[36] The other explanation emphasizes the effect of psychological orientation and holds that youngsters are "*naturally* vulnerable to strong and purist kinds of ideological motivation."[37] With little experience in society, young people derive their expectations about the political only from the socialization efforts of the regime. Indoctrination provides them with an idealized picture of the system, which is usually quite different from actual social reality. When noticing any "unhealthy tendency" in the society, these newcomers to the system, full of illusions created by the regime, carry out the civic duty imposed on them by the authorities to fight against it. As soon as they try to transfer what they have learned from books to political acts, however, they quickly realize the gap between the picture drawn by regime propaganda and the actual political reality in society. For example, when they try to fight power abusers, they elicit reprisals from those in power. Young people might follow the proper procedures to report such events to higher authorities and expect them to intervene on their behalf. Unfortunately, such moves will not bring the desired intervention of higher authorities. Even if the authorities decide to intervene, the results may not be satisfactory. "Seen from the point of view of the adolescents—especially when that view is sharpened by the vivid and uncompromising clarity that is given all of us at that age and so cruelly taken away somewhere around our twenty-first birthday—the normal channels of political communication are moss-strewn with elderly compromise."[38] When realizing the huge gap between their own expectations about the performance of the political community created by the socialization efforts of the regime and the political realities in the society, young people grow to resent the existing political institutions. Naturally, they will challenge them.[39]

The generational effect model, in contrast, attributes the relationship between age and unconventional political acts to the intergenerational shift of basic value priorities. Younger generations usually have different experiences in their formative years from those of older generations. As Ronald Inglehart and Hans Klingemann explain, "there are certain basic orientations, developed during one's pre-adult years, which tend to persist through later life."[40] Different generations in China have totally different experiences during different stages of their lives. Unlike people in their sixties and seventies, people in their fifties did not experience foreign invasion, soaring inflation, and civil war. People in their twenties and some in their thirties can hardly have any experiences of intensive political indoctrination, not to mention of the Cultural Revolution. The spread of modern communication, the dramatic reduction of the ability of the CCP to control people's private lives, and the economic and political reforms carried out after 1979 must have had significant impacts on the value priorities of the younger generation. Different from life-cycle effects, these basic value orientations do not change with age. Once acquired, such orientations continually influence people's behavior over their entire lives.

Influenced by ideas of liberty and democracy, the younger generation in China gives higher priority to self-expression and independence. As its basic value orientation and value priorities are fundamentally different from those of older people, the younger generation is unlikely to accept traditional social norms and the existing rules of the game in society. Perceiving fundamental differences between their goals and those of elites, young people tend to engage in resistance to challenge the established political order. Given the nature of the data, I am unable to test between the life-cycle model and generational effect model. But, more important, the two models may complement rather than contradict each other. We may not wish to deny either the life-cycle or the generational model to explain people's political behavior in Beijing because both of them contain far too much good sense to be irrelevant. In fact, the life-cycle model *makes* sense only if it also takes into account social and political changes in a society.[41]

As with other participatory modes in Beijing, people's access to grapevine rumors increases the likelihood of their engagement in resistance activities to express their opinions. Since bargaining between resisters and government officials is conducted not through language but through noncompliant behavior, normative power acquired from their knowledge of government policies does not give participants any help. Although the relationship between unofficial information and resistance looks familiar, the causal link between them must be fundamentally different from the one between information and the participatory mode encouraged by the regime. The major impact of information on resistance, I expect, is to help participants reduce risks associated with such political activities. To understand the impacts of grapevine rumors on resistance, an examination of certain unique features of the political process common to authoritarian regimes is in order.

One unique characteristic of societies ruled by people rather than by law is that government policies change from time to time. Changes may result from either the arbitrary decision of supreme leaders or the uninstitution- alized power struggles within leadership groups. China is no exception to this rule. PRC history contains many episodes of uninstitutionalized policy change. Consequently, both the ability of government officials to punish those who dare to challenge their authority and the ability of participants to defeat corrupted government officials fluctuate with the shifting of the political atmosphere and government policies. For example, during the campaign of "punishing criminals without mercy" (*yanda*) in the late 1980s, the central government established quotas of criminals to be executed. The pressure to fulfill these quotas during the campaign made many lower courts sentence to death criminals whose crimes should have been pun- ished with only twenty years in prison. Local government officials did not hesitate to use such opportunities to punish disobedient subordinates. In fact, many people were labeled rightists during the anti-rightist movement in 1957 simply because *danwei* leaders needed to meet the quotas assigned to their organization and picked people they didn't like to fulfill the quotas. Government officials are not free from the influences of such policy fluc- tuations either. During anti-corruption campaigns, corrupt officials who would be simply criticized if caught at some other time may have to serve prison terms for the same offense. Although resistance in grassroots orga- nizations is usually ignored by the authorities, such acts may lead to a full investigation into leaders of these organizations during certain political campaigns.

In the Chinese political system, the timing of one's acts can not only determine the success or failure of such political activities but also change the risks associated with them. To reduce the risks and maximize the gains of their political actions, participants need to make sure no major changes in the political atmosphere and government policy loom in the near future. Since this information is not available from official channels, people who want to "test the temperature before jumping into the water" must look to unofficial channels. The association between unofficial information and resistance also suggests that people's participation in such political activi- ties is more likely to be goal-oriented behavior rather than simply an ex- pression of frustration.

Owing to political constraints, measuring people's political attitudes in China is much more difficult than examining their political behavior. At the time of this survey, survey researchers were not allowed to ask many attitudinal questions. At best, survey researchers could measure people's value orientation indirectly. To infer people's value priorities, I asked if respondents thought "persons sympathetic to the Gang of Four should be allowed to publish." This kind of question, usually used by researchers to measure respondents' political tolerance, also measures respondents' value preferences. Under the rule of the Gang of Four, people were encouraged to use acts of resistance to rebel against the bureaucratic establishment (the capitalist roaders). When Deng Xiaoping resumed power after the Cultural Revolution, people's engagement in these acts to challenge the bureaucratic establishment was formally banned by "reform" leaders. The analysis reveals that people who are sympathetic to the Gang of Four are more likely to choose acts honored by those radical leaders to express their opinions, even though those leaders disappeared from the political arena a long time ago and the current leadership in China strictly prohibits people from using those political acts to articulate their interests. Clearly, participants' value priorities play an important role in shaping their decision to choose resistance to express their opinions.

Although far from conclusive, the findings that resistance in Beijing is associated with father's education, mother's occupation, age, and the most important political resource found thus far in China—grapevine rumors—in conjunction with the previous finding that resistance correlates to the overall participatory index strongly and positively, suggest that the resource model explains people's participation in resistance activities better than the deprivation model.

Cronyism

Cronyism includes two political acts: interest articulation through instrumental personal ties and ceremonial bribery. Whereas the former "mingles instrumental intentions with personal feeling," the latter involves a more "straightforward exchange of favors for material gain or compensatory favors."[42] Engaging in these acts requires participants to make material investment in certain government officials without a guarantee that the investment will bring the desired returns. Since more than one channel of interest articulation exists, we want to know who under what conditions uses such acts to articulate their interests.

Studies of unconventional political participation in liberal democracies may help us to understand this puzzle. They reveal that when conventional channels of communication fail to bring participants what they want, some turn to other channels to deliver their message to the authorities. What the other channels of communication might be can only be determined by the political process in a society. In many liberal democratic countries, the "last desperate acts of citizens . . . are usually collective action in the form of protest."[43] People choose to protest because such actions are protected by the constitution in those societies. More important, the political process in those societies requires participation in collective form to be taken seriously by government officials.

In China, the regime can suppress any collective political actions and deny protesters any gains without worrying about the possibility of losing in the next election. As there is little possibility for participants to get what they want from protests, citizens do not choose to express their opinions this way. Without this option, according to students of communist participation, citizens can only turn away from the political authorities and refuse to deal with the government, thus becoming "apathetic and ignorant."

Although this argument is logically correct, it presents two major problems. First, with most aspects of their lives controlled by the government, can people avoid dealing with it? Can they afford to become apathetic and ignorant toward politics? For example, if a person wants to get an apartment from his work unit and the leader refuses to allocate one to him, what is he going to do? Is he going to give up or try to find some other way to deal with the leader? By the same token, if a person is purged by her *danwei* leader, is she going to allow herself to be trampled upon or try to fight back to protect herself? In such a situation, few people can afford to stand idly by and wait for government officials to take advantage of them. Instead, they must find other ways to communicate with the political authorities and to protect their interests. For example, when people realize that they cannot launch strikes against management, some of them turn to an individualized version of the strike—a slowdown on the job—to fight management. Such a reaction applies not only to citizens in China but also to people in other former communist societies. Empirical studies of political participation in the Soviet Union demonstrate that apathy and ignorance did not necessarily characterize Soviet citizens even under the rule of Leonid Brezhnev.[44]

The second problem with such an argument is that there might be other ways for people in China to effectively express their opinions. Although it is true that the institutional arrangements in China prevent people from using such acts as strikes and demonstrations to express their opinions, they do allow people to work at the policy implementation stage to articulate their interests. Because lower-echelon bureaucrats in China have great discretionary power to implement government policies, the political process actually allows citizens who failed to influence government policy formulation to persuade those officials to ignore policy made by the government and even to twist government policy at the implementation stage to protect their interests. Cronyism is one of many ways for people in China to persuade government officials to do so.

As with other political activities, the major challenge facing participants in cronyism is to find a way to change the hierarchical relationship between themselves and government officials to make those officials pay attention to their requests. Whereas in other acts participants usually need to articulate their requests loudly and collectively to be heard by government officials, participation in the policy implementation stage requires participants to speak quietly and privately with government officials. To persuade government officials to take care of their interests, participants offer bureaucrats something they want in exchange for their help. In doing so, participants manage to turn the hierarchical relationship between themselves and bureaucrats into one of exchange.

Cronyism as a political act always has certain costs associated with it. To get what they want, people need to invest in government officials, either by supplying material goods or providing services officials need. When engaging in such acts, participants are actually wagering what they have in their own hands for something they may get in the future. Similar to commercial investments, these investments come with no guarantee of returns. Making the deal even more risky, "investors" can never participate in exchanges explicitly. Because such exchanges are strictly prohibited by the regime, the deal can only be made in a covert manner. As a result, misunderstandings and miscommunications add more risks for investors. It is thus not unusual for lower-echelon bureaucrats in China to accept material goods and enjoy the services offered by their subordinates and then refuse to provide the desired benefits. Moreover, since cronyism is outlawed by the regime, both parties to such transactions are liable to punishment by the authorities. Although bureaucrats are usually the major targets of regime retaliation, citizens, too, would at least lose their investment.

Cronyism can also provoke an action-reaction spiral in participants' organizations. If one person begins to send gifts to leaders of the organization or tries to become their protégé, other people in the same organization will be forced to do the same if they don't want to be left behind. Since cronyism is not designed to increase the total resource base available for the organization to be distributed among its employees, but instead is aimed at competing for already allocated resources, more people joining the competition can only make the situation for everyone in the organization worse.

Therefore, those who dare to initiate such an action-reaction spiral are usually severely punished by their colleagues.

Given the unique nature of cronyism, it is hard to imagine people choosing to pursue expressive benefits this way. Participants must aim at pursuing instrumental benefits deemed crucial for themselves or their family members or friends. Given the widespread corruption in today's China, some organizational actors may engage in cronyism to pursue their organizational interests. For example, factory managers in today's China may send gifts to government officials at higher levels in exchange for resources crucial for their factory rather than for themselves.

The political dynamics of cronyism in China suggest that the resources required for such acts must be different from those required for people to engage in other political activities. Since cronyism usually requires participants to make material investments, I expect that people with resources to pursue their goals through other means would prefer to choose other political activities. For example, those familiar with government policy on an issue of concern to them and clear that bureaucrats have failed to implement government policy properly would be more likely to make appeals or engage in adversarial activities to confront those bureaucrats than to send them gifts in exchange for favors. For the same reason, people having personal contacts with government officials at higher levels usually prefer to persuade higher-level officials to intervene on their behalf to overrule improper or unpopular decisions made by local government officials when facing the same situation. Those without resources to articulate their interests through conventional and not-so-costly channels of communication tend to choose cronyism to articulate their interests. In other words, cronyism appeals to disadvantaged groups in Chinese society. Those who lack other political resources, who are incapable of attracting other political actors to come to their aid in their dealings with local bureaucrats, and who expect their requests through normal channels to be ignored by government officials are more likely to be forced into such an exchange relationship to give up what they have in exchange for what they want.[45]

Arguing that cronyism belongs to disadvantaged groups in China does not imply, however, that engagement in cronyism requires no resources on the part of participants. Engagement does require resources but somewhat different ones from those required for people to engage in other political activities. To establish the exchange relationship with government officials, participants must have something to offer of interest to the officials they are dealing with. To establish an exchange relationship, participants must have material resources they can invest and know the proper way to deal with a complicated situation. In other words, they must know how to make the investment properly under delicate circumstances.

In addition to the material resources mentioned above, people's psychological orientations also play important roles in shaping their choice of political acts to pursue their goals. For example, scholars have found repeatedly that people's political behavior is influenced "by prevailing social norms about what is or is not proper behavior—by peer group influences, by the norms operative in friendship groups or social organizations to which the individual belongs and by the norms generally held in the community in which the individual lives."[46] An important social norm familiar to students of political participation is the sense of civic duty. The finding that civic duty can prompt people to vote is not new. What is new and important but neglected by some students of political participation is that the same psychological orientation which prompts people to engage in certain political acts may prevent them from choosing certain other acts to pursue their goals. Even though a participant knows that certain political acts can bring desired benefits, the understanding that such acts can damage the authorities, the society, and the nation, as well as the feeling that one has denied allegiance to the society by engaging in them, may prevent a participant from choosing those political acts to pursue his or her goals. In short, there might be certain express costs associated with cronyism. "Not everyone can employ this strategy," observes Andrew Walder in his study of *guanxi* in Chinese enterprises. "Many workers simply disapprove of this way of doing things and refuse to *lower* themselves."[47] A story told by a worker in an interview clearly demonstrates how certain psychological resources become a liability and deter people from engaging in cronyism to pursue their interests:

> I hesitated to engage in those [cronyist] activities because I understand the implication of these activities to society. If everyone in the society engages in these activities, it would definitely destroy not only the regime but also the nation. In the past, I tried very hard to use other means available to me to resolve my problem. Even if I could not achieve what I wanted, I didn't engage in these activities. Morally, it is unacceptable to me. However, when I realized that many cadres, some of them the highest leaders of the country, allowed their children or relatives to use the dual-price system to make money for themselves, I was finally awakened. If they don't care about our country, why should I care about it? I would say I am not a fool and know how to make use of the system. The reason that I did not want to engage in those activities is because I don't think it is proper for a responsible person to do that. However, after realizing that leaders are pursuing not the collective interests of the

state but only their own family's, why should I shy away from those acts? To tell you the truth, I am quite successful in getting what I want from the authorities now that the psychological barrier is gone.[48]

Expressive costs of cronyism must be shaped by people's normative belief system. Normative beliefs can be divided into social and individual beliefs. Social normative beliefs are "the individual's beliefs about what 'society' (i.e., most other people, his 'significant others,' etc.) 'says' he should do (i.e., social or group norms)."[49] Individual normative beliefs encompass "evaluations of how well political institutions conform to a person's sense of what is right, how well the system of government upholds the basic political values and norms in which he believes, and how well authorities conform to his sense of what is right and proper behavior."[50] Individual normative belief systems are shaped by participants' specific and diffused support. Specific support refers to satisfaction-dissatisfaction with policy outputs from the government and diffused support refers to generalized positive-negative affect for the political community, for the values, norms, and institutions of the regime, and for the authorities.[51]

At the time of this survey, it was still impossible for researchers to measure specific and diffused support of citizens in China directly. Therefore, I designed two questions to infer diffused support of respondents. One question asked people's attitudes toward political study. Political study sessions are an important institution used by the regime to socialize people in China to official norms. Whereas people identifying themselves with the authorities ideologically have no objection to this institution, people lacking diffused support usually dislike or even hate this political institution. Another question asked whether respondents felt any restrictions in talking about politics and governmental affairs with other people. Those whose normative belief systems are comparable to that required by the authorities and those who have positive affects for the values, norms, and institutions of the regime should not have anything to hide from the authorities. They should not feel any restrictions in talking politics and governmental affairs with other people. However, those who believe their own political attitudes are substantially different from official doctrine, who perceive substantial difference between their normative belief system and that required by the authorities, and those who have negative affects for values, norms, and institutions of the regime tend to believe they should be cautious in revealing their attitudes to other people. Thus they feel restrictions in talking about politics and governmental affairs with others. As revealed in Table 8.3, nearly 40 percent of respondents reported feeling restrictions in talking about politics and governmental affairs in Beijing. Although people who

Table 8.3   Feelings of restriction in discussing politics

Percentage who report they . . .	Percent (N)
Feel free to discuss politics	56.5 (428)
Don't feel free to discuss politics	38.2 (289)
No answer	5.3 (40)
Total	100 757

Note: Measured by the question, "If you wanted to discuss political and governmental affairs, are there some people you definitely wouldn't turn to, that is, people with whom you feel it is better not to discuss such topics?"

do not feel any restrictions in talking about politics do not necessarily have diffuse support toward the regime, we can safely conclude that people who feel such restrictions lack diffuse support toward the authorities.

Table 8.4 presents the results of multiple regression analysis on cronyism. The analysis reveals that participation in cronyism is associated with the types of residences in which people in Beijing live. People living in shared courtyards are more active in choosing cronyism to express their opinions than people living in other types of houses.

There are three major types of housing in Beijing—apartment buildings, private courtyards, and courtyards shared with others (*dazayuan*). Private courtyards are not only more comfortable but also give residents privacy. They are the most desirable places to live. Unfortunately, there are only a limited number of private courtyards available in Beijing and most of them are occupied by high-ranking government officials. A more practical choice for higher-status people is apartments. Although apartment living is not as comfortable as living in private courtyards, it is much better than residing in shared courtyards because apartments provide residents with their own bathroom and kitchen, while people living in shared courtyards must share these facilities with other people. Because of the land shortage, most residences constructed in the past twenty years are apartment buildings.

The housing supply in Beijing is the responsibility of the *danwei*. However, not every *danwei* can afford to build residences for its employees. As a general rule, the higher the status of the *danwei*, the better the chance it will raise money and get the necessary permissions to build residences for its employees. Employees of higher-status *danwei*, especially people working at government organizations or state institutions, which are capable of building houses for their employees, have gradually moved from shared courtyards to apartment buildings over the past twenty years. Arguing that

Table 8.4   Multiple regression on cronyism

Independent variables	Unstandardized coefficients[a]
Marital status[b]	−.22**
Type of place where respondent lives[c]	.19**
Grapevine rumors	.19**
Evaluation of influences of local government[d]	.15*
Cautious about talking about politics with other people[e]	.22***
Father's education[f]	−.01*
Attitude toward political study[g]	.15***
Idea on disagreement with government policies[h]	.30***

Note: N = 641; constant = −.51; adjusted R^2 = .08.

[a] The dependent variable is the principal component transformation of the participatory variables belonging to this mode.

[b] Coded as 1 if married, 0 if single.

[c] Coded as 1 if courtyard shared with others, 0 if other type of residence.

[d] Measured by the question, "Let's now discuss the local government. How much effect do you think its activities have on your day-to-day life? Do they have a great effect, some effect, or none?" Answers were coded as 1 if some effect, 0 if other.

[e] Measured by the question in Table 8.3. Answers were coded as 1 if yes, 0 if no.

[f] By years of formal schooling.

[g] Measured by the question, "Generally speaking, do you like to participate in political study? Do you like it very much, relatively enjoy it, not like it so much, or not like it at all?" Answers were coded from 1 ("not like it at all") to 4 ("like it very much").

[h] Measured by the question, "In your opinion, should anyone be allowed to disagree with certain policies of the government?" Answers were coded as 1 if yes, 0 if no.

*$p < 0.1$ **$p < 0.05$ ***$p < 0.01$.

most residents of apartment buildings are people working in higher-status *danwei* does not imply that people working at lower-status *danwei* do not have any chance to move into apartment buildings. Occasionally, some lower-status *danwei* may have the opportunity to purchase a few apartments for their employees. Since housing demands in lower-status *danwei* are always higher than supply, and since most people want to move into apartments, the purchase of apartments by an organization would definitely trigger furious competition for those apartments. Of course, politically resourceful people within an organization have a better chance to win such a competition and thus move into an apartment building, leaving their rooms in shared courtyards to the disadvantaged people in the organization. Such a selection process makes the type of housing a person lives in an important indicator of socioeconomic status. Whereas people working for higher-status *danwei* or resourceful employees in lower-status *danwei* tend to live in apartments, disadvantaged people remain in shared court-yards. Lacking resources to articulate their interests in other ways, people living in shared courtyards may be forced to offer what they have to gov-ernment officials in exchange for benefits they desire.

The analysis also reveals that respondents' father's educational achieve-ment is negatively associated with their engagement in cronyism—people from less-educated families are more likely to choose cronyism to articulate their interests. As I discussed in the previous section, political resources in China are transferable between generations. Resources such as information on government policies and personal contacts possessed by one person in the family may be transferred to another in the same family. It is also not unusual for one member in the family to represent others in making appeals to the authorities. Less-educated fathers in China can hardly have those important political resources for themselves, not to mention lend any of them to their children. Lacking such important sources to borrow political resources to compensate for their own shortages, children from less-edu-cated families in China are in disadvantageous positions as compared to children from other families.

However, although people living in shared courtyards and belonging to less-educated families are at a disadvantage in resources required for them to articulate their interests through other participatory activities, they might be more resourceful than other people when it comes to cronyism. Because cronyism is prohibited by the regime, neither party can clearly specify the terms and conditions of the proposed exchange. Such con-straints create a major difficulty for both parties in the proposed transac-tion. Before making their investment in any government officials, partici-pants must make sure that the official they are dealing with will provide them with the desired benefits after accepting their gifts and services, and will not turn the gifts over to the authorities and blame them for bribing government functionaries to increase their credentials. By the same token, unless officials can be sure that the person who proposed the deal would not report it to the authorities after receiving the desired benefits and charge them with asking for bribes, they usually dare not accept any offer, no matter how attractive it might be. As in commercial transactions, a power broker who can provide certain kinds of guarantees to both parties is usually required to facilitate the proposed transaction.

People living in shared courtyards contact their neighbors on a daily basis. Through such contacts intimate relationships and friendships with at least some neighbors develop. As suggested by a Chinese proverb, "dis-tant relatives may not be as good as nearby neighbors" (yuanqin buru jinlin). When they need to deal with the authorities, many neighbors offer one another help. Neighbors can either serve as power brokers themselves or help others to locate qualified people to serve as power brokers. The social network developed from shared courtyard living can compensate for the lack of political resources of lower-status people to accelerate the proposed transactions in cronyism.

Of course, the most likely power brokers are participants' family members. But sometimes people cannot persuade other members in the family to give them the desired help in cronyism. Since the father is still the person who makes the major decisions in Chinese families, his attitude toward cronyism plays an important role in determining whether the family can render participants any help in locating a power broker to facilitate such transactions.[52] For educated fathers, the means and ends in pursuing their goals must be compatible. Even if they do not support the regime, even if they know cronyism can help their children to resolve their problems, and even if they want to help their children to achieve their goals, the belief that cronyism is not the proper means for people of their caliber to pursue their interests can still prevent them from helping their children to identify, locate, and hunt for power brokers. Some fathers would also block the way for other family members to render the child such help, fearing it would "lower" the family. Less-educated parents are more likely to be influenced by changes in the social normative belief system in the society and thus less likely to have such psychological burdens. Moreover, without resources to help their children pursue their goals through other political acts, they might be able to justify engaging in cronyism. Precisely because they do not have many resources to help their children pursue their goals through other means, less-educated fathers would actively mobilize other family members and all the connections in their social network to help their children facilitate such proposed transactions.

Access to unofficial information increases the probability that people will get involved in cronyism to pursue their interests. As with acts of resistance, participants in cronyism need to make sure that they are not selected and used by the authorities as an example of government zeal to clean up corruption. Given the political risks associated with cronyism for the parties involved, both parties will want to make sure that the political atmosphere of the society is stable before striking any deals. Having access to information about the political situation facilitates proposed transactions by reducing the expected political costs associated with them.

In addition to political risks, there are the investment risks already described. The situation facing both parties in cronyism is quite similar to anarchy in international relations. There is no enforcement agency to provide any kind of guarantee for the parties involved. For their own protection, participants usually want to know the behavior pattern of government officials before striking any deal with them. Specifically, they want to make sure that the officials involved (1) have accepted gifts or services from someone in the past; (2) do not "accept" gifts and then turn them over to the authorities to show their honesty and scrupulousness; and (3) have a history of keeping their promises rather than welcoming gifts but refusing to render the expected help. Finally, participants want neither to overspend on gifts, and so appear insincere, nor underspend and insult the official they are dealing with. None of this information is in the public domain, and the only way for people to get it is, of course, from grapevine rumors.

Respondents' marital status is found to be correlated to cronyism—singles in Beijing are more active in cronyism than married couples. Singles are more active in cronyism not only because they have yet to acquire the necessary resources to pursue their goals through other means but also because they usually have an abundance of two resources deemed crucial for cronyism—time and money. Engaging in cronyism requires participants to make monetary investments. Cultivating good relationships with bureaucrats usually requires participants to spend a lot of time with them. For example, if leaders are fond of *majiang,* or bridge, the investor must prepare to spend time playing the game with them. Like business transactions, investments in cronyism, especially when participants aim at cultivating long-term personal ties with certain government officials, can fail to produce immediate returns for investors. Many investments of time and money cannot be justified, especially when participants plan to overspend on a certain government official to accumulate capital in the person and prepare to claim their investment for something crucial in the future. The utility and necessity of such investment can easily be challenged by other members of the family. No wife, for instance, would want her spouse to stay at a leader's house all night playing *majiang.* If she were to challenge the utility of the investment, her husband would have a hard time defending his actions, especially if he did not expect an immediate return. Without family obligations, singles have an easier time making such risky or long-term investments. They don't need to consult others before investing their time and money in government officials they feel would be useful for their goals.

As expected, respondents' belief systems significantly affect their decision to choose cronyism to pursue their interests. Clearly, the belief that individuals should be allowed to disagree with government policies is a necessary condition for people in Beijing to consider pursuing their own interests. Escape from the psychological shackles imposed by the regime increases the likelihood that people will articulate their interests through cronyism. Furthermore, people's awareness of the impact of local government on their daily lives makes an important difference in cronyism. Those who believe local government has great influence are found to be more actively engaged in cronyism. Since cronyism is designed not to change policies made by the central government but to influence the policy outputs of the local government, it is easy for us to understand why knowledge of local political processes makes a difference in cronyism. Finally, diffuse support is negatively associated with cronyism. As expected, while people in China who feel restricted in talking about politics and governmental affairs are more likely to choose cronyism to express their opinions, their attitudes toward political study are negatively correlated with cronyism. The more a person feels restricted in talking about politics, the more likely he or she will choose cronyism to pursue goals. The more a person dislikes political study sessions, the more likely he or she will choose cronyism when necessary. Those who feel restricted in talking about politics and governmental affairs have negative affects for the values, norms, and institutions of the regime. While people identifying themselves with the authorities ideologically usually have no objection to political study, people lacking diffused support tend to dislike this mobilizational mechanism. The finding that cronyism is negatively associated with participants' attitudes toward political study sessions but positively associated with people's feelings of restriction in talking about politics clearly demonstrates that the normative belief system of citizens in China shapes their choices of political acts to pursue their interests. While lacking diffuse support increases the tendency for people in Beijing to choose cronyism to articulate their interests, people with such psychological burdens voluntarily refrain from using acts of cronyism to pursue their goals.

Conclusion

Probably the most important finding of this chapter is that people's responses to structural constraints in society on their interest articulation are much more complicated than that suggested by students of political participation in communist societies. At the macrolevel, when "conventional ways" for people to express their opinion are blocked, rather than becoming apathetic and ignorant, citizens adapt themselves to system constraints and try to develop new ways to articulate their interests in the political system. At the microlevel, rather than abstaining from politics, people lacking resources for conventional participatory modes turn to acts requiring different resources to pursue their interests. The analysis demonstrates that the politicization process by which people become involved in politics is dynamic rather than static. Structural constraints of the political system and deficiencies of resources for individuals, rather than simply preventing people from engaging in politics to articulate their interests, push people to seek other means to achieve their goals. The actual choices of political acts used by individuals in society to pursue their interests are determined by both the tangible and the intangible resources possessed by the people concerned. Citizens will choose political acts that can maximize the utility of their resources to pursue their interests. As revealed in this chapter, people in Beijing lacking resources to pursue their goals through other means turn to cronyism to articulate their interests.

The analyses in previous chapters demonstrated that similar political acts under different institutional arrangements require different political resources on the part of participants. Institutional arrangements in a society change the resources required for alternative political activities. The analysis in this chapter further demonstrates that the impact of the same resources on different political acts under the same political institutions can be fundamentally different. For example, by helping participants realize their own rights under existing government policy and by providing them with normative power to support their requests when dealing with local government officials, information facilitates participation by increasing the confidence of participants in their potential for success in dealing with local officials. The function of the same resource—information from unofficial sources—on unconventional political acts fundamentally differs from the one demonstrated in the previous chapters. As the bargaining between participants and government officials through political acts studied in this chapter occurs through political acts rather than verbal communication, normative power has less use than it does for people dealing with governmental officials through such political acts as appeals and adversarial activities. Thus, rather than increasing the chances for participants to successfully persuade government officials to make desired concessions, information is found to facilitate participation in these unconventional political activities by reducing the various risks associated with them. By helping people to predict any possible change in the general political atmosphere in Chinese society and upcoming political campaigns, information reduces political risks associated with resistance. By helping people to predict the possible responses of government officials to their offers, information reduces the material risks—the risks that participants will lose their investments—associated with certain political activities.

The institutional arrangements in a society can not only shape new ways for people to express their opinions but also change the effects of people's psychological orientation on their political behavior. Certain psychological resources even become liabilities for people engaging in certain political activities in Beijing. For example, people's normative belief systems prevent people in China from choosing certain political acts to pursue their interests, even if they know such acts can bring them desired benefits. Diffuse support, which prompts participants to go to the ballot booth on the election day in China, *prevents* the same people from engaging in cronyism to pursue their interests. Regime-based trust is also found to be able to deter participants from engaging in acts prohibited by the authorities.

Institutional arrangements in China even create new dimensions of psychological orientation. Traditional conceptualizations of political efficacy divide psychological orientation into internal and external efficacy. Their unspoken assumption is that central efficacy must be linked with local efficacy. In other words, people who are confident of their ability to influence the decisions made by local government or the behavior of local government officials must believe that they can exert the same influence over the decisions made by the central government. Such an assumption is true in most societies but not in China. Because the system design in China allows people to change the way local officials implement government policy on an individual basis but prevents them from exerting influence on policies made by the central government, people without confidence in their ability to influence policy made by the central government may still be confident of their ability to influence the output of the government at the grassroots level. Such an institutional arrangement actually separates local efficacy from central efficacy. My analysis demonstrates that even without the feeling of central efficacy, local efficacy itself can still increase the probability that people will get involved in certain political acts to articulate their interests.

Finally, participants' experiences in the past can shape their current political behavior, although in a complicated way. The experience of political purges makes people more likely to get involved in elite-challenging political acts either to change the status quo or to protest, but only if they perceive that their current economic situation is worse than that of other people around them. If the previously purged have been fully rehabilitated and their current economic situation is no worse or even better than other people's, their willingness to take political risks to get involved in elite-challenging political acts will be reduced. The experience of being purged has definite negative effects on the willingness of people to take political risks. This finding contradicts the conventional wisdom that political purges make people antagonistic toward political authorities and willing to challenge them. In fact, the expected antagonism exists only if the current economic condition of the previously purged is still worse than that of others in the society. People's memory of the past is short. The current economic condition of the previously purged plays a far more important role in shaping people's political attitudes in general than the impacts of their past experiences on their particular political behavior.

9
Conclusion

This study portrays citizens in Beijing as participating in a wide range of political acts to articulate their private interests. Contrary to the conventional wisdom regarding communist countries, which holds that only "some kind of political participation does take place in these countries,"[1] people in Beijing are found to actively pursue their interests. As forcefully demonstrated in the book, only around one-tenth (10.4 percent) of respondents did not engage in any political act during the five-year period prior to the survey. Even leaving out "easy" political acts such as voting from the analysis, it still appears that roughly three-quarters of respondents (73.3) engaged in at least one participatory act described in this book to express their opinion during the same time frame. Political involvement in Communist China by private citizens is much more intensive than has been generally believed.

Moreover, contrary to mobilization theory, political participation in Beijing is not a unidimensional phenomenon wherein acts can be differentiated only by the initiative required on the part of participants. Instead, participatory activities utilized by people in Beijing to pursue their interests are found to be different from one another in the initiative required and risks involved and in their conflict dimension. Different combinations of these three dimensions cluster participatory acts in China into seven participatory modes—voting, campaign activities, appeals, adversarial appeals, cronyism, resistance, and election boycotts. Private citizens in Communist China engage in much more diversified political acts than has been believed.

The diversity and intensity of participatory activities in Beijing revealed in this study clearly contradict the claims made by many students of politics in communist societies, which describe participation there either as the product of regime-directed mobilization or "window dressing used by . . . leaders to obtain a veneer of legitimacy while enhancing their ability to mobilize citizens and check up on policy implementation."[2] Instead, this study confirms what Victor Falkenheim suggested more than ten years ago: that "organizational, social and political constraints notwithstanding, *significant nonritual* participation does take place in China, under conditions well understood by all participants."[3] The apparent contradiction between the well-accepted theories guiding the study of political participation in communist societies and the political reality in China suggests that a reevaluation of the conceptual framework for the study of citizen participation in general and in communist societies in particular is surely necessary.

Theoretical Reflections

Any attempt to reevaluate this conceptual framework must assess the effects of regime mobilization on people's behavior. It is true that communist regimes have tried to limit people's political activities within officially approved channels. It is also true that communist regimes have tried to exclude the previously participatory population from political life through "the disenfranchisement of the participant classes . . . and through liquidation, demobilization, intimidation and reeducation."[4] In addition, the regimes in both the former USSR and China attempted not only to remove the organizational bases in their societies to deter participants from expressing their opinions collectively, but also to convert citizens into "new socialist men" through thought reform and political indoctrination. But the question here is, facing the hostility of such regimes toward private interest articulation, deprived of organizational arrangements to aggregate their interests, and confronting thought reform aimed at transforming their psychological orientation, are citizens in communist societies necessarily mobilized into the political process as designed by the regime to carry out its predetermined goals, or do they become apathetic and ignorant and thus refrain from engaging in any political activities as suggested by many scholars of political participation in these societies?[5]

Although "no analysis of participation can ignore the regime's efforts [in those societies] to structure and limit citizen involvement in the political process,"[6] this book reveals that the effects of regime mobilization on people's behavior are much more complicated than had been originally realized by scholars of communist participation. The regime uses three mechanisms to shape people's political behavior in China: elimination of the organizational bases for people to articulate their interests collectively, "forced departicipation" of previously participatory groups, and political education to reshape people's psychological orientation. Examination of the effects of each of them shows an interesting paradox: while these mechanisms are successful in preventing people in China from articulating their interests collectively, they fail to confine private interest articulation to officially sanctioned channels.

Rather than preventing people from engaging in unauthorized political acts to express their opinions, removal of the organizational base "converts" collective political acts elsewhere into individually based political activities in China. For example, protest in the form of strikes and demonstrations, which usually require collective action elsewhere, is manifested in China in the form of whipping up public opinion and job slowdowns. Moreover, although the CCP successfully deters people from organizing together to campaign for candidates they like, the regime fails to prevent people from campaigning for candidates on an individual basis. Forced departication also fails to achieve its designed goals, that is, to prevent previously active groups from engaging in politics, especially in unauthorized participatory activities and modes to exert influence or to express their opinions. Had forced departication succeeded, we would find its targets refraining from acts prohibited by the authorities. The analysis shows that this is not the case in Beijing. Although political purges do influence people's behavior, such influences are mediated by people's economic situations. Political purges can silence the criticism of the previously purged and prevent them from engaging in unauthorized political activities only if they feel their current economic situation is better than other people's in the society. If the previously purged consider their own economic situation worse than others', their experiences increase rather than reduce the likelihood of their engaging in unauthorized political activities to express their opinions. This finding clearly demonstrates the limitation of the effects of political sanctions in "departicipating" previously active groups in society.

By the same token, if political education and thought reform help the regime to confine people's political acts to officially sanctioned channels, we should find that access to institutions used by the regime to transform people's psychological orientation into "new socialist men" (political study and the officially controlled news media) reduces participation in unauthorized political activities. The data analysis gives a different picture. People's attitudes toward political study and access to the news media neither diminish nor increase the likelihood of participation.

The limitations of regime mobilization in shaping people's political behavior are also demonstrated by the failure of the regime to alter the behavior pattern of lower-status people in society. Although the CCP tries to mobilize previously nonparticipating groups, such as lower-status people, to participate in politics, these efforts have failed to change behavior patterns. Contrary to CCP expectations, regime mobilization can neither increase the level nor alter the choices of political acts of people with a lower socioeconomic status. Citizens in this group are less likely to get involved in political acts authorized by the regime, such as elections and appeals. They are more likely to choose acts prohibited by the authorities, such as election boycotts, job slowdowns, and cronyism, to express their opinions.

These findings raise an interesting question for researchers, namely, why do the mobilizational efforts of the regime in China fail to prevent people from engaging in unauthorized political acts to pursue their interests but succeed in preventing them from choosing collective action? Previous discussions confirm that although lacking organized interest articulation in Chinese society is related to regime suppression, suppression by itself cannot be the major reason that people avoid organized political activities. The observed relationship between the hostility of the regime toward organized interest articulation and the fact that many people avoid choosing collective action to pursue their interests may be a spurious one. Instead, the success of the regime in preventing organized opposition from occurring should be attributed to the institutional settings in Chinese society.[7]

Although legislation in other societies may also be weak and political power within other administrations fragmented, the discretionary powers possessed by bureaucrats in China are different from those possessed by bureaucrats in other societies, qualitatively rather than quantitatively. For example, when government policy governing social welfare states that "families whose annual income is less than $4,000 get $500 per month per person from the government," even if bureaucrats can maneuver, the space and ability for them to do so is quite limited. However, when policy governing the same issue states that "each grassroots organization should give proper [shidang] subsidies to families with hardship," bureaucrats have much more freedom to maneuver when implementing the policy. Because bureaucrats in China are allowed to interpret government decisions according to love, hatred, and other personal, irrational, and emotional elements, institutional arrangements in the society attract interest articulation to policy at the implementation stage, when competition is situation-specific, involves fewer risks, and saves organizational costs for participants.

Another difference between institutions in urban China and those elsewhere is the installation of work units as the primary organization responsible for resource allocation. Such an arrangement fundamentally changes the way interests in Chinese society are organized. With most material and nonmaterial resources in urban China allocated to work units for distribution among their employees, people's interests inevitably involve work units rather than social strata across different sections in the society. Two major structural consequences follow. First, such an arrangement fragments the interests of people from the same social stratum working at different organizations. For example, employees of state enterprises in China get higher salaries, better housing, and better political treatment (*zhengzhi daiyu*) than employees of collective enterprises. People working for enterprises belonging to a ministry in the central government get higher salaries and better fringe benefits than people working in provincial-level state-owned factories.[8] As people in the same social stratum or the same occupational group working at different organizations have different interests, it is extremely difficult for people in urban China to break the barrier of work units to form cross-sectional interest groups to pursue their interests. Interests in urban China are simply not organized in such a way as to sustain the organization of cross-sectional associational interest groups.

Second, and no less important, by making the *danwei* the primary battlefield of resource competition, institutional arrangements in Chinese society fundamentally alter people's definition of interests and their relationship with other actors in the basic organization of the society. Within the primary battlefield of political competition, one person getting desired resources usually reduces the chances of other actors in the same organization receiving the same resources. Suppose a work unit gets ten apartments from the authorities to distribute among employees but has a hundred qualified people. If one person in the organization gets an apartment, it clearly means that the chances for other competitors are reduced by a fraction. This arrangement invalidates the crucial assumption of modern political science—that the outputs of government policy are infeasibility of exclusion and jointness of supply—at least for low-politics issues in China. Government policy there governing issues related to people's daily lives is not only divisible, but also limited in supply.

As interests in China are organized differently from those in other societies, the strategy required for political competition must also be different from those we are familiar with. Trying to make the government allocate more resources to the organizations participants are tied to may no longer be an appropriate strategy of interest articulation. As policy in China is usually vague, local leaders can always find a way to give additional resources allocated to their organization to someone else at their discretion. Even if participants can make the authorities appropriate more resources to the organization, there is no guarantee that participants themselves would get a share of these resources. Thus, rather than organizing people with similar attributes to lobby the government to appropriate more resources to the organization, the primary strategy of resource competition in China becomes persuading government officials responsible for distribution of the resources already appropriated to the organization to distribute them to the participant rather than to other people. As structural arrangements make the interests of political actors having similar attributes conflict with each other, collaboration with other political actors to lobby collectively becomes not only unnecessary but also irrational. Instead, exclusion—trying to persuade decision makers to appropriate resources to the participant rather than to other actors—becomes the primary strategy of political competition in urban China.

The study of China produces many "puzzling" findings, such as why information from unofficial channels rather than from the official media increases the probability of engagement in most participatory acts and modes in Beijing, why associational affiliation increases people's engagement in political acts not requiring interest aggregation, and why efficacy and trust are negatively rather than positively associated with certain participatory acts and modes. These findings can be easily understood when we appreciate the specific structural arrangements in Chinese society. The resources required for people to participate in politics must be linked to the strategies used by them to alter the hierarchical relationship between themselves and bureaucrats in the society. To persuade government officials to allocate resources to participants themselves rather than to other people, citizens in China usually need to "borrow" normative power from existing government policies or political power from other political actors to change the balance of power between themselves and government officials involved, or to turn the hierarchical relationship between themselves and bureaucrats into one of exchange. To borrow normative power from government policy, participants need to have knowledge of various government policies governing the issue at hand. To borrow political power from government officials, participants need to have access to officials able to influence and change decisions made by lower-echelon bureaucrats. To turn the hierarchical relationship between themselves and bureaucrats into an exchange, participants need to have material goods or services bureaucrats are interested in to induce them to strike deals. The analysis confirms that when the way people participate in politics changes, resources required for people to articulate their interests also change.

These results are important, not because they describe an interesting case unlike other societies, nor because the population was inaccessible for previous empirical work to outsiders, but because they show how institutional designs in a society determine *where* in the decision-making process people exert their influence, *how* people can alter the hierarchical relationship between themselves and government officials to pursue their goals, *what* resources are required for people to articulate their interests, and *who* in the society is more likely to choose *what* political acts to participate in. More important, this study demonstrates that when institutional settings in a society change, the whole political process—all the factors mentioned above—will change.

Although I conclude that participation in Beijing is no less common than in many other countries, it is not my intention to suggest that the political system in China is a democratic one. The concept of participation is derived from the notion of democracy, but the term "participation" in this study is deliberately uncoupled from its normative connotation and simply refers to efforts of people to influence their rulers. There are significant differences between citizen participation in Communist China and that in other societies. Such differences, however, lie neither in the frequency nor the effectiveness of participation, but elsewhere.

First, participation in China differs from that in many other societies in the stage of the decision-making process at which people assert their influence. While people in most other societies seek to influence government policy formation, people in urban China concentrate on influencing the way government policy is implemented. Almond and Verba's discussion of the difference between "citizens" and "subjects" illustrates this. Whereas citizens are "orientated to the system as a whole and to both the political and administrative structure and process," subjects' "orientation towards specifically input objects . . . approach[es] zero."[9]

Differences in the stages of the decision-making process over which influence is exerted lead to the second difference between political participation in Communist China and that in other polities—the repertories of acts and modes used by citizens in society to exert influence. Whereas the majority of people in liberal democracies participate in politics through voting, campaign activities, communal activities, and particularized contacts, people in China rely primarily on appeals, adversarial activities, resistance, and cronyism to fight for what they want.

The third difference lies in the impact of participation on the political system itself. Participation at the policy implementation stage, if successful, must destroy the ability of the administration to carry out the policies made by the authorities and corrupt government officials at various levels. If ordinary citizens in the society can change the way government policy is implemented, there can hardly be any government policy at all, not to mention accomplishment of the regime's public policy goals. The more responsive lower-echelon bureaucrats are to popular demands, the more likely the administration is to become paralyzed and fail to function. Some widely noticed problems in communist societies—such as inefficiency, waste, lack of state capacity, widespread corruption, and dysfunction of the administration—complained about by the CCP itself again and again in recent years are actually built into the system by its very institutional design. Deliberately blocking the way for ordinary people in society to articulate their interests at the policy implementation stage, system designs in many other societies greatly increase the possibility of achieving the goals of public policies as outcomes of government activities. Such designs may not be able to eliminate the maneuvering of bureaucrats at the policy implementation process. However, by greatly reducing the room for bureaucrats to maneuver, such designs greatly increase the capacity of administrations to function properly.

The fourth difference involves the impact of participation on people's psychological orientation toward the political community. Although political acts of citizens in both China and elsewhere may help participants get what they want, impacts of successful participation on people's psychological orientation can fundamentally differ from society to society. As revealed in this study, people's engagement in resistance and cronyism negatively correlate with efficacy and regime-based trust. If we believe that the relationship between participation and participants' psychological orientation is a recursive one and that participation can help shape participants' psychological orientation, then the negative relationship between participation in certain political acts and regime-based trust suggests that people's engagement in these activities makes them feel alienated from rather than identified with the political community.

Finally, the way people in a society participate in politics in turn affects the way interests therein are organized. As interest articulation in China is channeled to the policy implementation stage, both vertical ties between government officials and individual citizens and conflicts of interests among citizens with similar attributes working in the same organization not only develop but also are reinforced. The prevalence of social relationships produced by the structural arrangements in Chinese society further facilitates citizen participation in ways conducive to such societal relations. Therefore, the rather unique social structure in Communist China should be considered both as the structural cause and the consequence of the way in which people in the PRC participate in politics. More important, this social relationship can reproduce itself, and its reproduction will have a significant impact on the future of Chinese democracy.

The Future of Chinese Democracy

Two quotations epitomize the economic model used to predict democratization. First, "Perhaps the most widespread generalization linking political systems to other parts of society has been that democracy is related to the state of economic development."[10] Second, "The development hypothesis holds that higher levels of socio-economic development in a society lead to higher levels of political participation, and implicitly, to a shift from mobilized to autonomous participation."[11] This model is used not only by many scholars to predict the future of democratization in China but also by Chinese democratic practitioners to guide the opposition movement against the current communist regime. To many people, current CCP policy emphasizing economic development will sooner or later lead to its own demise. Will this expectation come true? Will recent economic development in Communist China lead to its democratization in the near future? We must carefully examine this development hypothesis before we can evaluate its validity.

Students of political development have long noticed the correlation between economic development and democratization. The model measures democracy through levels of autonomous political participation in society. When seeking causal links between economic development and democratization or increasing levels of autonomous participation, scholars emphasize the effects of economic, social, cultural, and psychological factors on people's participatory behavior. Some stress the impacts of industrialization and urbanization on people's psychological orientation, while others focus on the effects of education and information on people's political behavior.[12] Unfortunately, most theories explaining the association between economic development and political democratization ignore the effects of political factors on this alleged relationship.[13] Dankwart Rustow thus criticizes those who propose a simple relationship between economic development and political democratization as "jumping from the correlation between democracy and other factors to the conclusion that those other factors were responsible for democracy."[14]

One of the exceptions to this criticism is the explanation offered by Huntington and Nelson. In an attempt to explain the correlation between economic development and levels of participation, they propose that economic development transforms the basis of political participation in a society. According to them, "a simple theory of political modernization would suggest a clear displacement of more traditional bases (patron-client and communal groups) by more modern ones (class and party)."[15] When "many of the most important services that city government provides are distributed on a geographical basis: water supply, sewage disposal, and police and fire protection," people are required to deal with the government more frequently. People's ever increasing need to deal with government (generated by economic development) leads to "party-based participation."[16]

Careful examination of the theory offered by Huntington and Nelson shows that although it tells us why economic development generates the need for people to deal with government, it fails to specify why the need for people to deal with government would necessarily give birth to "democratic infrastructure," that is, associational interest groups and party-based politics in society, and transform the basis of political participation. What we are given here is a simple correlation between the need for people to deal with government and the emergence of party-based participation.

As demonstrated in this book, although both economic development and structural design in China generate the need for people to deal with government, the basis of politics does not change. New group-based politics has failed to replace traditional politics in urban China. People's ever increasing need to deal with government has not developed group- or party-based political participation in the society. Since institutional arrangements fail to transform the way interests in urban China are organized and rearrange the relationship among political actors with similar attributes, traditional politics still serves urban Chinese well in their interest articulation. The case in China reveals that increases in the level of participation may not necessarily be accompanied by the transformation of the basis of politics in a society. Unless such a transformation occurs, participation in a society remains on the output side of the policy process and democratic infrastructure cannot easily emerge.

One of the reasons many scholars ignore the important influence of the transformation of institutional settings on the process of political democratization is that economic development *usually* brings with it several changes that facilitate the proposed transformation. First, the socialization of economic life, which is both the cause and the consequence of economic development, tends to generate many new sources of power and control, which should fundamentally change the way people's interests in society are organized. With the emergence of new sources of power, traditional organizations such as family, kinship, and village are no longer able to provide basic needs to societal members. People thus need to seek new organizations to represent their interests.

Second, with economic development and the emergence of new sources of power and control, decision-making centers in society move away from traditional organizations such as family, kinship, and village to larger geographically based administrations. As decision-making centers move away from people's daily lives, decisions made by the government gradually acquire two important attributes: the infeasibility of exclusion and the jointness of supply. If the decisions made by family, kinship, and village affect only their members, decisions made by more widely geographically based administrations now affect all people with similar attributes in society. Such a change should tie the interests of people with similar attributes together.

Third, the birth of a legal-rational, impartial, and neutral organization—a "bureaucracy"—to serve as an instrument of enforcement and execution of decisions made by government makes it difficult, if not impossible, for the general populace to use traditional strategies like particularism to pursue their interests. As citizens are pushed to the policy formulation stage to exert their influence, group and group-based politics become necessary. Government decisions now affect many people, and competing voices would want to reach decision makers to influence government decisions. Since groups usually have a stronger voice than a single person, people with similar attributes would have incentives to form groups that aggregate their interests to bargain with government collectively. Autonomous social classes; regional groups; occupational groups; and institutional, nonassociational, anomic, and associational interest groups gradually emerge in society.[17] Although economic development should generate the need for people to deal with government, it is the concomitant changes of institutional settings accompanying economic development in some societies that lead to the transformation of political bases.

The regime in Communist China, unlike that in many other developing societies, puts every aspect of the private lives of ordinary citizens under its control. Direct involvement in economic life makes the government in China the direct and sometimes the only supplier of material and nonmaterial resources important to people's daily lives. Thus tension between the state and society in China is not only generated by economic development but also accelerated by the society's structural arrangements. As it does elsewhere, economic development in China creates strong incentives for people to deal with the government.

Economic development in urban China until today has failed to bring about concomitant change in the way interests are organized in society, however. The installation of work units in China shifts the institution responsible for people's basic needs from one type of traditional organization—family, kinship, and village—to another type of traditional one, the *danwei*. The survival of the work unit despite the recent reforms prevents basic social organizations representing people's interests from being transferred from traditional to modern, or cross-sectional, interest groups. Moreover, economic development has also failed to bring about changes of political logic in Chinese society. As the work unit remains the decision-making center in urban China, government decisions regarding daily issues for most people in society are still subject to exclusion and have yet to undergo jointness of supply. In addition, without the emergence of a legal-rational, impartial, and neutral bureaucracy, people in China can still use the traditional strategy of particularism to pursue their interests. Since the primary strategy of interest articulation for the urban population in China is exclusion of, rather than cooperation with, people with similar attributes, group and party-based politics remains not only unnecessary but also irrational for most participants.

John Duncan Powell's study of the transformation of clientelist politics in peasant society points out the salient characteristics of governments based on such systems: "the limitation of clientelist politics is that it seems to be a transitional phenomenon—or, better put, appropriate and successful only under certain conditions, and then for a limited period of time."[18] Unfortunately, the expected transformation has yet to occur in urban China. Such a transformation does not simply depend on such factors as increases in the level of education among the general populace, urbanization, and the spread of communications. All these factors matter, but a crucial and usually forgotten dimension is the development of the institutional arrangements in society, which may or may not necessarily grow step by step along with economic development. Until social, economic, and political developments in China reorganize private interests so that interests of people with similar social attributes no longer conflict, and until developments transform the nature of government decisions so that particularism can no longer provide people with most of what they want, politics in China will stay in its current form. Without new and group-based political activities emerging in China, increasing levels of participation will not give birth to a strong opposition movement to replace the current regime. Political participation in its current form, no matter how widespread, will not lead to democratization in China.

Transformation of the traditional polity into a modern or party-based one depends on the breakdown of the reproduction process of the rather unique social relationships in today's China. Two institutions can facilitate the proposed breakdown of that social relationship. One is the introduction of competitive elections at the national or provincial level, which should make traditional social relations "lose their predominantly personal character and evolve into more institutionalized machine politics" through the mobilizational efforts of elites.[19] The other is marketization, which will dramatically change the way in which private interests are organized and articulated. Such changes, it seems to me, are more likely to happen in rural China first.

As a result of de facto privatization, the government in rural China has gone from directly supplying material and nonmaterial resources to regulating the supply of those resources. Local officials in rural China now control fewer and fewer material and nonmaterial resources, and the market mediates interactions between peasants and government. As a result, the decision-making center in rural China has begun to move away from traditional organizations. For example, under the old system, village authorities were the only supplier of chemical fertilizer. The government provided fertilizer to each village, and village leaders allocated it among the peasants. With the introduction of the market mechanism, the government began to sell chemical fertilizer on the market, thus becoming its regulator. This "small" change actually has a revolutionary effect on politics in rural China. It ties the interests of people with the same attributes together. Villagers who used to compete with one another for chemical fertilizer now line up together to fight the government for lower prices. It also changes the strategy required for effective interest articulation in rural China. While the dual price system still existed, individuals in rural China could try to persuade government officials to sell them chemical fertilizer at the controlled price. However, when the government abolished the dual price system, peasants were left with only one way to get what they want: working collectively to change government price policy. By changing the way in which interests in rural China are organized, marketization has begun to create a basis for group politics therein.[20] Although the argument that the transformation to "new politics" is more likely to happen in rural rather than urban China seems to contradict what has been suggested by students of political development, the logical structure of the argument is compatible with the causal reasoning offered by those scholars.

If the emergence of certain institutional arrangements is crucial for political development in a society, we would expect democratization in China to proceed through one of the following three possible paths. The first one is "peasant evolution" in rural China. As marketization reorganizes interests in Chinese villages and transforms the strategies required for peasants to articulate their interests, it becomes more and more difficult for people in rural China to use the old strategy, particularism, to articulate their interests. People are thus pushed by their own interests to form various groups to lobby collectively with the authorities. However, low levels of education, lack of information on politics and governmental affairs, and lack of organizational skills may delay the formation of interest groups in the countryside, preventing the emergence of a new politics in rural China in the near future.

Alternatively, if the current economic reforms, especially marketization, in rural areas expand to urban China, the *danwei* system would dissolve. Marketization would require the government in urban China to withdraw from economic life. This development would rearrange interest organization in urban China in a way similar to that of other developing countries. As in rural China, such a change would also make interest articulation at the policy implementation stage through particularism become more and more difficult. The logic of politics in urban China today would gradually give way to a new one. When the current political foundation could no longer cope with such changes in society, new bases would emerge in urban China. However, if these changes, especially marketization and the collapse of the *danwei* system, occur in urban China, we may see a faster change in Chinese politics because the urban population is better prepared for such a transformation than the rural population, in terms of education, information, and organizational skills.

Finally, in today's China, some important issues facing citizens are collective by nature and cannot be resolved through particularism. Consider official corruption and inflation. These problems jeopardize the interests of the overwhelming majority of the population simultaneously, and there is no way for people to deal with them individually through particularism. If the government handles them poorly, these two issues can quickly mobilize people in both rural and urban China to oppose the government collectively and overthrow the current regime.

Because the first two paths to democracy in China come about through the transformation of interest organization in the society and the emergence of a democratic infrastructure to sustain a new politics, they are more likely to bring stable democracy to China. The future of any democracy coming from the third path is more likely to be uncertain. Since reorganization of interests crucial for the formation of the democratic infrastructure—associational interest groups and political parties—has yet to develop in the society, a new politics brought about by "revolution" would not have the necessary social structure to long sustain it. Unless an issue-oriented opposition movement temporarily mobilized by a problem facing the majority of citizens can quickly change the way interests in the society are organized and the government functions, to deliberately create democratic infrastructures, the postrevolutionary polity would be more likely to return to a traditional form than to develop into a stable democracy. "Dynastic change" in such a situation is more likely to be the product of revolution than the evolution of a new polity.

Appendix: Sample Design

Population

The population sampled in this study consisted of all noninstitutionalized Beijing residents eighteen years of age or older, residing in family households in eight urban districts at the time of the survey. The survey was conducted from December 12, 1988, to January 10, 1989.

Sample

A stratified multistage sampling procedure with probabilities proportional to size (PPS) measures was employed to select the sample. A special stratification technique, paired selection, was used in the sample design. Designs based on two random selections from each stratum have two main advantages. First, for fixed number selections, it is the farthest we can take stratification and still compute the variance from the sample data alone. Second, these comparisons permit simple formulas for computing the variance.[1]

The primary sampling units (PSUs) employed were street offices (*jiedao banshichu*). The units of selection of the second stage (SSUs) were neighborhood committees (*juweihuei*). Family households were used at the third stage.

Sample Frame

For selecting PSUs, the 1987 National Population Databook[2] was used as the basic material to construct the sampling frame. The number of family households for each unit was taken as the measure of size (Mos) in the PPS selection process.

For the successive stages, data were obtained from the Public Security Bureau of the Beijing Municipal Government. In places without household registration, lists were obtained from field counts.[3]

Sample Size

To limit sampling error to an acceptable level, first, we calculated the sample size of a simple random sample (SRS) that satisfied the precision requirement. Second, we modified this SRS size with some adjustment factors to get the real sample size. The required precision level is expressed as the allowed range of sampling error:

$$\Delta = t \cdot se(y)$$

For our survey Δ is set at 0.05. Since $0.05 = 1.96$ standard errors, the confidence interval of the sample is 95 percent.

When the finite population correction (fpc) is ignored, the sample size of an SRS is

$$n_{srs} = \frac{t^2 \cdot s^2}{\Delta^2}$$

S^2 is the element variance of the population. In practice this is unknown and it must be estimated or guessed.[4] There are no past surveys of similar variables in China to help us estimate s^2. Nevertheless, most parameters are proportions (P). We chose the "safe" choice by selecting the maximum $s^2 = 0.25$ ($s^2 = PQ$), corresponding to $P = 0.5$. Therefore,

$$n_{srs} = \frac{2^2 \times 0.25}{(0.05)^2} = 400$$

The above SRS size was modified by the design effect (deff) of this complex sample design. Examination of many surveys of similar design and size in other countries showed that most surveys have a design effect of 2 or lower value.[5] We chose deff = 2 as the adjustment:

$$n' = n_{srs} \times deff = 400 \times 2 = 800$$

This figure is further adjusted by an estimated response rate of $R = 0.85$.

$$n = \frac{n'}{R} = \frac{800}{0.85} = 941$$

Allocation of Sample Size at Different Stages

Let

a = the number of sample PSUs

b = the number of sample SSUs within each sample PSU

c^* = the planned average number of sample family households within second-stage units

m = the planned subsample size within PSUs

$m = bc^*$

$n = a \cdot m$

Cluster sampling ordinarily results in greater variance than a sample of the same number of elements selected individually. But the cost per element is lower, sometimes much lower, for cluster sampling than for element sampling. However, when clustering has substantial and opposing influences on cost and on variance, economic design depends on estimating and balancing those influences. The optimum (most economical) subsample size can be expressed as[6]

$$m_{opt} = \left[\frac{C_a \cdot (1 - roh)}{c \cdot roh} \right]^{1/2}$$

where C_a is the cost per PSU and c is the cost per sample household. The effects of clustering on variance come largely from two sources. First, the selection consists of actual clusters of the physical distribution of the population. Second, the distribution of the population in those clusters is generally not random. Instead, it is characterized by some homogeneity that tends to increase the variance of the sample. C_a is estimated as 200 renminbi (RMB) and c is estimated as 5 RMB. Usually, roh is lower than 0.1, hence roh = 0.1 is used here:

$$m_{opt} = \sqrt{\frac{200}{5} \cdot \frac{(1 - 0.1)}{0.1}} = \sqrt{40 \times 9} \approx 19$$

A convenient figure of $m = 20$ is taken as the subsample size per sample PSU.

The Number of Sample PSUs. The number of sample PSUs is

$$a = \frac{n}{m} = \frac{941}{20} \approx 47 (PSUs)$$

The Number of Strata. Since this is a paired selection design, the number of strata could be calculated as

$$H = \frac{a}{2} = \frac{47}{2} \approx 23.5$$

The Allocation at Lower Stages. For the second, we have $b = 2$ (neighborhood office); for the third, $c^* = 5$ (household units).

Sampling Fraction and PPS Selection Equation

The sampling fraction is

$$f = \frac{941}{1,585,000} = 0.00059369 \approx \frac{1}{1,684}$$

Within each stratum, all family households have an equal probability of selection, which is expressed by the PPS selection equation:

$$f_h = \frac{a_h \text{Mos}_\alpha}{\Sigma \text{Mos}_\alpha} \cdot \frac{b \text{Mos}_{\alpha\beta}}{\text{Mos}_\alpha} \cdot \frac{c^*}{\text{Mos}_{\alpha\beta}} = \frac{a_h b d^*}{\text{Mos}_h}$$

Since this is a paired selection design $a_h = 2$. For later stages, $b = 2$, therefore:

$$f_h = \frac{2 \times 2 \times c^*}{\text{Mos}_h}$$

In the above equations, Mos_α is the measure of the size of the αth PSU, and $\text{Mos}_{\alpha\beta}$ is the measure of the size of the βth SSU within the αth PSU. $\text{Mos}_h = \Sigma \text{Mos}_\alpha$ which is the stratum size.

It should be noticed that c^* is the planned number of sample households within each second-stage unit, not necessarily the real number to be interviewed (d). When the measure of size of the second-stage unit ($\text{Mos}_{\alpha\beta\tau}$) is not equal to the real size ($N_{\alpha\beta\tau}$) at the time of survey, the real number of households should be:

$$c = \frac{c^*}{\text{Mos}_{\alpha\beta}} \times N_{\alpha\beta}$$

Selection of One Adult Respondent from Each Household

Since the sampling unit is the household, the interviewer was instructed to select one adult respondent from each household. A procedure applied successfully for years at the Survey Research Center at the University of Michigan and elsewhere was used.[7] A cover sheet was assigned to each sample household; it contained a form for listing the adult occupants and a table of selection. At the time of the first contact with the household, the interviewer listed each adult separately on one of the six lines of the form; each was identified in the first column by his relationship to the head of the household, for example, wife, son, brother, boarder. In the next two columns the interviewer recorded the sex and the age of each adult. The interviewer then assigned a serial number to each adult; first the males were numbered in order of decreasing age, followed by the females in the same order. Then the interviewer consulted the table of selection for the number of adults to be interviewed.

Cover sheets were prepared containing the eight types of selection tables in the correct proportions. Where sample addresses were available in advance, the central office of the Opinion Research Center of China assigned specifically to each address its own cover sheet with a selection table. However, advance listings were not available for sampling unlisted segments, nor for newly discovered or newly constructed dwellings. For these, packs of cover sheets were stapled together, and the interviewer was instructed to assign the next cover sheet at the time of the first contact with residents at the address, in a strictly defined order. Each of these, whether they resulted in interviews or "not-at-homes" or refusals, had to be returned to the office for checking.

Response Rate

Of the 941 questionnaires delivered, 794 were returned. Of those returned, 37 were incomplete. Some respondents answered the questions on their personal background but skipped "politically sensitive" questions. Other respondents answered most of the "politically sensitive" questions but refused to give their socioeconomic status. I excluded those questionnaires from the data, leaving 757 effective questionnaires, which represents a response rate of 80 percent.

Notes

1. Introduction

1. Norman H. Nie and Sidney Verba, "Political Participation," in Fred Greenstein and Nelson Polsby, eds., *Handbook of Political Science,* vol. 4, *Nongovernmental Politics* (Reading, Mass.: Addison-Wesley, 1975), p. 4.
2. For discussion, see Sidney Verba, Norman H. Nie, and Jae-on Kim, *Participation and Political Equality: A Seven Nation Comparison* (Chicago: University of Chicago Press, 1978), p. 53. See also Lester Milbrath and M. L. Goel, *Political Participation: How and Why Do People Get Involved in Politics?* (Chicago: Rand McNally, 1977); Robert E. Lane, *Political Life: Why People Get Involved in Politics* (New York: Free Press, 1959).
3. Herbert McClosky, "Political Participation," in David L. Sills, ed., *International Encyclopedia of the Social Sciences* (New York: Macmillan and Free Press, 1968), vol. 12, pp. 252–253; Myron Weiner, "Political Participation: Crisis of the Political Process," in Leonard Binder, James Coleman, Joseph LaPalombara, Lucian Pye, Sidney Verba, and Myron Weiner, *Crises and Sequences in Political Development* (Princeton: Princeton University Press, 1971), pp. 164–165; Sidney Verba and Norman H. Nie, *Participation in America: Political Democracy and Social Equality* (New York: Harper and Row, 1972).
4. Nie and Verba, "Political Participation," p. 4.
5. See, for example, Carl J. Friedrich and Zbigniew Brzezinski, *Totalitarian Dictatorship and Autocracy* (Cambridge, Mass.: Harvard University Press, 1956). See also Hannah Arendt, *The Origins of Totalitarianism* (New York: Harcourt Brace Jovanovich, 1951); Zbigniew Brzezinski, *The Permanent Purge: Politics in Soviet Totalitarianism* (Cambridge, Mass.: Harvard University Press, 1956); Alex Kassof, "The Administered Society: Totalitarianism without Terror," *World Politics,* 16(4) (July 1964): 558–575; T. H. Rigby, "Traditional, Market, and Organizational Societies and the USSR," *World Politics,* 16(4) (July 1964): 539–540.

6. Carl J. Friedrich, Michael Curtis, and Benjamin R. Barber, *Totalitarianism in Perspective: Three Views* (New York: Praeger, 1969), p. 126.

7. See Harry Eckstein and David E. Apter, *Comparative Politics: A Reader* (New York: Free Press, 1963), p. 434. See also Bertram D. Wolfe, "The Durability of Soviet Totalitarianism," in Alex Inkeles and Kent Geiger, eds., *Soviet Society: A Book of Readings* (Boston: Houghton Mifflin, 1961), pp. 648–659.

8. Friedrich and Brzezinski, *Totalitarian Dictatorship,* pp. 161–171.

9. See, among others, Gordon H. Skilling and Franklyn Griffiths, eds., *Interest Groups in Soviet Politics* (Princeton: Princeton University Press, 1971); Gordon H. Skilling, "Interest Groups and Communist Politics Revisited," *World Politics,* 36(1) (October 1983): 1–27; David S. G. Goodman, ed., *Groups in the People's Republic of China* (Armonk, N.Y.: M. E. Sharpe, 1981); Victor C. Falkenheim, ed., *Citizens and Groups in Contemporary China* (Ann Arbor: University of Michigan Center for Chinese Studies, 1984).

10. Alan P. L. Liu, *Political Culture and Group Conflict in Communist China* (Santa Barbara, Calif.: Clio Books, 1976), p. 5.

11. It has been suggested that social development, especially exposure to the media, change of residence, factory work, and increases in education, is related to political participation. See Karl W. Deutsch, "Social Mobilization and Political Development," *American Political Science Review,* 55(3) (September 1961): 493–514; Alex Inkeles and David H. Smith, *Becoming Modern: Individual Change in Six Developing Countries* (Cambridge, Mass.: Harvard University Press, 1974).

12. Deutsch, "Social Mobilization," pp. 493–514; Daniel Lerner, *The Passing of Traditional Society: Modernizing the Middle East* (New York: Free Press, 1958).

13. Ted Gurr, "Causal Model of Civil Strife: A Comparative Analysis Using New Indices," *American Political Science Review,* 62(4) (December 1968): 1104. See also Joseph Greenblum and Leonard Pearlin, "Vertical Mobility and Prejudice: A Socio-Psychological Analysis," in Reinhard Bendix and Seymour M. Lipset, eds., *Class, Status, and Power: A Reader in Social Stratification* (New York: Free Press, 1953), pp. 480–491.

14. For discussion, see Weiner, "Political Participation," pp. 165–175.

15. Joseph LaPalombara, "Monoliths or Plural Systems: Through Conceptual Lenses Darkly," *Studies of Comparative Communism,* 8(3) (Autumn 1975): 305–332.

16. Joseph LaPalombara, "Political Participation as an Analytical Concept in Comparative Politics," in Sidney Verba and Lucian W. Pye, eds., *The Citizen and Politics: A Comparative Perspective* (Stamford, Conn.: Greylock Publishers, 1978), p. 172.

17. Ibid., p. 171.

18. Robert S. Sharlet, "Concept Formation in Political Science and Communist Studies: Conceptualizing Political Participation," in Frederic J. Fleron, Jr., ed., *Communist Studies and Social Science: Essays on Methodology and Empirical Theory* (Chicago: Rand McNally, 1969), p. 250.

19. His justification for including these kinds of activities in political participation is that they are voluntary. See James R. Townsend, *Political Participation in Communist China* (Berkeley: University of California Press, 1969), pp. 4–6.

20. Sidney Verba, Norman H. Nie, and Jae-on Kim, *The Modes of Democratic Participation: A Cross-National Comparison* (Beverly Hills, Calif.: Sage Publications, 1971);

Verba and Nie, *Participation in America;* Verba, Nie, and Kim, *Participation and Political Equality,* pp. 51–52.

21. See Verba, Nie, and Kim, *Participation and Political Equality;* Verba, Nie, and Kim, *Modes;* Verba and Nie, *Participation in America.*

22. Alex Inkeles and Raymond A. Bauer, *The Soviet Citizen: Daily Life in a Totalitarian Society* (Cambridge, Mass.: Harvard University Press, 1959), p. 7.

23. Seweryn Bialer, *Stalin's Successors: Leadership, Stability, and Change in the Soviet Union* (New York: Cambridge University Press, 1980), p. 166.

24. Ibid., pp. 166–167.

25. Ibid., p. 167.

26. Ibid., p. 166.

27. It is true that recent changes in the former Soviet Union and Eastern European countries are exceptions to this observation. These events provide scholars of citizens' political acts in those societies with a remarkable opportunity to study the conditions under which "high" and "low" politics in communist societies meet. Nonetheless, study of the conditions facilitating such changes is beyond the scope of this work. I would like to point out that recent changes in the former Soviet Union and many Eastern European countries do not refute Bialer's observation. The separation of high politics and low politics and the separation of opposition and dissent have existed in those countries for more than forty years. During that period, although the existing structure and political institutions did not provide a mechanism for citizens to influence the selection of high-level government officials, people were still intensely and regularly involved in politics at local levels.

28. The word "opposition," according to Leonard Schapiro, "in its English usage, . . . so far as politics is concerned, . . . [has] a peculiarly English connotation. It belongs to the period when, in the aftermath of the Glorious Revolution and of the doctrine of Locke, the idea took root that the 'party' of opposition stood 'opposed' to the administration of the day, the 'party' of government, ready and anxious to take its place. In this manner changes in administration could occur peaceably without the whole fabric of society being convulsed in a revolution . . . Now plainly in this sense 'opposition' as a political term is ill-adapted to communist regimes in which rival political parties are not tolerated, where the fiction of unanimity is maintained if need be by force, and where changes of administration are normally the result of, or accompanied by, dramatic power struggles among the top leaders . . . [The] critics [in communist countries] in no sense formed an 'opposition' who wished to replace . . . administrations with one of their own. All they claimed was the right freely to criticise what they believed to be the faults of [the] administration; and the right to advocate changes of policy which they believed to be desirable. Their action should more properly be described as 'dissent'—a term which implies a claim to criticise and disagree with the policy of the government, but without any intention or plan of replacing that government by one composed of its critics." See Leonard Schapiro, ed., *Political Opposition in One-Party States* (New York: John Wiley and Sons, 1972), pp. 2–3.

29. See Schapiro, *Political Opposition,* pp. 2–3; Andrew J. Nathan, *Chinese Democracy* (New York: Alfred A. Knopf, 1985), pp. 24–26.

30. Jerry F. Hough, "The Party Apparatchiki," in Gordon H. Skilling and Franklyn Griffiths, eds., *Interest Groups in Soviet Politics* (Princeton: Princeton University Press, 1971), p. 88.

31. For discussion, see among others Jerry F. Hough, *The Soviet Union and Social Science Theory* (Cambridge, Mass.: Harvard University Press, 1977), pp. 120–124; Falkenheim, *Citizens and Groups,* p. 4.

32. Gabriel A. Almond, "Introduction: A Functional Approach to Comparative Politics," in Gabriel A. Almond and James S. Coleman, eds., *The Politics of the Developing Areas* (Princeton: Princeton University Press, 1960), p. 13.

33. For discussion, see ibid., p. 12.

34. Roy C. Macridis and Bernard E. Brown, *Comparative Politics: Notes and Readings* (Pacific Grove, Calif.: Brooks/Cole Publishing, 1990), p. 201.

35. For discussion, see among others Stephen Skowronek, *Building a New American State: The Expansion of National Administrative Capacities, 1877–1920* (Cambridge: Cambridge University Press, 1982); Peter Hall, *Governing the Economy: The Politics of State Intervention in Britain and France* (New York: Oxford University Press, 1986); John G. Ikenberry, David A. Lake, and Michael Mastanduno, eds., *The State and American Foreign Economic Policy* (Ithaca, N.Y.: Cornell University Press, 1988); James March and Johan Olsen, *Rediscovering Institutions* (New York: Free Press, 1989); Douglass C. North, *Institutions, Institutional Change, and Economic Performance* (Cambridge: Cambridge University Press, 1990).

36. Graham Allison, *Essence of Decision: Explaining the Cuban Missile Crisis* (Boston: Little, Brown, 1971); Morton H. Halperin, *Bureaucratic Politics and Foreign Policy* (Washington, D.C.: Brookings Institution, 1974).

37. For a detailed discussion of the methods of communication in China, see Michel Oksenberg, "Methods of Communication within the Chinese Bureaucracy," *China Quarterly,* 57 (January–March 1974): 1–39.

38. Max Weber, *From Max Weber: Essays in Sociology,* ed. and trans. H. H. Gerth and C. Wright Mills (New York: Oxford University Press, 1946), p. 215.

39. Ibid., p. 216.

40. Ibid., p. 220.

41. See Martin K. Whyte and William L. Parish, *Urban Life in Contemporary China* (Chicago: University of Chicago Press, 1984), p. 25.

42. Andrew G. Walder, "Organized Dependency and Cultures of Authority in Chinese Industry," *Journal of Asian Studies,* 43(1): 51–76; Andrew G. Walder, *Communist Neo-Traditionalism: Work and Authority in Chinese Industry* (Berkeley: University of California Press, 1986).

43. Andrew G. Walder, "Factory and Manager in an Era of Reform," *China Quarterly,* 118 (June 1989): 242–264. See also Jean C. Oi, "Communism and Clientelism: Rural Politics in China," *World Politics,* 37(1) (October 1984): 238–266; John P. Burns, *Political Participation in Rural China* (Berkeley: University of California Press, 1988); Falkenheim, *Citizens and Groups,* especially articles by John Burns, Richard P. Suttmeier, and Lynn T. White III.

44. James Scott found that "a large proportion of individual demands, and even group demands, in developing nations reach the political system, not before laws are passed, but rather at the enforcement stage." James Scott, "Corruption, Machine

Politics, and Political Change," *American Political Science Review*, 63 (December 1969): 1142.

45. See among others Walder, "Organized Dependency," pp. 53–56.
46. For example, Arthur F. Bentley believes no "interest" can be considered to exist unless it manifests itself in group actions. By assuming that there are no effective individual interests, Bentley was able to claim that all things involving government are determined by conflicting group pressures. See Arthur F. Bentley, *The Process of Government* (Evanston, Ill.: Principia Press, 1949), p. 211. David Truman, in his well-known book *The Governmental Process*, argues that certain government policies would lead to disturbances and dislocations. "These disturbances inevitably produced associations—of owners, workers, and farmers—operating upon government to mitigate and control the ravages of the system through tariffs, subsidies, wage guarantees, social insurance and the like." See David B. Truman, *The Governmental Process: Political Interests and Public Opinion* (New York: Alfred A. Knopf, 1958), p. 61.
47. E. E. Schattschneider, *The Semi-Sovereign People: A Realist's View of Democracy in America* (New York: Holt, Rhinehart and Winston, 1960), p. 2.
48. Walder, "Communist Social Structure and Workers' Politics," in Victor C. Falkenheim, ed., *Citizens and Groups in Contemporary China* (Armonk, N.Y.: M. E. Sharpe, 1981), p. 47.
49. Ibid.
50. For cross-national data, see among others, Verba, Nie, and Kim, *Participation and Political Equality*, pp. 80–93.
51. Ibid., p. 81.
52. Ibid.
53. This is not contradictory to the situation in liberal democracies. In the United States, the standard socioeconomic model does not explain why citizens engage in particularized contacts, activities aimed at benefiting participants' private interests. "But for particularized contacts we see a contrast," point out Verba and Nie. "The standard socioeconomic model does not explain why citizens engage in these activities, a finding consistent with our earlier findings that these are activities carried out by citizens from across the socioeconomic spectrum and that they are not dependent on a more general psychological involvement in politics. Not only does particularized contacting produce different benefits, it derives from a process quite different from the one that leads to other activities." See Verba and Nie, *Participation in America*, p. 135.
54. Verba, Nie, and Kim, *Participation and Political Equality*, pp. 80–93.
55. Ibid., p. 1.
56. Sidney Verba, "The Parochial and the Polity," in Sidney Verba and Lucian W. Pye, eds., *The Citizen and Politics: A Comparative Perspective* (Stamford, Conn.: Greylock Publishers, 1978), p. 3.
57. In contrast to Verba, Nie, and Kim, Milbrath and Goel define political participation as "those actions of private citizens by which they seek to influence or to support government and politics" (see Milbrath and Goel, *Political Participation*, p. 2). Samuel Huntington and Joan Nelson think participation is "activity by private citizens designed to influence governmental decision-making"; see Samuel Huntington and

Joan M. Nelson, *No Easy Choice: Political Participation in Developing Countries* (Cambridge, Mass.: Harvard University Press, 1976), p. 4. Robert Sharlet proposes a definition of political participation "relevant to the functional inputs of the policy-making process"; see Robert S. Sharlet, "Concept Formation in Political Science and Communist Studies: Conceptualizing Political Participation," *Canadian Slavic Studies*, 1(4) (Winter 1967): 640–649, reprinted in Fleron, *Communist Studies*, p. 245. James Townsend believes political participation includes "all those activities through which the individual consciously becomes involved in attempts to give a particular direction to the conduct of public affairs, excluding activities of an occupational or compulsory nature." Although his study is influenced by the totalitarian mode, in his definition of political participation, interest articulation is still the core concept. For him the initiatives of activities should originate from individuals, and the aim of activities is to direct the policy to be characterized as political participation. See Townsend, *Communist China*, p. 4.

58. Theodore Friedgut includes involvement of the ordinary citizen by the government as a form of political participation in the Soviet Union. See Theodore H. Friedgut, *Political Participation in the USSR* (Princeton: Princeton University Press, 1979), pp. 13–20.

59. According to Townsend, elections in China perform the following functions: first, the education of both masses and cadres in the operation of socialist democracy; second, the creation of higher incentives for fulfilling production goals and carrying out party policies. See Townsend, *Communist China*, pp. 115 and 135–136.

60. Interviews with people who work in the Institute of Rural Development of the Research Center for Rural Development, conducted in February 1988.

61. See among others Verba and Nie, *Participation in America*; Verba, Nie, and Kim, *Participation and Political Equality*.

62. Huntington and Nelson, *No Easy Choice*, p. 6.

63. A detailed description of the sampling procedure is attached as an appendix.

64. W. Phillips Shively, *The Craft of Political Research* (Englewood Cliffs, N.J.: Prentice-Hall, 1974), p. 56.

65. See among others Chen Chongshan and Mi Xiuling, *A Study of Media Communication Effects in China* (Shenyang: Shenyang Publishing House, 1989); Stanley Rosen, "Public Opinion and Reform in the People's Republic of China," *Studies in Comparative Communism*, 22(2/3) (Summer/Autumn 1989): 153–170.

66. Survey researchers in the West use two different methods to calculate response rates. Some calculate the response rate based on the ratio between questionnaires collected by researchers and the original sample. Others do so on the basis of the "net sample"—the original sample minus locations that are not dwelling units or dwelling units that are vacant, or, in a small number of cases, residents with language problems. Almost all Chinese researchers calculate response rates based on the net sample, and survey nonresponse rate in China simply represents the percentage of refusals in the sample.

67. The most famous campaigns were the anti-rightist movement in 1957 and the Cultural Revolution from 1966 to 1976. During those campaigns, scores of people were purged and many families were separated by the authorities for expressing independent views or for criticizing the CCP.

68. Wayne DiFranceisco and Zvi Gitelman, "Soviet Political Culture and 'Covert Par-

ticipation' in Policy Implementation," *American Political Science Review*, 78(3) (September 1984): 603–621.

2. Forms of Citizen Participation in Beijing

1. For a detailed discussion of the history and the changes in the People's Congress system in China, see among others James R. Townsend, *Political Participation in Communist China* (Berkeley: University of California Press, 1969), pp. 103–144; Andrew J. Nathan, *Chinese Democracy* (New York: Alfred A. Knopf, 1985), pp. 193–223; John P. Burns, *Political Participation in Rural China* (Berkeley: University of California Press, 1988); Victor C. Falkenheim, "Political Participation in China," *Problem of Communism*, 27 (May–June 1978): 18–32; Bruce J. Jacobs, "Elections in China," *Australian Journal of Chinese Affairs* 25 (1991): 171–199; Barrett L. McCormick, "China's Leninist Parliament and Public Sphere: A Comparative Analysis," in Barrett L. McCormick and Jonathan Unger, eds., *China after Socialism* (Armonk, N.Y.: M. E. Sharpe, 1996), pp. 29–53; Barrett L. McCormick, *Political Reform in Post-Mao China: Democracy and Bureaucracy in a Leninist State* (Berkeley: University of California Press, 1990).
2. Electoral Law of the People's Republic of China, Peking, 1953, art. 5., in Theodore Chen, ed. and trans., *The Chinese Communist Regime* (New York: Praeger, 1967), p. 65.
3. "The electoral law for the [National People's Congress] and local people's congresses of the [People's Republic of China] (adopted by the Second Session of the Fifth NPC on 1 July 1979 and revised in accordance with the 'Resolution on the Revision of Certain Stipulations of the Electoral Law for the NPC and Local People's Congresses of the PRC,' adopted by the Fifth Session of the Fifth NPC on December 10, 1982)." The English translation appears in *Foreign Broadcast Information Service, Daily Report, People's Republic of China (FBIS-Chi)*, 82-243 (December 17, 1982): K14–K21.
4. Ibid., p. K14.
5. Ibid., p. K14. For discussion, see Nathan, *Chinese Democracy*, p. 196; John P. Burns, *Political Participation in Rural China* (Berkeley: University of California Press, 1988), pp. 88–89.
6. Nathan, *Chinese Democracy*, p. 196.
7. *Questions and Answers on the Election System*, a handbook for local officials published by the Masses' Publishing House, as cited in Nathan, *Chinese Democracy*, p. 196.
8. See "NPC to Probe Signature Incident," *Beijing Review*, 32 (July 17–23, 1989): 10–11.
9. Interviews with officials of the National People's Congress, conducted in Beijing, October 1993.
10. For discussion, see Nathan, *Chinese Democracy*, pp. 191–223.
11. For discussion of elections in Beijing and other places in China, see ibid., pp. 193–233.
12. See among others Martin K. Whyte and William L. Parish, *Urban Life in Contemporary China* (Chicago: University of Chicago Press, 1984).
13. Interviews with officials of Haidian District, conducted in Beijing, 1988.

14. For discussion of the differences between plebiscitary elections and limited-choice elections, see Alex Pravda, "Elections in Communist Party States," in Guy Hermet, Richard Rose, and Alain Rouquié, eds., *Elections without Choice* (New York: John Wiley and Sons, 1978), pp. 175–186.

15. There were different opinions on the uses of elections. Officials in the Central Organization Department of the CCP, especially those in the Young Cadres Bureau, lobbied for elections for the leaders of work units, especially after 1984 and 1985, when the government adopted a policy to promote "third-echelon" cadres. They believed newly promoted cadres had to go through the scrutiny of their constituents. Ironically, the Office of Political System Reform of the CCP, under Bao Tong, strongly opposed the election of managers, claiming that for a manager to run a factory well, he or she has to make decisions based on market demands. Elections on the shop floor would force managers in factories to respond to the demands of their constituents. Such behavior patterns would definitely jeopardize their ability to respond to the market. Therefore, Bao himself predicted that elections for leaders would only decrease the productivity of enterprises. Those who worked in the Young Cadres Bureau, by contrast, claimed that low productivity in Chinese enterprises mainly resulted from dissatisfaction of workers with their managers. The best way to resolve these tensions was to let workers choose their own leaders. Neither side won the debate and the actual attitude of the government was a laissez-faire-type response. The Central Organization Department of the CCP advocated such elections, and the Central Committee has never issued a formal document to make such elections a mandatory requirement. Interview with Wu Guoguang, who used to work at the Office of Political System Reform of the CCP Central Committee under Bao Tong; he was expelled from the CCP after June 4, 1989. At the time of the interview in 1990, he was a visiting Luce Fellow at Columbia University.

16. Reports on the elections of leaders of work units first appeared in the Chinese official news media in 1980. According to Xinhua, the Foreign Language Printing House was the "first to have all workshop heads elected by workers . . . [The] nominations came from the workers. During the elections . . . of 23 former workshop leaders, 13 were re-elected. Ten were dropped." See "Xinhua Praises Elected Leaders of Beijing Printing Plant," *FBIS-Chi*, 80-023 (February 1, 1980): R1. In the Geyang County Company, "all leaders below the company level are elected democratically once a year . . . [They] are elected by the workers by secret ballot instead of being appointed from above." See "Jiangxi Company Adopts Democratic Election of Leaders," *FBIS-Chi*, 80-025 (February 5, 1980): O6.

17. "Xinhua Praises," *FBIS-Chi*, 80-023, p. R1.

18. See "Jiangxi Company," *FBIS-Chi*, 80-025, p. O7.

19. For discussion, see Andrew G. Walder, "Communist Neo-Traditionalism: An Introductory Essay," in *Communist Neo-Traditionalism: Work and Authority in Chinese Industry* (Berkeley: University of California Press, 1986), pp. 1–27.

20. See Hong Yung Lee, *The Politics of the Chinese Cultural Revolution: A Case Study* (Berkeley: University of California Press, 1978).

21. The pledge to abolish political campaigns was first made by Deng Xiaoping in 1979 and reconfirmed by CCP Propaganda Department Director Wang Renzhong. When tested by the incident involving "Bitter Love" (a controversial movie attacked by

conservatives), Hu Yaobang invoked Deng's pledge and successfully blocked spill-over effects of the criticism. See "The News from Beijing Is That Economics Is the Overriding Task and That China Will Certainly Not Organize a Political Move-ment," *Hong Kong Hsin Wan Pao*, August 31, 1981. The English translation appears in *FBIS-Chi*, 81-169 (September 1, 1981): W1.

22. Victor C. Falkenheim, "Political Participation in China," *Problems of Communism*, 27 (May–June 1978): 25.

23. Ibid., p. 24.

24. See among others Nathan, *Chinese Democracy*, pp. 193–223; Burns, *Rural China*, pp. 94–95; Falkenheim, "Political Participation," p. 25.

25. Mao Zedong, "Some Questions Concerning Methods of Leadership," in *Selected Readings from the Works of Mao-Tsetung* (Beijing: Foreign Language Press, 1971), p. 290.

26. For discussion of the mass line in China, see Townsend, *Communist China*, pp. 72–74. See also Burns, *Rural China*, pp. 23–28; Harry Harding, "Maoist Theories of Policy-Making and Organization," in Thomas W. Robinson, ed., *The Cultural Rev-olution in China* (Berkeley: University of California Press, 1971), pp. 117–142; "Resolutions on Certain Questions in the History of Our Party since the Founding of the People's Republic of China," *Beijing Review*, 27 (July 6, 1981): 10–39.

27. Andrew G. Walder, "Factory and Manager in an Era of Reform," *China Quarterly*, 118 (June 1989): 252.

28. Article 42 of the Chinese constitution reads, "Citizens of the People's Republic of China have the right as well as the duty to work." From the *Constitution of the People's Republic of China* (Beijing: Foreign Languages Press, 1983), p. 35.

29. There is a three-month probation period (*shiyong qi*) for new employees. After this is successfully passed, it is very hard to be fired.

30. Walder, "Factory and Manager," p. 253.

31. The Chinese government knows of this tactic. In the Socialist Education Movement of 1962–63, the government put those whom it called "First Grade Commune Members" or "First Grade Workers" in the category of people who should be put back in control. According to an internal document ("Policy Issues of the Socialist Education Movement"), certain kinds of people who were not enemies of the regime but acted as tyrants at different places caused great trouble for the government.

32. Victor Falkenheim reports that "when villagers had grievances it was customary for wives to stand in the doorways of their homes hurling imprecations, often for *several days in a row*." Falkenheim, "Political Participation," p. 25, italics added.

33. Personal interview with engineer who worked at the Petroleum Machinery Manu-facturing factory in Beijing in the summer of 1988.

34. Jerry F. Hough, "The Party Apparatchiki," in Gordon H. Skilling and Franklyn Griffiths, eds., *Interest Groups in Soviet Politics* (Princeton: Princeton University Press, 1971), p. 49.

35. Townsend, *Communist China*, p. 154.

36. Ibid., p. 157.

37. For discussion, see Charles E. Lindblom, *The Policy-Making Process* (Englewood Cliffs, N.J.: Prentice-Hall, 1968), pp. 64–65.

38. The procedure is called mass evaluation (*qunzhong pingyi*).

39. General Office of the Central Committee of the CCP and General Office of the State Council, eds., *Xinfangxue Gailun* (Beijing: Huaxia Publishing House, 1991), p. 22.
40. Article 41, *Constitution of the PRC*, p. 34.
41. For discussion of the function of the agencies dealing with people's complaints, see General Office, *Xinfangxue Gailun*, pp. 88–103.
42. Interview with a retired high school teacher, conducted in Beijing, January 1989.
43. General Office, *Xinfangxue Gailun*, p. 183.
44. Ibid.
45. For a discussion of this function of newspapers in China, see Nathan, *Chinese Democracy*, p. 154.
46. Ibid.
47. Xinhua, December 14, 1979, in *FBIS-Chi*, 79-242 (December 14, 1979): L6–L7; quoted in Burns, *Rural China*, p. 140.
48. Interview with Wu Guoguang, conducted in New York, October 1990.
49. Xu Xing, "Internal Mechanisms of the Information Monopoly," *Kai Fang* (Open Magazine), 42 (June 1990): 53.
50. See Burns, *Rural China*, p. 141.
51. Interview with a journalist of Xinhua, conducted in Beijing, February 1989.
52. For a theoretical discussion, see Steffen W. Schmidt, Laura Guasti, Carl Landé, and James Scott, eds., *Friends, Followers, and Factions: A Reader in Political Clientelism* (Berkeley: University of California Press, 1977). For the situation in China, see Walder, "Neo-Traditionalism," and Jean C. Oi, "Communism and Clientelism: Rural Politics in China," *World Politics*, 37(1) (October 1984): 238–266.
53. See among others Ezra F. Vogel, "Voluntarism and Social Control," in Donald W. Treadgold, ed., *Soviet and Chinese Communism: Similarities and Differences* (Seattle: University of Washington Press, 1967), pp. 168–184. See also Susan L. Shirk, *Competitive Comrades: Career Incentives and Student Strategies in China* (Berkeley: University of California Press, 1982).
54. Walder, "Neo-Traditionalism," pp. 147–153.
55. The concept is borrowed from Kenneth Waltz, *Theory of International Politics* (New York: McGraw-Hill, 1979).
56. Ibid., p. 18.
57. Ibid., p. 40.
58. Walder, "Neo-Traditionalism," p. 151.
59. Ibid., p. 169.
60. For a discussion of *guanxi*, see Andrew J. Nathan, *Peking Politics, 1918–1923: Factionalism and the Failure of Constitutionalism* (Berkeley: University of California Press, 1976), pp. 27–58; Walder, *Neo-Traditionalism*, pp. 179–186.
61. "In 1956, small numbers of workers or students in certain places went on strike. The immediate cause of these disturbances was the failure to satisfy some of their demands for material benefits, of which some should and could have been met, while others were out of place or excessive and therefore could not be met for the time being. But *a more important cause was bureaucracy on the part of leadership*." Mao Tse-Tung, "On the Correct Handling of Contradictions among the People," in *Selected Works of Mao Tse-Tung* (Beijing: People's Press, 1977), vol. 5, p. 395, italics added.
62. Article 28 of the 1975 constitution and article 45 of the 1978 constitution.

63. Burns, *Rural China,* p. 154.

64. Interview with Zhao Hongliang, one of the major organizers of the strike in 1987, conducted in New York, October 1990. He actively participated in the democracy movement in 1989 and escaped from China after June 4, 1989. He now lives in Toronto.

65. "Horizontal connections" refers to those activities in which people in different sectors across the society join together, which is strictly prohibited in China. "Vertical connections" are activities undertaken by people within each sector of society, which are more likely to be tolerated by the regime even if the scope is rather extensive.

66. In late April, a rumor spread through Beijing that a jeep owned by the Public Security Bureau of the Beijing Municipal Government hit a female student of Beijing Normal University and fled the scene, leaving the girl dead on the spot. Many Beijing residents believed this story and got very angry with the government. In fact, there had been a traffic accident. In that accident, a female student was hit by a trolley bus on her way back from Tiananmen Square. When the rumor spread, the Beijing Municipal Government and the Public Security Bureau tried every way they could to refute it and denied the students' allegations. After the details of the incident were published in the *Beijing Ribao,* the story became that the girl had been heavily beaten by policemen on the previous night, April 20, in front of Xinhuamen, the main gate of Zhongnanhai (where the State Council is located). The girl was supposedly so severely beaten in the head that she could not walk properly. Because of internal injuries, she could not control herself and had fallen down when the trolley passed by. The new version of the story was even more provocative than the previous one. This story was one of the most important factors inciting people to protest against the government in April 1989. A student leader told me under the condition of anonymity that the rumor was deliberately made up and spread by his group to mobilize the populace in Beijing to join the student movement. Interview with a student leader in New York, February 1990.

67. Interview with worker in the Petroleum Machinery Manufacturing factory in Beijing, March 1988.

68. Interview with Wang Xi, formerly a Ph.D. candidate in the history department, Columbia University, now teaching at Indiana University in Pennsylvania. He had daily contacts with workers at Chongqing Steel and Iron Corporation from 1973 to 1978.

69. Interview with worker in the Petroleum Machinery Manufacturing factory in Beijing, March 1988.

70. In traditional China, the administrator also played the role of judge. There has never been a separation of power between the judicial and the executive branches. Therefore, when people make appeals to courts, they are actually appealing to administrators at higher levels. People nevertheless believe that the courts are staffed by honest and upright officials who will help them resolve their problems.

71. One of the major participants in the Democracy Wall Movement (see next section in text), Fu Yuehua, claimed that she was raped by the leaders of a work unit. She resorted to every means available to her and finally sued that particular unit in court.

72. Interview with a judge in a district court in Beijing in 1988. In a recent example,

peasants in Shun Yi County near Beijing sued the township officials in court for violating contractual obligations. Originally the villagers had signed contracts with township officials. A few years later, after villagers began getting higher and higher returns from the fields, officials tried to change the content of the agreement with the villagers, asking them to pay more money to the government. The villagers refused and appealed to the county officials. The county officials refused to intervene. The villagers then sued the township officials in court and won the case. Interview with villagers conducted in Shun Yi, Beijing, July 1988.

73. According to Hong Yung Lee, big-character posters also served Mao's political purposes. They helped Maoist leaders to grasp what was going on at lower levels and to expose "hidden enemies," since those attacked were forced to respond. See Lee, *Cultural Revolution*, pp. 45–46.

74. See Nathan, *Chinese Democracy*, pp. 108–109. Article 13 of the 1975 constitution and article 45 of the 1978 constitution guaranteed citizens the right to "speak out freely, air their views fully, hold great debates and write big-character posters."

75. For the origin of Democracy Wall, see Ruan Ming, "When Hu Yaobang First Came to Power," *Minzhu Zhongguo*, 5 (December 1990): 71–72.

76. For discussion, see James D. Seymour, ed., *The Fifth Modernization: China's Human Rights Movement, 1978–1979* (Stanfordville, N.Y.: Human Rights Publishing Group, 1980), pp. 1–27.

77. Ruan, "Hu Yaobang," pp. 71–72.

78. Nathan, *Chinese Democracy*, p. 36.

79. The right to demonstrate was codified in article 87 of the 1954 constitution, article 28 of the 1975 constitution, article 45 of the 1978 constitution, and article 35 of the 1982 constitution.

80. The example of such use of demonstrations during the Cultural Revolution can be found in Lee, *Cultural Revolution*, p. 245.

81. Roger Garside cites events at the local level, where peasants demonstrated in front of party headquarters for several days and demanded that the authorities punish local officials who had abused their power. See Roger Garside, *Coming Alive: China after Mao* (London: Andre Deutsch, 1981), pp. 221–243.

82. The 1979 demonstration was led by Fu Yuehua, who helped the peasants organize a protest along Changan Street in January 1979. This demonstration led to the downfall of Hua Guofeng and Wang Dongxing. See among others Garside, *Coming Alive*, p. 249. In 1986, a protest to demand quicker economic and political reform began at the Chinese University of Science and Technology in Anhui Province. The movement quickly spread to Shanghai and Beijing. Again, students from Peking University led the demonstration at Tiananmen Square. It resulted in Hu Yaobang's resignation as party general secretary. And in the democracy movement of 1989, millions of people demonstrated at Tiananmen Square starting from April 27 through June 3. This time, the demonstrations ended in bloody suppression and the dismissal of Zhao Ziyang as party general secretary.

83. According to Wu Guoguang, a former senior official at the Political System Reform Office of the CCP, conservatives made use of demonstrations and advocated tightening control to avoid chaos. They believed "liberalism" had led to demonstrations and advocated dealing with protests by reemphasizing political education. Each

time, reformers were the losers in these power struggles intensified by demonstrations.

84. Right after the Beijing Municipal People's Congress passed the regulations to limit the right of citizens to demonstrate, some Tibetan students applied and got approval from the Public Security Bureau of the Beijing Municipal Government to demonstrate in Beijing to protest a novel published in *Renmin Wenxue* (People's Literature). They claimed that the novel had humiliated the Tibetan people.

85. For the text of the regulation, see " 'Text' of Beijing Regulations on Demonstrations," *FBIS-Chi*, 86-249 (December 29, 1986): R1–R2.

3. The Extent of Citizen Participation

1. For the distinction between conventional and unconventional participation, see among others Lester Milbrath and M. L. Goel, *Political Participation: How and Why Do People Get Involved in Politics?* (Chicago: Rand McNally, 1977), pp. 20–21; Donna Bahry and Brian D. Silver, "Soviet Citizen Participation on the Eve of Democratization," *American Political Science Review*, 84(3) (September 1990): 826; Samuel H. Barnes and Max Kaase, *Political Action: Mass Participation in Five Western Democracies* (Beverly Hills, Calif.: Sage Publications, 1979).

2. See among others Sidney Verba and Norman H. Nie, *Participation in America: Political Democracy and Social Equality* (New York: Harper and Row, 1972); Sidney Verba, Norman H. Nie, and Jae-on Kim, *Participation and Political Equality: A Seven Nation Comparison* (Chicago: University of Chicago Press, 1978); Milbrath and Goel, *Political Participation*.

3. The actual wording of the question was, "During the past five years, did you and/or your colleagues encounter any incompetent cadres or leaders abusing power?"

4. The actual wording of the question was, "In the past five years, when certain decisions of your work unit [*danwei*], such as salary raises, bonus distributions, apartment allotments, and children taking over parents' positions [*zinü dingti*] were made that you considered harmful and unjust, did you often, sometimes, rarely, or never do the following?"

5. The actual text of the question was, "Did you happen to have a chance to vote in the (1988 county-level) election?"

6. Alex Pravda, "Elections in Communist Party States," in Guy Hermet, Richard Rose, and Alain Rouquié, eds., *Elections without Choice* (New York: John Wiley and Sons, 1978), pp. 186–193.

7. For example, Verba and Nie detailed overreporting of turnout rates by 10 percent in survey studies in their classic study of political participation in America; see Verba and Nie, *Participation in America*, p. 30. See also Aage R. Clausen, "Response Validity in Surveys: Vote Report," *Public Opinion Quarterly*, 32 (Winter 1968–69): 588–606.

8. Clausen, "Response Validity," p. 589.

9. Theodore H. Friedgut, *Political Participation in the USSR* (Princeton: Princeton University Press, 1979), pp. 116–118.

10. See among others Bahry and Silver, "Soviet Citizen," p. 824; Rasma Karklins, "Soviet Elections Revisited: Voter Abstention in Noncompetitive Balloting," *American Po-*

litical Science Review, 80(2) (June 1986): 449–470; Philip C. Roeder, "Electoral Avoidance in the Soviet Union," *Soviet Studies,* 41(3) (July 1989): 462–483; Victor Zaslavsky and Robert J. Brym, "The Functions of Elections in the USSR," *Soviet Studies,* 30(3) (July 1978): 362–371.

11. Bahry and Silver, "Soviet Citizen," p. 824.

12. Barrett L. McCormick, "China's Leninist Parliament and Public Sphere: A Comparative Analysis," in Barrett McCormick and Jonathan Unger, eds., *China after Socialism* (Armonk, N.Y.: M. E. Sharpe, 1996), p. 41.

13. Barbara A. Anderson and Brian D. Silver, "Measurement and Mismeasurement of the Validity of the Self-Reported Vote," *American Journal of Political Science,* 30 (1986): 775.

14. Clausen reported a response error for American voters of 8.3 percent in the 1964 elections. Clausen, "Response Validity," p. 601.

15. Interview with work unit leaders in Beijing at the Petroleum Machinery Manufacturing factory as well as leaders at various levels in Peking University, conducted in mid-1988.

16. Friedgut detailed a similar technique used by officials in the Soviet Union to cross nonvoters off the lists. See Friedgut, *Political Participation,* pp. 116–117. McCormick documented the same phenomenon in China; see McCormick, "China's Leninist Parliament," p. 41.

17. Article 35 of the People's Congress Electoral Law states, "A voter, who is in another locality during the time of an election, may entrust another voter, by written authorization, with a proxy vote, but not without prior approval from the election committee." See "People's Congress Electoral Law, Adopted by the Fifth Session of the Fifth NPC on 10 December 1982," English translation in *Foreign Broadcast Information Service, Daily Report, People's Republic of China (FBIS-Chi),* 82-243 (December 17, 1982): K20.

18. The description is based on my experience in the election for deputies to the local people's congress for 1979–1981, when I attended Peking University. I refused to vote in that election, and an official from the election commission, who was the CYL secretary, arbitrarily assigned me a proxy voter; that person voted in the election instead. Other students in my class as well as those in other classes had similar experiences.

19. Since not every work unit held elections, I used a screener to identify those respondents whose work units held elections in the past five years. The actual question was, "During the past five years, were there any elections held in your work unit or neighborhood for the masses to choose their leaders?" For those people whose work units held elections in the past five years, a second question was asked: "In the election at your work unit, did you happen to vote?"

20. See Andrew G. Walder, *Communist Neo-Traditionalism: Work and Authority in Chinese Industry* (Berkeley: University of California Press, 1986), pp. 162–189.

21. The actual wording of the questions was, "Which one of these statements comes closest to describing your feelings when you went to the polls to cast your ballot in 1988? Did you vote because you hoped you could elect a person who represents your interests, because you thought it was your duty, because the leaders of your

work unit asked you to vote, or did you not feel anything in particular, or have you never thought about the issue?"

22. Raymond Wolfinger and Steven J. Rosenstone, *Who Votes?* (New Haven: Yale University Press, 1980), pp. 7–8.

23. The actual wording of the question was, "During county-level/work unit elections, did you often, sometimes, rarely, or never persuade your relatives or colleagues to go to briefing meetings in order to get to know the candidates?"

24. The actual wording of the question was, "During county-level elections/elections for leaders in your work unit, did you often, sometimes, rarely, or never campaign for certain candidates?"

25. The actual wording of the question was, "During the 1988 county-level elections/elections in your work unit, did you often, sometimes, rarely, or never persuade other people to boycott any unfair election?"

26. This is a composite variable. See the note to Table 3.1 for the composition of this item.

27. The actual wording of each question was, "Did you often, sometimes, rarely, or never tell him that he was wrong?" "Did you often, sometimes, rarely, or never demand equal treatment in front of your leaders?" "Did you often, sometimes, rarely, or never talk about the matter to the leader of your work unit?"

28. The actual wording of the question was, "Did you often, sometimes, rarely, or never complain through the bureaucratic hierarchy?"

29. See John Burns, *Political Participation in Rural China* (Berkeley: University of California Press, 1988), pp. 122–138.

30. James R. Townsend, *Political Participation in Communist China* (Berkeley: University of California Press, 1969), pp. 156–157.

31. The actual wording of the question was, "Did you often, sometimes, rarely, or never complain through the trade unions?"

32. "Did you often, sometimes, rarely, or never complain through various political organizations?"

33. "Did you often, sometimes, rarely, or never complain through deputies to various levels of people's congresses?"

34. "Did you often, sometimes, rarely, or never write to newspaper editors?"

35. "Did you often, sometimes, rarely, or never report to complaint bureaus?"

36. "Did you often, sometimes, rarely, or never 'apply for an audience' with higher authorities to appeal for help personally?"

37. "Did you often, sometimes, rarely, or never sue in court?"

38. "Did you often, sometimes, rarely, or never organize a group of people to fight against leaders?"

39. "Did you often, sometimes, rarely, or never whip up public opinion in the work unit against leaders?"

40. "Did you often, sometimes, rarely, or never write big-character posters?"

41. "Did you often, sometimes, rarely, or never go on strike?"

42. "Did you often, sometimes, rarely, or never join demonstrations?"

43. "Did you often, sometimes, rarely, or never deliberately engage in slowdowns?"

44. The actual wording of the question was, "We have heard that if a government policy

jeopardizes the interests of people in a unit and people cannot counter it, some people engage in slowdowns on the job. Has it ever happened in your work unit?"

45. The actual wording of the question was, "Did you often, sometimes, rarely, or never try to find relatives or acquaintances of those in charge and ask them for help?"

46. The questions read, "Did you often, sometimes, rarely, or never send those in charge gifts and ask for favors when you were not satisfied with government policies?" "Did you often, sometimes, rarely, or never send those in charge gifts and ask for favors when you were not satisfied with policy implementation?"

47. Each respondent was asked to identify the social issues that he or she felt needed to be resolved. Those respondents who could identify at least one social issue were asked whether or not they had worked with others to resolve the problem. The actual wording of the question was, "Have you ever worked with others to try to solve the [problems mentioned by the respondent in the screener]?"

48. The activities in this category include complaints to bureaucrats, working together with others to attempt to solve social problems, complaints through political organizations, letters to government officials, campaigns for candidates in elections for deputies to local people's congresses, complaints through deputies to people's congresses, letters to the editors of newspapers, persuading others to go to campaign or briefing meetings in elections for deputies to local people's congresses, reports to complaint bureaus, boycotting unfair elections for deputies to local people's congresses, going to court, writing big-character posters, taking part in strikes, and taking part in demonstrations.

49. Max Kaase and Alan Marsh, "Political Action: A Theoretical Perspective," in Samuel H. Barnes and Max Kaase, *Political Action: Mass Participation in Five Western Democracies* (Beverly Hills, Calif.: Sage Publications, 1979), pp. 40–41.

50. This definition is given in ibid., p. 41.

51. I would like to remind readers that the measurement of unconventional political actions in this study is far from comprehensive. Some questions that should be included in the questionnaire were deliberately avoided owing to a kind of self-censorship. Although the study was conducted during the most liberal period of the People's Republic of China, with the help of the most liberal group in the country, we still imposed certain constraints on ourselves in order to escape the attention of the authorities. During the survey, our top priority was avoiding the attention of bureaucrats. Many times, aspirations to scientific accuracy gave way to the goal of simply maximizing the possibility of successfully completing this study. No one, then, now, and in the future, can evaluate whether we have gathered the maximum information that might be gathered given the political atmosphere at that time. I can say only that we have done our best and at least succeeded in gathering a rather comprehensive data base.

52. A good example is the question on slowdowns in Beijing. There clearly exists a discrepancy between the figures given by our respondents regarding their own behavior and the figures given by our respondents about other people's behavior.

53. The only group-based activity found in this survey is working with others to solve social problems, and this act is cooperative rather than conflictual in its nature.

4. Modes of Political Participation in China

1. For example, Bernard Berelson, Paul Lazarsfeld, and William McPhee stated that "political involvement and participation are highly correlated with one another and for analytical purposes, interchangeable." See Bernard Berelson, Paul F. Lazarsfeld, and William N. McPhee, *Voting: A Study of Opinion Formation in a Presidential Campaign* (Chicago: University of Chicago Press, 1954), p. 24. Robert Lane and Lester Milbrath and M. L. Goel argued that political acts are hierarchical and that citizens who engage in the most difficult acts almost certainly engage in easier ones. See Robert E. Lane, *Political Life: Why People Get Involved in Politics* (New York: Free Press, 1959), pp. 92–94; Lester Milbrath and M. L. Goel, *Political Participation: How and Why Do People Get Involved in Politics?* (Chicago: Rand McNally, 1977), pp. 18–19 and 22–23.

2. James R. Townsend, *Political Participation in Communist China* (Berkeley: University of California Press, 1969), pp. 183 and 174.

3. For discussion, see among others Milbrath and Goel, *Political Participation;* Sidney Verba and Norman H. Nie, *Participation in America: Political Democracy and Social Equality* (New York: Harper and Row, 1972); Sidney Verba, Norman H. Nie, and Jae-on Kim, *Participation and Political Equality: A Seven Nation Comparison* (Chicago: University of Chicago Press, 1978).

4. Theodore H. Friedgut, *Political Participation in the USSR* (Princeton: Princeton University Press, 1979).

5. Victor C. Falkenheim, "Political Participation in China," *Problems of Communism*, 27 (May–June 1978): 22–26.

6. In their comparative study of participation and political equality, they systematically studied the modes of political participation in Yugoslavia. More important, they paid much attention to the similarities and differences among the modes found there and in six other countries. See Verba, Nie, and Kim, *Participation and Political Equality*.

7. Ibid.

8. Wayne DiFranceisco and Zvi Gitelman, "Soviet Political Culture and 'Covert Participation' in Policy Implementation," *American Political Science Review*, 78(3) (September 1984): 603–621.

9. Donna Bahry and Brian D. Silver, "Soviet Citizen Participation on the Eve of Democratization," *American Political Science Review*, 84 (September 1990): 821–847.

10. Verba, Nie, and Kim, *Participation and Political Equality*, p. 51.

11. Herbert B. Asher, Bradley M. Richardson, and Herbert F. Weisberg, *Political Participation: An ISSC Workbook in Comparative Analysis* (Frankfurt: Campus Verlag, 1984), p. 54.

12. Verba and Nie, *Participation in America*, p. 61.

13. See among others Stephen Skowronek, *Building a New American State: The Expansion of National Administrative Capacities, 1877–1920* (Cambridge: Cambridge University Press, 1982); Peter Hall, *Governing the Economy: The Politics of State Intervention in Britain and France* (New York: Oxford University Press, 1986); John G. Ikenberry, David A. Lake, and Michael Mastanduno, eds., *The State and American Foreign Economic Policy* (Ithaca, N.Y.: Cornell University Press, 1988); James March

and Johan Olsen, *Rediscovering Institutions* (New York: Free Press, 1989); Douglass C. North, *Institutions, Institutional Change, and Economic Performance* (Cambridge: Cambridge University Press, 1990).

14. Townsend, *Communist China*, p. 3.
15. Asher, Richardson, and Weisberg, *Political Participation*, p. 54.
16. Ibid., p. 53.
17. The attitudes of the regime toward certain political acts have changed over time. For example, with the relaxation of controls in the late 1980s and the gradual erosion of the ability of the state to control society, the chance of participants' being punished for their engagement in unauthorized political activities was greatly reduced, as, correspondingly, were the risks associated with them. The reduction of the risks associated with these activities should have attracted more people to engage in them, but this may not be the case in China. Since the variation of tolerance usually comes from the "good will" or indifference of particular political leaders rather than from institutionalized protection, no one knows when leaders might change their mind. Given the possibility that the good will of political leaders will change at any time, many people in China still refrain from engaging in such risky political acts.
18. Asher, Richardson, and Weisberg, *Political Participation*, p. 54.
19. Ibid.
20. Ibid.
21. Ibid., pp. 55–56.
22. Verba, Nie, and Kim, *Participation and Political Equality*, pp. 310–339.
23. Verba and Nie, *Participation in America*, p. 106.
24. A well-known exception is the attitude of the lower bureaucrats toward demonstrations before June 4, 1989. However, there is a special reason for this attitude. For discussion, see Tianjian Shi, "The Democratic Movement in China in 1989: Dynamics and Failure," *Asian Survey*, 30(2) (December 1990): 1186–1205.
25. Verba and Nie, *Participation in America*, pp. 61–63.
26. The discussion of principal component analysis is based on ibid., pp. 60–62, and George H. Dunteman, *Principal Component Analysis* (Beverly Hills, Calif.: Sage Publications, 1989), pp. 9–10.
27. For the elections in 1984, 62.6 percent of respondents could not remember whether there were more candidates than seats; 8.6 percent of respondents could clearly point out that the elections had one candidate per seat. For the elections in 1988, 50.5 percent of people forgot whether there were more candidates than seats. Only 7.2 percent of people told us the elections involved one candidate per seat.
28. Most participants, when making complaints through the bureaucratic hierarchy or political organizations, simply present officials with their difficulties and ask them to ignore "unfair" rules and regulations to help them. Few of them challenge government policy per se. Bureaucrats in China do not interpret such acts as hostile, and many of them even encourage their subordinates to make appeals to higher authority to shift their own responsibility *(maodun shangjiao)*, especially when they believe their subordinates have just cases but they can do little to help them.
29. Most studies of modes of political participation use the exploratory factor analysis

model. For example, Verba and Nie, *Participation in America;* Verba, Nie, and Kim, *Participation and Political Equality;* Bahry and Silver, "Soviet Citizen."

30. For discussion, see Scott J. Long, *Confirmatory Factor Analysis: A Preface to LISREL* (Beverly Hills, Calif.: Sage Publications, 1983), p. 13.

31. Ibid., p. 12.

32. The model tested here incorporates all variables and relationships examined in the exploratory factor model except voting for work unit elections. In contrast to People's Congresses, many work units in Beijing did not hold elections for leaders. Ideally, I should exclude those whose unit did not hold elections from the analysis. However, such an exclusion dramatically increases the number of missing values and thus creates another problem for the model. In the exploratory factor analysis model I coded all respondents who failed to show up at the ballot booth in work unit leader elections as nonvoters without differentiating the reasons behind their behavior. Confirmatory factor analysis requires researchers to clearly specify all relationships between observed variables and latent factors. Since the reason for nonvoting in work unit elections is that there are no such elections available, coding such people as nonvoters may create other problems for the model. Therefore, I decided to exclude voting behavior regarding work unit elections from the analysis in the confirmatory factor analysis model.

33. For the construction of high-order factor solutions, see Verba and Nie, *Participation in America,* appendix B2.B, pp. 356–358.

34. For data on other countries, see Verba, Nie, and Kim, *Participation and Political Equality,* Table A-10 in "Appendix A: The Modes of Participation," pp. 310–339.

35. Ibid., p. 329.

36. See ibid.

37. Verba and Nie, *Participation in America,* p. 66.

5. Understanding Voting in Beijing

1. For discussion see Richard G. Niemi and Herbert F. Weisberg, "The Study of Voting and Elections," in *Controversies in Voting Behavior* (Washington, D.C.: Congressional Quarterly, 1984), pp. 9–15.

2. Anthony Downs, *An Economic Theory of Democracy* (New York: Harper and Row, 1957), p. 260.

3. Niemi and Weisberg, "Study of Voting," p. 14.

4. Raymond Wolfinger and Steven Rosenstone, *Who Votes?* (New Haven: Yale University Press, 1980), p. 7.

5. William H. Riker and Peter C. Ordeshook, *An Introduction to Positive Political Theory* (Englewood Cliffs, N.J.: Prentice-Hall, 1973), p. 63.

6. For a discussion of voting in China in the 1950s and the 1960s, see James R. Townsend, *Political Participation in Communist China* (Berkeley: University of California Press, 1969), pp. 115–121. For voting in the former Soviet Union, see Howard R. Swearer, "The Functions of Soviet Local Elections," *Midwestern Journal of Political Science,* 5(2) (May 1961); Jerome Gilison, "Soviet Elections as a Measure of Dissent: The Missing One Percent," *American Political Science Review,* 62(3)

(September 1968): 814–826; Rasma Karklins, "Soviet Elections Revisited: Voter Abstention in Noncompetitive Voting," *American Political Science Review*, 80(2) (June 1986): 449–469; James R. Millar, ed., *Politics, Work, and Daily Life in the USSR: A Survey of Former Soviet Citizens* (Cambridge: Cambridge University Press, 1987); Philip G. Roeder, "Electoral Avoidance in the Soviet Union," *Soviet Studies*, 41(3) (July 1989): 345–364.

 7. Andrew J. Nathan, *Chinese Democracy* (New York: Alfred A. Knopf, 1985), pp. 90–91, 193–223, 225–229, 246–247.

 8. Angus Campbell, Philip E. Converse, Warren E. Miller, and Donald E. Stokes, *The American Voter* (New York: John Wiley and Sons, 1960), pp. 467–478; Sidney Verba, Norman H. Nie, and Jae-on Kim, *Participation and Political Equality: A Seven Nation Comparison* (Chicago: University of Chicago Press, 1978); Wolfinger and Rosenstone, *Who Votes?* p. 17.

 9. See Verba, Nie, and Kim, *Participation and Political Equality*, p. 226.

10. Donna Bahry and Brian Silver, "Soviet Citizen Participation on the Eve of Democratization," *American Political Science Review*, 84(3) (September 1990): 838.

11. Karklins, "Soviet Elections," p. 449–469.

12. The school structure in China is similar to that of the United States. Children enter school at age seven. They normally spend six years in primary school, three years in junior high, and another three years in high school. College education ranges from three years for technical institutions *(dazhuan)*, through four years for liberal arts colleges and institutes *(daxue)*, to five years for engineering schools and departments, and six to eight years for medical colleges. Graduate study normally ranges from three years for an M.A. and M.S. to six years for a Ph.D. However, during and after the Cultural Revolution, the government carried on numerous educational reform projects. In 1971, the government reduced elementary school to five years and combined secondary and high schools to encourage pupils to complete middle school education within five years. Although the schools gradually returned to the original post-1949 system after the Cultural Revolution, it is still difficult to infer people's level of education by years of formal schooling received. Moreover, many people's education was interrupted by the Cultural Revolution. Many educated youth were sent "up to the mountains and down to the villages" *(shangshan xiaxiang)* to be reeducated by workers and peasants. In 1977 when the government resumed college entrance examinations after a near ten-year suspension, some of these people passed the examinations and entered college. But most students who entered college in the first few years after 1977 had never completed a high school education and some of them had not even finished primary school. They had achieved a high school equivalency level *(tongdeng xueli)* through self-study. This made the relationship between formal years of schooling and the diplomas one received even more difficult to evaluate.

13. Wolfinger and Rosenstone, *Who Votes?* p. 18.

14. The concept of departicipation was introduced by Philip G. Roeder. See his "Modernization and Participation in the Leninist Developmental Strategy," *American Political Science Review*, 83(3) (September 1989): 859–884.

15. Yasumasa Kuroda found no significant correlation between income and political participation in Japan. See Yasumasa Kuroda, "Measurement, Correlates, and Sig-

nificance of Political Participation in a Japanese Community," *Western Political Quarterly,* 20(1) (March 1967): 660–668. For data on the Soviet Union, see Bahry and Silver, "Soviet Citizen," p. 838.

16. For the relationship between income and voter turnout, see Wolfinger and Rosenstone, *Who Votes?* pp. 25–26; M. Margaret Conway, *Political Participation in the United States* (Washington, D.C.: Congressional Quarterly, 1991), pp. 25–26; Norman H. Nie, G. Bingham Powell, Jr., and Kenneth Prewitt, "Social Structure and Political Participation: Developmental Relationships, Part I and Part II," *American Political Science Review,* 63(2) (June 1969): 361–378, and 63(3) (September 1969): 808–832; Lester Milbrath and M. L. Goel, *Political Participation: How and Why Do People Get Involved in Politics?* (Chicago: Rand McNally, 1977), pp. 96–98; Russell J. Dalton, *Citizen Politics in Western Democracies: Public Opinion and Political Parties in the United States, Great Britain, West Germany, and France* (Chatham, N.J.: Chatham House, 1988).

17. Verba, Nie, and Kim, *Participation and Political Equality,* p. 73.

18. Townsend, *Communist China,* p. 120.

19. I am borrowing from Sidney Verba, Norman H. Nie, and Jae-on Kim, *The Modes of Democratic Participation: A Cross-National Comparison* (Beverly Hills, Calif.: Sage Publications, 1971), p. 63.

20. Wolfinger and Rosenstone, *Who Votes?* p. 20.

21. Some poor people regularly receive subsidies that can range from 10 yuan to 20 yuan per month per person.

22. By middle- and higher-level officials, I mean those whose administrative ranking is higher than bureau-chief level (*si ju ji*).

23. It is based on the question, "Compared with Chinese families in general, would you say the economic situation of your family is—far below average, below average, average, above average, or far above average?" Since only six people claimed that they were far above average, I grouped them with those who chose "above average."

24. See Conway, *Political Participation,* pp. 25–26.

25. The three categories are: farm owners, clerical and sales workers, and government employees. See among others Bernard R. Berelson, Paul F. Lazarsfeld, and William N. McPhee, *Voting: A Study of Opinion Formation in a Presidential Campaign* (Chicago: University of Chicago Press, 1954); Seymour Martin Lipset, *Political Man: The Social Bases of Politics* (Garden City, N.Y.: Doubleday, 1960), pp. 196–197; Milbrath and Goel, *Political Participation,* p. 102; Wolfinger and Rosenstone, *Who Votes?* pp. 26–34.

26. See Milbrath and Goel, *Political Participation,* p. 103.

27. Stein Rokken and Angus Campbell, "Norway and the United States of America," *Citizen Participation in Political Life, International Social Science Journal,* 12(1) (1960): 69–99.

28. See David Butler and Donald Stokes, *Political Change in Britain: Forces Shaping Electoral Choice* (New York: St. Martin's Press, 1969).

29. Among fourteen students who claimed that they did not vote in the 1988 elections, nine were only eighteen years old at the time of the interview. During voter registration, they had not even reached the age of eighteen. Among the eight students who did not vote in the 1984 elections, seven were below the age of twenty-one at

the time of the survey. Obviously they could not have reached the age of eighteen by the time of the election. The case for the military is somewhat different. Our sample population was noninstitutionalized Beijing residents, aged eighteen or older, residing in family households. We did not expect there to be military people therein, and we did not adapt our questionnaire to their specific situation, which is totally unlike civilians'. Military personnel do not participate in local elections. Article 5 of the People's Congress Electoral Law in China states that "the PLA shall conduct separate elections, and regulations governing such elections shall be made separately." See the electoral law for the NPC and local people's congresses of the PRC (adopted by the second session of the Fifth NPC on July 1, 1979, and revised in accordance with the "Resolution on Revision of Certain Stipulations of the 'Election Law for the NPC and Local People's Congresses of the PRC,'" adopted by the fifth session of the Fifth NPC on December 10, 1982). English translation in *Foreign Broadcast Information Service, Daily Report, People's Republic of China (FBIS-Chi)*, 82-243 (December 17, 1982): K15. Today, in fact, we still know little about elections in the army.

30. Wolfinger and Rosenstone, *Who Votes?* p. 7.
31. The Ordinary Least Square model is inadequate when the dependent variable is discrete or ordinal because some of the important assumptions necessary for hypothesis testing are violated. First, it is unreasonable to assume that the distribution of errors for the ordinal dependent variable is normal, which is one of the crucial assumptions of the OLS model. Second, the OLS model assumes that the relationship between the dependent and the independent variables is a linear one, which is also not the case. In such a situation, "abandoning the linear model in favor of a nonlinear one, say by introducing polynomials in X or using logarithms" is usually desirable. For details, see John H. Aldrich and Forrest D. Nelson, *Linear Probability, Logit and Probit Models* (Beverly Hills, Calif.: Sage Publications, 1984), p. 26. Fortunately, the past quarter-century has seen an explosion in the development of methods for analyzing categorical data. Many multivariate statistical methods, such as probit analysis and logistic regression, have been developed to analyze the relationship between predictors and binary or ordinal dependent variables. From a mathematical point of view, the logit used in the logistic model is an extremely flexible and easily used function. It lends itself to meaningful interpretation. Effects in the logistic model refer to odds. The estimated odds at one value of x divided by the estimated odds at another value of x is an odds ratio. The odds ratio approximates how much more likely or unlikely it is for the outcome to be present among those with $x = 1$ than among those with $x = 0$, which is easy to understand. And the logistic model does not assume normal distribution of the variables. Some of our independent variables are continuous variables, such as education and income; others are ordinal and nominal, such as economic status and party affiliation. For analytical purposes, we may need to dichotomize them or to make continuous variables ordinal at some politically meaningful cutoff point. Logistic regression enables us to explain the differences among alternative categories, even if the distribution of the ordinal data is not normal. For a discussion of the logistic regression model, see David W. Hosmer and Stanley Lemeshow, *Applied Logistic Regression*

(New York: John Wiley and Sons, 1989). Note that the estimated coefficients in logistic regression are the logit function or natural log of the odds.

32. The odds of an event occurring are defined as the ratio of the probability that it will occur to the probability that it will not. For example, if the probability of voting and nonvoting is the same, the odds ratio is 0.5/0.5 = 1. If the odds ratio is 1/3, the probability of voting compared to nonvoting is 0.25/0.75. By the same token, if the odds ratio is 3, the probability of voting compared to nonvoting is 0.75/0.25. The equation of the logistic model in terms of the log of the odds can be written as

$$\log \left(\frac{Prob \ (voted)}{Prob \ (not \ voted)} \right) = B + B_1 X_1 + \ldots B_p X_p$$

If we prefer to think of odds, rather than log odds, the logistic equation can be written as

$$\frac{Prob \ (voted)}{Prob \ (not \ voted)} = e^{B_0 + B_1 X_1 + \ldots B_p X_p} = e^{B_0} \, e^{B_1 X_1} \ldots e^{B_p X_p}$$

To assess the goodness of fit of the model, logistic regression tests how likely it is for observed results to appear, given the parameter estimates. Since the likelihood is a small number less than 1, it is usual to use -2 times the log of likelihood as a measure of how well the estimated model fits the data. Specifically, the -2 log likelihood presented here tests the null hypothesis that the coefficients for the model with predictors within the model are 0 as compared to the constant only model, or the model without the predictors.

33. In creating design variables, I use the reference cell coding method. With this method, every variable represents the value of a certain category. This particular value is coded as 1 and all the others are coded as 0. The reference category is the lowest value of the variable, if not otherwise specified. The coefficients are estimates of the odds ratio of specific groups relative to that of the "control" or "reference" group. For comparisons of different coding techniques and their interpretation, see Hosmer and Lemeshow, *Applied Logistic Regression*, pp. 45–56.

34. Education is first collapsed into eight categories as shown in Figure 5.1, which are then entered into the equation as design variables, because the relationship between education and turnout is found to be curvilinear. No significant relationship is found between education and turnout when the impact of *danwei* is controlled. I then entered education into the equation as a continuous variable with and without those who received more than eighteen years of education whose turnout rate dropped. No significant relationship was found therein either.

35. Students and military people were coded as missing in the analysis. Many students did not vote in deputy elections, especially in 1984 because they had not reached the age of eighteen at the time. For the military, their elections are held separately and we still don't know the real reason for their not participating in either election.

36. One test looks at all of the variables in the equation and examines p-values. The results show that no variable measuring occupation is significantly correlated with voter turnout when the impact of the *danwei* is controlled. At the same time, all but one design variable measuring *danwei* are still significant in the equation.

37. With occupation in the equation, the −2 log likelihood is 32.056 with 9 degrees of freedom. Without occupation in the equation, the −2 log likelihood is 42.465 with 4 degrees of freedom. The change in G, or the likelihood ratio test, due to excluding or including occupation in the model, can be obtained by

$$ G = 2In \left[\frac{(likelihood \; without \; the \; variable)}{(likelihood \; with \; the \; variable)} \right] $$

The G has a chi-square distribution. The value of the test comparing the model with and without occupation in it is calculated as

$$ G = 42.465 - 32.056 = 10.409 $$

with 4 degrees of freedom—the p-value for the test $P[X^2(4) > 10.409] < 0.05$. The fact that the p-value is smaller than 0.05 suggests that the two models are different.

38. See among others Campbell et al., *The American Voter*; Milbrath and Goel, *Political Participation*, pp. 53–56; and Verba, Nie, and Kim, *Participation and Political Equality*, p. 121.

39. Sidney Verba and Norman H. Nie, *Participation in America: Political Democracy and Social Equality* (New York: Harper and Row, 1972).

40. Verba, Nie, and Kim, *Participation and Political Equality*, p. 121.

41. Ibid., p. 226.

42. Bahry and Silver, "Soviet Citizen," p. 838.

43. The use of p-value < 0.1 is based on work on linear regressions by R. B. Bendel and A. A. Afifi and on the work on logistic regressions by J. Mickey and S. Greenland. These authors showed that the use of a more traditional level (such as 0.05) often fails to identify variables known to be important. See R. B. Bendel and A. A. Afifi, "Comparison of Stopping Rules in Forward Regression," *Journal of the American Statistical Association*, 72 (1977): 46–53; J. Mickey and S. Greenland, "A Study of the Impact of Confounder-Selection Criteria on Effect Estimation," *American Journal of Epidemiology*, 129 (1989): 125–137.

44. Milbrath and Goel, *Political Participation*, p. 114. See also Lipset, *Political Man*, pp. 196–197; Wolfinger and Rosenstone, *Who Votes?* pp. 37–41. For data from Austria, India, Japan, and Nigeria, see Norman H. Nie, Sidney Verba, and Jae-on Kim, "Political Participation and the Life Cycle," *Comparative Politics*, 6(2) (January 1974): 319–340.

45. For discussion, see Verba and Nie, *Participation in America*, p. 139.

46. See Elaine Cummings and William E. Henry, *Growing Old: The Process of Disengagement* (New York: Basic Books, 1961).

47. Nie, Verba, and Kim, "Political Participation," p. 321.

48. Wolfinger and Rosenstone, *Who Votes?* p. 47; Verba and Nie, *Participation in America*, pp. 139–148.

49. Nie, Verba, and Kim, "Political Participation," p. 321.

50. Milbrath and Goel, *Political Participation*, pp. 116–118.

51. Nie, Verba, and Kim, "Political Participation," p. 321.

52. Women are found to vote more than men in two other countries. In Argentina women vote more frequently in elections than men by a small margin (83.7 percent

versus 82.7 percent). See Paul H. Lewis, "The Female Vote in Argentina, 1958–1965," *Comparative Political Studies,* 3 (1971): 425–441. When the impacts of socioeconomic variables are controlled, being a woman increases the probability of voter turnout in the former Soviet Union. See Bahry and Silver, "Soviet Citizen," p. 838.

53. Nie, Verba, and Kim, "Political Participation," pp. 319–340.
54. M. Lal Goel, *Political Participation in a Developing Nation: India* (New York: Asia Publishing House, 1975).
55. Replacing *danwei* with education and subjective evaluations of economic status with income in the equation causes the slow-down effect to disappear.
56. Verba and Nie, *Participation in America,* p. 145. Wolfinger and Rosenstone arrived at similar conclusions independently. For discussion, see Wolfinger and Rosenstone, *Who Votes?* pp. 58–60.
57. Studies of elections in China have found that dissidents in universities actively participated in local elections to promote their ideas as early as 1979, even though elections were far from democratic and the government tried to suppress those unauthorized expressions of independent opinion. Some of the democratic activists who ran in those elections were even elected. See Andrew J. Nathan, *Chinese Democracy* (New York: Alfred A. Knopf, 1985), pp. 193–223.

6. Campaign Activities and Election Boycotts

1. The county-level elections in China from 1979 to 1981 clearly demonstrated the danger of citizen-initiated campaigns to end the monopolistic political control of the CCP and made the authorities in China even more hostile to campaign activities aimed at influencing high-politics issues. During these elections, the major struggle between democrats and the authorities was over the limits of Chinese democracy. According to Andrew Nathan, "the election-law revisions of 1982 made clear once again the official view of what the limits of Chinese democracy should be," and "the congress also cleared up the ambiguities of article 30, which candidates had used to defend their right to conduct election propaganda." Andrew J. Nathan, *Chinese Democracy* (New York: Alfred A. Knopf, 1985), p. 223.
2. For analysis of the situation, see James R. Townsend, *Political Participation in Communist China* (Berkeley: University of California Press, 1969), pp. 134–135.
3. Nathan, *Chinese Democracy,* pp. 193–223.
4. J. Bruce Jacobs, "Elections in China," *Australian Journal of Chinese Affairs,* 25 (January 1991): 183.
5. Andrew G. Walder, *Communist Neo-Traditionalism: Work and Authority in Chinese Industry* (Berkeley: University of California Press, 1986), p. 175.
6. For detailed discussion of the nomination process in China, see among others John P. Burns, *Political Participation in Rural China* (Berkeley: University of California Press, 1988), pp. 91–94; Jacobs, "Elections in China," pp. 183–186.
7. For example, Nathan documented struggles over candidate nomination at various universities in the early 1980s; see Nathan, *Chinese Democracy,* pp. 199–223. Jacobs talked about the struggle over candidate nomination in Nanjing; see Jacobs, "Elections in China," pp. 183–186.

8. In Nanjing, Jacobs reported that the interval between the nomination of candidates and the formal election was less than a month. See Jacobs, "Elections in China," pp. 183–186.

9. Interview with Su Shaozhi, conducted in New York, January 1990.

10. Jacobs, "Elections in China," p. 183.

11. Ibid.

12. Raymond Wolfinger and E. Steven Rosenstone, Who Votes? (New Haven: Yale University Press, 1980), p. 18.

13. Victor C. Falkenheim, "Political Participation in China," Problems of Communism, 27 (May–June 1978): 25.

14. Interview with workers at the Petroleum Machinery Manufacturing factory in Beijing, 1988.

15. Jacobs, "Elections in China," p. 199.

16. Alex Pravda, "Elections in Communist Party States," in Guy Hermet, Richard Rose, and Alain Rouquié, eds., Elections without Choice (New York: John Wiley and Sons, 1978), p. 181.

17. Jacobs, "Elections in China," p. 199.

18. Rasma Karklins, "Soviet Elections Revisited: Voter Abstention in Noncompetitive Voting," American Political Science Review, 80(2) (June 1986): 445; Jerome Gilison, "Soviet Elections as a Measure of Dissent: The Missing One Percent," American Political Science Review, 62(3) (September 1968): 819; Everett M. Jacobs, "Soviet Local Elections: What They Are, and What They Are Not," Soviet Studies, 22 (July 1970): 61–76; Philip G. Roeder, "Electoral Avoidance in the Soviet Union," Soviet Studies, 41(3) (July 1989): 463.

19. For discussion, see Hannah Arendt, The Origins of Totalitarianism (New York: Harcourt Brace Jovanovich, 1951), pp. 172–177; Hans Gerth and C. Wright Mills, Character and Social Structure: The Psychology of Social Institutions (New York: Harcourt, Brace and World, 1953), pp. 405–455; Karl A. Wittfogel, Oriental Despotism: A Comparative Study of Total Power (New York: Vintage, 1957), pp. 149–160.

20. Max Kaase and Alan Marsh, "Political Action: A Theoretical Perspective," in Samuel H. Barnes and Max Kaase, eds., Political Action: Mass Participation in Five Western Democracies (Beverly Hills, Calif.: Sage Publications, 1979), p. 27.

21. See Gabriel A. Almond and Sidney Verba, The Civic Culture: Political Attitudes and Democracy in Five Nations (Princeton: Princeton University Press, 1963), p. 88.

22. Interview with garment factory owner, Beijing, January 1988.

23. Neighborhood committees are responsible for crime watch. Many of them, however, have overplayed their role and intruded in people's lives. Since most people assigned crime-watch duty are retired women, Beijing residents call them "footbinding police," in reference to the tradition elderly women carry on of binding their feet.

7. Appeal Activities in Beijing

1. Adversarial activities and guanxi are dealt with separately in the next chapter.

2. James Townsend, Political Participation in Communist China (Berkeley: University of California Press, 1969), p. 73.

3. Ibid.
4. E. E. Schattschneider, *The Semi-Sovereign People: A Realist's View of Democracy in America* (New York: Holt, Rinehart and Winston, 1960), p. 2.
5. Lowell Dittmer, "Public and Private Interests and the Participatory Ethic in China," in Victor C. Falkenheim, ed., *Citizens and Groups in Contemporary China* (Ann Arbor: University of Michigan Center for Chinese Studies, 1987), Michigan Monographs in Chinese Studies, vol. 56, pp. 27–33.
6. Ted Robert Gurr, *Why Men Rebel* (Princeton: Princeton University Press, 1970), pp. 34–35.
7. Herbert Simon, *Models of Man* (New York: John Wiley and Sons, 1957), p. 241.
8. William H. Riker and Peter C. Ordeshook, *An Introduction to Positive Political Theory* (Englewood Cliffs, N.J.: Prentice-Hall, 1973), p. 21.
9. Albert O. Hirschman, *Exit, Voice, and Loyalty: Responses to Decline in Firms, Organizations, and States* (Cambridge, Mass.: Harvard University Press, 1970), pp. 30–31.
10. Ibid., p. 31.
11. For discussion of aggression and rebellion, see among others Gurr, *Why Men Rebel*; Edward Muller, *Aggressive Political Participation* (Princeton: Princeton University Press, 1979).
12. Theodore H. Friedgut, *Political Participation in the USSR* (Princeton: Princeton University Press, 1979), p. 224.
13. For discussion, see Lester Milbrath and M. L. Goel, *Political Participation: How and Why Do People Get Involved in Politics?* (Chicago: Rand McNally, 1977), pp. 45–46.
14. For the study of political culture in communist countries, see among others Frederick C. Barghoon, "Soviet Russia: Orthodoxy and Adaptiveness," in Lucian Pye and Sidney Verba, eds., *Political Culture and Political Development* (Princeton: Princeton University Press, 1965), pp. 450–511; Richard R. Fagen, *The Transformation of Political Culture in Cuba* (Stanford: Stanford University Press, 1969); Richard H. Solomon, *Mao's Revolution and the Chinese Political Culture* (Berkeley: University of California Press, 1971); Robert C. Tucker, "Culture, Political Culture, and Communist Society," *Political Science Quarterly*, 88(2) (June 1973): 173–190; Robert C. Tucker, "Communist Revolutions, National Cultures, and the Divided Nations," *Studies in Comparative Communism*, 7(3) (Autumn 1974): 235–245; Archie H. Brown and Jack Gray, eds., *Political Culture and Political Change in Communist States* (New York: Holmes and Meier, 1977). For the study of political culture in the Third World, see Samuel Huntington and Jorge I. Dominguez, "Political Development," in Fred Greenstein and Nelson Polsby, eds., *Handbook of Political Science*, vol. 3, *Macropolitical Theory* (Reading, Mass.: Addison-Wesley, 1975), pp. 1–114.
15. See Archie Brown, ed., *Political Culture and Communist Studies* (Armonk, N.Y.: M. E. Sharpe, 1985), p. 177. Gabriel Almond also distinguishes three versions of political culture in communist countries: (1) the official or ideological political culture that is a mix of exhortation and imputation, (2) the operational political culture or what the regime is prepared to tolerate and believes it has succeeded in attaining, and (3) the real political culture based on evidence such as opinion surveys and other kinds of research or on inferences drawn from the media or official statements. See

Gabriel A. Almond, "Communism and Political Culture Theory," *Comparative Politics,* 15(2) (January 1983): 131–134.

16. Wayne DiFranceisco and Zvi Gitelman, "Soviet Political Culture and 'Covert Participation' in Policy Implementation," *American Political Science Review,* 78(3) (September 1984): 603–621; Donna Bahry and Brian Silver, "Soviet Citizen Participation on the Eve of Democratization," *American Political Science Review,* 84(2) (September 1990): 821–847.

17. Harry Eckstein, "Memorandum to Participants in Conference on Political Culture and Communist Studies," quoted in Kenneth Jowitt, "An Organizational Approach to the Study of Political Culture in Marxist-Leninist Systems," *American Political Science Review,* 68 (September 1974): 1174.

18. Margaret M. Conway, *Political Participation in the United States* (Washington, D.C.: Congressional Quarterly, 1991), p. 42.

19. Townsend, *Communist China,* p. 204.

20. Friedgut, *Political Participation,* p. 302.

21. DiFranceisco and Gitelman, "Soviet Political Culture," pp. 610–611.

22. Bahry and Silver, "Soviet Citizen," p. 833.

23. For example, one of the frequently used questions for gauging efficacy developed by Almond and Verba reads: "Suppose a law were being considered by the [appropriate national legislature specified for each nation] that you considered to be unjust or harmful. What do you think you can do?" Scholars who study participation in a broad array of countries use this question. A recent study of participation in the Soviet Union also used it to gauge respondents' competence. See DiFranceisco and Gitelman, "Soviet Political Culture," p. 620. But if government output has little to do with law, what can this measurement tell us? Government decisions in China are neither codified into law nor transferred to the general populace in society by law. Instead, those policies are usually transmitted to the general populace by formal government documents, oral reports, or newspaper editorials. When survey researchers ask respondents in China if they will do anything about "unjust" laws when not satisfied with certain government policies, the first thing that comes to respondents' minds is the criminal code. If researchers want to measure political efficacy or output effects in China by people's perceived ability to do something about an unjust law or by their estimated likelihood of being able to change the law, they are destined to fail.

24. There is another way to explain this psychological dimension, i.e., alienation. Nonetheless, I tend not to interpret this finding as evidence of alienation from the regime. Breaking away from official norms and beginning to be aware of individual rights are different from becoming alienated from the regime because they have little to do with political powerlessness, meaninglessness, normlessness or isolation, or "the explicit rejection, 'freely chosen by individuals, from what they perceive as the dominant values or norms of their society.'" See among others Ada W. Finifter, "Dimensions of Political Alienation," *American Political Science Review,* 64(2) (June 1970): 390–391; Kenneth Keniston, *The Uncommitted: Alienated Youth in American Society* (New York: Harcourt, Brace and World, 1965), p. 455.

25. Lucian Pye, "Culture and Political Science: Problems in the Evaluation of the

Concept of Political Culture," *Social Science Quarterly*, 53(2) (September 1972): 285–296.

26. Interview with a professor of the Beijing University Department of Economics and Foreign Trade, conducted in Beijing, September 1988.

27. Since the requirements of orthogonality and univocality of scales are not met in our case (except for appeals, there is a common activeness dimension of participation in Beijing), the underlying scores may be correlated with one another; but correlation among component scores will not correctly reflect the underlying correlations among the factors when the oblique model is assumed. For discussion, see Jae-on Kim and Charles W. Mueller, *Factor Analysis: Statistical Methods and Practical Issues* (Beverly Hills, Calif.: Sage Publications, 1978). To avoid the additional complexities associated with multiple component scores, I tried to use the five appeal acts in another principal component analysis. The results show that all belong to a single dimension. Thus, I built a principal component score in the second analysis, which I use in the following analysis.

28. Although it seems that people aged sixty-two to seventy-one are substantially less likely to make appeals than most other age groups, except those of the youngest people in our survey, the relationship demonstrated in the table is not significant.

29. For discussion, see Milbrath and Goel, *Political Participation*, p. 115.

30. Political culture literature has revealed a "stunning finding from the standpoint of communist efforts to create a socialist personality." East Germans were found to display higher levels of political efficacy, greater interest in politics, and more positive attitudes toward minorities as compared to West Germans. See Russell J. Dalton, "Communists and Democrats: Attitudes toward Democracy in the Two Germanies" (paper delivered at the Annual Meeting of the American Political Science Association, Washington, D.C., 1991), p. 7.

31. Fang Zhongyan, "Yuyanlouji," in Wu Chucai, ed., *Guwenguanzhi* (Zhongyan Publishing House, 1976), p. 423.

32. For discussion, see Andrew G. Walder, *Communist Neo-Traditionalism: Work and Authority in Chinese Industry* (Berkeley: University of California Press, 1986).

33. They found that the people most alienated from the regime and from other people were the most "self-initiated and active." See DiFranceisco and Gitelman, "Soviet Political Culture," pp. 610–611.

34. "Even with social background taken into account, people with a stronger sense of personal influence, greater interest in politics, greater faith in people, and support for state control over civil liberties were more involved in conventional political activities." See Bahry and Silver, "Soviet Citizen," p. 835.

35. Seweryn Bialer, *Stalin's Successors: Leadership, Stability, and Change in the Soviet Union* (Cambridge: Cambridge University Press, 1980), pp. 166–167.

36. Gurr, *Why Men Rebel*, p. 24.

37. J. M. V. Whiting, "The Frustration Complex in Kwoma Society," *Man*, 44 (November–December 1944): 140–144; quoted in Gurr, *Why Men Rebel*, p. 34.

38. Ibid., pp. 34–35.

39. Bahry and Silver, "Soviet Citizen," p. 836.

40. Ibid.

41. Gabriel A. Almond and Sidney Verba, *The Civic Culture: Political Attitudes and Democracy in Five Nations* (Princeton: Princeton University Press, 1963), p. 188.

42. For the history and political consequences of the "up to the mountains and down to the villages" phenomenon, see Thomas P. Bernstein, *Up to the Mountains and Down to the Villages: The Transfer of Youth from Urban to Rural China* (New Haven, Conn.: Yale University Press, 1977); and Anita Chan, Richard Madsen, and Jonathan Unger, *Chen Village: The Recent History of a Peasant Community in Mao's China* (Berkeley: University of California Press, 1984).

43. Alex Inkeles and David H. Smith, *Becoming Modern: Individual Change in Six Developing Countries* (Cambridge, Mass.: Harvard University Press, 1974), p. 136.

44. Ibid., pp. 154–163.

45. Ibid., p. 158.

46. Ibid., p. 159.

8. Adversarial Activities, Resistance, and Cronyism

1. Anita Chan, Richard Madsen, and Jonathan Unger, *Chen Village: The Recent History of a Peasant Community in Mao's China* (Berkeley: University of California Press, 1984), p. 108.

2. Bad class labels were inherited from the father's line, but even a mother's label could affect her children. See Richard Curt Kraus, *Class Conflict in Chinese Socialism* (New York: Columbia University Press, 1981), pp. 21–22; William L. Parish and Martin King Whyte, *Village and Family in Contemporary China* (Chicago: University of Chicago Press, 1978), pp. 100–101.

3. See Gabriel A. Almond and Sidney Verba, *The Civic Culture: Political Attitudes and Democracy in Five Nations* (Princeton: Princeton University Press, 1963), p. 80.

4. Ibid., p. 88.

5. Seweryn Bialer, *Stalin's Successors: Leadership, Stability, and Change in the Soviet Union* (Cambridge: Cambridge University Press, 1980), pp. 166–167.

6. Almond and Verba, *Civic Culture*, p. 88.

7. Lester Milbrath and M. L. Goel, *Political Participation: How and Why Do People Get Involved in Politics?* (Chicago: Rand McNally, 1977), p. 57.

8. Stephen C. Craig, Richard G. Niemi, and Glenn E. Silver, "Political Efficacy and Trust: A Report on the NES Pilot Study Items," *Political Behavior,* 12 (September 1990): 290.

9. For discussion, see Seymour Martin Lipset, *Political Man: The Social Bases of Politics* (Garden City, N.Y.: Doubleday, 1960), pp. 97–130.

10. Ibid., p. 109.

11. Genevieve Knupfer, "Portrait of the Underdog," *Public Opinion Quarterly,* 11 (1947): 114.

12. Ibid., pp. 103–114.

13. Andrew G. Walder, *Communist Neo-Traditionalism: Work and Authority in Chinese Industry* (Berkeley: University of California Press, 1986), p. 175.

14. Kenneth Waltz, *Theory of International Politics* (New York: McGraw-Hill, 1979), p. 172.

15. Interview with workers at the Petroleum Machinery Manufacturing factory in Beijing, November 1988.
16. Alan Marsh and Max Kaase, "Background of Political Action," in Samuel H. Barnes and Max Kaase, *Political Action: Mass Participation in Five Western Democracies* (Beverly Hills, Calif.: Sage Publications, 1979), pp. 106–112.
17. For discussion, see ibid., p. 106.
18. See among others, Sidney Verba, Norman H. Nie, and Jae-on Kim, *Participation and Political Equality: A Seven Nation Comparison* (Chicago: University of Chicago Press, 1978), pp. 80–111; Sidney Verba and Norman H. Nie, *Participation in America: Political Democracy and Social Equality* (New York: Harper and Row, 1972); Milbrath and Goel, *Political Participation*.
19. Verba, Nie, and Kim, *Participation and Political Equality*, p. 80.
20. James R. Townsend, *Political Participation in Communist China* (Berkeley: University of California Press, 1969), pp. 145–146.
21. In the process of data manipulation, I tried several ways to group people's *chushen* and their *chengfen* (personal categorization). None of them revealed any significant impact on people's engagement in adversarial activities.
22. Ronald Inglehart and Hans D. Klingemann, "Ideological Conceptualization and Value Priorities," in Samuel H. Barnes and Max Kaase, *Political Action: Mass Participation in Five Western Democracies* (Beverly Hills, Calif.: Sage Publications, 1979), p. 207.
23. Ted Robert Gurr, "Psychological Factors in Civil Violence," *World Politics,* 20 (January 1968): 245–278; Ted Robert Gurr, *Why Men Rebel* (Princeton: Princeton University Press, 1970); Edward Muller, "A Test of a Partial Theory of Potential for Political Violence," *American Political Science Review,* 66(3) (September 1972): 928–959; Edward Muller, *Aggressive Political Participation* (Princeton: Princeton University Press, 1979); Barbara Farah, Samuel H. Barnes, and Felix Heunks, "Political Dissatisfaction," in Samuel H. Barnes and Max Kaase, *Political Action: Mass Participation in Five Western Democracies* (Beverly Hills, Calif.: Sage Publications, 1979), pp. 409–486.
24. Gurr, *Why Men Rebel,* p. 30.
25. Charles Tilly, Louise Tilly, and Richard Tilly, *The Rebellious Century* (Cambridge, Mass.: Harvard University Press, 1975); Michael Lipsky, "Protest as a Political Resource," *American Political Science Review,* 62(4) (December 1968): 1144–1158.
26. Russell J. Dalton, *Citizen Politics in Western Democracies: Public Opinion and Political Parties in the United States, Great Britain, West Germany, and France* (Chatham, N.J.: Chatham House, 1988), pp. 67–68.
27. Lipset, *Political Man,* p. 100.
28. Ibid., pp. 118–119.
29. Dalton, *Citizen Politics,* p. 67.
30. Joel D. Aberbach and Jack L. Walder, "Political Trust and Racial Ideology," *American Political Science Review,* 64(4) (December 1970): 1199–1220.
31. Ibid., p. 1209.
32. Inglehart and Klingemann, "Ideological Conceptualization," p. 204.
33. Parish and Whyte, *Village,* p. 211.

34. Ibid., p. 213.

35. Marsh and Kaase, "Background," p. 101.

36. Ibid.

37. Ibid.

38. Ibid.

39. Ibid.

40. Inglehart and Klingemann, "Ideological Conceptualization," p. 210.

41. Marsh and Kaase, "Background," p. 102.

42. Walder, *Neo-Traditionalism*, pp. 179–180.

43. Dalton, *Citizen Politics*, pp. 60–61.

44. For recent data on political participation in the Soviet Union, see Donna Bahry and Brian Silver, "Soviet Citizen Participation on the Eve of Democratization," *American Political Science Review*, 84 (September 1990): 821–847.

45. For example, Samuel Huntington and Joan Nelson believe that disadvantaged people usually lack such resources as information, contacts, money, and time, are often divided, and tend to expect their requests to be ignored, all of which would be obstacles to their engaging in political action. Samuel P. Huntington and Joan M. Nelson, *No Easy Choice: Political Participation in Developing Countries* (Cambridge, Mass.: Harvard University Press, 1976), p. 120. Thus, disadvantaged people are apt to conclude that their efforts to exert influence on government policy are futile even "on matters where government is viewed as relevant." They tend to be unable to engage in conventional political activities.

46. Martin Fishbein, "Attitude and the Prediction of Behavior," in Martin Fishbein, ed., *Readings in Attitude Theory and Measurement* (New York: John Wiley and Sons, 1967), p. 96.

47. Walder, *Neo-Traditionalism*, p. 184 (italics added).

48. Interview with a young worker in a state-owned enterprise, Beijing, November 1988.

49. Fishbein, "Attitude and the Prediction of Behavior," p. 489.

50. David Easton, *A Systems Analysis of Political Life* (New York: John Wiley and Sons, 1965), p. 79.

51. For discussion of specific and diffuse support, see ibid., pp. 267–274.

52. Martin King Whyte and William L. Parish, *Urban Life in Contemporary China* (Chicago: University of Chicago Press, 1984), p. 173.

9. Conclusion

1. Jeffrey W. Hahn, *Soviet Grassroots: Citizen Participation in Local Soviet Government* (Princeton: Princeton University Press, 1988), p. 38.

2. Ibid., p. 30.

3. Victor C. Falkenheim, "Political Participation in China," *Problems of Communism*, 27 (May–June 1978): 31–32 (italics added).

4. Philip G. Roeder, "Modernization and Participation in the Leninist Developmental Strategy," *American Political Science Review*, 83(3) (September 1989): 863.

5. For example, Roeder states that "enforced departicipation" might be a more appropriate term to describe citizen involvement in politics in the former Soviet Union.

See Roeder, "Modernization," pp. 859–884. DiFranceisco and Gitelman go further and argue that Soviet citizens dismissed official channels of participation as a mere formality. See Wayne DiFranceisco and Zvi Gitelman, "Soviet Political Culture and 'Covert Participation' in Policy Implementation," *American Political Science Review*, 78(3) (September 1984): 603–621. Donald Barry has even called participation in organizations in communist societies "sham participation at best." See also "Notes and Views, Correspondence," *Problems of Communism*, 25 (September–October 1976): 93–96.

6. Donna Bahry and Brian Silver, "Soviet Citizen Participation on the Eve of Democratization," *American Political Science Review*, 84(2) (September 1990): 840.

7. Collective action in the 1989 democracy movement proves the point. People engage in collective political action and take to the streets in protest not simply because the government relaxes control. Rather, people in Beijing and other cities successfully organize themselves to engage in collective action as a result of multiple government policies. The double-digit inflation and the widespread corruption hurt almost everybody in the society and few, if any, could escape their impact. More important, the nature of these problems made it impossible for citizens to resolve them through the particularism found in this study. When the interests of private citizens can only be pursued through collective action, no matter what the government does or threatens to do, people will mobilize to pursue their interests collectively.

8. Andrew G. Walder, *Communist Neo-Traditionalism: Work and Authority in Chinese Industry* (Berkeley: University of California Press, 1986), pp. 35–56.

9. Gabriel A. Almond and Sidney Verba, *The Civic Culture: Political Attitudes and Democracy in Five Nations* (Princeton: Princeton University Press, 1963).

10. Seymour Martin Lipset, "Some Social Requisites of Democracy: Economic Development and Political Legitimacy," *American Political Science Review*, 53(1) (March 1959): 72.

11. Samuel P. Huntington and Joan M. Nelson, *No Easy Choice: Political Participation in Developing Countries* (Cambridge, Mass.: Harvard University Press, 1976), p. 42.

12. See among others Daniel Lerner, *The Passing of Traditional Society: Modernizing the Middle East* (New York: Free Press, 1958), p. 60; Lipset, "Some Social Requisites," pp. 69–105; G. Bingham Powell, *Contemporary Democracies: Participation, Stability, and Violence* (Cambridge, Mass.: Harvard University Press, 1982), pp. 37–39.

13. Dankwart A. Rustow, "Transitions to Democracy: Toward a Dynamic Model," *Comparative Politics*, 2(3) (April 1970): 337.

14. Ibid.

15. Huntington and Nelson, *No Easy Choice*, p. 55.

16. Ibid., pp. 58–59.

17. Gabriel A. Almond, "Introduction: A Functional Approach to Comparative Politics," in Gabriel A. Almond and James S. Coleman, eds., *The Politics of the Developing Areas* (Princeton: Princeton University Press, 1960), p. 33.

18. John Duncan Powell, "Peasant Society and Clientelist Politics," *American Political Science Review*, 64 (June 1970): 422.

19. Huntington and Nelson, *No Easy Choice*, p. 58.

20. This argument seems contrary to what happened in Beijing in 1989 when students

and urban residents but not peasants demonstrated. However, the event confirms rather than refutes my hypothesis. The double-digit inflation and the corruption of government officials prompted students to protest more than their desire for democracy. These issues have two salient characteristics. First, they influence every citizen's private life; second, the patron-client type of participation could not help in such cases. The crisis, from its start, exceeded the capabilities of the existing political structure and organizations, and the essence of the issues demanded new patterns of interest articulation and required the establishment of associational groups for interest aggregation. When the government changed its policy on inflation, which had effectively mobilized urban residents against it on June 4, 1989, the way of life in urban areas returned to "normal." Without a continuing crisis horizontal lines of solidarity fade quite rapidly. For a discussion of the social origins of the democracy movement in 1989, see Tianjian Shi, "The Democratic Movement in China in 1989: Dynamics and Failure," *Asian Survey,* 30(12) (December 1990): 1188–1194.

Appendix

1. Leslie Kish, *Survey Sampling* (New York: John Wiley and Sons, 1965), pp. 123–127.
2. Ministry of Public Security, *Population Statistics by City and County of the People's Republic of China, 1987* (Beijing: Map Publishing House of China, 1988).
3. There are many newly built residences in Beijing that have not been assigned to any police station. People who live there do not hold legal household registration.
4. Kish, *Survey Sampling,* p. 51.
5. Leslie Kish and M. Frankel, "Balanced Repeated Replications for Standard Errors," *Journal of the American Statistical Association* 65(1970): 1071–1091.
6. Kish, *Survey Sampling,* pp. 263–272.
7. Ibid., pp. 398–400.

Index

Abuse, of power. *See* Power abuse
Active-competitive orientation, 67–68
Activeness component, 123–124, 124, 128
Activism, 21, 43, 68, 69
Adversarial activity, 120–121, 233–245; and complaints, 120, 121, 233; dimensions of, 123, 133; and factor analysis, 129, 133, 135, 138; and appeals, 198
Age, 167–176; and appeals, 209, 210–211, 212, 217, 218–220, 230, 317n28; and adversarial activity, 235; and resistance, 250–251
Agenda setting, 9, 12, 15
Aggregation, of interests. *See* Interest aggregation
Alienation, 275, 316n24
Almond, Gabriel, 21
Anonymity, 63–64
Anti-rightist movement, 78, 84, 147–148, 294n67
Apathy, 110, 111, 191, 254, 264, 269
Appeal, 198–232; kinds of, 120; and work units, 120, 202, 210, 213, 224; and conflict, 120, 226–229; dimensions of, 123, 133; and factor analysis, 129, 133, 138; and confrontation, 139, 220–224, 231; and government, 139–140, 199, 206, 208, 212, 216, 217; and elections, 142; and resources, 201–202; and age, 209, 210–211, 212, 217, 218–220, 230, 317n28; and information, 209, 212, 215, 216, 217, 218, 222, 223, 224, 225, 226, 230, 231, 238, 240; and gender,

209, 212, 216–220, 231, 240, 242–243; and high politics, 216, 238, 239; and low politics, 216, 238, 239; and men, 216–220, 231, 242; and news media, 238; and management, 239–241; and cronyism, 256; and psychological orientation, 316n24. *See also* Complaint
Articulation, of interest. *See* Interest articulation
Audience seeking, 126, 131, 137, 233
Authoritarianism, 241–242

Bahry, Donna, 205
Bao Tong, 296n15
Bargaining, 47–48, 70, 73–74, 97
Bauer, Raymond, 6
Beijing Municipal People's Congress, 87
Belief, 258, 263–264, 266
Benefit. *See* Cost-benefit; Expressive benefit; Instrumental benefit
Bialer, Seweryn, 6
Big-character poster, 84–86, 94, 102, 107, 116, 122, 123, 300n73
Blue-collar worker, 153, 154, 160, 161
Boycott, 180, 190–197; and persuasion, 44; and survey research, 44; and elections, 44, 100, 107, 111; and protest, 44, 108; use rate, 94; and resistance, 122, 132; and principal component analysis, 126, 127; and factor analysis, 131, 133, 135, 137, 138; dimensions of, 133; and bureaucracy, 181; and government, 181; and mobilization, 271

ness component, 125, 128; of 1988, 125, 145, 151, 152, 157, 165; of 1984, 125, 151, 152, 157; and principal component analysis, 127, 128; and factor analysis, 129, 130, 131, 133, 135, 137, 138; and cross-national comparison, 140; and benefit, 143, 144, 149, 152, 154, 162, 177; and civic duty, 143, 144, 154, 188–189; and status, 145–156, 163–164, 168–169, 172, 173, 174, 176, 177; and education, 147, 148, 311n34; and resources, 149; and cadre, 153, 160, 161, 166, 176, 178, 296n15; and men, 169, 170–174, 175, 312n52; and gender, 169–176, 178, 179, 242–243, 312n52; and women, 169–176, 178, 242–243, 312n52; of 1979–1981, 182; reform in, 182; changes in, 190; and withdrawal, 191; and news media, 193; and information, 193, 197; and grapevine rumor, 197; functions of, 294n59; and law, 302n17; and military, 309n29, 311n35; and students, 311n35, 313n57. *See also* Campaign; Choice

Election of 1984, 125, 151, 152, 157

Election of 1988, 125, 145, 151, 152, 157, 165

Elections of 1979–1981, 182

Elite: and totalitarian model, 1, 2; and communism, 7; contestation among, 36; and private interests, 106; and mobilization theory, 112, 140; and resistance, 245, 246–248, 250

Entrepreneur, 150, 194–196

Exchange: and hierarchy, 18, 20, 102, 111, 273; and patron-client relationship, 44–45; and *guanxi*, 69; use rate, 107; and cronyism, 121, 256–257

Exclusion, infeasibility of, 17, 272, 276–277

Expressive benefit: and policy formulation, 19; and status, 19; and psychological orientation, 143; and elections, 143, 144, 154, 177; and boycott, 191; and appeals, 199, 200, 229, 231; and adversarial activity, 235; and cronyism, 256. *See also* Cost benefit; Instrumental benefit

Factor analysis, 128–140. *See also* Statistical method

Falkenheim, Victor, 269

Family, 82–83, 210–211, 216, 244–245, 283, 284, 286–287

Farmer, 153

Father, 192, 196, 261, 262

Foreign Language Printing House, 40

Formulation, of policy. *See* Policy formulation

Freedom, 37, 119

Friedgut, Theodore H., 93, 204

Fu Yuehua, 299n71, 300n82

Gang of Four, 87, 245, 248, 253

Gender: and elections, 169–176, 178, 179, 242–243, 312n52; and politicization, 171, 174; and work units, 171–172; and economic status, 172, 173; and mobilization, 174, 219; and campaigns, 185, 188; and appeals, 209, 212, 216–220, 231, 240, 242–243

Gift-giving, 67–70; legality of, 21; use rate, 94, 102, 107; and tradition, 108; and hierarchy, 111; and conflict, 118; and cronyism, 121, 122; and principal component analysis, 126, 128; and factor analysis, 131, 132, 137

Gitelman, Zvi, 205

Government: and control, 1–2, 14, 39, 114; and modernization, 3; expansion of, 4; and conflict, 13; and resources, 19, 22, 24, 74, 90, 204; and elections, 35–36, 39, 93, 95, 104, 110, 119, 143, 149, 176, 181, 296n15; and political activity, 55, 89–91; and letters, 63–66; and Cultural Revolution, 78; and posters, 84–86; and demonstrations, 86; and work units, 90, 91, 13015; and complaints, 94, 101, 306n28; and civic duty, 100; and campaigns, 119, 180, 184; approval of, 128; and appeals, 139–140, 199, 206, 208, 212, 216, 217; and boycott, 181; influence on, 185; and equality, 192; and living standard, 194; disagreement with, 206, 208, 212, 216, 217, 224; ignoring of, 222, 225; and military, 229; and cronyism, 233; and resistance, 233; and adversarial activity, 233–234; and mobilization, 269–271; and unauthorized activity, 306n17. *See also* State enterprise; State organization

Graduate education, 146–147, 148. *See also* Education

Grapevine rumor: use rate, 30; and campaigns, 185–187; and boycott, 192, 193; and elections, 197; and appeals, 209, 212, 215, 216, 217, 222, 224, 225, 231, 240; and resistance, 251–252, 253; and cronyism, 262–263. *See also* Information

169, 174, 176, 177; and campaigns, 184;
and living standard, 194; and appeals, 208,
213, 221, 224, 225, 230; and resistance,
246; and mobilization, 270–271. *See also*
Economic status; Rank
Soviet Union (former): and politics, 6, 113,
291n27; and elections, 93, 165, 171, 176,
178; and appeals, 201–202, 216, 223, 224;
and apathy, 254; and suppression, 269
Special Issues of Collections of Letters from
the Masses (*Qunzhong Laixin Zhaibian
Tekan*), 65
State. *See* Government
State enterprise, 155, 156, 158, 159, 160, 161,
164, 172, 173, 272
State organization, 155, 156, 158, 159, 160,
161, 164, 172, 173
State vs. society, 2–3
Statistical method, 26–27, 92–93, 124–140,
157, 310n31, 311nn32,33, 312n37, 317n27.
See also Survey research
Status. *See* Economic status; Rank; Socioeco-
nomic status
Strategic reserve, 61–62
Strike, 70–77, 94; and bureaucracy, 71, 73,
298n61; and Mao Zedong, 71, 298n61; and
individual, 74, 110, 270; use rate, 102, 107;
and protest, 108; and risk, 116; and resistance, 122; and principal component analysis, 125
Struggle. *See* Conflict
Student, 36, 152, 153, 222, 309n29, 311n35,
313n57, 321n20. *See also* Youth
Subjectivity, and status, 151–152, 163–164,
174, 213, 223
Suffrage, 35
Supply, jointness of, 17, 272, 277
Suppression, 4, 44, 106, 115, 269, 271. *See
also* Departicipation; Purge
Survey research, 25–30, 89–93; and education, 29, 146–147; and boycott, 44; and
work units, 47; and elections, 95–96, 98–
99, 144–145; and patron-client relationship, 102; and frequency data, 103; and politicization, 155; and resistance, 253; sample
design, 283–287; and response rate,
294n66; and unconventional acts, 304n51.
See also Statistical method

Thought reform, 147–148, 169, 269, 270
Tiananmen Square demonstration, 16, 85, 87

Totalitarian model, 1–2, 3, 44, 182, 293n57
Townsend, James, 5, 204
Trade union: and lifetime employment, 48;
and education, 58; and mobilization, 58;
and complaints, 58–59, 94, 101, 120, 198;
and income, 59; and persuasion, 59; and
power, 59; and strikes, 71; and principal
component analysis, 128; and factor analysis, 130, 136. *See also* Labor; Worker
Traditional culture, 82, 108, 174, 175, 176,
213, 276, 277, 278, 280, 299n70
Transportation, 71–73

Unauthorized activity, 270, 306n17
Unconventional activity, 106–110, 111, 246,
253–254, 264–266, 304n51
United States, 174
Universal suffrage, 35
Upward accountability, 13
Urban population, 38
USSR. *See* Soviet Union (former)

Verba, Sidney, 5, 21, 113, 117, 123, 145, 165,
203, 293nn53,57
Voluntary action, 183, 185, 190, 240, 243–
244
Voting. *See* Election

Walder, Andrew, 14, 18, 242
Waltz, Kenneth, 68
Wang Dongxing, 85, 300n82
Wang Renzhong, 296n21
Warring States Period, 60
Weber, Max, 10–11
Wei Jingsheng, 85
White-collar worker, 153, 154, 160, 161, 162,
163
Whyte, Martin, 13
Withdrawal, from politics, 70, 191, 195, 269
Women: and elections, 169–176, 178, 242–
243, 312n52; and psychological orientation,
174; and economic status, 175; and mobili-
zation, 175, 176; and campaigns, 188; and
appeals, 216–220, 231; and Mao Zedong,
218–219; and Cultural Revolution, 219;
and retaliation, 242–243. *See also* Gender
Worker, 46, 150, 153, 154, 160, 161, 162,
163, 239–242. *See also* Labor; Trade union
Work unit (*danwei*): and government, 13–
15, 90, 91; and mobilization, 13–15, 154,
162, 177; and interest articulation, 14;